The Law and Strategy
of Biotechnology Patents

BIOTECHNOLOGY

JULIAN E. DAVIES, *Editor*
Pasteur Institute
Paris, France

16. N. First and
    F. Haseltine (editors)   *Transgenic Animals*

17. C. Ho and
    D. Wang (editors)   *Animal Cell Bioreactors*

18. I. Goldberg and
    J. S. Rokem (editors)   *Biology of Methylotrophs*

19. J. Goldstein (editor)   *Biotechnology of Blood*

20. R. Ellis (editor)   *Vaccines: New Approaches to Immunological Problems*

21. D. Finkelstein and
    C. Ball (editors)   *Biotechnology of Filamentous Fungi*

22. R. H. Doi   *Biology of Bacilli: Applications to Industry*

23. J. Bennett and
    M. Klich   *Aspergillus: Biology and Industrial Applications*

24. J. Davies and
    W. Reznikoff
    (editors)   *Milestones in Biotechnology: Classic Papers on Genetic Engineering*

25. K. Sibley (editor)   *The Law and Strategy of Biotechnology Patents*

The Law and Strategy
of Biotechnology Patents

Edited by

Kenneth D. Sibley

Butterworth–Heinemann

Boston London Oxford Singapore Sydney Toronto Wellington

Library of Congress Cataloging-in-Publication Data

The Law and strategy of biotechnology patents / edited by Kenneth D.
  Sibley.
          p.   cm. — (Biotechnology series ; 25)
    Includes index.
    ISBN 0-7506-9444-0 (acid-free paper)
    1. Biotechnology—United States—Patents.   I. Sibley, Kenneth D.
  II. Series: Biotechnology ; 25.
KF3133.B56L39   1994
346.7304'86--dc20
[347.306486]   93-39393
                                                                    CIP

British Library Cataloguing-in-Publication Data

A catalogue record for this book is available from the British Library.

Butterworth–Heinemann
313 Washington Street
Newton, MA 02158

10 9 8 7 6 5 4 3 2 1
Printed in the United States of America

William M. Atkinson, Esquire
Bell, Seltzer, Park & Gibson, P.A.

David E. Broome, Jr., Esquire
North Carolina State University

Brian P. O'Shaughnessy, Esquire
Mason, Fenwick & Lawrence

James R. Cannon, Esquire
Bell, Seltzer, Park & Gibson, P.A.

Shawn P. Foley, Esquire
Lerner, David, Littenberg, Krumholz & Mentlik

Virginia C. Bennett, Esquire
Bell, Seltzer, Park & Gibson, P.A.

Kenneth D. Sibley, Esquire
Bell, Seltzer, Park & Gibson, P.A.

James D. Myers, Esquire
Bell, Seltzer, Park & Gibson, P.A.

Robert W. Glatz, Esquire
Bell, Seltzer, Park & Gibson, P.A.

CONTENTS

Foreword by Charles E. Hammer   xiii
Preface   xv
Acknowledgments   xvii

PART I: INTRODUCTION

1. General Information   1
Kenneth D. Sibley
  1.1   Using the Patent Statute Requires Planning   2
  1.2   An Overview of the Content and Chapters   2
  1.3   A Brief Overview of the Patent Statute   3
  1.4   A Case Study: The Production of Acetone with *Clostridium*
      Acetobutylicum   6
      References   9

2. Patent Claims   11
Kenneth D. Sibley
  2.1   The Central Role of Patent Claims   11
  2.2   General Rules of Claim Interpretation   12
  2.3   The Practical Interpretation of Patent Claims   14
  2.4   Examples of Patent Claims in Biotechnology   16
      References   23

3. The Legal Decision-Making Process   27
William M. Atkinson
  3.1   The Patent Application Process   27
  3.2   Proceedings on Issued Patents   36
  3.3   Miscellaneous Matters   41
      References   43

4. Ownership of Tangible and Intellectual Property   49
David E. Broome, Jr.
  4.1   Tangible Property versus Intangible Property   49
  4.2   Trade Secret Issues   53
  4.3   Ownership of Intellectual Property   54
      References   58

PART II: BASIC REQUIREMENTS OF PATENTABILITY

5. Patentable Subject Matter   61
Brian P. O'Shaughnessy

	5.1	Statutory Subject Matter	61
	5.2	Practical Utility	69
	5.3	Operability	71
		References	72

6. Novelty and the Public Domain   75
James R. Cannon
	6.1	The Anatomy of Anticipatory Prior Art	76
	6.2	When Is Prior Art Properly Applied to a Claim?	80
	6.3	Rule 1.131—Removing Prior Art by a Showing of Prior Inventorship	86
		References	88

7. Nonobviousness   93
Shawn P. Foley
	7.1	The Basic Test	94
	7.2	The Scope and Content of the Prior Art	94
	7.3	The Person Having Ordinary Skill in the Art	95
	7.4	Differences between the Prior Art and the Claimed Invention—The Invention as a Whole	97
	7.5	Objective Evidence of Nonobviousness	101
	7.6	*Prima Facie* Obviousness	104
	7.7	Inventive Step and Nonobviousness Compared	110
	7.8	Conclusion	111
		References	111

PART III: SPECIAL ISSUES IN BIOTECHNOLOGY PATENTS

8. Discolsure Requirements   117
Kenneth D. Sibley
	8.1	The Enablement Requirement and Claim Scope	117
	8.2	The Best-Mode Requirement	126
	8.3	The Deposit Requirement	127
	8.4	The Written-Description Requirement	130
	8.5	The Claim Definiteness Requirement	132
		References	133

9. Collaborative Research   137
Kenneth D. Sibley
	9.1	Inventorship Issues in Collaborative Research	137
	9.2	Correcting Inventorship	147
	9.3	Prior Art Issues in Collaborative Research	148
		References	151

10. Competitive Research   **153**
      Kenneth D. Sibley
      10.1   Priority of Invention under the First-to-Invent System   154
      10.2   Applying the First-to-Invent System to Inventions Made
             Outside the United States   164
      10.3   Interference Procedure: Initiation of Interferences   164
      10.4   Priority under the First-to-File System   166
             References   167

11. Plant Biotechnology   **171**
      Virginia C. Bennett
      11.1   Plant Patents   171
      11.2   The Plant Variety Protection Act of 1970   175
      11.3   Trade Secrets   177
      11.4   Plants as Tangible Property   178
      11.5   Utility Patents   178
      11.6   The Strategy of Protecting Plants   179
      11.7   International Considerations in Plant Protection   180
             References   183

12. Foreign Patents   **187**
      Kenneth D. Sibley
      12.1   Avoiding Forfeiture of Foreign Patent Rights   188
      12.2   Choosing Where to File Foreign Applications   190
      12.3   Strategy: Preserve Foreign Rights and Defer Foreign Costs   191
      12.4   An Approach to Securing Foreign Patents   194
      12.5   Conclusion   198
             References   198

PART IV: PATENT LITIGATION

13. Substantive Aspects of Patent Litigation   **201**
      James D. Myers, Brian P. O'Shaughnessy, and Robert W. Glatz
      13.1   The Patent Grant   202
      13.2   Patent Infringement   203
      13.3   Patent Validity in the Courts   216
      13.4   Patent Enforceability in the Courts   219
      13.5   Estoppel Applied to the Accused Infringer   223
             References   223

14. Procedural Aspects of Patent Litigation   **231**
      James D. Myers and Robert W. Glatz
      14.1   Steps Taken Prior to a Lawsuit   231
      14.2   Initiating the Suit   232

14.3   The Discovery Phase   235
14.4   Determination of the Issues   242
14.5   Alternative Dispute Resolution and Settlement   247
         References   247

         Index   253

Kenneth Sibley and his colleagues in this book have undertaken and met a challenging task—addressing and explicating a complicated area of law in relation to a complicated new science. The task is important; the necessity of guidance in this area is increasingly apparent to those in both the legal and the scientific professions. The processes and techniques broadly called biotechnology are yielding tangible and specific discoveries, which in this as in any other area of invention require protection for attribution and use. Such protection is, for this technology, affected by the long development time required for discovery and application, as well as by the extent to which uses often are not conventionally understood or characterized. This is, after all, a technology that uses and changes life and living organisms. Attention to this fact is requisite to gain that protection necessary for both development efforts and eventual product application.

All parties involved with biotechnology commercialization—including lawyers, researchers and inventors, entrepreneurs, venture capitalists, investment bankers, technology development and transfer agents, and university administrators—will find here clear and useful information on a host of issues particular to life-based technology. Such specific issues are placed within a practical framework of information on the central role of patent claims, statutory subject matter, novelty, nonobviousness, disclosure considerations, and operation of the judicial system in relation to patents. Contributors reveal the extent to which biotechnology merges established law with new imperatives. Countries may treat patents for plants and animals differently. Europeans, for instance, until recently did not permit patents on animals, reflecting the complex implications of patenting life-based discoveries.

Strategic issues in writing a patent are made complex by the interdisciplinary nature of biotechnology. Collaborative research, funding from several sources, the requirement for continuing research, and a highly competitive environment require that approach, claims, and disclosure be well understood and laid out. The ultimate result from a patent is for the inventor and the public to benefit from commercializing the technology, of course, but in this technology certain restrictions and competitive concerns may make a smooth path to this result more difficult. As always, there are likely to be disputes and infringements requiring litigation. The pharmaceutical industry is well developed to handle these challenges, but biotechnology is demanding new tactics because of additional complications in defining improvements.

The nature and interrelationships of such content and issues are presented with admirable clarity and usefulness in *The Law and Strategy of Biotechnology Patents*. The book will serve as a solid resource for any person working at that point where law and biotechnology necessarily—and increasingly—meet.

Charles E. Hamner, DVM, Ph.D.
President, North Carolina Biotechnology Center

This book had its inception in a series of articles on patent law that appeared in *BT Catalyst,* a publication of the North Carolina Biotechnology Center. These articles led to a series of articles on patent law appearing in *SIM Industrial Microbiology News,* the magazine of the Society of Industrial Microbiology. The *SIM* articles then led to the invitation to prepare this book.

The current era of biotechnology patent law has been evolving, with the biotechnology industry, for more than 10 years. Numerous decisions have been handed down by the federal courts and the U.S. Patent and Trademark Office. Yet there is still considerable confusion on how the patent laws operate with respect to biotechnology inventions. Some of this confusion is over basic issues of patent law such as patentable subject matter, novelty, and nonobviousness. Often, however, confusion arises from other sources such as the legal decision-making process itself, the role of patent claims to the operation of the patent statute, or international aspects of patent law.

The legal decision-making process is, in a sense, the "scientific method" of law, but questions of biotechnology patent law are often fruitlessly debated without considering the judicial process by which they are actually decided. Patent claims are the legal definition of an invention, but often "inventions" are discussed without any reference to patent claims. Finally, countless inventions are jeopardized or forfeited each year because of misunderstanding the differences between U.S. patent law and the patent laws of other jurisdictions. Hence, the purpose of this book is to explain biotechnology patent law, with special emphasis on each of these problem areas. Hopefully *The Law and Strategy of Biotechnology Patents* will convey that there is a strategy to patent law: not strategy in the sense of gamesmanship or taking unfair advantage of the patent system, but strategy in the sense of planning in advance so that patent considerations may follow research and development in a logical and orderly fashion.

ACKNOWLEDGMENTS

I would like to acknowledge Mark Dibner, Karyn George, and all their colleagues at the North Carolina Biotechnology Center who made the *BT Catalyst* articles that led to this book possible; George Somkuti, who made the *SIM Industrial Microbiology News* articles that led to this book possible, and Julian Davies, who read these articles and suggested this book.

Laurel DeWolf and Marilyn Rash at Butterworth–Heinemann have been steadfast in their editorial support, the chapter authors have graciously given their time and effort so that this book might contain more than a single person's views, Joyce Paoli and Sharon Eccleston devoted considerable time to preparing the manuscript, and my colleagues at Bell, Seltzer, Park & Gibson have given me the flexibility to undertake this project.

Most of all I would like to thank my wife, Barbara, for her patience, support, and understanding through the many nights and weekends it took to bring this book to completion.

PART

I

Introduction

General Introduction

Kenneth D. Sibley

Three situations and events in the early 1980s combined to establish biotechnology patent law as a specialty area of legal practice. First, biology researchers were increasingly developing new techniques that had substantial commercial applications.[1] Second, in an effort to strengthen the patent system, the U.S. Congress created the Court of Appeals for the Federal Circuit to hear all appeals in patent cases.[2] Finally, the U.S. Supreme Court opened the door to obtaining patents on living things in the well-known case of *Diamond v. Chakrabarty*.[3]

It is now widely accepted that the Federal Circuit has succeeded in making patents more valuable investments.[4] Basic and applied research in the biological sciences continues to progress at a rapid rate, and the level of commercial interest and activity appears high.[5] However, it is often felt that the patent system itself, at least in the area of biotechnology, is capricious and unpredictable. There is thought to be little uniformity as to which patent applications are allowed and which are not, and little rationality in what patents are held valid and infringed.[6] Perhaps this is a natural consequence when patent laws are used in a research community that has not been heavily involved with patents previously.[7] Nevertheless, given the importance of the patent system in encouraging continued investment in biotechnology research, the effort the Federal Circuit has expended in clarifying the patent laws, and the diligent professionalism of the Examining Corps in the U.S. Patent and Trademark Office in applying these laws, this perception is unfortunate.

1.1   USING THE PATENT STATUTE REQUIRES PLANNING

Although the patent system is not capricious, its use does require considerable planning and forethought. This is particularly true in the area of biotechnology, where it can be fairly easy to formulate a new idea or hypothesis, but whether that hypothesis will prove accurate is a matter of great uncertainty until it is tried, and the effort required to try it is considerable. However, the competitive nature of biotechnology research tends to require that patents be pursued at an early stage before every possible variable in a new proposal has been confirmed. What's more, as research in a new area progresses, investigators encounter surprises, learn more, and formulate new ideas that may be inventive themselves. Finally, if publications are to be pursued concurrently with patents—as is often the case in biotechnology—the window of opportunity available to make decisions affecting patents will be smaller. This is because once a publication occurs, its contents enter the public domain (either immediately or after a grace period, depending on the country in which patent protection is sought).

In summary, at the time when a patent strategy for a planned course of research should be initiated, decisions need to be made based on limited data concerning unpredictable technology that will have consequences far into the future. If the wrong decisions are made, the ability to protect the fruits of an extremely expensive line of research may be severely jeopardized. Clearly, people involved with biotechnology patents need to treat the pursuit of those patents as a strategic undertaking. They must plan their strategies and include in them a way to protect broad and fundamental concepts, as well as to accommodate the surprises that may be encountered as the research progresses.

1.2   AN OVERVIEW OF THE CONTENT AND CHAPTERS

The purpose of this book is to provide an overview of biotechnology patent law, emphasizing the basic tools and concepts that must be understood to formulate a successful patent strategy. It is not intended to be a complete treatment of patent law. For that, reference should be made to additional works such as Chisum's multi-volume treatise on patent law,[8] Kayton's extensive patent bar course text,[9] or Harmon's review of the law established by the Federal Circuit.[10] Nevertheless, this book provides sufficient citations and resource materials throughout the chapters so that even those already acquainted with patent law will find it a useful resource.

The book is divided into four parts. Part I, in addition to this introductory chapter, includes chapters on patent claims (Chapter 2), the legal decision-making process (Chapter 3), and ownership of tangible and intellectual property (Chapter 4). The chapter on patent claims is included because patent claims are centrally important to the operation of the patent laws, yet, surprisingly, they tend to be overlooked in discussions of patent issues. The chapter on the legal decision-making process emphasizes that substantive patent issues are decided in the context of a carefully structured decision-making system. Obviously, no one can anticipate how an issue might be decided without understanding how the system for making that decision works. Finally, the chapter on ownership of tangible and intellectual property is included because understanding who owns a particular technology is fundamental to deciding how to protect that technology.

Part II, Basic Requirements of Patentability, includes three chapters that cover the requirements its title implies: patentable subject matter (Chapter 5), novelty (Chapter 6), and nonobviousness (Chapter 7). Part III, Special Issues in Biotechnology Patents, includes chapters on disclosure requirements (Chapter 8), collaborative research (Chapter 9), competitive research (Chapter 10), plant biotechnology (Chapter 11), and foreign patents (Chapter 12). A complete understanding of patent claims based on Chapter 2 would be particularly helpful before reading chapters 5 through 10.

Part IV, Patent Litigation, returns to issues of the legal decision-making process addressed earlier in Chapter 2 by exploring patent litigation in greater detail. To give greater emphasis to the decision-making process itself, substantive aspects of patent litigation (primarily validity and infringement) are addressed first in Chapter 13, while the procedural aspects of patent litigation are examined separately in Chapter 14. Hopefully, Chapter 14 will make abundantly clear that rules that are "merely" procedural can have an effect on the outcome of a substantive issue.

The remainder of this introductory chapter is devoted to a brief overview of the patent statute (section 1.3), followed by a case study in section 1.4 of the patent litigation that occurred shortly after World War I over Dr. Chaim Weizmann's process for producing acetone from maize. Apart from being an extremely interesting historical development, this case study is presented to make the point that complex technical issues in the area of biology are not new to the courts. Such issues have been presented to the courts and dealt with successfully by them for many years.

1.3 A BRIEF OVERVIEW OF THE PATENT STATUTE

The current patent statute was enacted in 1952 and is codified as Title 35 of the U.S. Code. A review of the details of this law and the reforms it made is set forth in the well-known "Federico's Commentary."[11] The two most basic areas of confusion on how this statute functions are: (1) what rights are granted by a patent and (2) what standards must be met to obtain a patent. A brief discussion of these two issues follows.

1.3.1 The Patent Grant: Only the Right to Exclude
A patent grants only the right to *exclude others* from practicing an invention,[12] and *not* the affirmative right to practice the invention. This is a fundamental rule underlying the patent system, and confusion on this point can have serious consequences. For example, the fact that someone obtains a patent on a new product does not mean that product will not infringe an earlier patent on a more basic invention. The

earlier patent in a case such as this is referred to as a *blocking* patent and is said to "dominate" the later patent. If the only commercially feasible product is one that is covered by both the earlier and later patents, then the patents are said to block one another, and neither patent holder can move forward without obtaining a license from the other (an arrangement known as a *cross-license*).

The statutory rule ensures that the patent system encourages continuing research and new inventions by rewarding every inventive contribution in a field, rather than by simply rewarding the first contribution to a field. The ability of utility patents to dominate one another is a major reason that the law and business of patent licensing is such an important offshoot of patent law in general.[13]

1.3.2   The Requirements for Patentability

Coincidentally, the case that provides one of the best general summaries of the criteria for patentability is the lower court decision that set the stage for *Diamond v. Chakrabarty*: the decision *In re Bergy*.[14] The author of *Bergy* was Judge Giles Rich, who was instrumental in drafting the current patent statute.[15] He later was elevated to the Court of Appeals for the Federal Circuit and is among the most highly regarded patent jurists in the federal courts. Perhaps sensitive to the fact that these decisions would usher in a new era of patent law, Judge Rich took the opportunity to set forth a detailed "anatomy" of the patent statute.

In *Bergy*, Judge Rich was primarily concerned with explaining the statutory subject matter requirement. As a preamble, he explained the general operation of the Patent Statute as follows:

> *Anatomy of the Patent Statute*
>
> The reason for our consideration of the statutory scheme in relation to its Constitutional purpose is that we have been directed to review our prior decisions . . . and we find . . . an unfortunate and apparently unconscious, though clear, commingling of distinct statutory provisions which are conceptually unrelated, namely, those pertaining to the categories of inventions in § 101 which may be patentable and to the conditions for patentability demanded by the statute for inventions within the statutory categories, particularly the nonobviousness condition of § 103. The confusion creeps in through such phrases as "eligible for patent protection," "patentable process," "new and useful," "inventive application," "inventive concept," and "patentable invention." The last-mentioned term is perhaps one of the most difficult to deal with unless it is used exclusively with reference to an invention which complies with every condition of the patent statutes so that a valid patent may be issued on it.
>
> The problem of accurate, unambiguous expression is exacerbated by the fact that prior to the Patent Act of 1952 the words "invention," "inventive," and "invent" had distinct legal implications related to the concept of patentability which they have not had for the past quarter century. Prior to 1952, and for sometime thereafter, they were used by courts as imputing *patentability*. Statements in the older cases must be handled with care lest the terms used in their reasoning clash with the reformed terminology of the present statute; lack of meticulous care may lead to distorted legal conclusions.
>
> The transition made in 1952 was with respect to the old term "invention," imputing *patentability*, which term was replaced by a new statutory provision, § 103, requiring *nonobviousness*, as is well explained and approved [by the Supreme Court] in *Graham*

v. John Deere Co. . . . Graham states that there are three explicit conditions, novelty, utility, and nonobviousness, which is true, but there is a fourth requirement, which alone, is involved here.

*   *   *

All of the statutory law relevant to the present cases is found in [the following four sections of the Patent Statute, Title 35 of the United States Code]:

Sec. 100   Definitions
Sec. 101   Inventions patentable [if they qualify]
Sec. 102   Conditions for patentability; novelty and loss of right to patent
Sec. 103   Conditions for patentability; non-obvious subject matter

. . . Achieving the ultimate goal of a patent under those statutory provisions involves, to use an analogy, having the separate keys to open in succession the three doors of sections 101, 102, and 103, the last two guarding the public interest by assuring that patents are not granted which would take from the public that which it already enjoys (matters already within its knowledge whether in actual use or not) or *potentially* enjoys by reason of obviousness from knowledge which it already has.

*   *   *

The first door which must be opened on the difficult path to patentability is § 101 (augmented by the § 100 definitions). . . . The person approaching that door is an inventor, whether his invention is patentable or not. There is always an inventor; being an inventor might be regarded as a preliminary legal requirement, for if he has not invented something, if he comes with something he knows was invented by someone else, he has no right even to approach the door. Thus, section 101 begins with the words "Whoever invents or discovers," and since 1790 the patent statutes have always said substantially that. Being an inventor or having an invention, however, is no guarantee of opening even the first door. What kind of an invention or discovery is it? In dealing with the question of kind, as distinguished from the qualitative conditions which make the invention patentable, § 101 is broad and general; its language is: "any . . . process, machine, manufacture, or composition of matter, or any . . . improvement thereof." Section 100(b) further expands "process" to include "art or method, and . . . a new use of a known process, machine, manufacture, composition of matter, or material." If the invention, as the inventor defines it in his claims (pursuant to § 112, second paragraph), falls into any one of the named categories he is allowed to pass through to the second door, which is § 102; "novelty and loss of right to patent" is the sign on it. . . .

*   *   *

The second door then, as we have already seen, is § 102 pursuant to which the inventor's claims are examined for novelty, requiring, for the first time in the examination process, comparison with the prior art which, up to this point, has therefore been irrelevant.

*   *   *

The third door, under the 1952 Act, is § 103 which was enacted *to take the place of the requirement for "invention."* [For present purposes it] will suffice to quote what the House and Senate reports . . . say about the third requirement, from which it will be seen that, again, the claimed invention for which a patent is sought must be compared with the prior art. We quote [citations omitted]:

Section 103, for the first time in our statute, provides a condition which exists in the law and has existed for more than 100 years, but only by reason of decisions of the courts. An invention which has been made, and which is new in the sense that the same thing has not been made [or known] before, may still not be patentable if the difference between the new thing and what was known before is not considered sufficiently great to warrant a patent. That has been expressed in a large variety of ways in decisions of the courts and in writings. Section 103 states this requirement in the title ["Conditions for patentability; non-obvious subject matter"]. It refers to the difference between the subject matter sought to be patented and the prior art, meaning what was known before as described in section 102. If this difference is such that the subject matter as a whole would have been obvious at the time [the invention was made] to a person [ordinarily] skilled in the art, then the subject matter cannot be patented. [Insertions and emphasis ours.]

If the inventor holds the three different keys to the three doors, his invention (here assumed to be "useful") qualifies for a patent, otherwise not; but he, as inventor, must meet still other statutory requirements in the preparation and prosecution of his patent application. . . . The point not to be forgotten is that being an inventor and having made an invention is not changed by the fact that one or more or all of the conditions for patentability cannot be met. Year in and year out this court turns away the majority of the inventors who appeal here because their inventions do not qualify for patents. They remain inventions nevertheless. It is time to settle the point that the terms *invent, inventor, inventive,* and the like are unrelated to deciding whether the statutory requirements for patentability under the 1952 Act have been met. There is always an invention; the issue is its patentability.[16]

1.4   A CASE STUDY: THE PRODUCTION OF ACETONE WITH *CLOSTRIDIUM ACETOBUTYLICUM*

Sometimes it is said that the federal courts do not have the technical expertise necessary to resolve the issues that arise in a patent dispute—particularly a dispute dealing with complex areas of biological research. This concern is misplaced. Setting aside the question of whether the public at large would place any confidence in a system where all decisions are made by technical experts, it should be noted that courts are called on to reach a final decision on technical questions where experts can differ. Furthermore, as will be pointed out later on, the courts have successfully dealt with complex technical questions for many years.

Most people involved with microbiology are familiar with the pioneering work of Dr. Chaim Weizmann on the fermentation of maize to produce acetone with *Clostridium acetobutylicum*. In brief, during World War I, Weizmann had been conducting basic research on this (and other) processes in England. Because of the British navy's need for a synthetic source for acetone, which was used to manufacture the explosive known as cordite, Weizmann was summoned to appear before the First Lord of the Admiralty, Winston Churchill. Churchill reportedly said, "Well, Dr. Weizmann, we need 30,000 tons of acetone. Can you make it?" Weizmann replied that he had produced only a few hundred cubic centimeters, but that "once the bacteriology of the process is established, it is only a question of brewing."[17] Weizmann's success with the process and his role in winning the support of the British government for the establishment of a Jewish homeland in Palestine apparently produced the apocryphal story that, when asked what reward he wanted for this service, Weizmann replied that he wanted "nothing for himself, only a country for his people."[18] Weizmann, of course, went on to become the first president of Israel in 1949.

Many people are not familiar with the long course of patent disputes over this process, which were dealt with by the British and the U.S. Courts in the 1920s and 1930s.[19] The disputes are noteworthy because the issues raised then are similar to, and as complex as, those encountered today in biotechnology patent disputes.

The disputes had their genesis in 1910, when Strange & Graham Ltd. was incorporated in England to develop synthetic rubber. This process required the commercial production of amyl or butyl alcohol, and Professor Perkin of Manchester University was hired to develop a fermentative process for producing these alcohols. Perkin hired Weizmann, who was at that time a junior demonstrator in chemistry under his direction at Manchester. Weizmann, in turn, recommended that Perkin also employ Professor Fernbach, under whom Weizmann had previously studied.

In 1911, Weizmann and Fernbach exchanged various bacteria. Among these, Fernbach provided Weizmann with "FB," a bacterium that fermented potato, but that was not an effective fermenter of maize. Potato was an undesirable starting material, however, because of its cost, and the company, therefore, considered it important to find a process that would work with maize.

Coincidentally, in March 1912, another employee of the company, Mr. Kane, found large quantities of acetone in the fermentation media. Though not useful for the production of synthetic rubber, acetone was an essential ingredient for the production of cordite. Apparently, the commercial significance of this finding was not appreciated at the time.

In June 1912, Strange & Graham was in the process of going public as the Synthetic Products Co. (SPC). The company issued a prospectus containing a paper by Professor Perkin that suggested it had a practical process for fermenting maize. Weizmann felt that this report was greatly exaggerated, criticized the paper, and was dismissed by Perkin. In September 1912, the company filed a provisional patent application that revealed the fact that, in the course of fermenting carbohydrate with a butyl-producing bacterium, acetone was produced simultaneously with the alcohol. After leaving Strange & Graham, Weizmann reviewed the literature of known butyl alcohol-producing bacteria. During 1913 and 1914, Weizmann studied these bacteria and other new bacteria he had isolated, and succeeded (among other things) in identifying a species that was particularly good at producing acetone from maize. This species was designated "BY." Before publishing these data, he was encouraged to file a patent application by Dr. Rintoul, the head of research at Nobel's Explosive Company.

As an aside, the circumstances of Rintoul's visit to Weizmann's lab are remarkable. In August 1914, Weizmann received a form letter from the British government inviting scientists to report inventions that might be useful to the war effort. Weizmann offered his process to the government, but received no reply.

Then, in February 1915, Rintoul visited Weizmann. Rintoul's visit had no stated purpose, and Weizmann himself had no idea why Rintoul was there. The conversation eventually turned to Weizmann's process, which Rintoul then and there offered to acquire on behalf of his firm at terms that were "dazzling." A contract was entered, but the Nobel plant blew up. Nobel requested release from the contract, which Weizmann granted.[20]

In April 1915, SPC entered into a contract with the British government to supply acetone for the war effort. Potatoes were used as the raw material. The minimum quotas in the contract were never met, however. Ultimately, in March 1916, the government took over the company's plant, discontinued SPC's process, and placed Weizmann in charge. Weizmann implemented his own process, using maize as the raw material and BY as the bacterium and succeeded in meeting the government's needs.

The plant was returned to SPC after the war, and Weizmann assigned his rights to Commercial Solvents Corp. SPC continued to practice Weizmann's process and Commercial Solvents sued for patent infringement. SPC argued, among other things, that Weizmann had "obtained" (that is, derived) his invention from SPC. SPC did not deny infringement.

The Trial Court decided in favor of Weizmann on all issues. Yet, it is noteworthy how close the defendants came to a successful process of their own. The only bacterium the defendants alleged that Weizmann obtained from them was FB, which the court found to be distinct from BY and of no help to Weizmann in isolating a useful bacterium for his own purposes. From 1912–1915, the defendants themselves continued to try to discover a better fermenter than FB, and they eventually succeeded in isolating a better strain, designated "FB.BB." The Judge commented:

> They do not seem, however, to have discovered [at that time] that FB.BB possessed these superior qualities, if, indeed, it did possess them. Had they done so, Dr. Weizmann's process would never have displaced the Defendant's. . . .

Furthermore, in May 1912 (just prior to Weizmann's dismissal), Kane isolated sample "No. 160" on behalf of the defendants. *After* the plant was returned to SPC, Kane subcultured No. 160 to prepare X160. X160, though not a pure culture, had all the characteristics of BY. Kane continued to subculture X160 and from it prepared "bacillus 251," which was pure BY. However, the defendants could not corroborate their allegation that they had used this bacterium before Weizmann's work and never alleged that Weizmann had obtained this particular bacterium from them.

Clearly, the British court properly explored the issues and reached a proper conclusion. Indeed, when the dispute arose in the United States, the U.S. court substantially adopted the views of the British Court.[21]

Of course, like most pioneering inventions, Weizmann's process did not shut out further invention in the area. For example, this was apparently one of the first fermentative processes reported to be phage-susceptible.[22] Commercial Solvents Corp. issued an improvement patent in 1928 concerning "immunized" (that is, phage-resistant mutant) cultures of *Clostridium acetobutylicum*[23] based on research addressed to solving this problem.

REFERENCES

1. *See generally* U.S. Congress, OFFICE OF TECHNOLOGY ASSESSMENT, BIOTECHNOLOGY IN A GLOBAL ECONOMY, OTA-BA-494 (Washington, DC: U.S. Government Printing Office, October 1991).
2. 28 U.S.C. § 1295; *see also* Cable Electric Products, Inc. v. Genmark, Inc., 770 F.2d 1015, 1032, 226 USPQ 881, 892 (Fed. Cir. 1985).
3. Diamond v. Chakrabarty, 447 U.S. 303, 100 S. Ct. 2204, 206 USPQ 193 (1980).
4. *See, e.g.*, *The Battle Raging over "Intellectual Property,"* BUSINESS WEEK, at 78 (May 22, 1989).
5. *See, e.g.*, STRATEGIC DEVELOPMENTS IN BIOTECHNOLOGY (1993) (published monthly by the North Carolina Biotechnology Center Institute for Biotechnology Information); G. Burrill and K. Lee, BIOTECH 93: ACCELERATING COMMERCIALIZATION (1992) (Ernst & Young's seventh annual report on the biotechnology industry).
6. *See, e.g.*, E. Marshall, *The Patent Game: Raising the Ante*, 253 SCIENCE 20 (July 5, 1991); L. Raines, *Protecting Biotechnology's Pioneers*, ISSUES IN SCIENCE AND TECHNOLOGY, 33 (Winter 1991–92).
7. *See generally* R. Eisenberg, Proprietary Rights and the Norms of Science in Biotechnology Research, 97 YALE L.J. 177 (1987).
8. *See* D. Chisum, Patents (1992) (published and regularly supplemented by Matthew Bender & Co., Inc.).
9. *See* I. Kayton, PATENT PRACTICE (5th ed. 1993) (in seven volumes) (published by the Patent Resources Institute, Inc. in connection with the patent bar review course of the Patent Resources Group, Inc., 2000 Pennsylvania Avenue, N.W., Suite 3450, Washington, DC 20006).
10. R. Harmon, PATENTS AND THE FEDERAL CIRCUIT (2d ed. 1991) (published by The Bureau of National Affairs, Inc., Washington, DC).
11. P. Federico, Commentary on the New Patent Act, 75 J. PAT. & TRADEMARK OFF. SOC'Y 161 (1993).
12. 35 U.S.C. § 154.
13. *See generally* WORLD INTELLECTUAL PROPERTY ORGANIZATION, GUIDE ON THE LICENSING OF BIOTECHNOLOGY (1992) (published by the World Intellectual Property Organization with the assistance of the Licensing Executives Society International); H. Mayer and G. Brunsvold, DRAFTING PATENT LICENSE AGREEMENTS (3d ed. 1991).
14. *In re* Bergy, 596 F.2d 952, 201 USPQ 361 (C.C.P.A. 1979).
15. *See generally* G. Rich, *Congressional Intent—Or, Who Wrote the Patent Act of 1952?*, in NONOBVIOUSNESS—THE ULTIMATE CONDITION OF PATENTABILITY (J. Witherspoon, ed. 1980).
16. Bergy, 596 F.2d 958–62.
17. C. Weizmann, Trial and Error, 219–20 (1950).
18. C. WEIZMANN: A BIOGRAPHY BY SEVERAL HANDS, 33 (M. Weisgal and J. Carmichael, eds. 1963).

19. Commercial Solvents Corp. v. Synthetic Products Co., 43 R.P.D. & T.M. Cas. 185 (Chancery Div. 1926).
20. *See* C. Weizmann, Trial and Error, 218–19 (1950).
21. Guaranty Trust Co. v. Union Solvents Corp., 54 F.2d 400, 12 USPQ 47 (D. Del. 1931), *aff'd*, 61 F.2d 1041, 15 USPQ 237 (3d Cir. 1932), *cert. denied*, 288 U.S. 614, 53 S. Ct. 405 (1933).
22. R. Erickson, *Bacteriophage Problems in the Dairy Industry*, DAIRY INDUSTRIES INTER-NATIONAL, at 42 (March 1980).
23. D. Legg, Art of Butyl-Acetonic Fermentation, U.S. Patent No. 1,668,814.

Patent Claims

Kenneth D. Sibley

The "claims" of a patent appear at the end of a patent and serve to define the "subject matter that the applicant regards as his invention."[1] Almost all patent law issues revolve around patent claims. Yet, there is an unfortunate tendency among lawyers and nonlawyers alike to debate patent law issues without any attention to patent claims. The purpose of this chapter is, accordingly, to describe what patent claims are and the functions they serve. Section 1 briefly reviews the reasons for the importance of patent claims, and section 2 provides some basic rules on how patent claims are interpreted. Section 3 explains how the basic rules of claim interpretation are applied in practice with a hypothetical set of patent claims for a basic biotechnology invention (monoclonal antibodies). Section 4 further illustrates patent claims with claims found today in U.S. patents issued in the biotechnology area.

2.1 THE CENTRAL ROLE OF PATENT CLAIMS

Nearly every significant issue in patent law relates to an "invention," including patentable subject matter, utility, novelty, nonobviousness, best mode, enablement, inventorship, and infringement. All of these issues require as precise a definition of the invention as possible. Since the precise definition of the invention is given by the claims, discussing issues such as these is futile without reference to the claims.

Patent claims are involved in every step of the patent process. For example, when an invention is searched for novelty and nonobviousness, draft claims usually are prepared to help define the search required. In a patent application, the claims usually are written first because the primary purpose of the rest of the application is to support and aid in interpreting the claims presented. When a patent application is examined in the U.S. Patent and Trademark Office, the wording of the claims almost always receives the patent examiner's primary attention. Finally, when a patent is enforced in the federal courts, the language of the claims is pivotal in deciding whether infringement has occurred. Hence, those who seek to understand the patent laws and use these laws in practice should have a sound understanding of how patent claims work.

2.2   GENERAL RULES OF CLAIM INTERPRETATION

General "rules" of law, particularly patent law, are often gross oversimplifications that can easily lead to error. Nevertheless, to understand patent claims, it is necessary to know a few general rules that usually (but not always) guide how these claims are written and interpreted.[2]

Claims may be directed to products (tangible things, such as chemical compositions, living things, and machines) or processes (a series of steps, such as a method of making a particular composition or a method of treating a particular disease). For brevity, the general rules that follow refer to product claims, but the same general rules also apply to process claims. Again, these rules are intended for introductory purposes only, and are by no means complete: important issues, such as the role of the doctrine of equivalents in determining infringement, are not addressed.

2.2.1   A Claim Covers a Product When It Reads on That Product

A claim "reads on" a product when everything described in the claim is found in that product (when all the elements or limitations of the claim are found in that product). Thus, claims generally are broader in scope when they contain fewer words. An important object in pursuing patent protection is to obtain the broadest claims available, because broad patent claims are more likely to cover an infringing product than narrow claims. Note that in biotechnology, the broadest claims practically available might not be the broadest claims that can be envisioned because of limitations placed on claim scope by the enablement requirement. The enablement requirement is discussed in greater detail in subsequent chapters.

2.2.2   A Claim Cannot Read on a Prior Art Product

Patent claims cannot be so broad that they cover a prior art product (i.e., a known product). If they do, they are not valid. In addition, patent claims cannot be so broad that they cover a product that, even though not in the prior art, was obvious in light of what was previously in the prior art. Thus, the goal of the patent applicant is to pursue claims narrow enough to exclude the prior art and obvious improvements of it, yet broad enough to cover competitive products that follow the invention.

The difference between what is obvious and what is not can be extremely subtle. More is said on the nonobviousness requirement in later chapters.

2.2.3 Claim Elements May Be Generic or Specific

An inventor may work with a single "species" in demonstrating his or her invention, but the claims might encompass multiple species. For example, a patent might show work only in mouse cells, but the claims might recite, and cover, any mammalian cell.

How far an inventor can go in extending the invention defined by the claims beyond his or her specific work is determined by, among other things, the enablement requirement and the nonobviousness requirement. If the claim is so broad that it encompasses nonobviousness subject matter, then it is unpatentable; if the claim is so broad that it encompasses speculative, unenabled subject matter, then, again, it is unpatentable.

2.2.4 Validity Is Assessed Separately for Every Claim in a Patent

Patents usually contain a variety of claims of varying scope so that even if some claims are later found invalid, other, narrower claims may remain valid. In general, it is easier to sustain the validity of narrower claims because they contain more elements that are not as likely to be found together in the prior art. Often, the precise form an invention will take when commercialized is unknown at the time a patent application is filed. Nevertheless, a narrow claim covering the commercially important versions of the invention should be included in an application whenever possible.

2.2.5 Claims Are Open-Ended Unless Made Close-Ended

If a claim is open-ended, then the addition of new features to a product does not avoid the claim covering that product. For example, if a claim is to "A DNA *comprising* elements A and B," then the manufacture of a DNA having elements A, B, and C would be covered by the claim. If a claim is close-ended, then the addition of meaningful new features may well avoid the claim covering the product. For example, if a claim is to "an isolated protein *consisting essentially of* chains A and B," then the manufacture of a protein having chains A, B, and C might not be covered by the claim.

2.2.6 The Limitations of Dependent Claims Are Not Imported into Their Base Claim

It is common for a claim element to be generically described in a basic claim and then specifically described in a dependent claim. It also is common, when a claim is open-ended, to add additional elements in dependent claims. Neither of these techniques limits the basic claim. In both cases the dependent claims, but not the basic claim, are narrower. If anything, limitations such as these placed in dependent claims clarify that the basic claim has a broader meaning than the dependent claims.

2.2.7   A Claim Can Cover a Subsequent Invention

This is a fundamental principle of patent law. The fact that someone obtains a patent claim covering an invention does not eliminate the possibility that the claim is dominated by an earlier patent on a more basic invention. Moreover, even if someone obtains a patent on a basic invention, others who further develop the work may be able to patent commercially significant versions of the earlier invention and possibly even prevent the developer of the basic invention from commercializing it.

2.2.8   Infringement of a Single Valid Claim
Constitutes Infringement of a Patent

If a party is found to infringe only a single valid claim in an issued patent, he or she can be liable for patent infringement.

2.3   THE PRACTICAL INTERPRETATION
OF PATENT CLAIMS

For the purpose of illustration, a set of hypothetical claims can be directed to the basic Köhler and Milstein hybridoma and monoclonal antibody technology.[3] Without particular regard to the prior art that might have been applied to this technology,[4] examples of claims that might have been pursued are as follows:

1.   A method of making cells useful for the production of monoclonal antibodies, said method comprising fusing an antibody-secreting B lymphocyte with an immortal cell to form a fusion product thereof.

2.   A method according to claim 1, wherein said immortal cell is a myeloma cell.

3.   A method according to claim 1, wherein said immortal cell is a mouse myeloma cell.

4.   A method according to claim 1, wherein said B lymphocyte is selected from the group consisting of human B lymphocytes and mouse B lymphocytes.

5.   An antibody-producing cell comprising the fusion product of a B lymphocyte and an immortal cell.

6.   A cell culture consisting essentially of antibody-producing cells according to claim 5.

7.   A method of producing monoclonal antibodies, comprising the culturing of an antibody-producing cell comprising the fusion product of a B lymphocyte and an immortal cell in a medium under conditions suitable for the production of antibodies therein, and collecting said antibodies from said media.

8.   A composition comprised of antibodies, wherein essentially all of said antibodies bind to the same epitope.

9.   A composition according to claim 8, wherein said antibodies bind to a protein.

10. A composition according to claim 9, wherein said antibodies bind to said protein at an affinity of at least 10^8 liters/mole.

11. A composition according to claim 10, wherein said antibodies are selected from the group consisting of IgG and IgM antibodies.

12. A composition according to claim 11, wherein said composition is lyophilized.

First, note that these 12 claims can be divided into four distinct categories:

1. Claims 1 through 4, directed to methods of making hybridomas
2. Claims 5 and 6, directed to a hybridoma cell *per se*
3. Claim 7, directed to a method of making monoclonal antibodies
4. Claims 8–12, directed to monoclonal antibody compositions

These four categories may well be patentably distinct from one another; that is, if one or more of the categories were determined to be unpatentable, the remaining categories still might be patentable. Clearly, patent protection for any one category could be very valuable. As a result, it is important to pursue as many distinct ways of defining the inventions arising from a particular technology as possible.

Claim 1 is a basic, or "independent," claim; claims 2 through 4 are "dependent" on claim 1. The limitations of the dependent claims are not imported back into the independent claim. Thus, claim 1 reads on the fusing of any antibody-secreting B lymphocyte with any immortal cell, regardless of the fact that claims 2 through 4 are directed to particular types of lymphocytes and immortal cells. The same is true for independent claim 8, directed to monoclonal antibodies *per se*, and claims 9–12 dependent thereon. For example, claim 8 covers compositions in any form, while only claim 12 is limited to covering lyophilized compositions.

No valid claim can read on a prior art product or process. Therefore, claim 8 might be invalid if monoclonal antibody compositions to a few highly repetitive immunogens had been known, because claim 8 covers such compositions. The validity of each claim is assessed separately, however. If monoclonal antibody compositions to proteins had not been known previously, then claim 9 might well have been valid even if claim 8 were invalid.

Claim 1 is generic as to the immortal cell, broadly covering any immortal cell. Claim 2 is more specific, and claim 3 still more specific. If it were highly unpredictable what types of immortal cells would work or not work in the fusion process, then claim 1 might have been considered unpatentable (as unenabled); claim 2, or perhaps just claim 3, still might have been patentable.

Note that claim 1 is open-ended, reciting a single "fusing" step. If subsequent inventions led to additional steps in the process, such as a third fusion step, then claim 1 still would cover the new process as long as the basic step was carried out. Further, it might be argued that the basic step covered either "directly" or "indirectly" fusing the lymphocyte with the immortal cell, particularly if the remainder of the patent were written to support such an interpretation.

Claim 8 is an example of a close-ended claim because it says "essentially all" of the antibodies in the composition bind to the same epitope. If claim 8 were not so limited, it would cover the possibility of other antibodies being included in the composition. It would also, however, clearly read on numerous polyclonal antibody compositions, and hence would be invalid.

If it were necessary to enforce a patent containing the foregoing claims, it might be decided, for any of a number of reasons, to enforce the patent against a party who possessed the monoclonal antibodies but was not involved in carrying out the fusion, did not possess the hybridoma cell line, and did not produce the antibodies from the cell line. Such a party might not directly infringe any of claims 1 through 7, but would directly infringe claims 8 through 12. Of course, other means exist for establishing infringement of claims 1 through 7. They will be discussed in subsequent chapters.

In an actual lawsuit, it might be that for reasons of anticipation, obviousness, and enablement, only claims 11 and 12 remained valid, and someone accused of infringement might have avoided using monoclonal antibodies in lyophilized form to avoid infringing claim 12. If, nevertheless, the accused infringer used a monoclonal antibody composition in which (a) the antibodies bound to a protein, (b) the antibodies bound to the protein at an affinity of at least 10^8 liters/mole, and (c) the antibodies were either IgG or IgM antibodies, then infringement of claim 11 would be established and he or she would have infringed the patent. Note that there are circumstances that can render even a valid and infringed patent unenforceable. These will be discussed in subsequent chapters.

2.4 EXAMPLES OF PATENT CLAIMS IN BIOTECHNOLOGY

To better illustrate some patent claims in the area of biotechnology, claims from some well-known issue U.S. patents will follow. These claims are organized approximately by subject matter. Since they are taken from actual patents, it would be improper to comment on how they might be interpreted: as later chapters will show, interpreting claims requires extreme care and consideration. However, the reader may wish to consider generally how these claims might be interpreted in light of the previous discussion.

2.4.1 Materials Isolated from Nature

Pasteur's patent[5] is an example of an early patent on a naturally occurring organism provided in a new, nonnatural form. Claim 2 of it reads as follows:

> 2. Yeast, free from organic germs of disease, as an article of manufacture.

A more recent example of a patent on a naturally occurring organism, isolated from nature, is the New England Medical Center patent for Lactobacillus strains.[6] Claims 1 and 2 read as follows:

> 1. A biologically pure culture of bacteria of a Lactobacillus species, said bacteria being characterized in that they have the same ability to attach mucosal cells of the

human intestinal tract as that exhibited by the *Lactobacillus* bacteria deposited in the American Type Culture Collection and given ATCC Accession No. 53103.

   2. The culture of claim 1, having ATCC Accession No. 53103.

An example of a patent on a naturally occurring protein isolated from nature is the Genetics Institute patent for erythropoietin,[7] claim 1 of which reads as follows:

   1. Homogeneous erythropoietin characterized by a molecular weight of about 34,000 daltons on SDS PAGE, movement as a single peak on reverse phase high performance liquid chromatography and a specific activity of at least 160,000 IU per absorbance unit at 280 nanometers.

This claim was, however, subsequently held invalid as both overly broad and indefinite in the litigation between Genetics Institute and Amgen.[8]

The Amgen claims to isolated DNA encoding erythropoietin that were held valid and infringed (other claims were held invalid) in Amgen's litigation with Genetics Institute include the following:

   2. A purified and isolated DNA sequence consisting essentially of a DNA sequence encoding human erythropoietin.

* * *

   4. A procaryotic or eucaryotic host cell transformed or transfected with a DNA sequence according to [claim 2] in a manner allowing the host cell to express erythropoietin.

Claim 1 of the Systemix patent for human hematopoietic stem cells[9] states:

   1. A cellular composition comprising human hematopoietic stem cells with fewer than 5% of lineage committed cells, wherein said hematopoietic stem cells are characterized as Thy-1+, capable of self-regeneration in a coculture medium and differentiation to members of the lymphoid and myelomonocytic hematopoietic lineages.

2.4.2 Biotechnology Techniques

The Cohen and Boyer patent issued to Stanford University in 1980 for recombinant DNA procedures (the patent had been pending since 1974)[10] includes the following as claims 1 and 2:

   1. A method for replicating a biologically functional DNA, which comprises:

     transforming under transforming conditions compatible unicellular organisms with biologically functional DNA to form transformants; said biologically functional DNA prepared in vitro by the method of:

     (a) cleaving a viral or circular plasmid DNA compatible with said unicellular organism to provide a first linear segment having an intact replicon and termini of a predetermined character;

(b) combining said first linear segment with a second linear DNA segment, having at least one intact gene and foreign to said unicellular organism and having termini ligatable to said termini of said first linear segment, wherein at least one of said first and second linear DNA segments has a gene for a phenotypical trait, under joining conditions where the termini of said first and second segments join to provide a functional DNA capable of replication and transcription in said unicellular organism;

growing said unicellular organisms under appropriate nutrient conditions; and isolating said transformants from said parent unicellular organisms by means of said phenotypical trait imparted by said biologically functional DNA.

2. A method according to claim 1, wherein said unicellular organisms are bacteria.

Claims to additional methods and to products *per se* were issued in a counterpart patent to Cohen and Boyer in 1988,[11] with the three product claims reading as follows:

9. As an article of manufacture, a cloned biologically functional circular recombinant DNA molecule capable of selection and replication in a host cell comprising: a first DNA segment containing an intact extrachromosomal replicon recognized by said host cell, said first segment being joined to a second DNA segment having foreign DNA derived from a source which does not exchange genetic information with said host cell.

10. An article of manufacture according to claim 9, wherein said host cell is a unicellular organism.

11. An article of manufacture according to claim 9, wherein said host cell is a prokaryotic organism.

The patent for cloning vehicles issued to Genentech in 1987 had been pending in one form or another for nearly 10 years and received much attention when it issued.[12] It includes the following claims:

1. A recombinant DNA cloning vehicle suited for transformation of a microbial host comprising:

(a) a homologous control region which regulates expression of a structural gene and
(b) a DNA insert comprising codons for a preselected functional heterologous polypeptide or polypeptide intermediate therefore characterized in that the DNA insert is operably linked to and in proper reading frame relative to the said control region and the host transformed thereby is capable of expressing the preselected heterologous polypeptide or polypeptide intermediate therefor under the control of the said control region and in recoverable form.

2. A recombinant cloning vehicle according to claim 1 wherein the control region is essentially identical to a control region ordinarily present in the chromosomal DNA of a bacterial species that serves as the host for transformation.

* * *

4. A recombinant cloning vehicle according to claim 2 wherein said polypeptide is the A chain of human insulin.

Some of the claims of the Cornell University "gene gun" patent[13] read as follows:

1. A method for introducing particles into cells comprising accelerating particles having a diameter sufficiently small to penetrate and be retained in a preselected cell without killing the cell, and propelling said particles at said cells whereby said particles penetrate the surface of said cells and become incorporated into the interior of said cells.

*   *   *

19. The method as in claim 1, wherein said particles comprise inert particles associated with a biological substance.

*   *   *

21. The method as in claim 19, wherein said substance is selected from the group consisting of organelles, vesicles, proteins, and nucleic acids.

Claim 1 of the Thomas Cech patent for ribozymes[14] reads as follows:

1. An enzymatic RNA molecule not naturally occurring in nature having an endonuclease activity independent of any protein, said endonuclease activity being specific for a nucleotide sequence defining a cleavage site comprising single-stranded RNA in a separate RNA molecule, and causing cleavage at said cleavage site by a transesterification reaction.

Finally, a basic claim in one of the original Kary Mullis polymerase chain reaction (PCR) patents[15] reads as follows:

1. A process for amplifying at least one specific nucleic acid sequence contained in a nucleic acid or a mixture of nucleic acids wherein each nucleic acid consists of two separate complementary strands, of equal or unequal length, which process comprises:

   (a) treating the strands with two oligonucleotide primers, for each different specific sequence being amplified, under conditions such that for each different sequence being amplified an extension product of each primer is synthesized which is complementary to each nucleic acid strand, wherein said primers are selected so as to be sufficiently complementary to different strands of each specific sequence to hybridize therewith such that the extension product synthesized from one primer, when it is separated from its complement, can serve as a template for synthesis of the extension product of the other primer;
   (b) separating the primer extension products from the templates on which they were synthesized to produce single-stranded molecules; and
   (c) treating the single-stranded molecules generated from step (b) with the primers of step (a) under conditions that a primer extension product is synthesized using each of the single strands produced in step (b) as a template.

2.4.3 Diagnostic Techniques

The Falkow and Moseley patent for DNA probes[16] includes the following as claim 1:

> 1. A method for detecting the presence of a pathogen in a clinical sample suspected of containing said pathogen, said method comprising:
>
> depositing said sample on an inert support;
> treating said sample to affix genetic material of any of said pathogen present in said sample to said support in substantially single stranded form at substantially the same site on said support where said sample was deposited;
> contacting said fixed single stranded genetic material with a labeled probe having a nucleotide sequence of at least about 25 bases at least substantially complementary to a nucleotide sequence of a structural gene characteristic of said pathogen, said contacting being under hybridizing conditions at a predetermined stringency; and
> detecting duplex formation on said support by means of said label.

The first claim in the Hybritech monoclonal sandwich assay patent[17] reads as follows:

> 1. A process for the determination of the presence or concentration of an antigenic substance in a fluid comprising the steps of:
>
> (a) contacting a sample of the fluid with a measured amount of a soluble first monoclonal antibody to the antigenic substance in order to form a soluble complex of the antibody and antigenic substance present in said sample, said first monoclonal antibody being labelled;
> (b) contacting the soluble complex with a second monoclonal antibody to the antigenic substance, said second monoclonal antibody being bound to a solid carrier, said solid carrier being insoluble in said fluid, in order to form an insoluble complex of said first monoclonal antibody, said antigenic substance and said second monoclonal antibody bound to said solid carrier;
> (c) separating said solid carrier from the fluid sample and unreacted labelled antibody;
> (d) measuring either the amount of labelled antibody associated with the solid carrier or the amount of unreacted labelled antibody; and
> (e) relating the amount of labelled antibody measured with the amount of labelled antibody measured for a control sample prepared in accordance with steps (a)–(d), said control sample being known to be free of said antigenic substance, to determine the presence of antigenic substance in said fluid sample, or relating the amount of labelled antibody measured with the amount of labelled antibody measured for samples containing known amounts of antigenic substance prepared in accordance with steps (a)–(d) to determine the concentration of antigenic substance in said fluid sample, the first and second monoclonal antibodies having an affinity for the antigenic substance of at least about 10^8 liters/mole.

2.4.4 Plant Science

The following is representative of the claims in the first utility patent encompassing plants *per se*:[18]

7. A monocotyledonous plant capable of producing seed having an endogenous free tryptophan content of at least about one-tenth milligram per gram dry seed weight, wherein the seed is capable of germinating into a plant capable of producing seed having an endogenous free tryptophan content of at least about one-tenth milligram per gram dry seed weight.

Other claims representative of those found on plants *per se* are the following, taken from a patent on hybrid corn issued to Pioneer Hi-Bred:[19]

1. Hybrid corn seed designated 3471.
2. A hybrid corn plant and its plant parts produced by the seed of claim 1.

*   *   *

4. A hybrid corn plant with the phenotypic characteristics of the hybrid plant of claim 2.

An illustrative claim for a plant tissue culture technique is the following, taken from a patent to Lubrizol Genetics:[20]

1. A method for the production of an organogenic tissue culture comprising cells of *Glycine max* comprising culturing an immature embryo of *Glycine max* to form an organogenic callus culture on a medium comprising BAP at a concentration between about 10 µM and about 15 µM and minor elements at a concentration between about four and about six times normal concentration of the micronutrients of MS medium such that germination of the embryo is prevented and organogenic shoot production is promoted.

Calgene's patent for, among other things, the use of the polygalacturonase gene in antisense to control the ripening of plants such as tomato[21] includes the following claims:

8. A DNA construct comprising a DNA sequence of at least 15 base pairs of a DNA sequence encoding tomato polygalacturonase (PG) joined, in the opposite orientation for expression, 5' to the 3' terminus of a transcriptional initiation region functional in plants.

*   *   *

14. A tomato plant cell comprising a DNA construct according to [claim 8].

2.4.5 Animal Science

The Ohio University patent for the genetic transformation of zygotes[22] includes the following claims:

1. A method of obtaining a mammal characterized as having a plurality of cells containing exogenous genetic material, said material including at least one gene and a control sequence operably associated therewith, which, under predetermined conditions,

express said gene under the control of said control sequence in a cell of said mammal, which comprises:

(a) introducing exogenous genetic material into a pronucleus of a mammalian zygote by microinjection, said zygote being capable of development into a mammal, said genetic material including at least one gene and a control sequence operably associated therewith, thereby obtaining a genetically transformed zygote;

(b) transplanting an embryo derived from the genetically transformed zygote into a pseudopregnant female capable of bearing the embryo to term; and

(c) allowing the embryo to develop to term;

where said gene and control sequence are selected so that the gene is not activated in such manner and degree as would prevent normal development of the embryo to term.

* * *

7. The method of claim 1 in which the zygote is allowed to develop in vitro to the morula or blastocyst stage prior to transplantation.

The "Harvard mouse" patent,[23] the first patent on an animal *per se*, includes the following claims:

1. A transgenic non-human mammal all of whose germ cells and somatic cells contain a recombinant activated oncogene sequence introduced into said mammal, or an ancestor of said mammal, at an embryonic stage.

2. The mammal of claim 1, a chromosome of said mammal including an endogenous coding sequence substantially the same as a coding sequence of said oncogene sequence.

* * *

11. The mammal of claim 1, said mammal being a rodent.

12. The mammal of claim 11, said rodent being a mouse.

The Biogen patent for the production of recombinant proteins in animal milk[24] illustrates claims to a manufacturing process employing a transgenic mammal:

1. A process for the production and secretion into mammal's milk of an exogenous recombinate protein comprising the steps of:

(a) producing milk in a transgenic mammal characterized by an expression system comprising a casein promoter operatively linked to an exogenous DNA sequence coding for the recombinant protein through a DNA sequence coding for a signal peptide effective in secreting and maturing the recombinant protein in mammary tissue;

(b) collecting the milk; and

(c) isolating the exogenous recombinant protein from the milk.

2.4.6 Therapeutic Compounds, Methods, and Compositions

A large number of patents issue each year on compounds, new therapeutic methods of treatment that employ known compounds, and compositions for treating various disorders in humans, animals, and plants. The following claims illustrate those found in such patents.

Claims to a method of combating retroviruses in a patent issued to Research Corporation[25] read as follows:

> 1. A method for inhibition of a retrovirus which comprises administering to a host a composition comprising an inhibitory effective amount of a peptide of 3 to about 11 amino acids containing the amino acid sequence Phe-X-Gly, wherein X is any amino acid.
>
> 2. The method of claim 1 wherein X is selected from the group consisting of phenyl-alanine, tryptophane, tyrosine, naphthylalanine, alanine, leucine, glycine, valine and isoleucine.
>
> 3. The method of claim 2 wherein X is phenylalanine, leucine or glycine.
>
> 4. The method of claim 1 wherein the retrovirus is HIV (AIDS) virus.

An NYU patent concerning live vaccines for the treatment of bacterial-mediated diarrheal diseases such as cholera and typhoid[26] includes the following claims:

> 1. A plasmid which comprises a gene coding for an immunologically active, conjugably transferable, non-toxic, heat-labile *Escherichia coli* enterotoxin and a gene coding for a non-toxic, heat-stable *Escherichia coli* enterotoxin.
>
> 2. The plasmid of claim 1, further comprising transposon 3.
>
> 3. A strain of *Escherichia coli* comprising the plasmid of claim 1.
>
> *   *   *
>
> 13. A live vaccine comprising the *Escherichia coli* of claim 3 and a sterile, pharmaceutically acceptable carrier.

Mycoherbicide compositions and methods of treatment are claimed in a Mycogen patent[27] as follows:

> 1. A composition for controlling wild poinsettia and weedy spurges comprising a herbicidally effective amount of novel isolate of the fungus *Alternaria euphorbiicola*, having the identifying characteristics of deposit NRRL 18056, in association with an inert agricultural carrier.
>
> 2. A process for controlling wild poinsettia which comprises applying a herbicidally effective amount of the fungus *Alternaria euphorbiicola*, having the identifying characteristics of deposit NRRL 18056, onto said wild poinsettia or onto the situs of said wild poinsettia.

REFERENCES

1. 35 U.S.C. § 112, paragraph two.
2. *See generally* A. Deller, PATENT CLAIMS (2d ed. 1971) (published and supplemented by Clark Boardman Callaghan); R. Faber, LANDIS ON MECHANICS OF PATENT CLAIM DRAFTING (3d ed. 1991) (published by the Practicing Law Institute, Inc.); I. Aisenberg,

ATTORNEY'S DICTIONARY OF PATENT CLAIMS (1985) (published and supplemented by Matthew Bender); T. Greer, WRITING AND UNDERSTANDING U.S. PATENT CLAIMS—A PROGRAMMED WORKBOOK (1979) (published by the Michie Company); CLAIMING BIOTECHNOLOGICAL INVENTIONS (B. Eisen and J. Williams, eds. 1985) (published by the American Intellectual Property Law Association).

3. G. Köhler and C. Milstein, *Continuous Cultures of Fused Cells Secreting Antibody of Predefined Specificity,* 256 NATURE 495 (1975).

4. *See, e.g.,* D. Yelton and M. Scharff, *Monoclonal Antibodies,* 68 AMERICAN SCIENTIST 510 (1980) (and references cited therein).

5. L. Pasteur, Manufacture of Beer and Yeast, U.S. Patent No. 141,072.

6. S. Borbach and B. Goldin, *Lactobacillus* Strains and Methods of Selection, U.S. Patent No. 4,839,281.

7. R. Hewick and J. Seehra, Method for the Purification of Erythropoietin and Erythropoietin Compositions, U.S. Patent No. 4,677,195.

8. Amgen, Inc. v. Chugai Pharmaceutical Co., 927 F.2d 1200, 18 USPQ2d 1016, 1029–31 (Fed. Cir.), *cert. denied,* 112 S. Ct. 169 (1991).

9. A. Tsukamoto *et al.,* Human Hematopoietic Stem Cell, U.S. Patent No. 5,061,620; *see also* M. Chase, *Systemix Wins a Controversial Patent On a Human Cell; Shares Rise Sharply,* WALL STREET JOURNAL (November 1, 1991) at B5.

10. S. Cohen and H. Boyer, Biologically Functional Molecular Chimeras, U.S. Patent No. 4,237,224.

11. S. Cohen and H. Boyer, Biologically Functional Molecular Chimeras, U.S. Patent No. 4,740,470.

12. K. Itakura and A. Riggs, Recombinant Cloning Vehicle Microbial Polypeptide Expression, U.S. Patent No. 4,704,362; *see also* R. Baum, *Genentech Receives Key Biotechnology Patent,* CHEMICAL & ENG. NEWS (Nov. 9, 1987) at 5.

13. J. Sanford *et al.,* Method for Transporting Substances into Living Cells and Tissues and Apparatus Therefor, U.S. Patent No. 4,945,050.

14. T. Cech *et al.,* RNA Ribozyme Polymerases, Dephosphorylases, Restriction Endoribonucleases, and Methods, U.S. Patent No. 4,987,071; *see also* A. Gibbons, *Molecular Scissors: RNA Enzymes Go Commercial,* 251 SCIENCE 521 (Feb. 1, 1991).

15. K. Mullis, Process for Amplifying Nucleic Acid Sequences, U.S. Patent No. 4,683,202; *see also* K. Mullis *et al.,* Process for Amplifying, Detecting, and/or Cloning Nucleic Acid Sequences, U.S. Patent No. 4,683,195.

16. S. Falkow and S. Mosley, Specific DNA Probes in Diagnostic Microbiology, U.S. Patent No. 4,358,535.

17. G. David and H. Greene, Immunometric Assays Using Monoclonal Antibodies, U.S. Patent No. 4,376,110.

18. K. Hibberd *et al.,* Tryptophan Overproducer Mutants of Cereal Crops, U.S. Patent No. 4,642,411.

19. R. Seifert *et al.,* Hybrid Corn Plant and Seed, U.S. Patent No. 4,737,596.

20. U. Barwale and J. Widholm, Whole Plant Regeneration via Organogenesis and Somaclonal Variation in Glycine Species, U.S. Patent No. 4,857,465.

21. W. Hiatt *et al.,* PG Gene and Its Use in Plants, U.S. Patent No. 4,801,540.

22. T. Wagner and P. Hoppe, Genetic Transformation of Zygotes, U.S. Patent No. 4,873,191.

23. P. Leder and T. Stewart, Transgenic Non-Human Mammals, U.S. Patent No. 4,736,866.

24. H. Meade and N. Lonberg, Isolation of Exogenous Recombinant Proteins from the Milk of Transgenic Mammals, U.S. Patent No. 4,873,316.

25. W. Gallaher, Method of Prevention or Treatment of AIDS by Inhibition of Human Immunodeficiency Virus, U.S. Patent No. 4,880,779.
26. W. Maas and C. Gyles, Mutant Enterotoxin of *E. coli,* U.S. Patent No. 4,761,372.
27. J. Riley and H. Walker, Biological Control of Wild Poinsettia and Other Weedy Spurges with a Fungal Pathogen, U.S. Patent No. 4,755,208.

The Legal Decision-Making Process

William M. Atkinson

Obtaining and enforcing patent rights requires involvement in a legal system that can be mind-boggling for the uninitiated. Although success in this system almost always requires the advice of an attorney, anyone who regularly deals with patent issues should become familiar with at least the basic rules of patent practice. The purpose of this chapter is to provide insight into basic administrative and judicial decision-making processes that make up our current patent system.

The patent system in the United States is governed by federal law set forth in statutes enacted by Congress[1] and in regulations issued by the Commissioner of Patents.[2] These statutes and regulations often are the subject of court decisions, which also must be consulted when seeking a patent. In addition, the U.S. Patent and Trademark Office (PTO) publishes the *Manual of Patent Examining Procedure* (MPEP) as a reference work on the practices and procedures of patent applications before the PTO. The MPEP does not have the force of law, but it is a convenient reference source in this area.

3.1 THE PATENT APPLICATION PROCESS

All U.S. patents are issued by the PTO, an agency within the U.S. Department of Commerce. The PTO is located in Arlington, Virginia, just outside of Washington,

DC. The PTO examines all U.S. patent applications, issues all U.S. patents, and conducts certain proceedings relating to patents already issued.

3.1.1 Patent Examiners

The PTO employs approximately 1900 patent examiners,[3] who are responsible for examining each patent application that is filed. In 1991 alone, approximately 178,000 patent applications were filed.[4]

All patent examiners have one or more college degrees in the various technical areas and, in some cases, the law. Many of the biotechnology examiners have advanced degrees and even postdoctoral experience. Regardless of their legal training or experience, all patent examiners are required to attend an eight-week training course on patent law and procedure during their first year on the job. The course covers all aspects of the PTO's patent application process, from filing to examination to the issuance of U.S. patents.

Besides the training, the PTO offers examiners the opportunity to take advanced courses covering specialized areas of patent law throughout their tenure in the PTO. Many examiners also attend law school in the evenings at one of the universities in the Washington, DC, area.

Part of an examiner's training, of course, occurs on the job. In the beginning, an examiner's work is closely watched by a supervisory primary examiner (SPE), who must review and sign all of the examiner's work. As an examiner gains experience, he or she is allowed more autonomy. The ultimate goal is to give each examiner the authority to make decisions concerning patent applications with only minimum supervision.

In order to gain this autonomy, the examiner must complete two separate review programs. In the first, or "partial signatory authority" program, the examiner is given the authority to make preliminary decisions on the merits of patent applications for six months without supervisory approval. The SPEs within each Examining Group and the group director oversee this program. After the review period ends, the cases the examiner acted on during the review period are gone over. If minimum standards for quality and quantity are met, the examiner's partial signatory authority is made permanent.

Two years after completing the partial signatory program, the examiner may enter the "full signatory authority" program. In this, the examiner is allowed to make final decisions concerning patent applications without prior supervisory approval. At the end of the review period, again six months, the cases he or she acted on are evaluated against minimum quality and quantity standards. If these standards are met, the examiner's full signatory authority is made permanent. Examiners earning full signatory authority are called "primary examiners."

Despite the review process, an examiner's work is monitored throughout his or her career as part of the PTO's system of controlling the average time that patent applications are pending within the patent office. The monitoring system focuses on the pace of the examiner in processing applications. For each patent application he or she considers, an examiner is awarded one "count" the first time he or she considers the merits of a given application and another "count" when the application is "disposed of"; that is, when it is allowed, abandoned, or appealed to the Board of Appeals and Interferences. Decisions made by the examiner between the first decision and the final disposition of the application are not credited toward the examiner's performance. This motivates examiners to complete work on any given application as quickly as possible.

Taking into consideration the varying technical difficulty of the applications and each examiner's level of experience, each examiner is assigned an expectancy that governs the rate at which he or she must move docket items. By surpassing this expectancy, an examiner can earn financial rewards for efficient service.

Every year, a sample of each examiner's work is rated against minimum quality standards as well. If it is outstanding, he or she may earn financial awards for excellent service.

3.1.2 Patent Filings

All patent applications filed in the PTO are reviewed by a series of "divisions" or "groups" within the PTO. First the applications go to the Application Division, where they are reviewed for compliance with a number of formal filing requirements.[5] Next, applications are classified, based on their technical content, according to the PTO's classification system.[6] Then they are assigned to the Examining Group responsible for the particular technologies that they cover.[7]

In certain cases, when the technology is sensitive in nature or may affect national security, applications are assigned to the Security Group, or Group 220, for examination.[8] Security applications are examined like any other applications. However, unless the security designation is removed later, these applications are never allowed to enter the public domain. This means that such applications, even when patentable, are never allowed to issue as U.S. patents and are never included in any interference proceeding.[9]

A goal of the classification process is to ensure that applications are assigned to an examiner who has the relevant technical expertise.[10] Although the PTO's classification system may make little sense to the average layperson, its sophistication and detail provide a degree of consistency and quality to the examination process. People who understand the classification system often know ahead of time what Examining Group, if not which examiner, will be assigned a given application. Biotechnology applications most frequently go to Group 180.

3.1.3 The Examination Process

3.1.3.1 Before the Examiner. The heart of the PTO operation is the examination process. In this stage of the patent application process, technically and legally trained examiners again review the application for matters of form and also examine the application on its merits to determine the patentability of the inventions claimed. Once in the Examining Group, the applications are assigned to a Group Art Unit, where they are further assigned to an examiner based on internal classification procedures.[11] Once assigned to a particular examiner, the applications generally are examined in order of filing date,[12] although in practice each examiner has some limited discretion to study the applications as he or she wishes for expediency and as a matter of personal preference.

However, an examiner's discretion in picking and choosing among the applications is limited by the requirement that all applications be examined within controlled time periods.[13] To help examiners and their supervisors in this and other processes, the PTO has a computerized system to track each application at each stage of the application process. Each examiner and supervisor is provided with a series of periodic reports that update and document the progression of the individual dockets. Supervisors also receive a report on the overall docket of the Art Unit and Examining Group.

Most of the examination process involves reviewing applications for patentability according to the patent statutes and regulations. These statutes and regulations provide the standards against which all applications are measured for patentability. For the most part, examiners judge the patentability of application claims according to 35 U.S.C. §§ 101–103 and 112. Each of these statutes is discussed in greater detail in other chapters of this book.

The first step in judging the patentability of an application is to identify what constitutes prior art to a given application.[14] This process focuses primarily on the date the application was filed but it is governed by section 102, as well as by various decisions from the U.S. Supreme Court, the U.S. Court of Appeals for the Federal Court, and the Board of Patent Appeals and Interferences.

After identifying what constitutes prior art to a given application, the examiner must search for the specific prior art that is relevant. This searching process is the most time-consuming part of the examination process and usually takes up the majority of an examiner's workday. The examiner searches for relevant prior art throughout the process. In practical terms, however, the search mostly is performed before the examiner makes the initial "office action" on the application.[15]

To assist the examiner, copies of previously issued U.S. patents and selected foreign patents and technical articles are classified in "shoes," or files, located within the examiner's Art Unit.[16] These reference materials relate to the technology for which the examiner's Art Unit is responsible. Should the examiner feel that a broader search is required, however, other search files within the PTO also are available. These reference files are constantly reorganized and updated to keep abreast of new technologies, while making the search process as simple as possible. This is done to streamline the application process and to ensure that the examiner has access to the most relevant prior art.[17]

In addition to the sources just discussed, examiners have access to a large, centrally located, technical library containing books and periodicals related to all sorts of technology.[18] This library also provides access to all foreign patents and published patent applications. Furthermore, in the mid-1980s, the PTO established its own on-line database, the Automated Patent System (APS), which allows computerized full-text searching of U.S. patents and selected foreign patent abstracts. Terminals for the APS system and other commercial databases are available within each examiner's Art Unit.

Consequently, each examiner has at his or her disposal numerous tools to identify and locate copies of relevant prior art. The system is not perfect, of course, but the PTO makes a great effort and spends huge sums of money to assure that each application is examined with the most pertinent prior art. Anyone faced with an infringement claim is free to contest the validity of the patent in either a reexamination proceeding within the PTO or in a court of law.

Once the examiner identifies and locates the pertinent prior art, the claims of the application are examined on their merits. In most instances, the examiner initially will object to the application on matters of form or will reject the patent's claims on the basis of the prior art or other statutory grounds.[19] If the examiner rejects the claims on the basis of prior art, the specific prior art is provided to the patent applicant[20] along with an explanation of the reasoning behind the rejection.[21] Of course, if everything is in order, the examiner may allow the claims on first action—although this is uncommon for biotechnology applications.[22]

When going over a patent application, the examiner essentially wears two hats. In one sense the examiner is responsible for protecting the public from invalid patents and wears the hat of a public prosecutor building a case against the patentability of the claims.[23] In this regard, he or she bears the burden of establishing a *prima facie* case of unpatentability.[24] In the other sense, however, the examiner is also the judge and jury, trying facts during the examination process. In this sense, he or she has to guard against an over-zealous application of the patent laws to the detriment of the patent applicant.[25] Typically, in a biotechnology-related application, the examiner initially raises a number of objections in an effort to identify potential inconsistencies in the applicant's case.

If the examiner initially rejects the application, the patent applicant has up to six months[26] from the date of the examiner's decision to challenge it or to make amendments to the application.[27] When challenging the decision, the applicant can present evidence, such as additional prior art, affidavits, or technical declarations, to persuade the examiner to alter the initial decision.[28] Whether he or she agrees with the examiner's decision or not, the applicant also can choose to amend the application in the hope of satisfying the examiner's concerns.[29] Such amendments may relate to matters of form or may substantively alter the scope of the protection sought.

In either case, after the patent applicant responds to the examiner's Office Action, the case is returned to the examiner for reconsideration. After considering the applicant's response, including any evidence presented by the applicant, the examiner again judges the merits of the application (usually within two months in accordance with the PTO's internal guidelines). The examiner either allows the application or continues to reject it on the same or modified grounds.

If the examiner is not persuaded that the initial decision is incorrect or obviated, a "final rejection" usually will be issued.[30] The final rejection can contain modified grounds if the modification is necessitated by the applicant's response. If a new point for rejection is set forth that is not necessitated by the applicant's response, the second office action must be nonfinal, and the applicant is given another six months to respond to the new point.[31]

Even if the examiner issues a final rejection, the patent applicant is offered another chance to respond.[32] The response, however, may be refused by the examiner unless it puts the application in condition for allowance or in a better posture for appeal.[33] In the alternative, the applicant may forego further reconsideration by the examiner and appeal the decision to the Board of Patent Appeals and Interferences.[34]

3.1.3.2 Before the Board. If the applicant chooses to appeal, both the applicant and the examiner must inform the Board of Patent Appeals and Interferences in writing of their respective positions.[35] The applicant also may request an oral hearing before the board.[36]

The board is made up of approximately 60 examiners-in-chief, each of whom has a law degree and is experienced in the examination process.[37] Each appeal is assigned to a panel of three board members (or in some special cases five or seven board members) who review the evidence in the record and the arguments of both sides. The board then decides whether to affirm the examiner's rejection in whole or in part, to make additional objections or rejections, or to reverse the examiner's decision.[38]

The board does not have the authority to allow the application. In practical terms, however, if the board reverses the examiner's position, he or she usually will allow the application without making any more rejections.[39] If the patent applicant accepts the decision of the board, the application is returned to the examiner for further action consistent with the board's decision.[40]

3.1.3.3 Additional Appeals. A patent applicant who is not satisfied with the board's decision may follow any one of three routes. The applicant may (1) sue the Commissioner of Patents in the U.S. District Court for the District of Columbia,[41] (2) appeal the board's decision directly to the Federal Circuit,[42] or (3) refile the application to restart the examination process.[43] The last alternative, however, usually will result in the same rejection that was affirmed by the board, unless additional evidence is presented to the examiner or amendments are made to the application.[44]

Before choosing any of these alternatives, the applicant may ask the board to reconsider its decision.[45] If none of the alternatives is chosen, the application is returned to the examiner for action consistent with the status of the claims remaining in the application.[46]

3.1.3.4 Civil Suits Under Section 145. Generally, it is rare when a patent applicant who is dissatisfied with the board's decision chooses to file a civil suit against the Commissioner of Patents rather than appeal to the Federal Circuit to obtain a patent. Nevertheless, the applicant has the right to sue, and from time to time this right has been used. The advantage of this course of action resides in the ability of the patent applicant to have his or her invention evaluated on the basis of traditional forms of testimonial and demonstrative evidence in addition to the written record generated before the PTO.[47]

Applicants tempted to proceed in this manner should be warned, however, that suing the commissioner can be very expensive. Section 145 provides that all expenses incurred by the commissioner in defending Section 145 actions shall be borne by the patent applicant. While this provision may not always have been enforced in the past, the current PTO solicitor recently indicated publicly that the agency intends to enforce this provision, even to the extent of requiring the applicant to pay for expert testimony on behalf of the commissioner.[48]

The District Court may not order the PTO to issue a patent but it may set aside the decision of the board if it is based on clearly erroneous factual findings or an error in law.[49] If the patent applicant wins the suit against the commissioner, the matter will be sent back to the PTO for action consistent with the District Court's decision. Although it is possible that the examiner still will reject the application, the claims generally will be allowed if the court sets aside the board's decision.

If the patent applicant is dissatisfied with the decision of the District Court, the matter may be appealed to the Federal Circuit for review in much the same manner as if the board's decision had been appealed directly to the Federal Circuit in the first place.[50] The record on appeal, however, will be the record adduced before the District Court rather than just the paper record considered by the board.[51]

3.1.3.5   Appeals to the Federal Circuit.   The far more common approach of patent applicants dissatisfied with the board's decision is to appeal directly to the Federal Circuit. The Federal Circuit has exclusive appellate jurisdiction over most, if not all, patent-related matters, whether of administrative or judicial origin.[52]

If an appeal of a board decision is taken to the Federal Circuit, the appeal generally is assigned to a three-judge panel for review.[53] Although it is very rare, the full court (12 judges) may hear the appeal if the case presents an important legal issue.[54]

The Federal Circuit's authority to review the decisions of the board is limited by the traditional standards of appellate review; that is, it is bound by the factual findings of the board unless it finds them to be clearly erroneous.[55] Legal decisions embodied in the board's decision, however, are reviewed by the court anew.[56]

After considering the briefs of the patent applicant and the PTO solicitor (who represents the Commissioner of Patents before the court) and, if requested, the oral arguments of the parties, the court renders a decision on the merits of the appeal. The court can pronounce its decision in one of three ways: (1) by judgment under Federal Circuit Rule 36, (2) by a nonprecedential opinion,[57] or (3) by a precedential opinion.[58]

A judgment under Federal Circuit Rule 36 is, by definition, a complete affirmation of the board's decision.[59] This mode of disposing of an appeal is rendered without comment when the court unanimously determines that the board's decision was not based on clearly erroneous factual findings or erroneous legal conclusions.

Nonprecedential opinions generally are short opinions aimed primarily at telling the losing party why it lost. Cases are disposed of in this manner when, in the panel's view, the issues involved in the appeal do not add significantly to the body of law. Consequently, nonprecedential opinions contain little discussion of the facts involved in the appeal and often only a cursory discussion of the merits of the court's decision. As the name indicates, such opinions are nonprecedential and cannot be cited as precedent. They can, however, form the basis of claim preclusion, issue preclusion, judicial estoppel, or law of the case, where appropriate, to insure finality to the dispute.[60] Nonprecedential opinions are not published in the *Federal Reporter*, but recent opinions dealing with patent law issues are published by the Bureau of National Affairs, Inc. in the *United States Patent Quarterly*.

Precedential opinions are full-fledged opinions of the court and contain a discussion of the relevant facts and law underlying the court's decision. As the name implies, precedential opinions may be cited as precedent.[61] All precedential opinions of the Federal Circuit are published in the *Federal Reporter*, and all such opinions involving patent law issues are published in the *United States Patent Quarterly*.

Decisions of the Federal Circuit are binding on the board and the PTO.[62] Accordingly, if the court reverses the board's decision, the matter will be sent back to the board for further action consistent with the court's decision. Like the board, the Federal Circuit does not have the authority to issue patents or even to order the commissioner to issue a patent.[63] As a result, even after a reversal of the board's decision, the examiner may, after obtaining approval from the Deputy Assistant Commissioner for Patents, institute new grounds of rejection. Practically speaking, however, if the patent applicant is successful on appeal to the court, the PTO usually will allow the application to issue on receipt of the court's decision.[64]

If the patent applicant is unsuccessful on appeal to the Federal Circuit, the patent applicant may ask reconsideration by the Federal Circuit panel that rendered the opinion and the Federal Circuit *in banc*.[65] These reviews are discretionary to the court, however, and are rarely granted.

3.1.3.6 Review by the U.S. Supreme Court.   Finally, the patent applicant who is dissatisfied with the decision of the Federal Circuit may file a petition for a writ of *certiorari* for the U.S. Supreme Court to review the Federal Circuit decision.[66] Such petitions are rarely granted.[67]

3.1.4 Post-Examination Processes

3.1.4.1 In General.   If at any stage of the examination process the claims of a given patent application are allowed by the examiner, the application passes to the PTO's Allowed Files Division, where it is processed for issuance as a U.S. patent.[68] After the application has been allowed, however, the applicant may submit any necessary amendments to the application before it issues.[69] These amendments are sent to the examiner for consideration and may be entered if good and sufficient cause is shown why the amendment was not submitted earlier. This right to submit amendments is limited, however, and should not be used as a way of making changes that could have or should have been made during the examination process.

3.1.4.2 Interference Proceedings.

After being allowed, an application may become involved in an interference proceeding with another allowed patent application or an issued patent.[70] Interference proceedings are necessary because of the statutory mandate that only *one* patent may issue for each invention.[71] This does not mean, of course, that a given commercial product may not be covered by more than one valid and enforceable patent. Rather, it means that two patents of the same scope may not issue to two different inventors.

Interference proceedings can be initiated by a patent applicant[72] or the examiner.[73] Once initiated, interference proceedings are handled by the board. Unlike the single-party appeals just discussed, however, they involve opposing parties before the board (they are *inter partes*, rather than *ex parte* proceedings). The goal of an interference proceeding is to determine which inventor has priority to the invention and thus should receive a patent.[74]

The United States is the only country that determines the right to hold a patent on a "first-to-invent" basis and, as a result, it is the only country to hold interference proceedings. All other countries instead award priority on a "first-to-file" basis. As the United States seeks to harmonize its patent laws with those of other countries, this aspect of U.S. patent practice may well become obsolete. Until it does, however, the current interference system remains in full force and looms as a prospect for any patent applicant.

While a substantive discussion of the rules of interference practice is beyond the scope of this chapter, the importance of maintaining records to prove the dates of an invention's conception and its first reduction to practice remains paramount. As will be seen in later sections of this chapter and this book, even if this evidence is not needed to obtain a patent, it can be crucial in defending against an attack on the validity of the patent in an interference context before the board or in a priority or infringement context in court.

The interference proceeding is more akin to litigation than it is to typical *ex parte* (i.e., single party) examination. This is because interference proceedings are conducted *inter partes* (i.e., between two or more opposing parties) and thus are adversarial in nature. In an interference proceeding, each party is afforded a limited right to discovery[75] and may present dispositive motions to the board similar to motions for summary judgment under Rule 56, Fed.R.Civ.P.[76]

The outcome of the interference proceeding determines which, if either, of the two parties is entitled to a patent.[77] In the appropriate case, the result of the interference contest may form the basis of later claims of interference estoppel, *res judicata*, or administrative estoppel.[78] Accordingly, involvement in an interference proceeding can seriously affect a party's rights under the patent system as well as any defensive efforts against others owning patents adverse to its interests.

A party not satisfied with the decision of the board in an interference proceeding may sue its opponent in the U.S. District Court[79] or appeal directly to the Federal Circuit.[80] These dual routes of review are similar to those just discussed with respect to appeals from the *ex parte* decisions of the board.

An appeal to the Federal Circuit is available as a matter of right to the party dissatisfied with the District Court's decision.[81] Whether the Federal Circuit's decision is based on a direct appeal from the board or from the District Court, a petition for writ of *certiorari* may be filed in the U.S. Supreme Court.[82]

3.2   PROCEEDINGS ON ISSUED PATENTS

The patent grant gives the patent owner the right to exclude all others from making, using, or selling the inventions covered by the patent.[83] In some limited circumstances, this right prohibits others from making, using, or selling essential parts of a claimed invention.[84] Concomitant to the right to exclude is the right to receive royalties or other consideration in exchange for agreeing not to enforce the right to exclude. Thus, the licensing of patent rights in many respects is an industry unto itself.

3.2.1   Patent Litigation

Because of their intrinsic value, patent rights often become involved in litigation in both federal and state courts. Many types of disputes may arise, ranging from infringement to validity to enforceability to priority to inventorship to ownership to damages. Because of the variety, disputes may arise in either federal or state courts. Chapter 13 is devoted to the substantive aspects of patent litigation, and Chapter 14 examines the procedural aspects of patent litigation. This section provides an overall perspective on how patent litigation fits into the legal decision-making process as a whole.

3.2.1.1   Federal or State Court?   To be in the federal system, litigation concerning patent rights must either "arise under any Act of Congress relating to patents"[85] or be based on principles of diversity.[86] Any dispute not falling within one of these categories must be brought in state court.[87]

Whether a particular cause of action "arises under any Act of Congress relating to patents" is governed by the "well-pleaded" complaint rule.[88] This rule focuses on whether the plaintiff has asserted a right or interest that would be defeated or sustained by the construction given to the patent laws.[89] The following is a partial list of issues that may properly be raised in federal court under Section 1338:

- Declaratory judgment suits regarding the invalidity of patents[90]
- Priority contests involving interfering patents[91]
- Suits to enjoin threatened patent infringement[92]
- Patent infringement suits[93]

- Mandamus actions against the PTO for denying a filing date because of an unsigned bank check[94]
- Suit seeking reinstatement to the patent bar by someone suspended from practice before the PTO[95]
- Compensation suits for infringement against the Tennessee Valley Authority[96]
- Actions to enforce the settlement agreement of a patent infringement suit[97]
- Declaratory judgment suits for noninfringement[98]
- Ancillary proceedings concerning enforcement of discovery requests from another suit involving patent infringement[99]
- Suits seeking determination of inventorship, and co-ownership and correction of inventorship[100]
- Suits seeking judicial review of the refusal of the Commissioner of Patents to revive an abandoned patent application[101]
- Declaratory judgment suits for infringement[102]

In contrast to the preceding list, the following are issues that do not "arise under" the patent laws and thus may be brought in federal court only where diversity exists:

- Priority contests not involving interfering patents[103]
- Suits by anyone claiming to be an assignee of a patent[104]
- Contract disputes arising out of patent license agreements[105]
- Suit to recover unpaid royalties under patent license agreements[106]
- Patent license disputes in federal court solely on the basis of diversity[107]
- Breach of license suits[108]
- Contract disputes to determine priority of inventorship[109]
- Declaratory judgment suits seeking relief from installment payments under assignment agreements[110]

These matters also may be brought in state court according to the governing personal jurisdiction and venue requirements of the state involved.

Although a discussion of the requirements for personal jurisdiction and proper venue are beyond the scope of this chapter, both must be considered in filing patent suits, just as in more traditional disputes. These requirements are discussed in greater detail in Chapter 14.

In certain types of patent suits, specific statutory provisions limit the courts in which the suits may be filed. For example, suits against the United States seeking compensation for use of a patented invention by the government must be brought in the U.S. Court of Federal Claims (formerly, the U.S. Claims Court).[111] Certain suits, such as those that relate to reviews of decisions by the Board of Patent Appeals and Interferences in *ex parte* patent applications, must be brought in the U.S. District Court for the District of Columbia.[112]

3.2.1.2 Questions of Law and Fact. Regardless of where or in what court patent litigation proceeds, it usually involves numerous issues of both fact and law.

Because of the deference given to someone trying fact on appeal, it is important to understand whether a given issue is one of fact or one of law. The following is a list of some issues related to patents that are considered questions of fact:

- Anticipation of properly interpreted claims under Section 102[113]
- Commercial success under Section 103[114]
- Differences between a claimed invention and prior art under Section 103[115]
- Diligence under Section 102(g)[116]
- Disclosure of best mode under Section 112, first paragraph[117]
- An "exceptional" case under Section 285[118]
- Infringement of properly interpreted claims under Section 271[119]
- Infringement under the doctrine of equivalents (whether the accused device performs substantially the same function in substantially the same way to achieve substantially the same result as does the claimed invention)[120]
- Intent to deceive for inequitable conduct[121]
- Level of skill in the art under Section 103[122]
- Materiality of prior art for inequitable conduct[123]
- The meaning of terms in a patent specification[124]
- Noninfringement under the reverse doctrine of equivalents[125]
- The scope and content of prior art under Section 103[126]
- Structural equivalence under Section 112, sixth paragraph[127]
- Sufficiency of written description under Section 112, first paragraph[128]
- The meaning of arguments made to the PTO for purposes of claim interpretation or prosecution history estoppel[129]
- Utility under Section 101[130]
- Willful infringement[131]

In contrast, the following are considered questions of law:

- Claim interpretation[132]
- Claim definiteness under Section 112, second paragraph[133]
- The conception of an invention[134]
- Construction of a count in an interference proceeding[135]
- Enablement under Section 112, first paragraph[136]
- The existence of an implied license[137]
- Identity of claims for double patenting under Section 101[138]
- Inequitable conduct after determining materiality and intent to deceive the PTO[139]
- Obviousness under Section 103[140]
- "On sale" under Section 102(b)[141]
- "Public use" under Section 102(b)[142]
- Prosecution history estoppel under the doctrine of equivalents[143]
- Reduction to practice of an invention[144]
- Repair versus reconstruction of a patented invention[145]
- What constitutes prior art under Section 102[146]

- Whether a particular equivalent under the doctrine of equivalents is precluded by the prior art or whether a hypothetical claim could have been legally issued by the PTO[147]

3.2.1.3   Jury Trials.

Whether a particular issue is one of fact or law is important for several reasons, not the least of which concerns who may determine the issue. For the most part, unless the parties agree to a nonjury trial, factual issues are within the province of the jury under the Seventh Amendment to the U.S. Constitution. Legal issues, on the other hand, are primarily for the judge. However, it is proper for the judge in any given case to allow the jury to decide legal as well factual issues.[148] This is particularly true when the ultimate issue is a legal question based on factual questions, such as obviousness under Section 103.[149]

When legal questions are given to the jury to decide, however, the judge must be very careful to properly instruct the jury on the legal significance of its factual findings. It is the court's ultimate responsibility to ensure that the law is correctly applied. The judge should explain the intricacies of the law to the jury and order the jury to return a general verdict on the legal issues in addition to specific answers to the underlying factual questions.[150] In this way, the judge will be able to decide whether the jury's general verdict is consistent with its underlying factual determinations.

When the general verdict on a legal issue is harmonious with the factual findings of the jury, judgment on the general verdict will be entered. When the general verdict of the jury is inconsistent with its factual determinations, however, the court may enter judgment in accordance with the jury's factual determinations, return the matter to the jury for further deliberation, or order a new trial. If the jury's factual findings are themselves inconsistent, the court will not enter judgment and may either seek further deliberations from the jury or order a new trial.[151]

Even when the parties demand a jury trial, the Federal Circuit has held on many occasions that the litigants have a right to a jury trial, not a jury verdict.[152] In so holding, the court was validating the provisions of the Federal Rules of Civil Procedure that allow for any of the issues that may be present in a patent case to be decided apart from the jury, such as through summary judgment,[153] through a motion for judgment (formerly a directed verdict),[154] or through a renewed motion for judgment (formerly a judgment notwithstanding the verdict).[155] On the other hand, if the judge thinks the jury verdict is unsupported by the evidence, he or she may disregard the verdict and order a new trial.[156]

3.2.1.4   Standards of Proof.

Whether brought by the patent holder[157] or by the accused infringer,[158] the most common form of patent litigation involves allegations of patent infringement. Infringement issues, however, are rarely litigated alone. A person accused of patent infringement may raise any one of a number of defenses to the patent owner's claim of infringement. These include claims that the asserted patent is invalid, unenforceable, not infringed,[159] and, less frequently, the failure of the patent holder to mark the commercial products with the patent number,[160] intervening rights,[161] laches, or estoppel.[162] In almost all patent infringement suits, the issue of damages also will be tried.

Certain standards of proof are applicable on each of these matters. In that regard, patent owners must prove infringement by a preponderance of the evidence[163] and damages to a reasonable probability.[164] Accused infringers, however, generally are held to a higher standard in proving their defenses, one of clear and convincing evidence.[165] The following defenses must be proven by this standard:

- Patent invalidity (based on anticipation, obviousness, "on sale," "public use," prior invention, lack of enablement, failure to disclose best mode, lack of written description, or indefiniteness)[166]
- Unenforceability (based on inequitable conduct and its underlying findings of intent to deceive and materiality, unclean hands, or patent misuse)[167]
- Lack of utility[168]

With respect to laches and equitable estoppel, however, an accused infringer has to prove only the necessary elements of each defense by a preponderance of the evidence.[169]

The clear and convincing standard of proof that applies to invalidity and unenforceability defenses arises from the presumption of validity that applies to every issued patent.[170] The presumption of validity has no evidentiary value but it determines which party has the burden of going forward with evidence at the trial.[171] The party challenging the validity of the patent always carries the ultimate burden of proof.[172] Once the challenger has presented a *prima facie* case of invalidity, the burden of providing evidence supporting the validity of the patent shifts to the patent holder.[173] If the patent holder provides evidence that undermines the challenger's *prima facie* case, the challenger must respond with additional evidence.[174]

Although the presumption of validity may be overcome at any time, practically speaking, it is more difficult to overcome when the challenge to the validity of the patent is based on evidence that was considered by the PTO during the examination process.[175] This is because judges and juries usually defer to the decisions of the PTO on complex factual and legal questions, besides the traditional presumption that government agencies charged with administering the laws do so correctly.[176]

On some issues, the patent holder also faces the clear and convincing standard of proof:

- Prior invention (conception, diligence, and reduction to practice if the accused infringer proves a date of invention prior to the filing date of the patent in suit or provides invalidating evidence less than one year prior to the filing date of the patent in suit)[177]
- Willful infringement[178]
- Exceptional case[179]

3.2.1.5 Appeals. Regardless of which standard of proof applies, a judgment eventually will be entered once the issues are decided by the jury or the judge. This ends the first phase of the litigation.[180] Either party that is dissatisfied with any aspect of the judgment may appeal the matter to the appropriate appellate court. What court has jurisdiction to hear the appeal depends on the subject matter and jurisdictional basis on which the suit was brought.

If the suit was brought in Federal District Court on a matter "arising under" the patent laws, the District Court's judgment must be appealed to the Federal Circuit.[181] The same is true for patent suits against the government litigated in the U.S. Court of Federal Claims.[182] Matters brought in Federal District Court on the basis of diversity jurisdiction must be appealed to the respective regional U.S. Court of Appeals.[183] Finally, suits originating in state court must be appealed to whatever appellate court is allowed by state law.

The right to appeal is not the right to relitigate matters decided by the lower court.[184] Appellate courts may overturn the judgment of a lower court only if the judgment being reviewed is based on clearly erroneous factual findings,[185] erroneous legal determinations[186] or an abuse of discretion,[187] or if it is deficient in some matter of form.[188]

In this regard, the classification of issues as questions of fact or questions of law becomes paramount. Failing to consider these classifications in deciding whether to appeal and on what basis can doom any hope of obtaining relief. It also can subject the appealing party and its counsel to sanctions from the appellate court.[189] Understanding this may mean the difference between winning and losing any appeal.

The procedures of the various appeals courts differ widely. In the Federal Circuit, however, the procedures for handling appeals from the various district courts are the same as those regarding appeals from the PTO.

Finally, regardless of where the immediate appeal is taken, either party dissatisfied with any aspect of the appellate court's judgment may petition the U.S. Supreme Court to review the case by *certiorari*.

3.3 MISCELLANEOUS MATTERS

Patents also may become involved in any one of many administrative proceedings after they are issued. The most common of these are reissue proceedings and reexamination proceedings.

3.3.1 Reissue Proceedings

Section 251 of the patent statutes provides that a patent holder who believes that his or her patent is wholly or partly defective or invalid may file a reissue application to correct the patent in the PTO.[190] The reissue statute is remedial in nature, but does not allow correction unless a sufficiently recognizable error has been made in its procurement.[191] Not all defects may be corrected by reissue. Only those errors that occurred due to "inadvertence, accident, or mistake" may be corrected.[192] The failure to file a divisional application following a restriction requirement is not correctable through reissue.[193]

As long as the reissue application is filed within two years of the issue date of the original patent, however, the claims of the patent may be broadened unless doing so would be the same as allowing the patent holder to "recapture" subject matter that was given up during the original patent application.[194] The reissue process is not designed to allow the patent holder a second chance at the original patent application.[195]

Once a reissue application is filed, the claims of the application are examined again against the prior art, but the examination process is expedited.[196] Any type of prior art recognized under Section 102 may be considered by the PTO in a reissue proceeding. Remember, however, that the presumption of validity that applies to issued patents under Section 282 does not apply to reissue applications.[197] As a result, the burden of proof on the examiner of a reissue application is the same as it is regarding any *ex parte* application, that is, a preponderance of the evidence.

If the claims of the reissue application are patentable, the patent holder must surrender the issued patent in favor of the reissued patent.[198] The reissued patent then may be asserted just as any other issued patent.

The reissue process also protects the rights of the public. That is, there can be no liability for the infringement of a reissued claim prior to the reissue date unless the reissued claim is substantially identical in scope to a claim of the original patent. Plus, in certain limited circumstances, a court may hold that "intervening rights" exist and deny damages for infringement after the date the reissue patent issues. The court also may refuse to grant an injunction barring further infringement.[199]

On the whole, the reissue process works well. It allows the patent holder to obtain relief from unintentional errors in the patent, while at the same time keeping in mind the right of the public to make decisions based on the public record.

3.3.2   Reexamination Proceedings

Issued patents also may wind up before the PTO in a reexamination proceeding.[200] Unlike a reissue proceeding, which may be initiated only by the patent holder,[201] a reexamination proceeding may be initiated by any member of the public, including the Commissioner of Patents and the patent holder.[202]

Such a proceeding may be initiated by bringing to the PTO's attention through a properly filed request any patent or printed publication that the requester believes raises a "substantial new question" as to the patentability of the claimed invention.[203]

If the patent examiner who is assigned the request agrees that a substantial new question of patentability has been raised, the reexamination request is granted.[204] Once the request has been granted, the application is examined against the cited prior art under normal *ex parte* procedures, except that an expedited schedule is followed.[205] The requester is not involved in the proceeding after the request is granted, although the record generated is available for public inspection.[206]

At the conclusion of the reexamination proceeding a reexamination certificate is issued announcing the status of the patent claims.[207] Any substantial modification in the scope of the claims will give rise to intervening rights in the public, just as in the reissue context.[208]

REFERENCES

1. 35 U.S.C. § 1 *et seq.*
2. 37 C.F.R. parts 1, 3, 5, and 7.
3. COMMISSIONER OF PATENTS AND TRADEMARKS ANNUAL REPORT, Fiscal Year 1991, p. 58.
4. COMMISSIONER OF PATENTS AND TRADEMARKS ANNUAL REPORT, Fiscal Year 1991, p. 60.
5. *See generally* MPEP chapter 500.
6. 35 U.S.C. § 9; MPEP § 903.
7. MPEP § 504.
8. 37 C.F.R. § 5.3; MPEP §§ 120, 130.
9. MPEP § 130.
10. 35 U.S.C. § 9; MPEP §§ 903.01, 903.02.
11. MPEP § 903.08(b).
12. MPEP § 708.
13. 37 C.F.R. § 1.101; MPEP § 708.
14. 35 U.S.C. § 102; MPEP §§ 706.02, 904.
15. MPEP § 904.
16. MPEP § 901.07.
17. MPEP § 903.02(a).
18. MPEP § 901.06(a).
19. MPEP § 706.
20. MPEP § 707.05(a).
21. MPEP § 706.02.
22. MPEP § 1302.14.
23. *See* Graham v. John Deere Co., 383 U.S. 1, 18, 148 USPQ 459 (1966).
24. *In re* Fine, 837 F.2d 1071, 1074, 5 USPQ2d 1596 (Fed. Cir. 1988).
25. MPEP § 706.
26. 35 U.S.C. § 133; *see also* MPEP §§ 710, 710.1.
27. 37 C.F.R. § 1.111; MPEP § 714.02.
28. 37 C.F.R. §§ 1.131, 1.132.
29. 37 C.F.R. § 1.111(c).
30. 37 C.F.R. § 1.113; MPEP § 706.07.
31. MPEP § 706.07(a).
32. 37 C.F.R. § 1.116(a).
33. 37 C.F.R. § 1.116; MPEP §§ 714.12, 714.13.
34. 35 U.S.C. § 134; 37 C.F.R. §§ 1.113(a), 1.191; MPEP § 706.07.
35. 37 C.F.R. §§ 1.192, 1.193.
36. 37 C.F.R. § 1.194.
37. 35 U.S.C. § 7; MPEP § 1203.
38. 37 C.F.R. § 1.196.
39. 37 C.F.R. § 1.198; MPEP § 1214.07.
40. 37 C.F.R. § 1.197.
41. 35 U.S.C. § 145; 37 C.F.R. § 1.303.
42. 35 U.S.C. § 141; 37 C.F.R. § 1.301.
43. 35 U.S.C. § 120.
44. MPEP § 706.07(b).
45. 37 C.F.R. § 1.197(b); MPEP § 1214.03.

46. 37 C.F.R. § 1.197(c); MPEP § 1214.06.

47. 35 U.S.C. § 145; Gould v. Quigg, 822 F.2d 1074, 1076, 3 USPQ2d 1302 (Fed. Cir. 1987); Burlington Indus., Inc. v. Quigg, 822 F.2d 1581, 1584, 3 USPQ2d 1436 (Fed. Cir. 1987).

48. Remarks of PTO Solicitor Fred McKelvey to the Chemical Practice Committee of the American Intellectual Property Law Association, October 1991.

49. Gould v. Quigg, 822 F.2d 1074, 1079, 3 USPQ2d 1302 (Fed. Cir. 1987).

50. 28 U.S.C. § 1295(a)(4)(c).

51. Gould v. Quigg, 822 F.2d 1074, 1077, 3 USPQ2d 1302 (Fed. Cir. 1987).

52. 28 U.S.C. §§ 1292(c), 1295.

53. Fed. Cir. R. 47.2.

54. Fed. Cir. R. 35.

55. *In re* Wilder, 736 F.2d 1516, 1520, 222 USPQ 369 (Fed. Cir. 1984).

56. *In re* Caveney, 761 F.2d 671, 674, 226 USPQ 1 (Fed. Cir. 1985).

57. Fed. Cir. R. 47.8(b).

58. Fed. Cir. R. 47.8(a).

59. Fed. Cir. R. 36.

60. Fed. Cir. R. 47.8(b).

61. Fed. Cir. R. 47.8(a).

62. 35 U.S.C. § 144.

63. *In re* Clemens, 622 F.2d 1029, 1039, 206 USPQ 289 (CCPA 1980); *In re* Fisher, 448 F.2d 1406, 1407, 171 USPQ 292 (CCPA 1971); *In re* Ruschig, 379 F.2d 990, 993, 154 USPQ 118 (CCPA 1967).

64. MPEP § 1216.01.

65. Fed. Cir. R. 35, 40.

66. 28 U.S.C. § 2101(e); Sup. Ct. R. 11.

67. Sup. Ct. R. 10.

68. *See generally*, MPEP chapter 1300.

69. 37 C.F.R. § 1.312; MPEP §§ 714.15–16(e).

70. 35 U.S.C. § 135; 37 C.F.R. §§ 1.601–90.

71. 35 U.S.C. § 101.

72. 37 C.F.R. §§ 1.604, 1.607.

73. 37 C.F.R. § 1.605.

74. MPEP § 2301.01.

75. 37 C.F.R. § 1.687.

76. 37 C.F.R. § 1.633.

77. 37 C.F.R. § 1.658.

78. 37 C.F.R. §§ 1.658, 1.663.

79. 35 U.S.C. § 146.

80. 35 U.S.C. § 141. A dissatisfied party's right to appeal directly to the Federal Circuit is subject to the right of the other party to have the board's decision reviewed first by the District Court under Section 146.

81. 28 U.S.C. § 1295(a)(4)(c).

82. 28 U.S.C. § 2101(e).

83. 35 U.S.C. § 154.

84. *See* 35 U.S.C. § 1.271(b), (c), (f).

85. 28 U.S.C. § 1338.

86. 28 U.S.C. § 1332.

87. *See, e.g., In re* Oximetrix, Inc., 748 F.2d 637, 223 USPQ 1068 (Fed. Cir. 1984).
88. Christianson v. Colt Indus. Operating Corp., 486 U.S. 800, 808–09, 108 S. Ct. 2166, 2173–74, 7 USPQ2d 1109 (1988).
89. Dubost v. United States Patent and Trademark Office, 777 F.2d 1561, 1564, 227 USPQ 977 (Fed. Cir. 1985).
90. C.R. Bard, Inc. v. Schwartz, 716 F.2d 874, 219 USPQ 197 (Fed. Cir. 1983).
91. *See* Albert v. Kevex Corp., 729 F.2d 757, 221 USPQ 202 (Fed. Cir. 1984).
92. Chemical Engineering Corp. v. Marlo, Inc., 754 F.2d 331, 222 USPQ 738 (Fed. Cir. 1984).
93. Air Products & Chemicals, Inc. v. Reichhold Chemicals, Inc., 755 F.2d 1559, 225 USPQ 121 (Fed. Cir. 1985); Yarway Corp. v. Eur-Control USA, Inc., 775 F.2d 268, 227 USPQ 352 (Fed. Cir. 1985).
94. Dubost v. United States Patent and Trademark Office, 777 F.2d 1561, 227 USPQ 977 (Fed. Cir. 1985).
95. Wyden v. Commissioner of Patents and Trademarks, 807 F.2d 934, 231 USPQ 918 (Fed. Cir. 1986).
96. Alco Standard Corp. v. Tennessee Valley Authority, 808 F.2d 1490, 1 USPQ2d 1337 (Fed. Cir. 1986).
97. Joy Mfg. Co. v. National Mine Service Co., 810 F.2d 1127, 1 USPQ2d 1627 (Fed. Cir. 1987).
98. Cordis Corp. v. Medtronic, Inc., 835 F.2d 859, 5 USPQ2d 1118 (Fed. Cir. 1987).
99. Solarex Corp. v. Arco Solar, Inc., 870 F.2d 642, 10 USPQ2d 1247 (Fed. Cir. 1989).
100. MCV, Inc. v. King-Seeley Thermos Co., 870 F.2d 1568, 10 USPQ2d 1287 (Fed. Cir. 1989).
101. Morganroth v. Quigg, 885 F.2d 843, 12 USPQ2d 1125 (Fed. Cir. 1989).
102. Lang v. Pacific Marine & Supply Co., 895 F.2d 761, 13 USPQ2d 1820 (Fed. Cir. 1990).
103. Albert v. Kevex Corp., 729 F.2d 757, 221 USPQ 202 (Fed. Cir. 1984).
104. Beghin-Say International, Inc. v. Ole-Bendt Rasmussen, 733 F.2d 1568, 221 USPQ 1121 (Fed. Cir. 1984).
105. *In re* Oximetrix, Inc., 748 F.2d 637, 223 USPQ 1068 (Fed. Cir. 1984).
106. Schwarzkopf Development Corp. v. Ti-Coating, Inc., 800 F.2d 240, 231 USPQ 47 (Fed. Cir. 1986).
107. *In re* Innotron Diagnostics, 800 F.2d 1077, 231 USPQ 178 (Fed. Cir. 1986).
108. Ballard Medical Products v. Wright, 823 F.2d 527, 3 USPQ2d 1337 (Fed. Cir. 1987).
109. Consolidated World Housewares, Inc. v. Finkle, 831 F.2d 261, 4 USPQ2d 1565 (Fed. Cir. 1987).
110. Speedco, Inc. v. Estes, 853 F.2d 909, 7 USPQ2d 1637 (Fed. Cir. 1988).
111. 28 U.S.C. § 1498(a).
112. 35 U.S.C. § 145.
113. Lindemann Maschinenfabrik GmbH v. American Hoist and Derrick Co., 730 F.2d ˙452, 1458, 221 USPQ 481 (Fed. Cir. 1984); *but see In re* Self, 671 F.2d 1344, 1351, 213 USPQ 1 (C.C.P.A. 1982).
114. Akzo N.V. v. U.S. Int'l Trade Comm'n, 808 F.2d 1471, 1480, 1 USPQ2d 1241 (Fed. Cir. 1986).
115. Loctite Corp. v. Ultraseal Ltd., 781 F.2d 861, 872, 228 USPQ 90 (Fed. Cir. 1985).
116. Bey v. Kollonitsch, 806 F.2d 1024, 1027–28, 231 USPQ 967 (Fed. Cir. 1986).
117. Dana Corp. v. IPC Limited Partnership, 860 F.2d 415, 418, 8 USPQ2d 1692 (Fed. Cir. 1988).

118. Reactive Metals & Alloys Corp. v. ESM, Inc., 769 F.2d 1578, 1582, 226 USPQ 821 (Fed. Cir. 1985).
119. SRI Int'l v. Matsushita Elec. Corp., 775 F.2d 1107, 1118, 227 USPQ 577 (Fed. Cir. 1985) (in banc).
120. Lemelson v. United States, 752 F.2d 1538, 1550, 224 USPQ 526 (Fed. Cir. 1985).
121. *In re* Jerabek, 789 F.2d 886, 889, 229 USPQ 530 (Fed. Cir. 1986).
122. Loctite Corp. v. Ultraseal Ltd., 781 F.2d 861, 872, 228 USPQ 90 (Fed. Cir. 1985).
123. *In re* Jerabek, 789 F.2d 886, 889, 229 USPQ 530 (Fed. Cir. 1986).
124. Perini America, Inc. v. Paper Converting Machine Co., 832 F.2d 581, 584, 4 USPQ2d 1621 (Fed. Cir. 1987).
125. SRI Int'l v. Matsushita Elec. Corp., 775 F.2d 1107, 1125, 227 USPQ 577 (Fed. Cir. 1985) (in banc).
126. Loctite Corp. v. Ultraseal Ltd., 781 F.2d 861, 872, 228 USPQ 90 (Fed. Cir. 1985).
127. D.M.I., Inc. v. Deere & Co., 755 F.2d 1570, 1575, 225 USPQ 236 (Fed. Cir. 1985).
128. Ralston Purina Co. v. Far-Mar-Co., Inc., 772 F.2d 1570, 1575, 227 USPQ 177 (Fed. Cir. 1985).
129. Hormone Research Foundation, Inc. v. Genentech, Inc., 904 F.2d 1558, 1567, 15 USPQ2d 1039 (Fed. Cir. 1990).
130. Moleculon Research Corp. v. CBS, Inc., 793 F.2d 1261, 1268, 229 USPQ 805 (Fed. Cir. 1986).
131. Bott v. Four Star Corp., 807 F.2d 1567, 1572, 1 USPQ2d 1210 (Fed. Cir. 1986).
132. Johnston v. IVAC Corp., 885 F.2d 1574, 1578–79, 12 USPQ2d 1382 (Fed. Cir. 1989).
133. Orthokinetics, Inc. v. Safety Travel Chairs, Inc., 806 F.2d 1565, 1576, 1 USPQ2d 1081 (Fed. Cir. 1986).
134. Hybritech, Inc. v. Monoclonal Antibodies, Inc., 802 F.2d 1367, 1376, 231 USPQ 81 (Fed. Cir. 1986).
135. De George v. Bernier, 768 F.2d 1318, 1321, 226 USPQ 758 (Fed. Cir. 1985).
136. Quaker City Gear Works, Inc. v. Skil Corp., 747 F.2d 1446, 1453, 223 USPQ 1161 (Fed. Cir. 1984).
137. Met-Coil Systems Corp. v. Korners Unlimited, Inc., 803 F.2d 684, 687, 231 USPQ 474 (Fed. Cir. 1986).
138. Interconnect Planning Corp. v. Feil, 774 F.2d 1132, 1138, 227 USPQ 543 (Fed. Cir. 1985).
139. *In re* Jerabek, 789 F.2d 886, 890, 229 USPQ 530 (Fed. Cir. 1986).
140. Panduit Corp. v. Dennison Mfg. Co., 810 F.2d 1561, 1568, 1 USPQ2d 1593 (Fed. Cir. 1987).
141. UMC Electronics Co. v. United States, 816 F.2d 647, 657, 2 USPQ2d 1465 (Fed. Cir. 1987).
142. Moleculon Research Corp. v. CBS, Inc., 793 F.2d 1261, 1266, 229 USPQ 805 (Fed. Cir. 1986).
143. Loctite Corp. v. Ultraseal Ltd., 781 F.2d 861, 870, 228 USPQ 90 (Fed. Cir. 1985).
144. D.L. Auld Co. v. Chroma Graphics Corp., 714 F.2d 1144, 1151, 219 USPQ 13 (Fed. Cir. 1983).
145. Dana Corp. v. American Precision Co., 827 F.2d 755, 758, 3 USPQ2d 1852 (Fed. Cir. 1987).
146. Panduit Corp. v. Dennison Mfg. Co., 810 F.2d 1561, 1568, 1 USPQ2d 1593 (Fed. Cir. 1987).
147. Wilson Sporting Goods Co. v. David Geoffrey & Assoc., 904 F.2d 677, 685, 14 USPQ2d 1942 (Fed. Cir. 1990).
148. Rule 49(b), Fed.R.Civ.P.

149. Railroad Dynamics, Inc. v. A. Stucki Co., 727 F.2d 1506, 1514–15, 220 USPQ 929 (Fed. Cir. 1984); Connell v. Sears, Roebuck & Co., 722 F.2d 1542, 1547, 220 USPQ 193 (Fed. Cir. 1983).

150. Structural Rubber Prods. Co. v. Park Rubber Co., 749 F.2d 707, 718–24, 223 USPQ 1264 (Fed. Cir. 1984).

151. Rule 49(b), Fed.R.Civ.P.

152. *See, e.g.*, Newell Companies, Inc. v. Kenny Mfg. Co., 864 F.2d 757, 763, 9 USPQ2d 1417 (Fed. Cir. 1988).

153. Rule 56, Fed.R.Civ.P.

154. Rule 50(a), Fed.R.Civ.P.

155. Rule 50(b), Fed.R.Civ.P.

156. Rule 59, Fed.R.Civ.P.

157. 35 U.S.C. § 271.

158. 28 U.S.C. § 2201 *et seq.*

159. 35 U.S.C. § 282.

160. 35 U.S.C. § 287.

161. 35 U.S.C. §§ 252, 307(b).

162. A.C. Aukerman Co. v. R.L. Chaides Construction Co., 960 F.2d 1020, 22 USPQ2d 1321 (Fed. Cir. 1992) (in banc).

163. Laitram Corp. v. Rexnord, Inc., 939 F.2d 1533, 1535, 19 USPQ2d 1367 (Fed. Cir. 1991).

164. Water Technologies Corp. v. Calco, Ltd., 850 F.2d 660, 671, 7 USPQ 1097 (Fed. Cir. 1988).

165. Intel Corp. v. U.S. Int'l Trade Comm'n, 946 F.2d 821, 829, 20 USPQ2d 1161 (Fed. Cir. 1991).

166. American Hoist & Derrick Co. v. Sowa & Sons, Inc., 725 F.2d 1350, 1360, 220 USPQ 763 (Fed. Cir. 1984).

167. FMC Corp. v. Manitowoc Co., 835 F.2d 1411, 1415, 5 USPQ2d 1112 (Fed. Cir. 1987).

168. Moleculon Research Corp. v. CBS, Inc., 793 F.2d 1261, 1269, 229 USPQ 805 (Fed. Cir. 1986).

169. A.C. Aukerman Co. v. R.L. Chaides Construction Co., 960 F.2d 1020, 1044–46, 22 USPQ2d 1321 (Fed. Cir 1992) (in banc).

170. 35 U.S.C. § 282.

171. Stratoflex, Inc. v. Aeroquip Corp., 713 F.2d 1530, 1534, 218 USPQ 871 (Fed. Cir. 1983).

172. American Hoist & Derrick Co. v. Sowa & Sons, 725 F.2d 1350, 1360, 220 USPQ 763 (Fed. Cir. 1984).

173. Ashland Oil, Inc. v. Delta Resins & Refractories, Inc., 776 F.2d 281, 291–93, 227 USPQ 657 (Fed. Cir. 1985).

174. Cable Elec. Prods., Inc. v. Genmark, Inc., 770 F.2d 1015, 1022, 226 USPQ 881 (Fed. Cir. 1985).

175. Hughes Aircraft Co. v. United States, 717 F.2d 1351, 1359, 219 USPQ 473 (Fed. Cir. 1983).

176. Polaroid Corp. v. Eastman Kodak Co., 789 F.2d 1556, 1560, 229 USPQ 561 (Fed. Cir. 1986); American Hoist & Derrick Co. v. Sowa & Sons, 725 F.2d 1350, 1360, 220 USPQ 763 (Fed. Cir. 1984).

177. United Shoe Machinery Corp. v. Brooklyn Wood Heel Corp., 77 F.2d 263, 264 (2d Cir. 1935); Mendenhall v. Astec Indus., Inc., 13 USPQ2d 1913, 1923 (E.D. Tenn. 1988), *aff'd*, 887 F.2d 1094, 13 USPQ2d 1956 (Fed. Cir. 1989) (table). The applicability of

the clear and convincing standard of proof to these issues is a somewhat open question inasmuch as the Federal Circuit has not expressly addressed the issue.

178. E.I. du Pont de Nemours & Co. v. Phillips Petroleum Co., 849 F.2d 1430, 1440, 7 USPQ2d 1129 (Fed. Cir. 1988).
179. Machinery Corp. of America v. Gullfiber AB, 774 F.2d 467, 471, 227 USPQ 368 (Fed. Cir. 1985).
180. Rule 54, Fed.R.Civ.P.
181. 28 U.S.C. §§ 1292(c), 1295(a)(1)–(2).
182. 28 U.S.C. § 1295(a)(3).
183. 28 U.S.C. §§ 1291, 1292(a)–(b); *In re* Innotron Diagnostics, 800 F.2d 1077, 1080 n. 4 (Fed. Cir. 1986).
184. Eaton Corp. v. Appliance Valves Corp., 790 F.2d 874, 877, 229 USPQ 668 (Fed. Cir. 1986).
185. Rule 52, Fed.R.Civ.P.
186. Heisig v. United States, 719 F.2d 1153, 1158 (Fed. Cir. 1983).
187. Rosemount, Inc. v. Beckman Instruments, Inc., 727 F.2d 1540, 1547–48, 221 USPQ 1 (Fed. Cir. 1984).
188. Loctite Corp. v. Ultraseal Ltd., 781 F.2d 861, 872, 228 USPQ 90 (Fed. Cir. 1985).
189. *See, e.g.,* Fromson v. Western Litho Plate & Supply Co., 853 F.2d 1568, 1570, 7 USPQ2d 1606 (Fed. Cir. 1988).
190. Green v. Rich Iron Co., Inc., 944 F.2d 852, 20 USPQ2d 1075 (Fed. Cir. 1991) (a court may not order a patent holder to seek reissue against his or her will).
191. *In re* Weiler, 790 F.2d 1576, 1579, 229 USPQ 673 (Fed. Cir. 1986).
192. *In re* Orita, 550 F.2d 1277, 1280, 193 USPQ 145 (C.C.P.A. 1977).
193. *In re* Watkinson, 900 F.2d 230, 14 USPQ2d 1407 (Fed. Cir. 1990).
194. Ball Corp. v. United States, 729 F.2d 1429, 1435–36, 221 USPQ 289 (Fed. Cir. 1984).
195. Hewlett-Packard Co. v. Bausch & Lomb Inc., 882 F.2d 1556, 1565, 11 USPQ2d 1750 (Fed. Cir. 1989).
196. 37 C.F.R. § 1.176.
197. *In re* Sneed, 710 F.2d 1544, 1550 n. 4, 218 USPQ 385 (Fed. Cir. 1983).
198. 37 C.F.R. § 1.178.
199. 35 U.S.C. § 252.
200. 35 U.S.C. §§ 301–07.
201. Green v. Rich Iron Co., Inc., 944 F.2d 852, 20 USPQ2d 1075 (Fed. Cir. 1991).
202. 35 U.S.C. §§ 301, 302; 37 C.F.R. §§ 1.510(a), 1.520.
203. 35 U.S.C. §§ 301, 302, 304.
204. 35 U.S.C. § 304; 37 C.F.R. § 1.515.
205. 37 C.F.R. § 1.550.
206. 37 C.F.R. § 1.550(e); MPEP § 2232.
207. 37 C.F.R. § 1.570.
208. 35 U.S.C. § 307(b).

4

Ownership of Tangible and Intellectual Property

David E. Broome, Jr.

As companies, universities, and inventors develop innovations, questions inevitably arise on how and where to file patents, whether to maintain the innovations as trade secrets, and whether to develop innovations in-house or to license out all or part of an invention. These are important questions, but first, two more basic questions must be answered or an entire commercialization strategy may be at risk of failing. These two initial questions are: What kind of innovation has been made? Who owns it?

While this book is primarily concerned with patents, anyone formulating a commercialization strategy for an invention must be aware of the other means that are available for protecting and exploiting an invention. It is even more important to know who has the legal authority to control the use of an invention. These issues are addressed in this chapter.

4.1 TANGIBLE PROPERTY VERSUS INTANGIBLE PROPERTY

The field of biotechnology has spawned many valuable new materials in recent years. The development of cell lines, hybridomas, genetically engineered plasmids, monoclonal antibodies, and various biological reagents has created opportunities for commercialization unknown only a few years ago. When a potentially valuable new material is developed, the technology manager has a decision to make. Such inventions are tangible pieces of property and, as such, are subject to control in ways similar to other types of tangible property. This control includes the sale, lease or bailment, or concealment (internal use) of the product. Biotechnology innovations also may be protected as intellectual property by patenting them. *Diamond v. Chakrabarty*[1] established that a living organism can qualify as a "manufacture" or "composition of matter" within the meaning of the U.S. patent statute.[2] As such, the organism can be patented if it meets the other criteria of the patent statute.

4.1.1 Federal Patent Law Rights Are Distinct from State Law Rights

Even though an innovation can be patented, the owner of the property is free to pursue other means of protecting his or her rights in the innovation and utilizing it. In *Aronson v. Quick Point Pencil Corp.*,[3] the U.S. Supreme Court established that the options available to the owner of intellectual property under state law are not limited by U.S. patent law, except when state law is inconsistent with the federal law governing patents. That is, unless the state law in question "stands as an obstacle to the accomplishment and execution of the full purposes and objectives of Congress," the state law governs.[4]

So, even though a biological property can be patented, patenting the invention may not be the way to proceed. A major reason often given for such a decision is that greater control of the property can be exercised by the licensor of a tangible property. For example, in order to patent a biological material in the United States and in most of the industrially developed countries of the world, the party applying for the patent may need to make a publicly available deposit of a viable sample of the material in question.[5] While the commercial use of the material may be prohibited after it is patented, there is no control over who can gain access to the material. In addition, it is not always easy to determine when another party is using the patented material. Because of the potential for unauthorized use, such access could easily hurt the competitive position of the patent applicant and be devastating to the value of the patented item. In addition, the patent term is limited to 17 years.[6]

For a variety of reasons, the owner of a biological invention may prefer not to make the item widely available. For example, a researcher may want to be sure that other researchers do not have access to the material until a particular line of research is completed or a paper is published. Or the inventor simply may want to control access to the material so that a particular academic or commercial competitor cannot obtain it, even for experimental, non-commercial uses.

Another reason for deciding not to patent an item is when it is only a precursor or a material involved in making the final commercial product. Because of the difficulty in knowing whether the patented material is being used by a third party, patenting (and the required deposit of material) is only of marginal value and may even damage the interests of the owner of the biological property.

4.1.2   Materials Derived from Human Donors

Many of the new biological materials being patented and licensed today have their origin in the human body. For example, in the recent case of *Moore v. Regents of the University of California*,[7] physicians used biological material removed from their leukemia patient to create a potentially valuable cell line, which then was patented. The patient sued the physicians and their employer, seeking to share in any income generated by the patented cell line. The *Moore* case asks an important question: What are the rights of the patient whose cells were used to make a product?

The plaintiff sought relief based on theories of fraud, conversion, breach of fiduciary duty, and absence of informed consent. The California Supreme Court held that Moore had stated a claim for a breach of duty to disclose to him that there was a research intent involved in the medical procedures being performed. Of more significance to this discussion, however, was the court's holding that the plaintiff had not stated a claim for conversion based on the physicians' use of his cells to create a patented cell line. The court further stated that the patented cell line was not the plaintiff-patient's property because the patented cell line was legally distinct from the cells removed from his body.

It is likely that there will be further challenges to ownership of cell lines and other biological materials and constructs that have their origins in tissues removed from human patients. Because these claims will be based on state laws relating to ownership and use of tangible property (see section 4.1.1), the courts of each state will decide the issues based on the laws of the state in question. Nevertheless, *Moore* has established a useful framework for future discussions and litigation of these issues.[8]

In addition, *Moore* confirms that issues relating to the ownership of tangible property are distinct from issues of inventorship and patent ownership. As the court stated:

> . . . the subject matter of the Regent's patent—the patented cell line and the products derived from it—cannot be Moore's property. This is because the patented cell line is both factually and legally distinct from the cells taken from Moore's body. Federal law permits the patenting of organisms that represent the product of "human ingenuity," but not naturally occurring organisms. . . . Thus, Moore's allegations that he owns the cell line. . .are inconsistent with the patent, which constitutes an authoritative determination that the cell line is the product of invention.[9]

4.1.3   Derivatives of Biological Materials

Researchers may or may not choose to apply for patents on new biological material they have created. Regardless of whether the material is patented, scientists often receive requests to share their creation with other scientists. The recipients use the materials in various types of research, often producing new materials in the process. When that happens, there may be a conflict between the supplier and the recipient. According to the *Moore* case, if the new material made by the recipient could be patented, the issue becomes one of state law relating to contract interpretation and tangible property ownership. It is not a question of inventorship. The supplier does not become a coinventor merely by supplying the material used as the basis for an invention. Of course, if the supplier and the recipient are actively collaborating, the possibility of a joint invention arises (see Chapter 9, Collaborative Research).

The need to bring some certainty to these situations in recent years has prompted tremendous growth in the development of agreements governing the rights of suppliers and recipients of such biological materials. One of the primary areas of concern in such "materials transfer agreements," or MTAs, concerns the parties' rights with regard to "derivatives" of the supplied material.[10]

There is no "standard" MTA; derivatives are described in these documents as anything from a material that could not have been made "but for" the supplied material, to an "unmodified" derivative, to a derivative material that U.S. patent law would recognize as an invention. The agreements also vary widely in what rights are given and received with regard to derivatives, however they may be defined. In an effort to bring some uniformity to this area, the National Institutes of Health has established a panel to devise a Uniform Biological Material Transfer Agreement. Such an agreement could gain general acceptance in the field.

4.1.4 The Use of Bailments to Transfer Biological Material

To take advantage of the established law as it relates to transfers of tangible personal property, many MTA's structure the transmittal of biological material as a bailment, rather than an outright transfer under which the recipient expects to own the received sample. A *bailment* is defined by *Black's Law Dictionary* as:

> A delivery of goods or personal property, by one person to another, in trust for the execution of a special object upon or in relation to such goods, beneficial either to the bailor or bailee or both, and upon a contract . . . to perform the trust and carry out such object and thereupon either to redeliver the goods to the bailor or otherwise dispose of the same in conformity with the purpose of the trust.[11]

The use of a bailment gives the supplier of the material a great degree of control over its subsequent use by the recipient. As can be seen from the definition, possession of the object passes from one party to the other in a bailment, but title does not. The bailment lasts only for the term set by the parties in their agreement, and then the property is returned. In addition, the use of the material and its progeny can be controlled under the terms of the bailment. That is, the supplier can place any chosen conditions on the use of the bailed property and, as long as those conditions are not illegal or contrary to public policy, they can be enforced.[12]

Of course the bailment does not exist in a vacuum. Usually, while a person may be the supplier of biological materials one day, that same person may be trying to obtain someone else's materials the next. Placing consistently difficult conditions on recipients may result in having equally difficult conditions placed on yourself in return or in being completely cut off from the supply of biological materials from your peers. Instead, a graduated approach is necessary, in which the supplier makes less valuable properties available under less stringent terms and insists on maximum protection and control only for materials that have been identified as the most valuable. Of course, any attempt to retain control over the transferred material hinges on the recipient's willingness to adhere to the terms of the transfer agreement. There may well be cases where the material is so valuable that its owner considers it best not to transfer the material at all, but rather to treat it as a trade secret.

4.2   TRADE SECRET ISSUES

When dealing with trade secrets, it is important to note that a wide range of matters can be protected. Tangible property (including cell lines, genetically engineered plasmids, and other biological materials), patentable inventions, and unpatentable "know-how" all can be protected as trade secrets. A trade secret is defined as any formula, pattern, device, or compilation of information that is used in someone's business and gives him or her an opportunity to obtain an advantage over competitors who do not know or use it.[13] Note that while this is the most common definition of trade secrets, state law governs this matter, and the law of the jurisdiction in question should be consulted for the relevant definition.

The issues involved in the ownership of trade secrets will be addressed later. This section will focus on why and how trade secret law is used to protect innovations in the field of biotechnology.

4.2.1   Why Trade Secrets Are Sometimes Used in Lieu of Patents

Ever since the landmark *Chakrabarty* case,[14] it has been clear that biological inventions may not be denied patent protection just because they consist of or involve living matter. Why then do those who develop new biotechnology sometimes choose to protect their innovations as trade secrets rather than through patenting? Some of the reasons were presented in section 4.1.4. This section will present additional reasons.

Besides deposit requirements, a U.S. patent has a 17-year life span, while a trade secret is unlimited in duration. A trade secret also may be protected worldwide for little expense, while worldwide patenting often proves costly. The inventor considering patenting an invention also must consider the likelihood of success when there is a need to enforce or defend the patent in an infringement action.

Choosing trade-secret protection is risky, however. There always is the chance that someone will independently invent the same thing or its equivalent, for example. In such an event, the trade secret is lost, the holder of the former trade secret has no remedy, and the second inventor may even be able to obtain a patent that would prevent the holder of the former trade secret from practicing the invention without a license from the patent holder.[15] Furthermore, once a trade secret becomes public, even though it does so in violation of an agreement to maintain secrecy, trade secret protection is lost and the public is free to use it.

4.2.2   How Trade Secrets Are Protected

Once someone has decided to protect an invention as a trade secret, what must be done to maintain the protection? Generally, the holder of a trade secret should be certain that employees, licensees or prospective licensees, prospective purchasers, and any visitors to the site where the trade secret is kept are aware of the confidential nature of the information or material. Usually, this is accomplished by having visitors sign a confidentiality agreement, that is, a contractual promise to maintain the confidential nature of the trade secret. In addition, when employees move on to other jobs, they should be reminded of their obligations regarding the confidentiality of the trade secret. The location of the trade secret also must be physically secure to prevent unauthorized access.[16]

Trade secrets are much better suited to the world of corporate research facilities than to the open academic environment of universities. The university culture, with its open academic exchange and rapid publication of research findings, makes it hard to protect trade secrets. While universities often license tangible biological property, they do so because it is simpler and cheaper to obtain such a license than to reproduce the entire process on the basis of the published record—not because the biological material is a trade secret. That is, the party wishing to use the biological material generally finds it more economical to pay a license fee and get a proven material rather than recreate an entire experimental process by following the recipe in a journal article.

As a final note, companies hiring researchers who are coming to the company directly from an academic environment should be particularly aware of the academic tradition of the open exchange of information and materials. Special care should be taken to inform such employees about the confidential nature of any information or materials that are being guarded as trade secrets.

4.3   OWNERSHIP OF INTELLECTUAL PROPERTY

This section will deal with the question of who owns the rights to patents and trade secrets developed in the course of the inventor's employment. First, it will look at the case of the employee working in the corporate environment. Next, the somewhat special case of the university-based inventor will be examined.

4.3.1   The General Rule Concerning Ownership of Employees' Inventions

In the seminal case of *U.S. v. Dubilier Condenser Corp.*,[17] the U.S. Supreme Court held that inventions made by employees who are "hired to invent" a specific item must be assigned to the employer upon the employer's demand. *Dubilier* further held that the employer may own the patent on an invention created by an employee hired for his or her inventive skills when the invention is within the scope of the employee's duties.

Nevertheless, it is a well-established general rule that the inventor owns the patent rights to his or her invention. He or she may not be forced to turn over ownership to an employer except under the conditions outlined in *Dubilier* or when there is an agreement (the employment contract) in which the employee promises to assign the rights to the employer.[18] To be assured of their rights and to avoid the uncertainties associated with judges and juries, employers generally include a requirement to assign patents in their employment contracts with employees.

4.3.1.2 Contracts to Assign Intellectual Property Rights. Agreements in which employees agree to assign their patent rights to their employers are enforceable and generally are upheld by the courts.[19] There seems to be a trend in the courts to construe these agreements more strictly against employers[20] and to limit their application to inventions in which the employer has a legitimate business interest. This probably is an attempt by the courts to equalize the often wide disparity in the bargaining power of the employer and the employee.

The employer who is sensitive to such issues will be careful in drafting the assignment provisions of the employment contract to be sure it does not try to achieve so much that a court might find it unenforceable. By limiting its rights, the employer may achieve greater certainty in areas that are of primary importance to the company's business.

Another area where the employer must be wary concerns state statutes. Several states, including California, North Carolina, Illinois, Minnesota, and Washington,[21] have adopted laws that limit the circumstances under which the employer can compel assignment by the employee-inventor. If an employment agreement fails to comply with the limitations imposed by the applicable state law, the agreement will be unenforceable.

These statutes vary in their methods and coverage—some are more favorable to the employer than the law would be, some are more favorable to the employee. In any event, employment contracts must conform to the law in that jurisdiction to be valid.

4.3.1.3 Express Contracts Versus the Employment Manual. In some cases, the employment contract says nothing about assigning patent rights but the employer has a policy, perhaps written into a separate employment manual, that addresses the issue. These situations are perhaps more common in the college and university settings than in the corporate environment.[22]

When there is no clear statement in the employment agreement that refers to the manual and incorporates it into the employment contract, the employer may have to show that the employee agrees to the terms of the employment manual in some other way. Typically this is done by demonstrating the employee's consent to the policy. That is, the employee's own conduct becomes the key to determining whether he or she acquiesces. Factors important in making the determination are: past behavior (whether the employee assigned previous patents to the employer); permitting the employer to pay for patenting costs and marketing activities; cooperating with the employer in such technology transfer activities; and complying with policy requirements. This compliance includes disclosing the invention on forms provided by the employer and not making any statements asserting the employee's claim to ownership of the invention.[23]

4.3.1.4 Shop Rights. Even in cases where the employer is not entitled to an assignment of the employee's patent rights, the courts have consistently held that the employer is entitled to a "shop right" to the invention. This occurs when the employee comes up with the invention during working hours and using his or her employer's materials and resources.[24]

A shop right is the employer's royalty-free, nonexclusive, and nontransferable license to use the employee's invention.[25] It is not assignable and its scope generally is limited by the nature of the employer's business, the character of the invention, the circumstances leading to its development, and the relation, conduct, and intent of the parties.[26]

4.3.2 Joint Ventures: Confidential Relationships

When parties have entered into a relationship (but not an employment relationship) to jointly accomplish a certain task, the courts have held that the inventions of one of the parties, even if communicated to the other party while involved in the joint undertaking, do not become the property of the other party. An example is *Saco-Lowell Shops v. Reynolds*,[27] where the plaintiff invented certain textile machinery and licensed it to the defendant. While collaborating with the defendant's employees under the license agreement, the plaintiff mentioned his ideas for improvements to the patented device. The defendant then obtained a patent on the improvement in his own name. The court held that this was improper, stating:

> . . . [the plaintiff] was the owner of the intangible property represented by the ideas embodied in the J frames; and whether they were covered by patent or not, he was entitled to protection against their use by one to whom he had disclosed them in the course of a confidential relationship.[28]

By paying attention to the principles of *Saco-Lowell*, the inventor who "brings to the table" intellectual property (patents, patentable ideas, or trade secrets) when establishing a relationship with a business partner or joint venturer can, by establishing the proper confidentiality in the relationship, protect himself or herself from losing control of future inventions made in the course of the business relationship. This protection is available even if the new inventions are disclosed to the other party in order to further the business venture.

4.3.3 The University Setting

As universities become more involved in the protection and licensing of intellectual property, there will be more conflict between individual inventors (usually faculty members) and their university employers concerning ownership of the intellectual property created by the inventor. Most universities by now have developed policies that govern the ownership and management of intellectual property, particularly patents. Most of these policies assert university ownership of inventions generated by faculty, other employees, and, sometimes, students.[29]

There have already been a number of disputes between faculty members and their university employers concerning the ownership of faculty inventions. For example, the confusion between the University of Pennsylvania and Professor Albert Kligman concerning rights to the patent for the anti-wrinkle cream, Retin-A, has been well documented.[30] To date, however, there is only one reported case that directly applies to this situation. In *Speck v. N.C. Dairy Foundation, Inc.*,[31] the North Carolina Supreme Court found that two professors at North Carolina State University did not acquire an ownership interest in an invention they made while conducting research at the university. The plaintiffs attempted to establish that a constructive trust existed based on their confidential report of the invention to the university (see section 4.3.2). The court rejected their argument, finding that the employees essentially were employed to invent. The court found the researchers' case was similar to that in *Houghton v. U.S.*,[32] where it was stated:

> It matters not in what capacity the employee may originally have been hired, if he be set to experimenting with the view of making an invention, and accepts pay for such work, it is his duty to disclose to his employer what he discovers in making the experiments, and what he accomplishes by the experiments belongs to the employer.

While *Speck* has been criticized,[33] it is clear that university ownership of faculty inventions serves several purposes. First, it ensures that faculty members will be able to continue to engage in research in their specialties. Also, consider what would happen if the rights to an invention were held by the inventor with no obligation to assign them to the university. Serious questions would arise (especially at state-supported institutions) concerning the use of university resources to develop an invention owned by an individual. Using university property for the financial benefit of an individual inventor inevitably would lead to public outcry and complaints from the legislature.

In addition, *Speck* helps research sponsors to enter into reasonably secure research relationships with university partners. For example, the sponsor would know that a research agreement is meaningful if it grants the sponsor certain rights to intellectual property arising out of the research project. Research sponsors also would find it easier to deal with a single institution regarding intellectual property rights than to have to reach separate agreements with every researcher at every institution where research is being sponsored.

Nevertheless, many cautionary notes are being sounded as universities become more involved in the ownership and commercialization of inventions. Some believe that the purpose of the university will be distorted or lost in the drive to find commercial uses for university-generated inventions. They fear these activities will destroy the judicially acknowledged distinctions between a university's academic core activities and ancillary activities. If this happens, activities previously sheltered from governmental and judicial intrusion would lose such protection.[34]

4.3.3.1   Outside Funding of University Research.   Rights to inventions developed by university researchers are subject to the same general principles that apply to employees in the corporate setting. Because most university research is supported by third-party funds, however, there are a few additional factors in the equation. Corporate funding of university research almost always includes a promise by the university that the sponsor of the research will have certain rights (often a right of first refusal to an exclusive, royalty-bearing license) to any inventions made in the course of the research project. These contractual obligations make it crucial for the university to own the rights to inventions by its researchers.

Where federal funding of university research is involved, federal regulations[35] generally impose several responsibilities on the recipient of the grant or contract with respect to inventions. Some of these regulations have an impact on the question of who owns the invention.

For example, federal regulations require the inventor to disclose the invention to the university, which then must report the invention to the federal agency sponsoring the research. The university then must advise the sponsoring federal agency whether it elects to retain title to the invention. Should the university choose to not retain title, the government agency may do so. In either case, the party retaining title may patent the invention and market the rights to private industry.

While it is generally accepted that the employer must have ownership of the intellectual property in order to carry out its responsibilities under the federal funding agreement, the view is not universal.[36]

The next years will see the law develop in this area, and clearer guidance will be provided by the courts. Meanwhile, the prudent university administration will examine its policies and employment agreements. Then the institution will be prepared to meet its obligations to research sponsors.

REFERENCES

1. Diamond v. Chakrabarty, 447 U.S. 303, 100 S. Ct. 2204, 65 L.Ed.2d 144, 206 USPQ 193 (1980).
2. 35 U.S.C. § 101.
3. Aronson v. Quick Point Pencil Co., 440 U.S. 257, 99 S. Ct. 275, 58 L.Ed.2d 254, 201 USPQ 1 (1979).
4. *Id.*
5. 37 CFR §§ 1.801–1.809; *see generally* I. Cooper, BIOTECHNOLOGY AND THE LAW, sec. 5.05.

6. 35 U.S.C. § 154.
7. Moore v. Regents of the University of California, 51 Cal.3d 120, 271 Cal. Rptr. 146, 793 P.2d 479 (1990).
8. Cooper, *supra* at note 5, sec. 11.03.
9. Moore, *supra* at note 7.
10. For a discussion of different types of MTAs, *see* Cooper, *supra* at note 5, sec. 11.03, pp. 11–69, 70.
11. BLACK'S LAW DICTIONARY, 179 (rev'd 4th ed).
12. For a full discussion of this subject, *see* Kirn, *The Treatment of Tangible Personal Property in Conjunction with Licensing of Patented Biotechnology*, III J. ASSN. UNIV. TECHNOLOGY MGRS. 59.
13. Restatement (First) of Torts (1939) at sec. 757, comment b.
14. Diamond v. Chakrabarty, *supra* at note 1.
15. *See, e.g.*, W.L. Gore & Assoc. v. Garlock, Inc., 721 F.2d 1540, 220 USPQ 303 (Fed. Cir. 1983), *cert. denied*, 469 U.S. 851 (1984).
16. Ruckelshaus v. Monsanto, 467 U.S. 986, 104 S. Ct. 2862, 81 L.Ed. 2d 815 (1984).
17. U.S. v. Dubilier Condenser Corp., 289 U.S. 178, 53 S. Ct. 554, 77 L.Ed. 2d 1114 (1933).
18. *Id.* at 289 U.S. 187; *see also* Annot., 153 ALR 983.
19. Annot., 153 ALR 983 at 995–1000.
20. Roberts v. Sears, Roebuck & Co., 573 F.2d 976, 197 USPQ 516 (7th Cir. 1978), *cert. denied*, 439 U.S. 860 (1978).
21. Cal. Labor Code sec. 2870–2872; N.C. Gen. Stat. sec. 66-57.1 and 57.2; Ill. Rev. Stat. sec. 301–303; Minn. Annot. Stat. sec. 181.78; Wash. RCN 49.44.140 and 150.
22. P. Chew, *Faculty-Generated Inventions: Who Owns the Golden Egg?*, 1992 WIS.L.REV. 259 at 285.
23. *Id.*, at pp. 289–90.
24. Quaker State Oil Ref. Co. v. Talbot, 315 Pa. 517, 174 A. 99 (1934) and Pure Oil Co. v. Hyman, 95 F.2d 22 (7th Cir. 1938).
25. Dubilier, *supra* note 17, at 289 U.S. 178.
26. Flannery Bolt Co. v. Flannery, 86 F.2d 43 (3d Cir. 1936).
27. Saco-Lowell Shops v. Reynolds, 141 F.2d 587, 61 USPQ 3 (4th Cir. 1944).
28. *Id.* at p. 598, citing Becher v. Contoure Laboratories, Inc., 279 U.S. 388.
29. Chew, *supra* note 22, at pp. 298–304. In addition, *see* B.J. Weidemier, *Ownership of University Inventions*, IV J. ASSN. UNIV. TECHNOLOGY MGRS. 1 for a good general discussion of the practical and legal aspects of this area.
30. *See* E. Marshall, *A New Wrinkle in Retin-A Dispute*, 256 SCIENCE 607 (May 1, 1992); E. Marshall, *Penn Charges Retin-A Inventor with Conflict*, 247 SCIENCE 1028 (March 2, 1990). *See also*, University of Houston v. Hwang (Cause No. 90-021705, Harris Co., Texas). (The University sued a former professor over ownership of intellectual property the professor allegedly made while at the university and failed to disclose.)
31. 311 N.C. 679, 319 S.E.2d 139 (1984).
32. 23 F.2d 386, 390 (4th Cir. 1928).
33. Chew, *supra* at note 22, pp. 298–304.
34. *See*, D. Sacken, Commercialization of Academic Knowledge and Judicial Deference, 19 J.C. & U.L 1.
35. 37 CFR, Ch. IV, Part 401 (1989).
36. Chew, *supra* at note 22, pp. 293–96.

PART
II

Basic Requirements
of Patentability

Patentable Subject Matter

Brian P. O'Shaughnessy

Section 101 of the federal patent statute promotes the progress of the useful arts, stating:

> Whoever invents or discovers any new and useful process, machine, manufacture, or composition of matter, or any new and useful improvement thereof, may obtain a patent therefor, subject to the conditions and requirements of this title.

As observed by Judge Giles Rich in *In re Bergy*, Section 101 has three requirements: "novelty, utility, and statutory subject matter."[1] The utility requirement can be subdivided into two distinct requirements: "practical utility" and "operability."[2] The novelty requirement is expanded in Section 102 of the patent statute and is discussed in detail in Chapter 6 of this book. The remaining three requirements of Section 101, statutory subject matter, practical utility, and operability, all present distinct and important issues for chemical and biological inventions. These three requirements are the focus of this chapter.

5.1 STATUTORY SUBJECT MATTER

Strictly speaking, Section 101 identifies all subject matter that is entitled to patent protection. That is, to qualify for patent protection, inventions must fall into one of the four enumerated categories: process, machine, manufacture, or composition of matter.[3]

The four categories are somewhat ambiguous. This is especially true today, where reasonable people may differ over whether a genetically altered cell that manufactures recombinant human proteins is a machine or a composition of matter. As a result, the statutory categories are little more than an example of the Constitutional prescription that patentable subject matter must promote the progress of the "useful arts."

5.1.1 Defining "The Useful Arts"

Defining what constitutes a contribution to "the useful arts" has long been a subject of debate. It must be more than a mere contribution to human knowledge, a bare scientific principle, or the discovery of something that occurs naturally. In *In re Joliot*,[4] the Court of Customs and Patent Appeals reexamined Article I, Section 8, Clause 8 of the U.S. Constitution, observing that:

> there was no implication that patents were to be granted for scientific discoveries, or hypotheses, but only to inventors for their discoveries in useful arts. Hence the statutory requirement that something of use in the useful arts must be produced and the correlative requirement that it must be fully disclosed so that those in the art can use it.

Some have reduced the issue to one of semantics, saying that discovery is finding the principle, and invention lies in devising a means of applying the principle and making it useful.[5] Thus, a discovery would not be patentable but an invention would be. Either way, it is safe to say that methods for usefully applying a law of nature or a scientific principle fall within the patentable classes of inventions as defined by the patent statute.

5.1.2 Products of Nature

An often-stated "principle" of patent law is that products of nature per se are not patentable. This statement is deceiving in its seeming simplicity, however. Numerous patented therapeutics and related processes draw on naturally occurring materials. Similarly, patent rights are frequently granted for certain proteins, growth factors, and gene sequences. These, too, might be called "products of nature," yet they are the subject of issued patents that have withstood challenge in the courts.

The only formal guide from the patent office is Section 706.03(a) of the *Manual of Patent Examining Procedure*, which states ". . . a thing occurring in nature, which is substantially unaltered, is not a 'manufacture.' " What then is an unpatentable, substantially unaltered product of nature?

A partial answer is provided by the Patent Office Board of Appeals in *Ex parte Prescott*.[6] In *Prescott*, an examiner had rejected claims directed to a process for inoculating a wart with a newly discovered bacteria that was capable of producing butyl and isopropyl alcohol in the absence of ethyl alcohol. In concluding that there was patentability, the board said:

> It seems to us that the purpose of the patent laws is to promote the progress of the useful arts and that when a useful result has been attained, the acts of the inventor should be viewed as an entirety instead of segregating them into steps and holding that each step is devoid of invention. The discovery of the specific bacteria, its isolation and the inoculation of a suitable mash therewith are all new and their combined result constitutes a definite advance in the art.[7]

Prescott suggests that the two most common instances where the discovery of so-called products of nature (products found in nature) can lead to patentable subject matter are: (1) isolation or purification to yield products not otherwise useful in their natural state, and (2) the use of the product in a novel and nonobvious process. In the latter case, the product itself is not being patented; rather, its use in a process is claimed.

In *Parke-Davis v. H.K. Mulford Co.*,[8] the court addressed the validity of a patent for adrenalin, known to raise blood pressure in the supradrenal glands. The inventor had discovered and claimed a "substance possessing the herein-described physiological characteristics and reactions of the supradrenal glands in a stable and concentrated form, and practically free from inert and associated gland-tissue." The court held that the inventor had not monopolized more than was fairly his due, stating:

> [H]e was the first person who had ever isolated a nonsalt substance relatively pure.
> . . . But, even if it were merely an extracted product without change, there is no rule that such products are not patentable. Takamine was the first to make it from the other gland-tissue in which it was found, and, while it is of course possible logically to call this a purification of the principle, it became for every practical purpose a new thing commercially and therapeutically. That was a good ground for a patent. . . . The line between different substances and degrees of the same substance is to be drawn rather from the common usages of men than from nice considerations of dialectic.[9]

A thorough analysis of the principle is found in *Merck & Co. v. Olin Mathieson Chemical Corp.*[10] In *Merck*, the alleged infringer, Olin, challenged the validity of Merck's patent for vitamin B_{12} as directed to a "product of nature." Prior to Merck's efforts, the product was known only as an anti-pernicious anemia factor and had been detected in the liver of cattle and in the by-products of certain microorganisms. Merck researchers discovered a product with the same activity in the fermentation broth of *Streptomyces griseus*. After a great deal of analysis, Merck researchers concluded that the product could be classified as a water-soluble vitamin, so it was given the designation B_{12}. Holding that the patent laws did not preclude issuance of a patent to a "product of nature" when the product otherwise complied with the requirements for patentability, the court made the practical observation that:

> All of the tangible things with which man deals and for which patent protection is granted are products of nature in the sense that nature provides the basic source materi-

als. The "matter" of which patentable new and useful compositions are composed necessarily includes naturally existing elements and materials.[11]

The court expressed Olin's defense by separating it into two doctrines: (1) that a patent may not be granted on an old product even though it is derived from a new source by a new and patentable process, and (2) that every step in the purification of a product is not a patentable advance, except, perhaps, as to the process itself, if the new product differs from the old "merely in degree, and not in kind."[12] Finding that the facts did not apply to both aspects of the defense, the court said of the first point:

> Until the patentees produced them, there were no such B_{12} active compositions. No one had produced even a comparable product. The active substance was unidentified and unknown. The new product, not just the method, had such advantageous characteristics as to replace the liver products. What was produced was, in no sense, an old product.[13]

As to the second aspect, the court observed:

> The fact, however, that a new and useful product is the result of processes of extraction, concentration, and purification of natural materials does not defeat its patentability.
>
> *   *   *
>
> The Court of Customs and Patent Appeals said [citation omitted]: ". . . if the process produces an article of such purity that it differs not only in degree but in kind it may be patentable. If it differs in kind, it may have a new utility in which invention may rest."
>
> *   *   *
>
> The compositions of the patent here have all the novelty and utility required by the Act for patentability. They never existed before; there was nothing comparable to them. If we regard them as a purification of the active principle in natural fermentates, the natural fermentates are quite useless, while the patented compositions are of great medicinal and commercial value. The step from complete uselessness to great and perfected utility is a long one. That step is no mere advance in the degree of the purity of a known product. From the natural fermentates, which, for this purpose were wholly useless and were not known to contain the desired activity in even the slightest degree, products of great therapeutic and commercial worth have been developed. The new products are not the same as the old, but new and useful compositions entitled to the protection of the patent.[14]

Similarly, in *Amgen, Inc. v. Chugai Pharmaceutical Co.*, the court addressed arguments that a patented DNA sequence encoding human erythropoietin (EPO) was an unpatentable product of nature. The court stated:

> The invention as claimed in the '008 patent is *not* as plaintiff argues the DNA sequence encoding human EPO since that is a nonpatentable natural phenomenon "free to all men and reserved exclusively to none." . . . Rather the invention as claimed in claim 2 of the patent is the "purified and isolated DNA sequence encoding erythropoietin."[15]

Thus, isolation and purification can form the basis for patentability of a product that is not a product of nature, as defined by the claims, even though it may exist in nature.

Indeed, nearly any affirmative manipulative step can make a natural product patentable under the statute, provided the resulting product meets the other criteria for patentability. In *Diamond v. Chakrabarty*, the Supreme Court observed that:

> the Committee Reports accompanying the 1952 Act inform us that Congress intended statutory subject matter to "include anything under the sun that is made by man."[16]

5.1.3 Living Things

The most dramatic development in the patent laws in the 1980s was the clarification of the patentability of living things.[17] A distinction should be drawn between claims directed to processes incorporating living things such as micro-organisms and claims to living things, per se. The former has long been recognized as patentable subject matter, whereas the latter has involved ardent debate.

In *Guaranty Trust Co. of New York v. Union Solvents Co.*,[18] the claimed process produced acetone and butyl alcohol via fermentation of a mash of natural substances rich in starch, namely, corn mash, by means of bacteria described and characterized in the patent. The court rejected the defendant's contention that the process was unpatentable since it was for the life process of a living organism. The court found it significant that the claim was not directed to bacteria, per se, but to a fermentation process employing bacteria discovered by the inventor. The distinction undoubtedly gave rise to patentable subject matter.[19]

Similarly, in *In re Mancy*,[20] the Court of Customs and Patent Appeals had before it a refusal to grant a patent to an inventor who claimed a process of producing a known antibiotic using a new strain of micro-organism. The micro-organism had been isolated from a soil sample and designated *Streptomyces bifurcus*, strain DS 23,219. The inventors' application showed how daunorubicin could be obtained from the aerobic cultivation of this novel strain of *Streptomyces*. The patent office refused to grant the patent on the grounds of obviousness in that several other strains of *Streptomyces* were known to produce daunorubicin. The court reversed the patent office on the obviousness issue and went on to discuss the nature of the invention as constituting patentable subject matter. The court said:

> We recognize the differences between this case and the situation in *Kuehl,* where the novel zeolite used as a catalyst in the claimed hydrocarbon cracking processes was itself the subject of allowed claims in the application. Here appellants not only have no allowed claim to the novel strain of *Streptomyces* used in their process but would, we presume (without deciding), be unable to obtain such a claim because the strain, while new in the sense that it is not shown by any art of record, is, as we understand it, a "product of nature."[21]

The court went on to observe that the claimed process was nonetheless "clearly within 35 USC 101" and that:

> . . . the public interest appears to be well served by encouraging the patenting of such inventions. While the patent will grant appellants a limited right to exclude others from producing daunorubicin by the use of *Streptomyces bifurcus,* the public receives not

only the knowledge of appellants' discovery but also access to *Streptomyces bifurcus* through its deposit with the Department of Agriculture.[22]

In the situation where applicants seek to claim living things in and of themselves, the patent office has asserted that living things constitute unpatentable subject matter. This position prompted the dual argument that living things per se are not patentable subject matter under Section 101 and, as living things, they are unpatentable products of nature. In a case like this, however, patentability will be found not on purification or use, but rather on affirmative manipulation to produce something novel and nonobvious.

In *Diamond v. Chakrabarty*, the Supreme Court addressed the patent office's refusal to grant a patent to Ananda Chakrabarty for a micro-organism that could break down the hydrocarbons in crude oil. The product was intended to be used in oil spills. Although the hydrocarbon degradative properties were not found in any naturally occurring bacteria, the patent office rejected the application, asserting that (1) micro-organisms are "products of nature," and (2) as living things they are not patentable subject matter under Section 101. The court found, however, that the "respondent's micro-organism plainly qualifies as patentable subject matter. His claim is not to a hitherto unknown natural phenomenon, but to a nonnaturally occurring manufacture or composition of matter—a product of human ingenuity 'having a distinctive name, character [and] use.' "[23]

The court rejected the position taken by the patent office that the existence of the Plant Patent Act of 1930 and the Plant Variety Protection Act of 1970 show Congressional intent that "manufacture" and "composition of matter" do not include living things. Citing the House and Senate committee reports, the court concluded that "the relevant distinction was not between living and inanimate things, but between products of nature, whether living or not, and human-made inventions." In so holding, the court observed that in 1873 the patent office had granted Louis Pasteur a patent on "yeast, free from organic germs of disease, as an article of manufacture," and that in 1967 and 1968 two patents had been directed to living micro-organisms.[24]

The court also rejected the argument that "micro-organisms cannot qualify as patentable subject matter until Congress expressly authorizes such protection"[25] by acknowledging that the inventions most benefiting mankind are those that "push back the frontiers of chemistry, physics, and the like" and that Section 101 employs broad language precisely because such inventions are unforeseeable.[26] Accordingly, *Chakrabarty* makes it clear that under Section 101, living things are not excluded from statutory subject matter.

In *Ex parte Hibberd*,[27] the principle of *Chakrabarty* was extended to include plants. In *Hibberd*, the Patent Office Board of Appeals reversed an examiner's rejection of claims directed to hybrid plant seeds, hybrid plants, and plant tissue cultures on the ground that Congress expressly provided for the protection of plants elsewhere. The examiner acknowledged that "in view of the decision in *Diamond v. Chakrabarty* . . . it appears clear that § 101 includes man-made life forms, including plant life."[28] But, the examiner contended, by enacting legislation specifically for the protection of plants (the Plant Patent Act [PPA] of 1930 and the Plant Variety

Protection Act [PVPA] of 1970), Congress had intended to make the PPA and the PVPA the exclusive forms of protection for plant life covered by those acts.

The appeals board reiterated the Supreme Court's acknowledgment that the use of the expansive terms "manufacture" and "composition of matter" indicated that Congress contemplated that the patent laws would be given wide scope and that statutory subject matter should include anything under the sun that is made by people.[29] Moreover, neither the plant-specific acts themselves nor their legislative histories expressed an intention to exclude any plant subject matter from protection under Section 101. Finally, the board rejected the examiner's position that the enactment of the plant-specific acts by implication narrowed Section 101 to exclude protection for plant life except under the express terms of those plant-specific acts. The board said:

> the overwhelming weight of authority is to the effect that repeals by implication are not favored and that when there are two acts on the same subject the rule is to give effect to both unless there is such a "positive repugnancy" or "irreconcilable conflict" that the statutes cannot co-exist.[30]

Finding no such positive repugnancy or irreconcilable conflict, the board concluded that plants had not been removed by implication from the category of statutory subject matter under Section 101.

After *Hibberd*, the principle of *Chakrabarty* was further extended by the board to include animals as well as plants. In *Ex parte Allen*,[31] the patent applicants had produced and claimed novel polyploid Pacific oysters of the species *Crassotrea gigus*, which were edible year-round. The board held it to be patentable subject matter under Section 101. Allen was, however, denied a patent for another reason: his invention was obvious.

Following *Allen* and amid considerable public debate, the patent office announced that it would from then on consider nonnaturally occurring, nonhuman, multicellular living organisms, including animals, to be patentable subject matter. On April 21, 1987, just days after the board's decision in *Allen*, the PTO issued a notice stating:

> The Patent and Trademark Office now considers nonnaturally occurring nonhuman multicellular living organisms, including animals, to be patentable subject matter within the scope of 35 USC Section 101.
>
> The board's decision [in *Allen*] does not affect the principle and practice that products found in nature will not be considered to be patentable subject matter under 35 USC 101 and/or 102. An article of manufacture or composition of matter occurring in nature will not be considered patentable unless given a new form, quality, properties or combination not present in the original article existing in nature in accordance with existing law.[32]

The notice went on to point out that patent claims encompassing humans were not permissible under the Constitution and suggested that this problem could be avoided by including the term "nonhuman" in the claims.

The first animal patent, P. Leder and T. Stewart, *Transgenic Non-Human Mammals,* U.S. Patent No. 4,736,866, was issued on April 12, 1988. This patent, sometimes referred to as the "Harvard mouse" patent, concerned genetically engineered nonhuman mammals containing an activated oncogene. The 1987 PTO policy and the 1988 issuance of the Harvard mouse patent generated considerable debate, all of which is beyond the scope of the present discussion.[33] The next three animal patents were issued on December 29, 1992.[34]

5.1.3.1   The European Experience with the Patenting of Living Things.   What constitutes statutory subject matter varies widely from country to country. The course of development under the European Patent Convention (EPC) is an example.

Article 53(b) of the EPC states that European patents are *not* available for:

> plant or animal varieties or essentially biological processes for the production of plants or animals; this provision does not apply to microbiological processes or the products thereof.

Thus, for new plants, the question under the EPC is whether that plant is a new "variety" or whether the process for producing that plant is "essentially biological." In deciding to allow Lubrizol patent EP122791, the European Patent Office (EPO) Board of Appeals stated that exclusions to patentability are to be "construed narrowly" and granted patent protection for both methods of modifying plant cells with certain Ti-plasmids and plants produced from them. The generic group of plants produced by this process was not a new variety because it did not meet the requirements of distinctness, uniformity, and stability, and the process involved sufficient intervention to render it *not* "essentially biological."[35] As discussed in Chapter 11, U.S. law is different in that utility patent protection could be obtained on a plant even if it were a new "variety."

The patentability of animals under the EPC was addressed when a counterpart to the Harvard mouse patent was filed in the European Patent Office. The application was initially rejected by the Examining Division, but the Technical Board of Appeals reversed this decision, applying an analysis similar to that applied for the Lubrizol plant patent.[36] In this case, however, the board remanded the case to the Examining Division for an analysis of whether the application complied with EPC Article 53(a). This article states that European patents shall not be granted for "inventions the publication or exploitation of which would be contrary to 'ordre public' or morality. . . ." For the Harvard mouse, the Examining Division ultimately concluded that the invention was patentable. The division stated that it must weigh three factors: the interest of mankind to remedy disease, the need to protect the environment from the dissemination of unwanted genes, and the need to avoid cruelty to animals. Emphasizing that its decision applied solely to the case at hand, the division stated that a test animal useful in cancer research could not be considered something immoral or contrary to public order in and of itself under Article 53(a).[37]

The patentability of plants and animals in Europe is still in a state of flux, and a draft Biological Patents Directive, which would clarify this area, remains under consideration.[38]

5.2   PRACTICAL UTILITY

The issue raised under the practical utility requirement is whether the claimed subject matter is useful. One example where this requirement has become an issue is the National Institutes of Health patent application on more than 2000 partial cDNA sequences.[39]

The practical utility requirement has been hotly debated since the mid-1960s, when the Supreme Court decided *Brenner v. Manson*.[40] In *Brenner*, the applicants claimed a process for producing certain known steroids. The application was initially rejected for failure "to disclose any utility for" the chemical compound produced by the process. The applicants responded with a reference showing a homologue with apparent tumor-inhibiting effects in mice. On review, the Board of Appeals held that "the statutory requirement of usefulness of a product cannot be presumed merely because it happens to be closely related to another compound which is known to be useful." The CCPA reversed the board, holding that "where a claimed process produces a known product it is not necessary to show utility for the product" so long as the product "is not alleged to be detrimental to the public interest."[41]

The Supreme Court rejected the CCPA's analysis and the applicants' arguments. The court, however, included their position that the process had utility because (1) the process worked, that is, it produced a compound, and (2) the compound that was produced belonged to a series of compounds then under serious scientific investigation. In holding that this was not sufficient to satisfy the utility requirement, the court explained:

> Whatever weight is attached to the value of encouraging disclosure and of inhibiting secrecy, we believe a more compelling consideration is that a process patent in the chemical field, which has not been developed and pointed to the degree of specific utility, creates a monopoly of knowledge which should be granted only if clearly commanded by the statute. . . . The basic *quid pro quo* contemplated by the Constitution and the Congress for granting a patent monopoly is the benefit derived by the public from an invention with substantial utility. Unless and until a process is refined and developed to this point—where specific benefit exists in currently available form—there is insufficient justification for permitting an applicant to engross what may prove to be a broad field.[42]

The utility requirement established in *Brenner v. Manson* was extended in *In re Kirk*,[43] where the CCPA upheld the Board of Appeals' Section 101 rejection of claims directed to 1-dehydro-6-methyl steroid compounds. The applicants in *Kirk* had stated that their derivatives constituted "a new class of compounds often possessing high biological activity" and that they were of value "on account of their biological properties or as intermediates in the preparation of compounds with useful biological properties." The examiner argued that the application failed to provide a "specific allegation of utility." The board agreed, saying that the claimed utility "is so general and vague as to be meaningless." The CCPA upheld the board, saying that "the nebulous expressions 'biological activity' or 'biological properties' "[44] failed to convey an explicit indication of the utility of the compounds and how to use them. Moreover, the court held that an affidavit submitted in response to the rejection showing a particular utility of the claimed compounds failed to cure the lack of utility since "it is what the compounds are *disclosed* to do that is determinative here."[45]

Judge Rich, long a scholar of the practical utility requirement, filed a vigorous and thoughtful dissent in *Kirk*.[46] Among other things, Judge Rich suggested that all chemical compounds should be considered useful per se within the meaning of Section 101.[47] Those concerned with the question of how the practical utility requirement will be interpreted and applied to new technologies in the future should carefully review Judge Rich's dissenting opinion.

The apparent stringency of the practical utility requirement was first clarified and relaxed in *Nelson v. Bowler*.[48] In *Bowler*, the Patent Office Board of Interferences had concluded that Bowler was the first to conceive and reduce the contested substituted prostaglandins to practice, and thus was entitled to the patent. The board held that Nelson's evidence did not show adequate proof of practical utility. Instead it demonstrated that, as with natural prostaglandins, the claimed compounds caused smooth muscle stimulation and modulation of blood pressure in rats. On appeal, the CCPA reversed the PTO, stating that the "board erred in not recognizing that tests evidencing pharmacological activity may manifest a practical utility even though they may not establish a specific therapeutic use."[49] In response to Bowler's arguments that the tests were inconclusive, the court held that "rigorous correlation is not necessary where the test for pharmacological activity is reasonably indicative of the desired response. . . . The controlling point is that these responses are evidence of pharmacological activity."[50]

In so holding, the court expressed its pragmatic view that:

> Knowledge of the pharmacological activity of any compound is obviously beneficial to the public. It is inherently faster and easier to combat illnesses and alleviate symptoms when the medical profession is armed with an arsenal of chemicals having known pharmacological activities. Since it is crucial to provide researchers with an incentive to disclose pharmacological activities in as many compounds as possible, we conclude that adequate proof of any such activity constitutes a showing of practical utility.[51]

In *Cross v. Iizuka*,[52] the courts took the practical utility analysis one step further. When determining practical utility, the Federal Circuit expressed its view that:

> a thorough analysis of the utility issue requires first, a determination as to what utility is disclosed, i.e., the stated utility, for the invention claimed in the application. Only after the stated utility has been determined, can a proper analysis be undertaken to determine if the stated utility complies with the "practical utility" requirement of § 101.[53]

The court acknowledged that stated utility often arises in a variety of forms. It is common in U.S. patent practice to express certain objectives that the claimed invention is sought to achieve; objectives that usually are in harmony with the perceived utility of the invention. The court reiterated that "when a properly claimed invention meets at least one stated objective, utility under § 101 is clearly shown."[54] Thus, if the stated objective or perceived utility is deemed to be useful[55] and if the claimed subject matter possesses such utility, there is patentable subject matter.

The court concluded that the applicants' original disclosure, for which utility was alleged to be lacking, adequately stated its practical utility in the form of a specific pharmacological activity, namely, inhibition of thromboxane synthetase. The fact that the activity was shown only by *in vitro* testing was not fatal to that showing.[56]

It would seem that the practical utility requirement of Section 101 is met where the utility of the claimed subject matter has been stated with particularity and shown adequately, though not conclusively, by testing methods generally accepted within the field.

5.3 OPERABILITY

The issue raised by the operability requirement is not whether the invention is useful, but whether the invention works.[57] For example, a perpetual-motion machine clearly would be useful, but it is questionable whether any such machine would work.[58]

Chemical and biological patent applications are frequently questioned on whether they satisfy the operability requirement. An extreme example is *In re Eltgroth*,[59] in which claim 1 read as follows:

> 1. The method of influencing the effective age of a living organism which comprises modification of the abundance of a specific isotope present in such organism.

In upholding the rejection of this claim under Section 101, the court said:

> Undoubtedly, the *alleged utility* of control of the aging process in living organisms and the significant beneficial results flowing therefrom is adequate. Yet, there is a conspicuous absence of proof thereof.[60]

Operability questions can arise in many situations. For example, in *Ex parte Balzarini*, the Patent Office Board of Appeals upheld an examiner's rejection of claims directed to methods of treating AIDS with known compounds and pharmaceutical compositions containing such compounds.[61] The board noted that "a disclosure of utility which corresponds in scope to the subject matter sought to be patented *must* be taken as sufficient to satisfy the utility requirement . . . *unless* there is reason for one skilled in the art to question the objective truth of the statement of utility or its scope." The board decided there was ample support for the position that the applicant's *in vitro* data was insufficient to establish the operability of the claimed inventions in humans. The board was careful to state that it was not requiring human clinical trials of the applicant. It did state, however, that there was no evidence of record that experimental models in this area could predict its efficacy in humans and that "it may well be" that nothing short of human clinical trials would be sufficient.[62]

New chemical compounds receive substantially different treatment under the operability requirement, which must be satisfied only with respect to the practical utility relied on by the applicant. If *in vitro* utility is enough to satisfy the practical utility requirement, then, clearly, *in vitro* data is sufficient to establish that the invention is operable *in vitro*.

REFERENCES

1. *In re* Bergy, 596 F.2d 952, 960, 201 USPQ 352, 361 (C.C.P.A. 1979).
2. *See, e.g., In re* Eltgroth, 419 F.2d 918, 922, 164 USPQ 221 (C.C.P.A. 1970) ("Undoubtedly, the alleged utility of control of the aging process in living organisms and the significant beneficial results flowing therefrom is adequate [to satisfy the utility requirement.] Yet, there is a conspicuous absence of proof thereof. . . ."); *see also* P. Goldstein, Copyright, Patent, Trademark and Related State Doctrines, 493 (2d ed. 1981) ("'Operability,' in the patent lexicon, is quite different from 'utility.' Operability's function is to assist in determinations of [a legitimate] reduction to practice. . . .").
3. *See, e.g., In re* Pardo, 684 F.2d 912, 214 USPQ 673 (C.C.P.A. 1982) ("Any process, machine, manufacture, or composition of matter constitutes statutory subject matter unless it falls within the judicially determined exceptions to section 101.").
4. *In re* Joliot, 270 F.2d 954, 123 USPQ 344 (C.C.P.A. 1959) (Rich, J., concurring).
5. 1 Lipscomb's Walker on Patents, p. 102.
6. *Ex parte* Prescott, 19 USPQ 178 (Bd. Pat. App. 1932).
7. *Id.* at 180–81.
8. Parke-Davis v. H.K. Mulford Co., 189 F. 95 (S.D.N.Y. 1911), *aff'd in part, rev'd in part,* 196 F. 496 (2d Cir. 1912).
9. *Id.* at 103.
10. Merck & Co. v. Olin Mathieson Chemical Corp., 253 F.2d 156, 116 USPQ 484 (4th Cir. 1958).
11. *Id.* at 488.
12. *Id.* at 489.
13. *Id.*
14. *Id.* at 489–90.
15. Amgen, Inc. v. Chugai Pharmaceutical Co., 13 USPQ2d 1737, 1759 (D. Mass. 1989) (citations omitted), *modified on other grounds,* 927 F.2d 1200, 18 USPQ2d 1016 (Fed. Cir. 1991).
16. Diamond v. Chakrabarty, 447 U.S. 303, 309, 100 S.Ct. 2204, 2207–08, 206 USPQ 193 (1980).
17. *See generally* K. O'Connor, *Patenting Animals and Other Living Things,* 65 SOUTHERN CAL. L. REV. 597 (1991).

18. Guaranty Trust Co. v. Union Solvents Co., 54 F.2d 400, 12 USPQ 47 (D. Del. 1931), *aff'd*, 61 F.2d 1041, 15 USPQ 237, *cert. denied*, 288 U.S. 614, 53 S. Ct. 405 (1933).
19. Guaranty Trust, 54 F.2d at 410.
20. *In re* Mancy, 499 F.2d 1289, 182 USPQ 303 (C.C.P.A. 1974).
21. *In re* Mancy, 182 USPQ at 306.
22. *Id.*
23. *Id.*
24. Chakrabarty, 447 U.S. at 314, note 9, 100 S. Ct. at 2210, note 9.
25. Chakrabarty, 447 U.S. at 314, 100 S. Ct. at 2210.
26. Chakrabarty, 447 U.S. at 316, 100 S. Ct. at 2211.
27. *Ex parte* Hibberd, 227 USPQ 443 (Bd. Pat. App. 1985).
28. Hibberd, 227 USPQ at 444.
29. *Id.*
30. *Id.*
31. *Ex Parte* Allen, 2 USPQ2d 1425 (Bd. Pat. App. 1987), *aff'd*, 846 F.2d 77 (Fed. Cir. 1988).
32. D. Quigg, Animals—Patentability, 1077 Official Gazette 24 (April 21, 1987).
33. *See generally*, U.S. Congress, Office of Technology Assessment, NEW DEVELOPMENTS IN BIOTECHNOLOGY: PATENTING LIFE—SPECIAL REPORT, OTA-BA-370 (Washington, DC: U.S. Government Printing Office, April 1989) at p. 12. *See also* Animal Legal Defense Fund v. Quigg, 932 F.2d 920, 18 USPQ2d 1677 (Fed. Cir. 1991).
34. T. Wagner and X.-Z. Chen, Virus-Resistant Transgenic Mice, U.S. Patent No. 5,175,385; P. Krimpenfort and A. Berns, Transgenic Mice Depleted in Mature T-Cells and Methods for Making Transgenic Mice, U.S. Patent No. 5,175,384; P. Leder and W. Muller, Animal Model for Benign Prostatic Disease, U.S. Patent No. 5,175,383.
35. *See* 5 WORLD INTELLECTUAL PROPERTY REPORT 212, 213 (August 1991) (published by BNA International, Inc., London, England).
36. *See* Harvard/Onco-mouse, [1990] EPOR 501.
37. *See* 6 WORLD INTELLECTUAL PROPERTY REPORT, 7–8, 21–22 (Jan. 1992).
38. *See* J. Hodgson, *European Patent Rules Emerge*, 10 BIO/TECHNOLOGY 1525 (Dec. 1992); N. Jones, *Biotechnological Patents in Europe—Update on the Draft Directive*, 12 EUROPEAN INTELLECTUAL PROPERTY REPORTS 455 (1992).
39. *See, e.g.*, R. Eisenberg, *Genes, Patents, and Product Development*, 257 SCIENCE 903 (Aug. 14, 1992); R. Adler, *Genome Research: Fulfilling the Public's Expectations for Knowledge and Commercialization*, 257 SCIENCE 908 (Aug. 14, 1992); T. Kiley, *Patents on Random Complementary DNA Fragments?*, 257 SCIENCE 915 (Aug. 14, 1992).
40. Brenner v. Manson, 383 U.S. 519, 86 S. Ct. 1033, 148 USPQ 689 (1966). *See generally* K. Sibley, *Practical Utility–Evolution Suspended?* 32 IDEA 203 (1992).
41. *Id.* at 383 U.S. 522, 86 S. Ct. 1035.
42. *Id.* at 383 U.S. 534, 86 S. Ct. 1041.
43. *In re* Kirk, 376 F.2d 936, 153 USPQ 48 (C.C.P.A. 1976).
44. Kirk, 376 F.2d at 941.
45. *Id.*
46. Kirk, 376 F.2d at 947–66, 153 USPQ at 266–81.
47. Kirk, 376 F.2d at 957, 153 USPQ at 275.
48. Nelson v. Bowler, 626 F.2d 853, 206 USPQ 881 (C.C.P.A. 1980).
49. Nelson, 626 F.2d at 856.

50. *Id.*
51. *Id.*
52. Cross v. Iizuka, 753 F.2d 1040, 224 USPQ 739 (Fed. Cir. 1985).
53. Cross, 753 F.2d at 1044.
54. Cross, 753 F.2d at 1045 note 9.
55. Cf. Brenner v. Mason, 383 U.S. 519, 86 S. Ct. 1033 ("biological activity" insufficient as an expression of utility despite the fact that the compounds were later shown to actually have therapeutic activity).
56. Cross, 753 F.2d at 1051 ("We perceive no insurmountable difficulty, under appropriate circumstances, in finding that the first link in the screening chain, *in vitro* testing, may establish a practical utility for the compound in question.").
57. *See generally* E. Walterscheid, *Insufficient Disclosure Rejections (Part II)*, 62 J. PAT. OFF. SOC'Y 229 (1980).
58. *See, e.g.*, Newman v. Quigg, 11 USPQ2d 1340 (Fed. Cir. 1989).
59. *In re* Eltgroth, 419 F.2d 918, 164 USPQ 221 (C.C.P.A. 1970).
60. Eltgroth, 164 USPQ at 223.
61. *Ex parte* Balzarini, 21 USPQ2d 1892 (Bd. Pat. App. 1991).
62. Balzarini, 21 USPQ2d at 1897.

6

Novelty and the Public Domain

James R. Cannon

The patentability of an invention depends to a large extent on what information is already in the public domain. The requirement that says an invention must be "novel" relative to that information is presented in a rather convoluted fashion in 35 U.S.C. § 102. The statute's seven subsections describe conditions that bar an invention from patent protection. Several of these subsections deal with whether the invention was somehow in the public domain at the time that the application was filed. An invention that falls within the scope of one of these subsections is said to be "anticipated" and is precluded from patent protection.

Of the seven subsections of Section 102, subsections (a) and (b) include most of the anticipatory information. These subsections read as follows:

A person shall be entitled to a patent unless—

(a) the invention was known or used by others in this country, or patented or described in a printed publication in this or a foreign country, before the invention thereof by the applicant for patent, or

(b) the invention was patented or described in a printed publication in this or a foreign country or in public use or on sale in this country, more than one year prior to the date of the application for patent in the United States. . . .

The terms of these subsections reflect the policy underlying the patent system: to reward an inventor who discloses and explains to the public the previously unknown technology behind his or her art. Subsection (a) bars protection for an applicant who only claims an invention that was previously known by others. Subsection (b) bars protection for an applicant who waits too long after placing an invention in the public domain. Each subsection bars patent protection for someone who, according to policy, should not be rewarded for a disclosure.

This chapter will discuss the boundaries of these deceptively simple-looking subsections, focusing on scenarios of interest to biotechnology.

6.1   THE ANATOMY OF ANTICIPATORY PRIOR ART

To qualify as anticipatory prior art under any of the subsections of Section 102, certain criteria must be met. First, an individual prior art act or document must disclose the elements of the claimed invention. Second, the prior art must be an "enabling" disclosure as defined by the first paragraph of Section 112. Third, the prior art must not fall within the "accidental anticipation" exception to these rules. Each of these criteria will be explored in the following sections.

6.1.1   All Claim Elements Must Be Present

Each of the claimed elements must be included in the reference, either expressly or inherently, for the reference to be anticipatory. As pointed out by the Federal Circuit in *Hybritech, Inc. v. Monoclonal Antibodies, Inc.*, an invention may not be anticipated by a combination of references.[1] Due to the imprecise nature of claim language, determining the presence or absence of all claim elements often is very difficult. *Hybritech* illustrates the critical point that if an invention is not anticipated, numerous arguments can show that it is nonobvious.

The test for anticipation is set forth in *Lewmar Marine Inc. v. Barient, Inc.*,[2] in which the Federal Circuit held "that which would *literally* infringe if later in time anticipates if earlier than the date of invention."[3]

The *Lewmar Marine* test is especially useful for demonstrating the relationship of "genus" claims and "species" claims in determining anticipation. As the terms suggest, a "genus" is a relatively broad class of items that somehow are generically related. A "species" is an individual item within a genus. If a species of the later-discovered and claimed genus is disclosed in a prior art reference, it anticipates the claimed genus. This is demonstrated by the *Lewmar* doctrine; if the species had come after the genus was disclosed, it would literally infringe the genus claim.[4] In contrast, if the species alone is claimed (as a "selection" invention), disclosure of the genus does not anticipate because it would not literally infringe the species claim. Thus, the prior disclosure of a generic chemical formula that encompasses a later-claimed specific chemical formula or species does not anticipate the species unless the species itself is disclosed "without any need for picking, choosing, and combining various disclosures not directly related to each other by the teachings of the cited reference."[5]

The exception to this general rule is that when a genus includes only a very limited number of species that are well-identified and closely related, explicit disclosure of the genus is considered an explicit disclosure of all included species.[6] It also should be noted that even though a species claim may not be anticipated by a prior disclosure, it still must be shown to be nonobvious under Section 103.[7]

6.1.2   The Prior Art Must Be Enabling

The prior art also must provide an enabling disclosure to be anticipatory; that is, it must adequately describe the invention so that a person of ordinary skill in the art could understand and make the invention.[8] The disclosure must be such that the skilled artisan could at least utilize the teachings of the reference in combination with his or her own knowledge to recreate the invention.[9] Not disclosing how to make the invention is excusable only when the method of making it would be obvious to the skilled artisan from the description of the invention itself.[10]

In re LeGrice[11] illustrates this issue. LeGrice applied for a plant patent on a "rosa floribunda plant." Photographs of the plants were included in British catalogs and a publication of the National Rose Society, and in each instance, the origin of the plants was attributed to the patent applicant. The court held that a mere photograph and description of the external characteristics of the plant did not bar patentability, since neither would teach the skilled horticulturist what starting materials would be required to produce this strain. Courts have applied the *LeGrice* court's analysis to hold nonanticipating a description of an antibiotic available from the fermentation broth of a strain of actinomyces isolated from the soil of the Chiba prefecture,[12] a cell line not yet deposited at a recognized depository,[13] and a bacterium that was available only from the applicant, who had not submitted it to a depository at the time of the prior art disclosure.[14]

Whatever embodies the claimed invention described in the prior art need not actually have been made; it is enough to simply indicate how the skilled artisan could do so.[15] It has been held, however, that a reference that fully discloses each element of a claimed compound but does not teach how to make the compound anticipates the claim if another reference adequately discloses a way of making it.[16] Note that if the method of making the invention is shown to be unsatisfactory, this is strong evidence that the disclosure is not enabling for anyone skilled in the art.[17]

Care should be taken in extending *LeGrice* too far. Recently, in *Ex parte Thomson*, the PTO distinguished *LeGrice* and held that claims to a cotton cultivar were properly rejected because seeds to the cultivar were commercially available in Australia.[18]

Where the question is whether the description of a novel biological material in a scholarly journal (rather than a trade publication) is enabling, preliminary indications are that the EPO sometimes takes a much *harsher* view than that currently taken in the United States. In the *Methylomonas* decision,[19] the EPO Technical Board of Appeals held that claims directed to a novel *Methylomonas* that was described in the journal *SZESZIPAR* and abstracted in *Chemical Abstracts* failed to satisfy the novelty requirement. The applicant argued that it was not possible to reproduce the microorganism from the description in the publications and that the microorganism had not been passed on to the public. The examiner, while acknowledging that the patent law required a prior art publication to enable the production of a claimed microorganism, expressed the following view:

(a) The purpose of any scientific publication is to make a certain teaching or discovery accessible to the public by a written description. Further, it is common in scientific circles, to pass on samples of, for example, microorganisms to other scientists, if they cannot be obtained directly from a depository.

(b) It may therefore be presumed that the readiness of the author of a scientific publication to pass on samples, is *implicitly contained* in such a scientific publication, and that already this implicit readiness, as applicant admits itself . . . is sufficient for the repeatability of the teaching of the publication. Finally, the author of a scientific article, which deals with nonreproducible micro-organisms, is aware that the passing on of a sample of said micro-organism is essential to ensure that the repeatability of the technical teaching of the scientific article in question. Without that, the publication would be only paper and meaningless.

(c) Consequently, in the present case the teaching of the publication . . . is to be considered as repeatable and, consequently, as anticipating the present claims, *no matter whether or not the sample was in fact passed on.*

The Board of Appeals agreed with the examiner, noting that if it were to decide otherwise: (1) the prior art would be nonuniform because there would be repeatable patent literature in which microorganisms were deposited and nonrepeatable journal literature, (2) examiners would be required to make lengthy and unreasonable investigations, and (3) it would be providing a grace period after publication where the EPC does not. It is currently unclear whether the EPO will continue this line of analysis or whether a similar line of analysis might arise in the United States. If so, the outcome most likely will be highly dependent on the facts of the particular case.

6.1.3 The Prior Art Has No Utility Requirement

Although utility is required by Section 101 for an invention to be patented, an anticipating prior art reference need not disclose a "practical utility" to anticipate the invention.[20] In *In re Hafner*, the applicant had filed within the requisite time period two German patent applications, followed by a U.S. application that combined the German applications into one. More than a year after the publication of one of the German applications, the applicant filed a continuation-in-part application based on the still-pending U.S. application. The applicant conceded that the German application did not disclose the utility required by the U.S. application. The continuation-in-part application did not receive the priority date of the earlier German application because of its failure to disclose the requisite utility, yet the applicant still was barred from patent protection under 102(b) because of the publication of the same document. The court in *In re Hafner* agreed that this rule created a double standard for inventions and prior art references, but stated that this double standard is "implicitly if not explicitly required by law."[21] Of course, method protection for the newly discovered use of the previously known (but useless) compound or structure may well be available.

6.1.4. Inherency—Discovery Without Invention

A reference may anticipate a claimed invention despite a startling new discovery that explains the mechanism behind the invention. If the new discovery, such as an unexpected property, is inherent in the invention as previously disclosed, the applicant is barred from obtaining a patent; even when the inventor's work is the discovered property now understood.[22] This doctrine, known as "inherency," was applied in *In re Wilder*.[23] The applicant in this case discovered that a specific additive known to be a member of a class of rubber preservatives was nontoxic to the skin. Almost all of the remaining members of the disclosed class of additives were toxic. The prior art was silent on the toxicity of any of the compounds but did specifically disclose the formulas of the nontoxic compounds as rubber preservatives. The court held that the unexpected property discovered by the applicant was irrelevant to the question of whether claims directed to the compounds as rubber preservatives were anticipated. The court stated that "proof [of nontoxicity] would not necessarily negate the fact that the reference does, in fact, *describe* those very compositions."[24]

6.1.5 Accidental Anticipation—Inherency Without Appreciation

The inherency doctrine is complicated. An exception known as "accidental anticipation" exists when the invention was accidentally and unintentionally practiced, and the practice of the invention was unappreciated by the practitioner. Put another way, "chance hits in the dark will not anticipate an invention."[25] The seminal case for the accidental anticipation doctrine, *Tilghman v. Proctor*,[26] regarded the production of fatty acids in numerous prior processes practiced "whilst the inventors were in pursuit of other and different results, without exciting attention and without even being known what was done or how it had been done. Accordingly, it would be absurd to say that this was an anticipation of Tilghman's discovery."[27] The broad concept of accidental anticipation set forth in *Tilghman* was later limited to include only circumstances in which there is no "assurance that the result can be reached another time," which is not present "unless the process is deliberate and the means understood."[28] In contrast, when "the result is a necessary consequence of what was deliberately intended,"[29] the invention is said to be anticipated. Factors to be considered in determining whether a previous practice anticipates the invention include the number and frequency of previous practices,[30] the prior practitioner's appreciation of the claim elements defining the invention in the prior practice (as opposed to appreciating the result of the claimed invention),[31] and the certainty that the prior event occurred.[32]

6.2 WHEN IS PRIOR ART PROPERLY APPLIED TO A CLAIM?

This section discusses the circumstances under which prior acts meeting the criteria just discussed fall within the provisions of the subsections of Section 102 and hence can be applied as prior art against patent claims.

6.2.1 A Comparison of Sections 102(a) and 102(b)

Section 102(a) bars an invention from patent protection if the invention was: (1) known or used by others in this country, or (2) patented or described in a printed publication in this or a foreign country before the applicant created the invention. Thus, the key date for this section is the date of invention. In contrast, Section 102(b) bars patentability if the invention was: (1) patented or described in a printed publication in this or a foreign country, or (2) in public use or on sale in this country for more than a year prior to the date of the application for patent in the United States. The key date for Section 102(b) is the date the patent application was filed. The U.S. patent system allows the inventor a one-year grace period from the date of first public disclosure of the invention either by publication, issued patent, public use, or being "on sale" to file a patent application to protect his or her rights in the invention.

The one-year grace period is quite different from the "absolute novelty" rule in many other countries, which bars patentability of an invention after the invention is publicly disclosed. In a practical sense, the U.S. grace period is advantageous for the inventor, because it allows him or her the time to learn about the commercial feasibility of the invention to determine whether the effort and expense of obtaining a patent are worth the investment.

The terms *known or used*, *in public use*, *on sale*, and *printed publications*, which appear in sections 102(a) and 102(b), have special meaning. The following sections describe the peculiarities of these terms and the issues they involve.

6.2.2 Printed Publications

The term *printed publication* was originally intended to have a literal meaning: a printed document available to the public designed to convey ideas to people.[33] The term now refers to information that is available to the public in a tangible form. "[D]issemination and public accessibility are the keys to the legal determination whether or not a prior art reference was 'published.' "[34] Thus, a "printed publication" need not actually be a printed page (although it very often takes this form), but may be a microfilm or microfiche, an audio or video tape, or a computer database.

Having defined the term, two key issues are raised. Is a particular collection of information accessible to the degree necessary to deem it "published"? If the information has been published, what is its date of publication? These issues are analyzed in more detail in the following sections.

6.2.2.1   Date of Publication.   For both sections 102(a) and (b), the publication date of a printed publication determines whether a reference is available as prior art. The general rule is that the publication date is the date the public gained access to the information regarding the invention.[35] The reference need not be accessible to everyone; access that is restricted to a specific sector of the public is enough if accessibility is shown to "raise a presumption that the public concerned with the art would know of the invention."[36] A document may be publicly available (and therefore published) even if no copies have been distributed, as long as an interested party could obtain a copy by simply requesting one.[37] For many references, the publication date is initially presumed to be the date borne by the reference. That date may be challenged and subsequently proven to be earlier or later by extrinsic evidence.[38] There are, however, recognized exceptions to this general rule. Documents delivered to specific addressees are considered to be published on the date of first receipt of the document rather than the date of mailing or shipment.[39] This can create uncertainty as to the actual date of publication (and, accordingly, the critical date for the invention) because different addressees most likely would receive individual copies on different days. This problem is illustrated by *Ex parte Albert*,[40] in which the applicant tried to prove that the date of publication of a reference known to have been printed on November 10 was actually sometime after November 25. The applicant introduced evidence that indicated that several libraries had received their copies of the reference after November 25. In holding the reference to be valid prior art, the board said that better evidence of the publication date would come from the U.S. Postal Service and the publisher of the reference because each could draw on past experience to describe the expected delay between publication and receipt by addressees. This places an enormous burden on the applicant, who must track down the information from the publisher and the postal service.

6.2.2.2   Types of Printed Publications.   Printed publications come in a number of different forms, such as seminar and conference papers, technical journals, library collections, and confidential documents. A great deal of information concerning biotechnology appears in one or more of these publication forms, each of which has its own unique body of law. The following sections address type of publication.

6.2.2.2.1   Seminars and Conferences.   As a starting point, it is important to note that the oral presentation of information, with nothing more, does not constitute a printed publication because nothing is "printed" as required by sections 102(a) and (b). Frequently, however, a public address on a topic of scientific interest is accompanied by a printed abstract, a slide presentation, or a brochure. Material of this sort may qualify as a printed publication by itself or in combination with the oral presentation. As with all printed publications, the inquiry focuses on factors such as the degree of accessibility to the information, the number of people with access to the information, and the form of the information.

Because there is no standard format for presenting, reviewing, and supplementing material at a seminar or conference, the case law on seminars and conferences as printed publications tends to be very specific. For example, a presentation given to between 50 and 500 people, a copy of which was available after the conference, was held to be a publication.[41] Similarly, an advance copy of a paper mailed to conference participants approximately a month prior to presentation also was held to be a publication. It was so judged even though the advance copy was different from the final copy, which was not available until 18 months after the conference.[42]

In contrast, in *Regents of the University of California v. Howmedica*,[43] a slide show unaccompanied by a printed document was judged not to constitute a printed publication. The *Howmedica* court determined that the limited duration of the lecture "could not disclose the invention to the extent necessary to enable a person of ordinary skill in the art to make or use the invention," and that the public did not have access to the slides prior to the critical date.[44] A pre-delivery review of a manuscript by a committee of five conference attendees was found to be a sufficiently limited distribution to support a finding that the manuscript was not a printed publication.[45] This holding was supported by evidence showing that the manuscript was understood to be confidential and that no copies were distributed at or available after the presentation. Similar facts also led to a holding of no publication in *National Semiconductor v. Linear Technology, Inc.*,[46] in which the members of a 10-person review committee understood that the papers they were examining were confidential until the date of the conference.

These cases provide little guidance as to whether a particular presentation is actually prior art. Of course, delaying any disclosure until a patent application is filed is the most certain course; however, other factors often require rapid publication of research findings. The best course in a situation such as this is to simply plan in advance so a logical patent strategy can be adapted to a publication schedule.

6.2.2.2.2 Collections of Single Manuscripts. As just described, the date of a publication generally is considered to be the date carried by the publication. However, many publications, such as undergraduate and master's theses, exist as only a single copy. Such documents usually are indexed and stored in a library upon receipt, where theoretically they are accessible to the public. Nevertheless, because of the detail contained in these documents, they can be extremely relevant prior art. If the validity of a patent is ever challenged in court, opposing counsel may expend considerable effort to locate such references.

Theses and dissertations generally are considered printed publications, with most of the case law focusing on the accessibility of the information in order to establish the publication date. An early case on single-copy documents held that the publication date of a thesis was the date the library received the document.[47] However, this holding was not followed by the court in *In re Tenney*,[48] which held that an unpublished German patent application available from a library on microfilm but improperly indexed was not a printed publication because it had not been widely circulated and, therefore, was not accessible.

The court in *Philips Electric & Pharmaceutical Industries Corp. v. Thermal & Electric Industries*[49] held that a properly indexed (therefore, accessible) German application was a published reference. *In re Tenney* was distinguished as mere misindexing of a reference. The court in *Philips* held that the proponent of the reference must prove accessibility by showing either: (1) actual dissemination of the reference, or (2) its availability to one skilled in the art. Similar reasoning led to a holding of delayed publication in *In re Bayer*.[50] The reference in question was a thesis kept in a university library. It was the library's practice to accumulate theses in a library office accessible only to library staff. At some later date, usually several months after receipt, each thesis would be processed by indexing, binding, and shelving. The Board of Patent Appeals held that the publication date was not the date of receipt, since on that date the document was not available to the public. However, the court noted that the author's thesis defense announced to the faculty that the thesis was available for inspection. Clearly, the members of the faculty qualify as skilled artisans who would be able to understand the thesis. On appeal, the court's decision was reversed on the grounds that the thesis was available only to those on the review committee rather than by the customary research channels; therefore, the probability of *public* knowledge of the contents was, for all practical purposes, zero. The court held that the publication date was the date of processing by the library.

The Federal Circuit has treated this issue consistently with the *Bayer* holding. In *In re Hall*,[51] a dissertation indexed according to customary library procedures was determined to be published upon indexing. In *In re Cronyn*,[52] an undergraduate thesis was indexed only under the author's last name, and the indexing system was a shoe box kept in the chemistry department library. Under this system, it was held that the reference was not reasonably accessible to the interested public.

6.2.2.2.3   Confidential Documents.   The general rule regarding confidential documents is that they are not printed publications because they are not accessible to the public. The confidentiality can be governmental or industrial,[53] and express or implied,[54] and still obstruct public access.

It should be noted that many documents considered to be confidential are actually only partially confidential, since the confidentiality expires after a predetermined period. Documents of this sort can be prior art after the confidentiality period expires. The issue of confidential documents arises most often when a government document is declassified. *Ex parte Harris*[55] held that declassified government documents on subsidized penicillin research were not published upon declassification. Instead, an overt act, such as an announcement that the documents were available or an actual publishing that communicated the contents of the documents to the public, was required for the documents to be considered public.

Grant applications and proposals for government-sponsored research and reports filed before the research was done can be particularly important sources of prior art. Such documents can be sought under the federal Freedom of Information Act (FOIA),[56] which may grant public access to a document (and cause the document to be prior art).[57]

In the *DuPont v. Cetus* case over the polymerase chain reaction patents, the district court held that information available to the public under the FOIA is published material and, therefore, it can be used as anticipatory prior art.[58] In *DuPont*, 10 years before the patent application, grant proposals allegedly disclosing the invention were submitted to the National Science Foundation and to the National Institutes of Health. Each proposal was accessible to the public under the FOIA. The court defined a printed publication as one that is "sufficiently accessible to members of the public who are interested in the art and exercise reasonable diligence"[59] and expressly rejected the defendant's contention that the standard should be whether the skilled artisan *would be likely* to have encountered the prior art. The court then noted that each of the proposals was filed and indexed by its title, author, institution, and grant number in published indexes of grants. The court also pointed out that the author was the preeminent researcher in this field.[60] Anyone familiar with this field would have been aware of the author's work and would have been interested in publications bearing his name. One of the grant proposals was cited as a source in at least one of the author's publications. As such, not only would the skilled artisan have access to the grant proposal, he or she also would have been directed to it by other publications. Consequently, the grant proposal was held to be an accessible printed publication.

6.2.3 Prior Use, Knowledge, and "On Sale"

This section describes circumstances under which acts by the patent applicant or someone else can negate patentability; namely, if the invention is "in use," "known," or "on sale" in this country.

Of note is the requirement that these anticipating activities must occur in the United States. The reason for including this requirement when the bill was drafted in 1836 is unclear, although the difficulty in proving activity on foreign soil may have been a factor, as well as the accessibility of the information to the U.S. public;[61] excluding foreign activity generally encourages domestic inventors to provide U.S. residents with access to the information in question. With the opening of worldwide markets, vastly improved communications, and open sharing of information between researchers, the driving forces behind requiring activity to take place in this country are no longer so strong. Consequently, removing this term from the statute is occasionally suggested.[62] Nevertheless, the requirement stands.

6.2.3.1 Prior Use. Section 102(a) bars patentability of an invention if the invention has been in *use* in this country by others prior to the applicant's date of invention. Section 102(b) similarly bars patentability if the invention was in *public use* in this country at least one year before the application's filing date. Despite the difference in terminology, Subsection (a) has been consistently interpreted to mean a use that is accessible to the public; a secret use generally is not sufficient.[63] It also has been held that the commercial but secret use of a machine does not constitute an anticipation under this section, although it might be used to establish first invention under Section 102(g).[64] However, a *single* public use with a commercial motive can be an anticipating use.[65]

An invention must be reduced to practice in order to qualify as a prior use under 102(a) or (b). "An inoperable invention or one that fails to achieve its intended result does not negative novelty."[66] The reduction to practice can take the form of actual successful use;[67] it does not require that the prior use be optimized or even as skillfully designed as the later invention.[68] In fact, the prior user need not understand how the invention works to anticipate an invention.[69]

Sometimes, an anticipatory prior use will be labeled an unsuccessful experiment. The argument is that because the prior user did not capitalize on the invention, the prior use must have been unsuccessful, so the invention was not put into practice. The Supreme Court validated this concept in *Brown v. Guild*,[70] which held that "The experiment . . . was a mere experiment, which was never repeated. It may have presented one or two ideas in advance of other machines, but it can hardly be said to anticipate the machine which we have described as Brown's."[71] Similarly, in *Washburn & Moen Mfg. Co. v. Beat 'Em All Barbed-Wire Co.*[72] public display of barbed wire for one day 16 years before a patent was issued on the invention was deemed insufficient to anticipate the invention.[73] As a comparison, a prior use that was confined to the laboratory has been held not to be an abandoned experiment.[74] As a result, questions in this area are very fact-sensitive, and the answers vary considerably from case to case.

As a technical matter, the Federal Circuit has held that experimental use is not an *exception* to the ban on public use but, rather, a factor that rejects an initial finding of public use.[75]

6.2.4 Known Inventions

Subsections (a) and (b) bar patentability when an invention is "known" by people other than the applicant before the applicant's date of invention. By "known," we mean that the invention is completely and adequately described. The known invention need not be reduced to practice to anticipate;[76] however, the Federal Circuit does require "knowledge of a complete and operative device."[77]

It is well established that an invention must be publicly known; secret or private knowledge of an invention will not rise to the level of prior art.[78] However, an unpublished, declassified government document can be enough evidence of knowledge to bar patentability.[79]

6.2.5 On Sale

Subsection (b) bars an invention when it has been on sale for more than a year before the filing of a patent application. The term *on sale* encompasses not only the actual sale of the invention but also any *offer to sell* it.[80] This is true even if no sale is made in the following year and even if the invention is taken from the market. It also is noteworthy that the "on sale" ban is limited to the sale of the invention itself. It does not include licensing or assigning potential patent rights to an invention to someone else.[81]

6.2.6 Experimental Use

Uses and sales are permitted under very limited circumstances while the invention is still being refined. So-called "experimental use" is limited to those scenarios in which all the circumstances indicate that the use or sale of the invention was for experimental purposes.[82] As recently stated by the Federal Circuit:

> Factors to be considered in deciding whether there is a public use include, for example, the length of the test period, whether any payment has been made for the device, whether there is a secrecy obligation on the part of the user, whether progress records were kept, whether persons other than the inventor conducted the asserted experiments, how many tests were conducted, and how long the testing period was in relationship to tests of other similar devices.[83]

Particularly persuasive is evidence that the use or sale was for technological purposes rather than for gathering information about market development or customer satisfaction. For example, in *In re Smith*[84] the inventor of a carpet cleaning product gave the product to 76 consumers and asked them to use the product for two weeks. No confidentiality agreement was in place, nor were any restrictions placed on the consumers' use of the product. The court held that the purpose of the test was to determine customer satisfaction and to gather information on a proper sales price and, thus, held that this activity barred the patenting of the product. In contrast, the Federal Circuit has held that the sale of steel alloy samples to airline companies for evaluation was not a bar to patentability. The inventor was in no position to fabricate samples for free and had no facilities to conduct the types of tests the aircraft manufacturers were able to conduct. There also was an unwritten agreement that the information exchanged by the parties was confidential.[85]

6.3 RULE 1.131—REMOVING PRIOR ART BY A SHOWING OF PRIOR INVENTORSHIP

As discussed in the preceding section, prior art that includes all the elements of a claimed invention bars the patentability of that invention. If such prior art exists and cannot be removed as an anticipating reference by arguing that not all claim elements are present, the applicant still may be able to remove the reference by a showing of prior inventorship. This process, known as "swearing behind" the reference, is available only for rejections under Sections 102(a), (e), and (g); Sections 102(b), (c), (d), and (f) preclude swearing behind either because the provisions are based on the date of filing rather than the date of inventorship (Sections 102[b] and [d]), or bar patentability due to other circumstances (Sections 102[c] and [f]).

6.3.1 When Can a Rule 131 Declaration Be Used?

Paragraph 1.131(a) of 37 C.F.R. provides that a showing that the invention of the application was "completed" before the date of the anticipating reference prevents the reference from barring patentability of the invention. Subsection (b) provides that prior "completion" of the invention can be shown in two ways, by showing that: (1) the invention was reduced to practice prior to the date of the reference, and (2) the invention was conceived before the reference date and was diligently reduced to practice. Not surprisingly, these rules mirror the rules regarding priority of invention.[86]

Although these rules at first glance appear to be relatively straightforward, in practice they raise many issues. The first is the geographic location where the invention was reduced to practice. Only reduction to practice in the U.S. is effective for the purposes of this rule; if the invention is reduced to practice only in a foreign country before filing the application, the earliest completion date for the invention is the filing date. Accordingly, the provisions of this rule are not available for such inventions.

A second issue is whether the inventor diligently reduced the invention to practice after conception. If this can be shown, then a Rule 131 Declaration can be used to show that the completion date for the invention is the date of conception. If, instead, the inventor did not diligently pursue reduction to practice, the completion date becomes the date of reduction to practice in the U.S. Since this will be later than the date of conception, it may not be sufficiently remote in time to swear behind the anticipating reference.

A third issue is the type of reference to be sworn behind. If the reference is a U.S. patent, the affidavit must show a completion date prior to the application date of the patent. If the reference is a foreign patent, the date of the reference is the publication date of that patent. If the reference is a printed publication, the date is the publication date of the document.

Of course, a Rule 131 Declaration cannot be used to swear behind an anticipating reference when the date of the reference falls outside the one-year grace period provided by Section 102(b). Another situation in which a Rule 131 affidavit cannot be used to eliminate an anticipating reference is when the reference is a U.S. patent that *claims* the identical invention claimed in the application. In such circumstances, the solution for the applicant is to begin interference proceedings so that priority between the inventors can be determined. Of course, interference proceedings are available only if the issue date of the U.S. patent is less than one year prior to the filing date of the application in question. If the patent's issue date precedes the filing date of the application by more than a year, the reference anticipates the invention under 102(b).

6.3.2 Content of a Rule 131 Affidavit

As already stated, the affidavit must show either: (1) a reduction to practice in this country prior to the date of the reference, or (2) conception in this country prior to the date of the reference followed by continuous diligence from before the reference date to a later reduction to practice in this country. Section 715.07 of the *Manual of Patent Examining Procedure* states that the declaration must include facts or documentary evidence that support such a showing. What this will entail in a given situation depends upon the circumstances. For example, a claimed device or article of manufacture can be shown to be reduced to practice by demonstrating that a physical embodiment of the device existed on a particular date. This can be done by the use of photographs, lab notebooks, test results, drawings, and the like.

If the reference only discloses part of the claimed invention, a declaration is sufficient if it shows prior possession of merely that part.[87] An example is a situation in which a reference discloses a chemical compound. To swear behind the reference to support a generic claim that includes the disclosed species, the one who is swearing must show possession of "so much of the invention as to encompass the reference disclosure."[88] Whether that is enough depends on the facts in the particular case.

It is neither necessary nor advisable to establish the precise date of conception or reduction to practice in a Rule 131 declaration. Instead, it is generally preferred to provide the necessary evidence in a manner that shows simply that the requisite conception or reduction to practice had occurred by the date of the reference. If the applicant were to definitely state that a certain date was the date of conception or the date of reduction to practice, such a statement is, at best, free information to an opponent and, at worst, an admission of no earlier date in a trial or an interference proceeding.

REFERENCES

1. Hybritech, Inc. v. Monoclonal Antibodies, Inc., 802 F.2d 1367, 231 USPQ 81 (Fed. Cir. 1986).
2. Lewmar Marine, Inc. v. Barient, Inc., 827 F.2d 744, 3 USPQ2d 1766 (Fed. Cir. 1987).
3. Lewmar, 3 USPQ2d at 1768.
4. *See, e.g.,* Corning Glass Works v. Sumitomo Electric U.S.A., 868 F.2d 1251, 9 USPQ2d 1962 (Fed. Cir. 1989).
5. *In re* Arkley, 455 F.2d 586, 172 USPQ 524, 526 (C.C.P.A. 1972).
6. *In re* Schaumann, 572 F.2d 312, 197 USPQ 5 (C.C.P.A. 1978).
7. *See* Merck & Co. v. Biocraft Laboratories, Inc., 874 F.2d 804, 10 USPQ2d 1834 (Fed. Cir. 1989).
8. Thus, it must satisfy the same standard as that required for an invention seeking patent protection under 35 U.S.C. § 112, first paragraph. Seymour v. Osborne, 78 U.S. (11 Wall.) 516 (1870).
9. *In re* LeGrice, 301 F.2d 929, 133 USPQ 365 (C.C.P.A. 1962); Akzo N.V. v. U. S. Int'l Trade Comm'n, 808 F.2d 1471, 1 USPQ2d 1241 (Fed. Cir. 1986).
10. Cohen v. United States Corset, 93 U.S. 366 (1876).
11. *In re* LeGrice, 133 USPQ 365.
12. *In re* Argoudelis, 434 F.2d 1390, 168 USPQ 99 (C.C.P.A. 1970).
13. *Ex parte* Lundak, 773 F.2d 1216, 227 USPQ 90 (Fed. Cir. 1985).

14. *In re* Mancy, 499 F.2d 1289, 182 USPQ 303 (C.C.P.A. 1974).
15. *In re* Donohoe, 766 F.2d 531, 226 USPQ 619, 621 (Fed. Cir. 1985).
16. *Id.*; *In re* Samour, 571 F.2d 559, 197 USPQ 1, 4 (C.C.P.A. 1978).
17. *In re* Wilder, 429 F.2d 447, 166 USPQ 545 (C.C.P.A. 1970); *In re* Wiggins, 397 F.2d 356, 158 USPQ 199, 202 (C.C.P.A. 1968).
18. *Ex parte* Thomson, 24 USPQ2d 1618 (Bd. Pat. App. 1992).
19. Decision of the Technical Board of Appeals dated 29 September 1988 Concerning European Application 84 103 754.2.
20. *In re* Hafner, 410 F.2d 1403, 161 USPQ 783 (C.C.P.A. 1969); *accord In re* Schoenwald, 964 F.2d 1122, 22 USPQ2d 1671 (Fed. Cir. 1992).
21. *In re* Hafner, 161 USPQ at 785.
22. General Electric Co. v. Jewel Incandescent Lamp Co., 326 U.S. 242, 67 USPQ 155 (1945).
23. *In re* Wilder, 429 F.2d 447, 166 USPQ 545 (C.C.P.A. 1970).
24. Wilder, 166 USPQ at 549.
25. United Chromium, Inc. v. International Silver Co., 60 F.2d 913, 917, 15 USPQ 51 (2d. Cir. 1932).
26. 102 U.S. 707, 711 (1881).
27. *Id.*
28. H.K. Regar & Sons v. Scott & Williams, 63 F.2d 229, 17 USPQ 81 (2d Cir. 1933). The Federal Circuit has framed the issue by stating "[T]o establish prior invention, there must be evidence that the alleged prior inventors appreciated at the time of their work all the elements of the invention." E.I. DuPont de Nemours Co. v. Phillips Petroleum Co., 849 F.2d 1430, 7 USPQ2d 1129 (Fed. Cir. 1988).
29. Regar, 63 F.2d at 231.
30. Bird Provision Co. v. Owens Country Sausage, 568 F.2d 369, 197 USPQ 134 (5th Cir. 1978).
31. Anthracite Separator Co. v. Pollock, 175 F. 108 (M.D. Pa. 1909); Clements Industries Inc. v. A. Meyers & Sons Corp., 712 F. Supp. 317, 12 USPQ2d 1874 (S.D.N.Y. 1989); United Chromium, 15 USPQ 51.
32. *In re* Marshall, 578 F.2d 301, 198 USPQ 344, 346 (C.C.P.A. 1978).
33. 1 W. Robinson, THE LAW OF PATENTS FOR USEFUL INVENTIONS § 325–27 (1890).
34. Constant v. Advanced Micro-Devices, Inc., 848 F.2d 1560, 7 USPQ2d 1057, 1062 (Fed. Cir. 1988).
35. *In re* Bayer, 568 F.2d 1357, 196 USPQ 670 (C.C.P.A. 1978); Massachusetts Institute of Technology v. AB Fortia, 774 F.2d 1104, 227 USPQ 428 (Fed. Cir. 1985).
36. *In re* Certain Caulking Guns, 223 USPQ 388, 396 (I.T.C. 1984).
37. *Id.*; Constant v. Advanced Micro-Devices, 848 F.2d at 1560.
38. Canron, Inc. v. Plasser American Corp., 474 F. Supp. 1010, 203 USPQ 440 (E.D. Va. 1978), *aff'd*, 609 F.2d 1075, 203 USPQ 641 (4th Cir. 1979).
39. Carella v. Starlight Archery, 595 F. Supp. 613, 224 USPQ 879, 885 (E.D. Mich. 1984), *aff'd*, 804 F.2d 135, 231 USPQ 644 (Fed. Cir. 1986); M.P.E.P. § 706.02.
40. *Ex parte* Albert, 18 USPQ2d 1325 (Bd. Pat. App. 1990).
41. Massachusetts Institute of Technology, 227 USPQ 428.
42. *Ex Parte* Brimm, 147 USPQ 72, 74 (Bd. Pat. App. 1963).
43. Regents of the University of California v. Howmedica, Inc., 530 F. Supp. 846, 210 USPQ 727 (D.N.J. 1981).
44. Howmedica, 210 USPQ at 738–39.

45. Hybritech, Inc. v. Abbott Laboratories, Inc., 4 USPQ2d 1001, 1007 (C.D. Cal. 1987), *aff'd*, 849 F.2d 1446, 7 USPQ2d 1191 (Fed. Cir. 1988).
46. National Semiconductor Corp. v. Linear Technology Corp., 703 F. Supp. 845, 8 USPQ2d 1359 (N.D. Cal. 1988).
47. Hamilton Libraries, Inc. v. Massengill, 111 F.2d 584, 45 USPQ 594 (6th Cir. 1940).
48. *In re* Tenney, 254 F.2d 619, 117 USPQ 348 (C.C.P.A. 1958).
49. Philips Electronic and Pharmaceutical Industries Corp. v. Thermal and Electronics Industries, Inc., 450 F.2d 1164, 171 USPQ 641 (3rd Cir. 1971).
50. *In re* Bayer, 568 F.2d 1357, 196 USPQ 670 (C.C.P.A. 1978).
51. *In re* Hall, 781 F.2d 897, 228 USPQ 453 (Fed. Cir. 1986).
52. *In re* Cronyn, 890 F.2d 1158, 13 USPQ2d 1070 (Fed. Cir. 1989).
53. Southwest Aerospace Corp. v. Teledyne Industries, Inc., 702 F. Supp. 870, 9 USPQ 1949 (N.D. Ala. 1988).
54. Aluminum Co. of America v. Reynolds Metals Co., 14 USPQ2d 1170 (N.D. Ill. 1989); Northern Telecom, Inc. v. Datapoint Corp., 9 USPQ2d 1577 (N.D. Tex. 1988), *aff'd in pert. part*, 908 F.2d 931, 936–37, 15 USPQ2d 1321, 1324–25 (Fed. Cir. 1990).
55. *Ex parte* Harris, 79 USPQ 439 (Comm'r Pats. 1948).
56. 5 U.S.C.A. § 525 (1992); *see generally* P. Hernon, PUBLIC ACCESS TO GOVERNMENT INFORMATION: ISSUES, TRENDS, AND STRATEGIES (2d Ed. 1988).
57. *See generally* D. Hodgins and J. Matula, *Government Grant Applications, Despite E. I. DuPont de Nemours v. Cetus, Are Not Necessarily Prior Art,* 74 J. PAT. OFF. SOC'Y 241 (1992); *see also* J. Avery, What Constitutes "Trade Secrets and Commercial or Financial Information Obtained From a Person and Privileged or Confidential," Exempt From Disclosure Under Freedom of Information Act (5 U.S.C.S. § 552(b)(4), 21 ALR Fed. 224; D. Jacoby, *The uses of FOIA and FOIL,* 16 TRIAL LAWYERS QUARTERLY 12 (1984).
58. E.I. DuPont de Nemours & Co. v. Cetus Corp., 19 USPQ2d 1174 (N.D. Cal. 1990).
59. *Id.* at 1185.
60. *Id.* at 1186.
61. 1 D. Chisum, PATENTS, § 3.05[5] (1992).
62. President's Commission on the Patent System, TO PROMOTE THE PROGRESS OF . . . USEFUL ARTS IN AN AGE OF EXPLODING TECHNOLOGY, 2, 3 (1966).
63. Revisor's Notes to the Patent Act of 1952; Carella v. Starlight Archery, 804 F.2d 135, 231 USPQ 644 (Fed. Cir. 1986). There are qualifications to this rule. First, the seminal case on this issue, Gaylor v. Wilder, 51 U.S. (10 How.) 477 (1850), stressed that the prior user's failure "to bring his invention to public" will not *per se* preclude it from being a public use. Second, case law indicates that the requirement at most means the absence of affirmative steps to conceal. *See* D.L. Auld Co. v. Chroma Graphics, 714 F.2d 1144, 219 USPQ 13 (Fed. Cir. 1983), in which the Federal Circuit held that a secret method used to produce a product will not bar another inventor from the grant of a patent on that method. Third, if the use must be public, there is little to distinguish prior use from prior knowledge. Some commentators believe that because prior knowledge may include concepts not reduced to practice, these should require a higher standard of publicity than a use clearly reduced to practice. 1 D. Chisum, PATENTS, § 3.05[2] (1992).
64. Gillman v. Stern, 114 F.2d 28, 46 USPQ 430 (2d Cir. 1940); *see also* Metallizing Engineering Co. v. Kenyon Bearing Auto Parts Co., 153 F.2d 516, 68 USPQ 54 (2d Cir. 1946).

65. Electric Storage Battery Co. v. Shimadzu, 307 U.S. 5, 41 USPQ 155 (1939); Harrington Mfg. Co. v. Powell Mfg. Co., 815 F.2d 1478, 2 USPQ2d 1364 (Fed. Cir. 1986).

66. United States v. Adams, 383 U.S. 39, 148 USPQ 479 (1966); *see also* Hycor Corp. v. Schleuter Corp., 740 F.2d 1529, 222 USPQ 553 (Fed. Cir. 1984).

67. Smith v. Hall, 301 U.S. 216, 33 USPQ 249 (1937).

68. *Id.*

69. DeForest Radio Co. v. General Electric Co., 283 U.S. 664, 51 S. Ct. 563 (1936).

70. 90 U.S. (23 Wall.) 181 (1874).

71. *Id.* at 210. Although this language is apparently telling, the holding of this case was based more on the fact that the allegedly anticipating machine was neither the same invention nor operative than on the experimental nature of the prior machine.

72. The Barbed Wire Patent, 143 U.S. 275, 12 S. Ct. 443 (1892).

73. As with Brown v. Guild, the Supreme Court characterized the prior use as an abandoned experiment in addition to citing other grounds for finding an invention to be novel. It is curious that this doctrine springs from these two cases in which the doctrine is of questionable import.

74. Corona Cord Tire Co. v. Dovan Chemical Corp., 276 U.S. 358, 48 S. Ct. 380 (1928).

75. TP Laboratories, Inc. v. Professional Positioners, Inc., 724 F.2d 965, 220 USPQ 577 (Fed. Cir. 1984).

76. *In re* Borst, 345 F.2d 851, 145 USPQ 554 (C.C.P.A. 1965).

77. Rosemount, Inc. v. Beckman Instruments, Inc., 569 F. Supp. 934, 218 USPQ 881 (C.D. Cal. 1983); *aff'd*, 727 F.2d 1540, 221 USPQ 1 (Fed. Cir. 1984).

78. Alexander Milborn Co. v. Davis-Bournonville Co., 270 U.S. 390, 46 S. Ct. 324 (1926).

79. *In re* Borst, 345 F.2d 851, 145 USPQ 554 (C.C.P.A. 1965).

80. CTS Corp. v. Piher Int'l Corp., 527 F.2d 95, 188 USPQ 419 (7th Cir. 1975).

81. Moleculon Research Corp. v. CBS, Inc., 793 F.2d 1261, 229 USPQ 809 (Fed. Cir. 1986).

82. Western Marine Elecs. v. Furano Electronics Co., 764 F.2d 840, 226 USPQ 334 (Fed. Cir. 1985).

83. Hycor Corp. v. The Schleuter Co., 740 F.2d 1529, 222 USPQ 553, 557 (Fed. Cir. 1984); *see also* Sinskey v. Pharmacia Ophthalmica Inc., 25 USPQ2d 1290 (Fed. Cir. 1992).

84. *In re* Smith, 714 F.2d 1127, 218 USPQ 976 (Fed. Cir. 1983).

85. Armco Inc. v. Cyclops Corp., 791 F.2d 147, 229 USPQ 721 (Fed. Cir. 1986).

86. 1 D. Chisum, PATENTS § 3.08[1] (1992).

87. *In re* Mulder, 716 F.2d 1542, 219 USPQ 189 (Fed. Cir. 1983).

88. *In re* Clarke, 356 F.2d 987, 148 USPQ 665 (C.C.P.A. 1966).

Nonobviousness

Shawn P. Foley

Section 103 of the Patent Statute of 1952 and the U.S. Supreme Court's decision in *Graham v. John Deere* eliminated much of the confusion over how the obviousness of patent claims is analyzed.[1] The entry of biotechnology into the world of intellectual property has created uncertainty in this area, however. Patent applicants frequently must overcome rejections on the basis of obviousness in biotechnology patent applications if they are to obtain patents.

The notion that the standard of obviousness under Section 103 might be different for biotechnological inventions was dispelled long ago when Judge Rich explained in *In re Papesch*:

> The problem of "obviousness" under section 103 in determining the patentability of new and useful chemical compounds, or, as it is sometimes called, the problem of chemical "obviousness," is not really a problem in chemistry or pharmacology or in any other related field of science such as biology, biochemistry, pharmacodynamics, ecology or others yet to be conceived. It is a problem of patent law.[2]

Patent rights to countless inventions have been lost because of uninformed assumptions that the inventions were obvious or the failure to appreciate that even an invention that appears to be obvious can be proven nonobvious.

Notwithstanding the comforting language of *Papesch*, one of the most formidable obstacles facing biotechnology patent applicants is satisfactorily resolving obviousness rejections by the Patent and Trademark Office. Perhaps thinking that the Federal Circuit has imposed a higher standard of inventiveness under Section 103 for biotechnology inventions, the patent office tends to allow a significantly smaller percentage of biotechnology applications compared to applications in other technologies. For example, the patent office rejected as obvious the claims to polyploid oysters in *Ex parte Allen*,[3] which indicated that animals would be statutory subject matter.

The challenge for biotechnology patent applicants is unusual because rejections based on the contention that the invention is obvious are often juxtaposed (and seemingly conflict) with rejections on the basis that skilled people would not know how to make or use the invention ("lack of enablement rejections" are discussed in Chapter 8). This situation must be approached delicately. A clear demarcation between the statutes must be maintained. Otherwise, arguments in response to an obviousness rejection (that the art was unpredictable) might be construed as an admission and used against the applicant in support of the lack of enablement rejection.

This chapter summarizes various substantive aspects of the law regarding Section 103 in a quasi-procedural context, while highlighting cases particularly relevant to biotechnology. The chapter also discusses additional dilemmas and briefly compares the requirements of Section 103 to its European statutory counterpart, the lack of inventive step.

7.1 THE BASIC TEST

A determination that an invention would have been obvious when it was made to someone of ordinary skill in the art under Section 103 is a conclusion of law based on fact.[4] The facts on which this legal conclusion is based include: (1) the scope and content of the prior art at the time the invention was made, (2) the differences between the prior art and the claims at issue, (3) the level of ordinary skill in the art at the time the invention was made, and (4) objective evidence of nonobviousness, if any.[5]

7.2 THE SCOPE AND CONTENT OF THE PRIOR ART

The scope of the prior art has been defined (somewhat redundantly) as all the prior art in the field of the inventor's endeavor and those arts reasonably pertinent to the particular problem with which the inventor was involved.[6] The rationale is that rejections based on a combination of teachings of references from nonanalogous arts should be precluded because an inventor could not possibly be aware of every teaching in every art. Thus, the circumstances surrounding the making of an invention are more closely approximated.[7] The term *pertinent art* ("art to which the subject matter sought to be patented pertains . . .") has been defined on the basis of the problem to be solved rather than the specific industry or trade that is faced with the problem and uses the invention.[8]

The scope and content of the prior art is limited in terms of time. Since Section 103 specifies that the determination of obviousness must be made *at the time the invention was made*, the prior art includes only references with effective dates that precede the date of invention. However, consistent with the provisions of Section 102(b) (discussed in Chapter 6), all patents, publications, public uses, or public sales with an effective date of more than one year prior to the inventor's application date constitute prior art.[9] This includes publications written by the inventors, which was O'Farrell's downfall.[10]

The use of patents as prior art references is not limited to what is described as the invention or to the problems that concerned the patentees.[11] Thus, a patent reference must be considered for everything it teaches by way of technology, not just the claimed invention.[12] This would include, for example, an inoperable device.[13] Moreover, the Supreme Court has held that the disclosure in an issued U.S. patent is effective as a reference under Section 103 as of its filing date, regardless of the fact that the disclosure is not available until the issue date of the patent.[14]

The scope of the prior art is not limited to patents, publications, public uses, or public sales. For instance, the Federal Circuit has held that an expert's firsthand practical knowledge of unsolved needs in the art is evidence of the state of the art.[15] Statements submitted to the Patent Office by applicants during prosecution may be properly considered as evidence of obviousness.[16] Further, a prior invention in the U.S. by someone who has not abandoned, suppressed, or concealed the invention constitutes prior art for purposes of Section 103, even though the invention was kept secret or the patent applicant otherwise had no personal knowledge of the prior invention.[17] An exception occurs when, at the time the claimed invention was made, both it and the prior invention were commonly owned or subject to an obligation of assignment to the same person.[18]

7.3   THE PERSON HAVING ORDINARY SKILL IN THE ART

Section 103 specifically states that obviousness is assessed with respect to the "person having ordinary skill in the art." As pointed out by Harmon, this standard requires inquiring who this person is, the skill this person has, and what this person knows.[19] The identity and skill of this person are discussed in the following sections; what this person is presumed to know is the prior art in the inventor's field and related fields.

7.3.1 Identifying the Person of Ordinary Skill

A person with ordinary skill in the art has been defined by the Federal Circuit as follows:

> The issue of obviousness is determined entirely with reference to a hypothetical "person having ordinary skill in the art." It is only that hypothetical person who is presumed to

be aware of all the pertinent prior art. The actual inventor's skill is irrelevant to the inquiry, and this is for a very important reason. The statutory emphasis is on a person of ordinary skill. Inventors, as a class, according to the concepts underlying the Constitution and the statutes that have created the patent system, possess something— call it what you will—which sets them apart from the workers of ordinary skill, and one should not go about determining obviousness under 103 by inquiring into what paten- tees (i.e., inventors) would have known or would likely have done, faced with the reve- lations of references. A person of ordinary skill in the art is also presumed to be one who thinks along the line of conventional wisdom in the art and is not one who under- takes to innovate, whether by patient, and often expensive, systematic research or by extraordinary insights, it makes no difference which.[20]

This person also is not a judge, a layman, someone skilled in remote arts, or a genius in the art at hand.[21] There is reason to believe that patent examiners are not consid- ered persons of ordinary skill in the art, even though they may have considerably more experience than the hypothetical person.[22]

A somewhat unusual aspect of biotechnology patent law is that arguments often involve a very high level of skill in the art in question. Some biotechnology inventions appear obvious, but to people who work in the field and are familiar with all the perplexing intricacies, difficulties, and surprises that must be over- come to actually make that invention, it would not be obvious at all. For example, in *In re O'Farrell*,[23] the applicants argued that those of ordinary skill in the arts of molecular biology and recombinant DNA technology were research scientists who had extraordinary skill in the relevant arts and were among the brightest biol- ogists in the world.[24]

7.3.2 Determining the Skill of the Hypothetical Person

The overriding consideration in determining the level of skill is to adhere to the statute, and focus on what would be obvious to someone of ordinary skill in the art at the time the invention was made.[25] Any one or more of the following non- inclusive factors may be considered in this determination: (1) the educational level of the inventor, (2) the type of problems encountered in the art, (3) the prior art solutions to those problems, (4) the speed with which innovations are made, (5) the sophistication of the technology, and (6) the educational level of active workers in the field.[26]

The level of skill in the art also may be determined by turning to information that otherwise does not qualify as prior art for purposes of Section 103, such as si- multaneous invention and internal company memoranda.[27]

The decision maker, be it judge, jury, or the PTO, is not required to possess or- dinary skill in the art. For that matter, the Federal Circuit has expressly rejected the argument that a Patent Office board's decision should be held invalid if its members lack competency in the art relating to the claimed invention. The court also implied that an examiner's decision should be treated similarly.[28]

7.4   DIFFERENCES BETWEEN THE PRIOR ART AND THE CLAIMED INVENTION—THE INVENTION AS A WHOLE

This analysis begins with a key legal question—what is the invention claimed?[29] The statute requires the decision-maker (again be it judge, jury, or PTO) to view the invention "as a whole," which requires consideration of the claim in its entirety.

7.4.1 The Invention as a Whole

The Federal Circuit has made it clear that the claimed subject matter *as a whole* should not be reduced to merely the extent of the differences between the claimed invention and the prior art:

> Though it is proper to note the difference in a claimed invention from the prior art, because that difference may serve as one element in determining the obvious/nonobviousness issue, it is improper (even if erroneously suggested by a party) to consider the difference as the invention. The "difference" may have seemed slight (as has often been the case with some of history's great inventions, e.g., the telephone), but it may also have been the key to success and advancement in the art resulting from the invention. Further, it is irrelevant in determining obviousness that all or all other aspects of the claim may have been well known in the art.[30]

Hence the statute established by Congress requires that the invention as claimed be considered "as a whole" when considering whether that invention would have been obvious when it was made. For example, the patentability of a chemical compound cannot be determined by considering its structure while ignoring its properties. In the leading case of *In re Papesch*,[31] the Court of Customs and Patent Appeals held that claims directed to certain trialkyl hetero-aromatics were nonobvious and, thus, patentable over prior art disclosing a methyl homologue. Papesch had discovered that the claimed compounds possessed unexpectedly potent anti-inflammatory activity. An affidavit to this effect, which also demonstrated the lack of pharmacological activity of the prior art compound, was submitted to the patent office during prosecution.

The examiner said that the contribution to the art was the discovery of a single new property, which by itself seemed inadequate to support a claim for an otherwise obvious chemical homologue and that was not limited to a method of use. The board affirmed the examiner's finding, essentially concluding that the claimed compounds would have been obvious "beyond a shadow of a doubt" to a chemist. Therefore, the affidavit evidence was insufficient because there was no doubt to resolve.

The court concluded that the board committed a fundamental error of law because it did not consider the affidavit evidence, thus failing to decide patentability on the basis of the claimed invention as a whole, that is, the structure *and* properties of the compounds:

> From the standpoint of patent law, a compound and all of its properties are inseparable; they are one and the same thing. The graphic formulae, the chemical nomenclature, the

systems of classification and study such as the concepts of homology, isomerism, etc., are mere symbols by which compounds can be identified, classified, and compared. But a formula is not a compound and while it may serve in a claim to <u>identify</u> what is being patented, as the metes and bounds of a deed identify a plot of land, the <u>thing</u> that is patented is not the formula but the compound identified by it. And the patentability of the thing does not depend on the similarity of its formula to that of another compound but of the similarity of the former compound to the latter. There is no basis in law for ignoring any property in making such a comparison. An assumed similarity based on a comparison of formulae must give way to evidence that the assumption is erroneous.[32]

In *Hybritech, Inc. v. Monoclonal Antibodies, Inc.*,[33] the Federal Circuit concluded that the district court failed to consider the claimed invention as a whole and reversed its holding of invalidity for obviousness under Section 103. The claims of the patent at issue were directed to a process of using monoclonal antibodies in a sandwich assay, whereby a first labeled monoclonal antibody complexed with a target antigen to which it had a specific affinity was further complexed with a second monoclonal antibody that was bound to a substrate in order to determine the presence of the target antigen in a fluid sample. The claims also recited that the monoclonal antibodies had at least 10^8 liters/mole affinity, which distinguished the claims over the prior art during prosecution.[34]

The court carefully reviewed the 20 or so items of prior art and found that they "skirt[ed] all around but do not as a whole suggest the claimed invention, which they must, to overcome the presumed validity . . . <u>as a whole</u>."[35] For instance, it found that the prior art, taken in groups, disclosed the production of monoclonal antibodies, for example, *in vitro*; competitive assays using a single monoclonal antibody; sandwich assays using polyclonal antibodies; mapping epitopes on a known quantity of antigen; and a method for rapidly determining affinity constants for monoclonal antibodies, including constants encompassed by the claims. The collective prior art fell short of the mark:

> Focusing on the obviousness of substitutions and differences instead of on the invention as a whole, as the district court did in frequently describing the claimed invention as the mere substitution of monoclonal for polyclonal antibodies in a sandwich assay, was a legally improper way to simplify the difficult determination of obviousness.[36]

7.4.2 *In re Durden* and Process Inventions

The "invention as a whole" requirement was at issue in what has turned out to be one of the most significant decisions by the Federal Circuit, *In re Durden*.[37] The case dealt with insecticidal carbonates, yet this decision has had serious consequences for biotechnology, particularly the domestic industry. Briefly, Durden (Union Carbide Corporation) appealed the decision of the Patent Office Board of Appeals affirming the Section 103 rejection of a claim directed to a process for preparing certain pesticidal carbonate esters using specific heterocyclic oxime starting materials. The claim was affirmed over prior art that disclosed the recited process but with different reactants. Claims to both the products and the oxime reactants presented in two related applications had been held patentable. Durden, however, specifically admitted that apart from their novel and nonobvious starting materials and products, the claimed process was obvious.[38] The issue facing the Federal Circuit, aside from the use of patented starting materials and products, was whether a chemical process that was admittedly obvious was patentable because the specific starting material or the end product obtained were novel and nonobvious.

Durden argued that his process was patentable regardless of the similarities to the prior process because it employed a patentable starting material and a patentable product was produced. The CAFC disagreed:

> Of course, an otherwise old process becomes a <u>new</u> process when a previously unknown starting material, for example, is used in it which is then subjected to a conventional manipulation or reaction to produce a product which may also be new, albeit the <u>expected</u> result of what is done. But it does not necessarily mean that the whole process has become <u>unobvious</u> in the sense of § 103. In short, a new <u>process</u> may still be obvious, even when considered "as a whole," notwithstanding the fact the specific starting material or resulting product, or both, is not to be found in the prior art.[39]

Durden initially might have been innocuous. The panel emphasized that obviousness issues are to be decided in each case on the basis of the particular fact situation, not by "black letter" rules. It resisted the temptation to state a clear, general rule by which all similar cases could be decided. The irony is that despite the CAFC's refusal to lay down a general rule, *Durden* has been applied enthusiastically by the U.S. Patent Office, particularly in applications directed to biotechnology.[40] The result has been that patentability is often denied for many types of biotechnological process claims, such as those drawn to producing recombinant therapeutic proteins using recombinant host cells.

The consequences of applying *Durden* to biotechnology patent applications are considered devastating by some elements of the U.S. biotechnology industry, particularly in cases where the final product, for example, the recombinant protein, is not patentable itself. In a case such as this, importing products made abroad from an unpatented process is not an act of infringement even though a U.S. patented starting material (such as the recombinant host cell) is used. As discussed in Chapter 13, this discriminatory effect, or loophole, created by Durden came to light in *Amgen v. Chugai*. The legislative efforts (the Boucher Bill) to overrule *Durden* by amending sections 103 and 271 are also discussed in Chapter 13.

The 1990 Federal Circuit decision in *In re Pleuddemann*[41] was initially regarded as limiting Durden's universal applicability. *Pleuddemann* also dealt with a nonbiotechnological subject. The patent application at issue disclosed organosilane coupling agents, which bond polyester resins to fiberglass filing material, thereby improving the mechanical properties of the resulting products. Specifically, Pleuddemann's coupling agents, the reaction product of an isocyanatoalkyl ester with an aminoorganosilane, imparted superior moisture resistance to mineral-filled unsaturated polyesters. The two independent claims at issue were directed to methods of using the coupling agents.

The first claim was drawn to a process for bonding a polymerizable material to a mineral filler, involving mixing the organosilane with a polymerizable material, then polymerizing the material to form a solid composite. The second independent claim was directed to a method for priming a surface having hydroxyl capabilities to improve its bonding to organic resins, involving wetting the surface with a solution of the organosilane and then drying the surface. Relying on *Durden* as support, the PTO rejected the claims as obvious over a previously issued patent by Pleuddemann that also was directed to organosilane coupling agents, together with admissions in the specification.

On appeal, Pleuddemann focused on the fact that the PTO had allowed claims directed to this new class of silane coupling agents and claims directed to the articles made by using these agents in a usual way. He argued that he was also entitled to the appealed claims directed to the process or method of using these organosilane agents in their usual way for bonding or priming. He also argued that the method of use claim should be allowed because the articles made by using the new bonding agents had superior moisture resistant properties.

The Federal Circuit reversed the decision of the board. It concluded that the board's decision was flawed in several respects, namely that it used hindsight in comparing the functioning of the new compounds with the functioning of the prior art organosilane compounds, effectively presuming that the new group of compounds was prior art. In a valiant effort to draw some helpful distinctions between *Durden* and other cases in this area, the court attempted to draw a distinction between processes of *making* and processes of *using*:

> From the standpoint of patent law, a compound and all of its properties are inseparable; they are one and the same thing. In re Papesch [citation omitted]. It is the properties of appellant's compounds as bonding/priming agents for certain polymers and fillers or support surfaces that give them their utility. As stated above, the compounds and their use are but different aspects of, or ways of looking at, the same invention and consequently that invention is capable of being claimed both as new compounds or as a new method or process of bonding/priming. On the other hand, a process or method of making the compounds is a quite different thing; they may have been made by a process which was new or old, obvious or nonobvious. In this respect, therefore, there is a real difference between a process of making and a process of using and the cases dealing with one involve different problems from the cases dealing with the other. *Durden* was a case involving only the patentability of a process of making a novel insecticide and the single claim on appeal was held to be directed to obvious subject matter in view of a prior art patent disclosing a very similar process using similar reactants notwithstanding the facts that there were unobvious starting material used and unobvious products obtained. We are not here concerned with a process of making bonding/priming agents but with the agents themselves in which the bonding/priming properties are inherent, for which reason we do not find *Durden* a controlling precedent as did the examiner and the board.[42]

Initially it appeared that *Pleuddemann* might provide some relief from the four-plus years of *Durden* rejections by suggesting that claims concerning a method of *using* a new, nonobvious starting material would fall outside the judicial boundaries of *Durden*. The PTO, however, also searching for clear instructions in this area, appears constrained to follow *Durden* until it is expressly reversed by the Federal Circuit.[43] Until some clearer guidance is provided, applicants should avoid admitting that their process is obvious apart from the materials it employs. Instead, they should emphasize how the differences in the materials used in their process lend unpredictability to that process.

7.5 OBJECTIVE EVIDENCE OF NONOBVIOUSNESS

The most common forms of objective evidence of nonobviousness include unexpected results, long-felt needs, prior failure of others, commercial success, skepticism by others, copying, acquiescence by licensing, and near-simultaneous development of the claimed invention. Such objective evidence (or secondary considerations) typically do not play a large part in the analysis of the obviousness issue during patent office prosecution because the inventor usually waits until the patent issues before starting substantial commercial activity.[44] If, however, the patent applicant properly presents objective evidence, the patent office must always consider this evidence in connection with the determination of obviousness.[45] In any given case, the objective evidence may be entitled to more or less weight, depending upon its nature and its relationship to the merits of the claimed invention.[46]

Applicants must comply with two requirements for the objective evidence to be given significant weight. First, a nexus between the evidence and the claimed invention must be established by applicant.[47] The term *nexus* is defined as a sufficient logical connection between the evidence and the patented invention, such that the evidence should be considered in the determination of nonobviousness.[48] For example, in the case of commercial success, a nexus is established when the applicant demonstrates that the invention disclosed and claimed in the application is commercially successful.[49] Second, the objective evidence submitted must be commensurate in scope with the claims. For example, in *In re Grasselli*,[50] experimental evidence limited to sodium was found to not be commensurate in scope with claims directed to a catalyst composition with an alkali metal.

7.5.1 Long-Felt Need and Prior Failure

Long-felt need is *not* a requirement for nonobviousness. Although a patent should issue only for new and nonobvious inventions, there is no requirement that people of ordinary skill have been aware of a problem and have been seeking solutions. The inventor is not required to be the winner of a race to a common goal. An invention may create a new need and still be nonobvious and, therefore, patentable.[51] However, recognition of a need and difficulties encountered by those skilled in the field are classical indications of nonobviousness.[52] The logic behind this type of evidence is that the existence of a defect creates a demand for its correction. Thus, it is reasonable to deduce that the defect would not have persisted if the solution, namely, the claimed invention, was obvious;[53] the amount of time that the need went unfulfilled and the failures by others must have occurred in the context of the same state of the art;[54] and that the inventor's solution was superior to prior solutions.[55]

The failure of others to provide a solution to a long-standing problem is substantiating proof of nonobviousness.[56] A prior failure may not be considered an indication that a later invention would have been obvious since the inventor would have known that some other approach should be tried.[57] If this reasoning were accepted, it would be progressively more difficult after a succession of failures to secure a patent on an invention that provided a solution to a long-felt need.[58] That there were other attempts and various combinations and procedures tried in the past does not render the later, successful one obvious.[59] The use of the applicant's "admission" of long-felt need as *prima facie* evidence of obviousness is contrary to logic as well as law.[60] On the other hand, a prior failure will not substantiate nonobviousness when the person that failed did not have knowledge of the best prior art and, most importantly, was not motivated to correct the problem because the result was satisfactory.[61]

7.5.2 Skepticism

The reactions of experts in the field of the claimed invention when it is disclosed to the public also have weight in determining obviousness. It is thought that these statements usually are truthful since they occur spontaneously, just after the disclosure of the invention, and in a nonadversarial setting. For example, the Federal Circuit has ruled that the skepticism of an expert, expressed before the inventor proved him wrong, is entitled to fair evidentiary weight.[62] The Supreme Court also has recognized the value of this type of evidence:

> [A]t the time Adams perfected his invention noted experts expressed disbelief in it. Several of the same experts subsequently recognized the significance of the Adams invention, some even patenting improvements on the same system.[63]

In a similar vein, an insight contrary to the understanding and expectations of the art indicates nonobviousness.[64] Contradicting accepted wisdom also is strong evidence of nonobviousness.[65]

7.5.3 Near-Simultaneous Invention

Simultaneous invention by others working under the same state of the art does not preclude patentability or prove obviousness: it is just one of the factors considered by a court en route to a decision on the issue. For instance, in *In re Merck*[66] the claims in reexamination centered on a method of treating mental disorders relating to depression by administering a certain oral dosage of amitriptyline. The Federal Circuit disagreed with the appellant's assertion that the board erred in relying on the contemporaneous, independent invention of four other groups who had used knowledge and concepts known in the art. The court found that this evidence was not essential in terms of obviousness. Nonetheless, it concluded that these simultaneous acts substantiated "the level of knowledge in the art at the time the invention was made."[67]

In contrast, the *Hybritech* court criticized the district court's reliance on near-simultaneous invention to support a conclusion of obviousness:

> Finding 10, which states that the invention was contemporaneously developed and disclosed in at least five publications and patents applications not listed above <u>and dated well after the filing date of the '110 patent but before its issuance</u> is irrelevant for purposes of 103 as interpreted by *Graham v. John Deere* [citation omitted], because obviousness must be determined as of the time the invention was made. Additionally, they are of little probative value in this case because they are dated December 1981 at the earliest, more than a year after the August 4, 1980 filing date here and roughly two years after conception occurred.[68]

7.5.4 Unexpected Results

To preface this discussion, the patent statute does not require that a patentable invention be superior to all prior art.[69] For that matter, finding that an invention is an improvement is not a prerequisite to patentability. It is possible for a claimed invention to be less effective than existing prior art but nevertheless meet the statutory criteria for patentability.[70] Regardless, the submission of evidence of unexpectedly superior properties or advantages of the claimed invention compared to prior art products or processes is common practice in chemical and biotechnology prosecution,[71] whether including it in the application as originally filed[72] or by the subsequent submission of a declaration or affidavit.[73]

Unexpected results must be established by factual evidence of a comparison between the claimed invention and the closest prior art. Mere arguments or conclusions in the specification are not enough.[74] Evidence of unexpected results may include data showing that a compound is unexpectedly superior in a property it shares with prior art compounds.[75] However, to be patentable, a compound need not excel over prior art compounds in all common properties: evidence that a compound is unexpectedly superior in one of a spectrum of common properties can be enough to rebut *prima facie* obviousness.[76] It is the applicants' burden to establish that the actual differences observed in the argued property (or properties) represent an "unexpected" improvement; that is, a difference in kind or degree over what one skilled in the art would have expected based on the collective teachings of the prior art.[77] For example, in *Ex parte Erlich*,[78] the patent office concluded that the evidence presented by the applicant merely established that the monoclonal antibodies produced by the claimed hybridomas differed in their specificity for the target antigen, which is exactly what one skilled in the art would have expected based on the prior art.

Where a product-by-process claim is rejected over a prior art product that appears to be identical, although produced by a different process, the burden is on the applicant to come forward with evidence establishing a nonobvious difference between the claimed product and the prior art product.[79]

7.6 *PRIMA FACIE* OBVIOUSNESS

The concept of *prima facie* obviousness during *ex parte* patent examination is merely a procedural mechanism to allocate, in an orderly way, the burdens of presenting evidence and persuasion between the examiner and the applicant.[80] The patent office has the initial burden under Section 103 to establish a *prima facie* case of obviousness.[81] Obviousness cannot be established by combining the teachings of the prior art to produce the claimed invention without some teachings or suggestions supporting the combination. Under Section 103, teachings of references can be combined *only* if there is some suggestion or incentive to do so.[82] While there must be some teaching, reason, suggestion, or motivation to combine existing elements to produce a claimed invention, it is not necessary that the cited references or prior art specifically suggest making the combination.[83] The suggestion can derive solely from the existence of a teaching, which someone of ordinary skill in the art would be presumed to know, and the use of that teaching to solve the same or a similar problem.[84] In other words, the references must expressly or implicitly suggest the claimed invention or *the examiner must present a convincing line of reasoning* as to why the skilled artisan would have found the claimed invention obvious in light of the references.[85] The extent to which the suggestion must be explicit in, or fairly inferred from, the references is decided on the facts of each case in light of the prior art and its relationship to the applicant's invention.[86]

Finally, the number of references relied on by an examiner is immaterial to the legal propriety of the *prima facie* case.[87] This burden can be satisfied only by showing some objective teaching in the prior art or knowledge generally available to someone of ordinary skill in the art that would have led him or her to combine the relevant teachings of the references.[88] An examiner must determine whether the prior art teaching would have appeared sufficient to someone of ordinary skill to suggest making a claimed substitution or other modification.[89]

The relative strength or weakness of the *prima facie* case is immaterial.[90] The concept is imprecise but it is relatively well developed in the area of chemical compositions.[91] For example, *prima facie* obviousness is well established in combining two compositions, each of which is taught by the prior art to be useful for the same purpose, in order to form a third composition that is to be used for the same purpose.[92] The procedure is not unique to the chemical arts, however. The fact that a *prima facie* case may be established or rebutted by different forms of evidence in various technologies does not restrict the concept to any particular field of technology.[93]

If examination at the initial stage does not produce a *prima facie* case of unpatentability, the applicant is entitled to a conclusion of nonobviousness.[94]

7.6.1 Structural Obviousness

The *In re Dillon in banc*[95] decision has stirred considerable controversy.[96] Nevertheless, it is the leading authority on the *prima facie* obviousness of chemical compositions. In reversing the ruling of an earlier Federal Circuit panel decision,[97] the *in banc* court reaffirmed that *prima facie* obviousness is properly established when there is structural similarity between the prior art and the claimed composition, and the prior art gives any reason or motivation to make the claimed composition.[98]

Dillon's claimed invention was directed to a hydrocarbon fuel composition comprising at least one tetra-orthoester in an amount sufficient to reduce particulate emissions during the combustion of the fuel. The prior art disclosed hydrocarbon fuel compositions containing tri-orthoesters for the purpose of dewatering and the use of water-scavenging tri- and tetra-orthoesters in nonhydrocarbon fluids. The board had found that the claims were obvious in view of the prior art teachings.

On appeal, Dillon urged that the prior art did not disclose or suggest that the tetra-orthoesters could be used to reduce particulate emissions. She also argued that a *prima facie* case had not been properly established since the conclusion was contrary to the ruling of *In re Wright*,[99] which indicates that *prima facie* obviousness requires that the prior art suggest the claimed compositions' properties and the problem the applicant was attempting to solve.

In response to the first argument, the Federal Circuit simply pointed out that the composition claims were not limited to the new use—they were distinct from the prior art only in terms of the orthoester. The court crushed Dillon's argument by overruling *In re Wright*, stating:

> Each situation must be considered on its own facts, but it is not necessary in order to establish a *prima facie* case of obviousness that both a structural similarity between a claimed and prior art compound (or a key component of a composition) be shown and that there be a suggestion in or expectation from <u>the prior art</u> that the claimed compound or composition will have the same or a similar utility <u>as one newly discovered by applicant</u>. To the extent that *Wright* suggests or holds to the contrary, it is hereby overruled. In particular, the statement that a *prima facie* obviousness rejection is not supported if no reference shows or suggests the newly-discovered properties and results of a claimed structure is not the law.[100]

The court cautioned that properties of a chemical compound must be considered in the overall evaluation of obviousness. For instance, the lack of any disclosure of useful properties of a prior art compound may indicate a lack of motivation to make related compounds, which would preclude establishing a *prima facie* case. However, "it is not correct that similarity of structure and a suggestion of *the activity of an applicant's compounds* in the prior art are necessary before a prima facie case is established."[101]

7.6.2   The Significance of *Prima Facie* Obviousness

Proper establishment of *prima facie* obviousness is significant because once it is established, the applicant is required to submit factual evidence to the contrary. Since any such evidence becomes part of the file history, it provides ammunition to an opposing party during litigation of the issued patent. For example, in *Merck & Co. v. Danbury Pharmacal Inc.*,[102] claims to a market-leading pharmaceutical product were held to be valid and admittedly infringed. Nevertheless, they were held unenforceable because rebuttal evidence had been submitted in a way that constituted "inequitable conduct." Submission of rebuttal evidence can be avoided by demonstrating that *prima facie* obviousness had not been properly established. Thus, the Section 103 rejection issued by the examiner must be carefully analyzed. The alleged *prima facie* case can be successfully attacked in numerous ways. In a number of cases, it has been held that compounds that seem to be close in structural similarity to prior art compounds are not obvious.[103] Other common arguments center about "obvious to try," "hindsight reconstruction," and a lack of a suggestion in the collective prior-art teachings to produce the claimed invention. The most significant of these in biotechnology is the "obvious to try" line of cases.

7.6.2.1 Obviousness and "Obvious to Try."   The Federal Circuit has repeatedly emphasized that "obvious to try" is not the standard under Section 103.[104] In *In re O'Farrell*,[105] the court expounded on that point in the context of a biotechnology invention. The claims at issue were directed at a method for producing a predetermined protein in stable form in a transformed host bacterium. The claimed method required preparation ("providing") of a cloning vector containing at least a substantial portion of a gene endogenous to the host bacterium, namely, the regulatory sequences (for RNA synthesis) and the protein-coding sequence (the structural gene) excluding the termination signal, linked at its distal end (3') in proper orientation and reading frame to a natural or synthetic heterologous gene encoding the predetermined protein. The heterologous gene had to contain sufficient DNA to result in expression of a fused protein large enough to confer stability to the predetermined protein when the resultant vector was used to transform the bacterium. The Board of Appeals upheld the obviousness rejection of the claims over a reference (*Polisky et al.*) published more than one year prior to the filing date of the application and coauthored by two of the named inventors. It reasoned that so much of the claimed method was disclosed in *Polisky* that making a protein by substituting the corresponding gene for that used in the reference (a frog ribosomal RNA gene), the substitution of which was suggested by the authors, would have been obvious to someone of ordinary skill in the art.

The applicants argued nonobviousness on the grounds that there was significant unpredictability in the molecular biology field at the time the invention was made, so the predictions in the *Polisky* reference constituted a mere invitation to try to make the claimed invention.

The Federal Circuit upheld the board's decision. It found that *Polisky* contained detailed enabling methodology for practicing the claimed invention, a suggestion to modify the prior art to practice the claimed invention, and evidence suggesting that it would be successful. Thus, the court made the legal conclusion that the claimed invention would have been obvious over *Polisky* alone or in combination with Bahl (disclosing a general method for inserting synthetic DNA into plasmids).

In the course of its discussion, the court expounded on the "obvious to try" conundrum. First, the court deduced that since even "obvious inventions would have been obvious to try," not all obvious-to-try situations necessarily result in nonobviousness:

> It is true that this court and its predecessors have repeatedly emphasized that "obvious to try" is not the standard under 103. However, the meaning of this maxim is sometimes lost. Any invention that would in fact have been obvious under 103 would also have been, in a sense, obvious to try. The question is: when is an invention that was obvious to try nevertheless nonobvious?[106]

Judge Rich then explained that the general rule had been directed mainly at two kinds of errors. In the first obvious-to-try situation, someone skilled in the art would have had to vary all parameters or try each of numerous choices before achieving success when the prior art gave either no indication of which parameters were critical or no direction as to which of many possible choices was likely to be successful. The second situation described by Judge Rich was the exploration of a new technology or a general approach that seemed to be a promising field of experimentation, where the prior art gave only general guidance as to the particular form of the claimed invention or how to achieve it. This scenario was present in *Hybritech v. Monoclonal Antibodies, Inc.*[107] In *Hybritech*, the court found that none of the prior art disclosed sandwich assays using two monoclonal antibodies. The prior art was characterized by the district court as "predicting" that the Kohler and Milstein breakthrough would lead to widespread use of monoclonal antibodies in immunoassays.[108] Notwithstanding its concession that the district court correctly found that the use of polyclonal antibodies in sandwich assays was well known, the Federal Circuit concluded:

> At most, these articles are invitations to try monoclonal antibodies in immunoassays but do not suggest how that end might be accomplished. To the extent the district court relied upon these references to establish that it would have been obvious to try monoclonal antibodies of 10^8 liters/mole affinity in a sandwich immunoassay that detects the presence of or quantitates antigen, the court was in error.[109]

The Federal Circuit, in two recent decisions concerning biotechnology inventions, distinguished *In re O'Farrell* factually on the issues of "obvious to try" and "reasonable expectation of success."

In *In re Vaeck*,[110] the court reversed the board's finding of *prima facie* obviousness. It concluded that the prior art contained neither: (1) a suggestion that would have motivated someone skilled in the art to make the substitution that constituted the difference between the claimed invention and the prior art, nor (2) a reasonable expectation of success in so doing.

The claimed invention was drawn to chimeric genes capable of expression in Cyanobacteria, comprising a promoter region linked to a DNA fragment encoding an insecticidally active *Bacillus* protein, hybrid plasmid vectors, Cyanobacterial strains, recombinant Cyanobacteria expressing the gene, and insecticidal compositions. The prior art included a primary reference that disclosed the expression in cyanobacteria of a chimeric gene encoding chloramphenicol acetyltransferase (CAT) (an antibiotic resistance-conferring gene) and secondary references that disclosed expression of *Bacillus* insecticidal protein genes in various *Bacillus* hosts and in *E. coli* with the stated purpose of obtaining large quantities of the protein. The examiner concluded that it would have been *prima facie* obvious to: (1) substitute the genes disclosed in the secondary references for the CAT gene to obtain high level expression, and (2) use cyanobacteria as heterologous hosts for expression of the claimed genes in view of the teachings of the primary reference that demonstrated this function. The board substantially agreed and, citing *O'Farrell*, added that obviousness does not require absolute certainty, only a reasonable expectation of success.

The Federal Circuit disagreed. With respect to the primary reference, it concluded that the expression of a CAT gene in cyanobacteria, without more, would not have rendered expression of an unrelated gene in cyanobacteria obvious. Likewise, the disclosures of the secondary references did not constitute a suggestion to express *Bacillus* insecticidal protein genes in cyanobacteria. The PTO argued that someone skilled in the art would have considered *Bacillus* and cyanobacteria interchangeable as hosts for expression of heterologous genes since both are members of the same taxonomic kingdom (*Procaryotae*) and other secondary references disclosed a certain amino acid sequence homology between bacteria and cyanobacteria. The Federal Circuit shot down this argument. It found that the respective bacteria were taxonomically distinct and that the evidence of the uncertainty regarding the biology of cyanobacteria relied on by the PTO weighed in favor of the opposite conclusion. Finally, the court concluded that the prior art indication that cyanobacteria are attractive hosts for expression of genes involved in photosynthesis (by virtue of their capability of undergoing oxygenic photosynthesis) did not constitute a suggestion the cyanobacteria would be equally attractive for expression of unrelated heterologous genes.

A similar conclusion was reached by the Federal Circuit in *Amgen v. Chugai*.[111] The court affirmed the district court's holding that the claimed invention was not invalid under Section 103, since the prior art presented merely an "obvious to try" situation unaccompanied by a reasonable expectation of success. The claims at issue were directed to purified and isolated genes encoding human erythropoietin (EPO) and host cells transformed with the gene. The district court had found that the inventor's unique probing strategy, that is, using two fully redundant sets of probes of relatively high degeneracy to screen a human genomic DNA (gDNA) library, and the extensive effort required to employ that method, made the claimed invention nonobvious over the prior art.[112]

On appeal, Chugai argued that at the time the invention was made, someone skilled in the art would have had a reasonable expectation of success in screening a gDNA library by the inventor's method. The CAFC disagreed in view of testimony on the record indicating the lack of experience in these probing techniques. Also important to the CAFC were the doubts that other experts in the field expressed as to whether they would have been successful, even if they had been in possession of various starting materials (EPO fragments) used by the inventor.

In the alternative, Chugai argued that the human EPO gene could have been found using a known monkey EPO gene as a probe and pointed to testimony of its expert that the overall homology of baboon DNA and human DNA was "roughly 90 percent."[113] The court reasoned that since neither the DNA sequence of the human EPO gene nor its exact degree of homology with the monkey EPO gene was known, and since the inventor had been unsuccessful at probing a human gDNA library with monkey cDNA until after he had isolated the EPO gene using the probing strategy, Chugai's argument amounted to, at most, an obvious-to-try scenario.

7.6.2.2 Monoclonal Antibodies and Obvious to Try. Administrative decisional authority on the issue of obviousness as it relates to monoclonal antibodies (Mabs) does not weigh in favor of applicants. The general rule applied by the Patent and Trademark Office basically is that claims directed to monoclonals specific to a given substance are *prima facie* obvious if the prior art disclosed that the substance is antigenic. After initial agreement by the PTO that Mabs were merely obvious to try,[114] in *Ex parte Erlich*[115] the board affirmed the obviousness rejection of claims to hybridoma cells that produced Mabs specific to human fibroblast interferon. The examiner rejected the claims over prior art that disclosed: (1) the antigenicity of human fibroblast interferon and human leucocyte interferon, (2) the Kohler and Milstein method of preparing Mabs specific to known antigens, and (3) Mabs specific to human leucocyte interferon, as well as to various other antigens.

The appellants' arguments of unpredictability concerning the production of antibodies in different animals in response to injection of the same antigen were to no avail. The board ruled that the production of the claimed monoclonals would have been obvious since human fibroblast interferon was a known antigen of unquestioned research interest as an antiviral or antitumor agent, and that one would have had a reasonable expectation of success in view of the production of Mabs specific to a related antigen.

In the recent decision *Ex parte Erlich*[116] (Erlich II), the board eliminated any doubt as to the manner in which monoclonal antibody subject matter was to be treated by the patent office. Confronted with virtually the same claimed subject matter as in the first *Erlich* decision (Erlich I) and further armed with *In re O'Farrell*, it affirmed the obviousness rejection in substantially identical wording. The differences are that the conclusion of reasonable expectation of success was predicated on the success other researchers had in adapting hybridoma technology broadly to other antigens (not just that monoclonals had been produced that were specific to a *related* antigen) and, of course, the discourse in *O'Farrell* on "obvious to try."[117]

7.6.3 Rebutting *Prima Facie* Obviousness

After a *prima facie* case of obviousness has been established, the burden of going forward with evidence and the burden of persuasion shifts to the applicant. The rebuttal is a showing of facts supporting a conclusion of nonobviousness. The facts may relate to any of the *Graham v. Deere* secondary considerations, including but not limited to unexpected results, commercial success, long-felt need, and failure of others. If rebuttal evidence of adequate weight is produced, the holding of *prima facie* obviousness, which is just a legal inference from previously uncontradicted evidence, is dissipated. Regardless of whether the *prima facie* case would have been characterized as strong or weak, the examiner must reconsider all of the evidence from scratch.[118]

7.7   INVENTIVE STEP AND NONOBVIOUSNESS COMPARED

In the European Patent Office (EPO) and a number of other jurisdictions, inventiveness is measured against the standard of "inventive step." Some suggest that the EPO Technical Board of Appeals has tried to harmonize its approach to analyzing inventive step with the approach taken by the Federal Circuit for analyzing obviousness.[119] Nevertheless, even with perfect harmony, different decision-making tribunals may reach different results on similar sets of facts.

It is interesting to note that the EPO took a significantly different view of the prophetic statements contained in the Polisky article, which was so damaging to the applicants in *In re O'Farrell,* in the *GENENTECH I/Polypeptide expression* decision.[120] Polisky was again viewed as the closest prior art. Claim 1 in this application (as amended for appeal) read as follows:

> 1. A recombinant plasmid suited for transformation of a bacterial host wherein the plasmid comprises a homologous regulon, heterologous DNA, and one or more termination codon(s), the heterologous DNA encoding a desired functional heterologous polypeptide or intermediate therefor which is not degraded by endogenous proteolytic enzymes, said DNA being positioned in proper reading frame with said homologous regulon between said regulon and the termination codon(s), whereby on translation of the transcription product of the heterologous DNA in a suitable bacterium, the resulting expression product is said desired functional polypeptide or intermediate therefor in recoverable form.

The examining division rejected this claim as lacking an inventive step over Polisky. The Technical Board of Appeals agreed that Polisky was the closest prior art, but viewed the statement on producing a functional eukaryotic protein as "speculative" and a mere reference to a "technical problem," namely, how to express heterologous polypeptides in bacteria as useful products. The solution, noted the board, was to insert the heterologous DNA in correct reading frame and to use an insert of sufficient size to encode a polypeptide that would resist degradation by proteolytic enzymes. The board viewed these solutions as neither suggested by Polisky nor apparent to those skilled in the art and, accordingly, granted the application.

One interpretation of these two decisions may be that speculative statements in prior publications are given more weight in the United States than in the EPO. However, the Federal Circuit in *O'Farrell* emphasized that the applicants *themselves* had published their invention more than one year prior to filing their application. A different group was involved in the *GENENTECH I/Polypeptide expression* application. Hence, another interpretation is that inventors may be held to a higher standard of nonobviousness (at least in the United States) when their own speculative statements become a part of the prior art. In any case, it is clear that highly fact-sensitive questions such as the "reasonable" expectations of people of ordinary skill in the art can easily be decided differently in different jurisdictions.

7.8 CONCLUSION

We are now in the later phase of the pioneering age of biotechnology. The Federal Circuit continues to decide biotechnology obviousness cases, and the Patent Office Examining Corps continues to look to these cases for guidance. Nevertheless, there is a lag in time between when a technology is presented to the patent office and when it reaches the Federal Circuit. Indeed, many of the cases recently decided by the Federal Circuit deal with patents filed more than a decade ago. Because of the significant public interests affected by biotechnology, the patent office tends to issue biotechnology patent applications carefully. While this course is prudent to an extent, when the patent office becomes overly cautious and unduly delays issuance of a patent, then the applicant with the resources to persevere can obtain a broad patent well after the technology has matured.[121] This is always a serious disruption to industry; if generic patent claims are to be issued, then the sooner they are issued, the sooner they will expire, or the sooner competitors can determine how to properly design around those claims. Hopefully, with the disposition of additional biotechnology cases by the Federal Circuit, the continued professionalism of the Patent Office Examining Corps in applying those cases, and the care and patience of patent applicants, a time of logical predictability in the law of nonobviousness of biological inventions soon will be reached. Until that time, the long-established principles in this area should be considered and applied to biotechnology inventions with care.

REFERENCES

1. *See generally* NONOBVIOUSNESS—THE ULTIMATE CONDITION OF PATENTABILITY (J. Witherspoon, ed. 1980).
2. *In re* Papesch, 315 F.2d 381, 137 USPQ 43, 47 (C.C.P.A. 1963).
3. *Ex parte* Allen, 2 USPQ2d 1425, 1427 (Bd. Pat. App. 1987).
4. Panduit Corp. v. Dennison Manufacturing Co., 810 F.2d 1561, 1 USPQ2d 1593, 1597 (Fed. Cir.), *cert. denied*, 481 U.S. 1052 (1987).
5. Graham v. John Deere Co., 383 U.S. 1, 17–18, 148 USPQ 459, 467 (1966).
6. *In re* Deminski, 796 F.2d 436, 442, 230 USPQ 313, 315 (Fed. Cir. 1986); Stratoflex, Inc. v. Aeroquip Corp., 713 F.2d 1530, 1535, 218 USPQ 871, 876 (Fed. Cir. 1983).
7. *In re* Wood, 599 F.2d 1032, 1036, 202 USPQ 171, 174 (C.C.P.A. 1979).
8. *See* 2 D. Chisum, PATENTS, § 5.03[1][b] (1992).

9. *In re* Foster, 343 F.2d 980, 988, 145 USPQ 166, 173 (C.C.P.A. 1965), *cert. denied*, 383 U.S. 966 (1966); *accord, In re* Kaslow, 707 F.2d 1366, 217 USPQ 1089, 1095 (Fed. Cir. 1983).
10. *In re* O'Farrell, 853 F.2d 894, 7 USPQ2d 1673 (Fed. Cir. 1988).
11. *In re* Lemelson, 397 F.2d 1006, 1009, 158 USPQ 275 (C.C.P.A. 1968).
12. EWP Corp. v. Reliance Universal Inc., 755 F.2d 898, 907, 225 USPQ 20, 25 (Fed. Cir. 1985), *cert. denied*, 474 U.S. 843 (1985).
13. Beckman Instruments, Inc. v. LKB Produckter AB, 892 F.2d 1547, 13 USPQ2d 1301, 1304 (Fed. Cir. 1989).
14. Hazeltine Research, Inc. v. Brenner, 382 U.S. 252, 86 S. Ct. 335, 15 L.Ed.2d 304, 147 USPQ 429 (1965); *see also* 35 U.S.C. § 102(e).
15. *In re* Piasecki, 745 F.2d 1468, 223 USPQ 785, 789 (Fed. Cir. 1984).
16. Constant v. Advanced Micro-Devices, Inc., 848 F.2d 1560, 7 USPQ2d 1057, 1063 (Fed. Cir. 1988).
17. E.I. duPont de Nemours & Co. v. Phillips Petroleum Co., 849 F.2d 1430, 7 USPQ2d 1129, 1134–35 (Fed. Cir. 1988), *on remand*, 711 F. Supp. 1205, 11 USPQ2d 1081 (D. Del. 1989).
18. duPont, 849 F.2d at 143 note 6, 7 USPQ2d at 1135 note 6.
19. R. Harmon, PATENTS AND THE FEDERAL CIRCUIT, 85 (2d ed. 1991).
20. Standard Oil Co. v. American Cyanamid Co., 774 F.2d 448, 227 USPQ 293, 297–98 (Fed. Cir. 1985).
21. Environmental Designs, Ltd. v. Union Oil Co., 713 F.2d 693, 218 USPQ 865, 869 (Fed. Cir. 1983).
22. Compaigne de Saint-Gobain v. Brenner, 386 F.2d 985, 987, 155 USPQ 417, 419 (D.C. Cir. 1967).
23. *In re* O'Farrell, 853 F.2d 894, 7 USPQ2d 1673 (Fed. Cir. 1988).
24. O'Farrell, 853 F.2d at 902, 7 USPQ2d at 1680.
25. Kloster Speedsteel AB v. Crucible, Inc., 793 F.2d 1565, 1574, 230 USPQ 81, 86 (Fed. Cir. 1986); Environmental Designs, Ltd., 218 USPQ at 869.
26. Orthopedic Equipment Co., Inc. v. All Orthopedic Appliances, Inc., 707 F.2d 1376, 217 USPQ 1281, 1285 (Fed. Cir. 1983).
27. *In re* Merck, 800 F.2d 1091, 231 USPQ 375, 380 (Fed. Cir. 1986) ("evidence of contemporaneous invention is probative of 'the level of knowledge in the art at the time the invention was made.'"); Newell Companies, Inc. v. Kenney Manufacturing Co., 864 F.2d 757, 766 note 12, 9 USPQ2d 1417, 1425 note 12 (Fed. Cir. 1988) (an internal memorandum, although not technically prior art, was admissible to show that others skilled in the art had suggested solutions to the problem that was the subject of the claims of the patent at issue).
28. *In re* Nilssen, 851 F.2d 1401, 7 USPQ2d 1500, 1501 (Fed. Cir. 1988).
29. Panduit Corp., 1 USPQ2d at 1597.
30. Jones v. Hardy, 727 F.2d 1524, 220 USPQ 1021, 1024 (Fed. Cir. 1984).
31. *In re* Papesch, 315 F.2d 381, 137 USPQ 43 (C.C.P.A. 1963).
32. Papesch, 315 F.2d at 3, 137 USPQ at 51 (emphasis in original).
33. Hybritech, Inc. v. Monoclonal Antibodies, Inc., 802 F.2d 1367, 231 USPQ 81 (Fed. Cir. 1986), *cert. denied*, 107 S. Ct. 1606 (1987).
34. Hybritech, Inc. v. Monoclonal Antibodies, Inc., 623 F. Supp. 1344, 227 USPQ 215, 219 (N.D. Cal. 1985) (reversed on appeal).
35. Hybritech, 231 USPQ at 93 (emphasis in original).
36. Hybritech, 231 USPQ at 93.

37. *In re* Durden, 763 F.2d 1406, 226 USPQ 359 (Fed. Cir. 1985).
38. Durden, 226 USPQ at 360.
39. Durden, 226 USPQ at 362.
40. *See, e.g.*, D. Chisum, A Retrospective: The First Decade of Federal Circuit Patent Law, AIPLA Bulletin, 72, 78 (Oct.–Nov. 1992); *see also Ex parte* Orser, 14 USPQ2d 1987 (Bd. Pat. App. 1990).
41. *In re* Pleuddemann, 910 F.2d 823, 15 USPQ2d 1738 (Fed. Cir. 1990).
42. Pleuddemann, 15 USPQ2d at 1741.
43. *See, e.g., Ex parte* Ochiai, 24 USPQ2d 1265 (Bd. Pat. App. 1992) (reviewing Durden, Pleuddemann, and other relevant decisions).
44. *In re* Sernaker, 702 F.2d 989, 217 USPQ 1, 7 (Fed. Cir. 1983).
45. Sernaker, 217 USPQ at 7.
46. Ashland Oil, Inc. v. Delta Resins & Refractories, 776 F.2d 281, 306, 227 USPQ 657, 674 (Fed. Cir. 1985), *cert. denied*, 475 U.S. 1017 (1986).
47. Cable Electric Products, Inc. v. Genmark, Inc., 770 F.2d 1015, 1027, 226 USPQ 881, 888 (Fed. Cir. 1985).
48. *Id.*
49. Demaco Corp. v. F. Von Langsdorff Lic., Ltd., 851 F.2d 1387, 7 USPQ2d 1222, 1226 (Fed. Cir. 1988).
50. *In re* Grasselli, 713 F.2d 731, 218 USPQ 769, 778 (Fed. Cir. 1983).
51. Leinoff v. Louis Milona & Sons, 726 F.2d 734, 740, 220 USPQ 845, 849 (Fed. Cir. 1984).
52. Graham v. John Deere Co., 383 U.S. 1, 17, 148 USPQ 459, 467 (1966).
53. Safety Car Heating & Lighting Co. v. All Orthopedic Appliances Co., 707 F.2d 1376, 217 USPQ 1281 (Fed. Cir. 1983).
54. Newell Companies, Inc. v. Kenney Manufacturing Co., 864 F.2d 757, 868, 9 USPQ2d 1417, 1426 (Fed. Cir. 1988); *Ex parte* Stern, 13 USPQ2d 1379, 1382 (Bd. Pat. App. 1989).
55. *In re* Cavanagh, 436 F.2d 491, 168 USPQ 466 (C.C.P.A. 1971).
56. Uniroyal v. Rudkin-Wiley, 837 F.2d 1044, 5 USPQ2d 1434, 1440–41 (Fed. Cir. 1988).
57. *Id.*
58. *Id.*
59. *In re* Dow Chemical Co., 837 F.2d 469, 5 USPQ2d 1529, 1531 (Fed. Cir. 1988).
60. *Id.*
61. *In re* Sneed, 710 F.2d 1544, 218 USPQ 385, 389–40 (Fed. Cir. 1983).
62. *In re* Piasecki, 745 F.2d 1468, 1475, 223 USPQ 785, 790 (Fed. Cir. 1984).
63. United States v. Adams, 383 U.S. 39, 52, 148 USPQ 479, 483–84 (1966).
64. Schenk AG v. Norton Corp., 713 F.2d 782, 218 USPQ 698, 700–01 (Fed. Cir. 1983).
65. W.L. Gore & Assoc. v. Garlock, Inc., 721 F.2d 1540, 1552, 220 USPQ 303, 312 (Fed. Cir. 1983), *cert. denied,* 105 S. Ct. 172 (1984).
66. *In re* Merck, 800 F.2d 1091, 231 USPQ 375 (Fed. Cir. 1986).
67. Merck, 800 F.2d at 1098, 231 USPQ at 380.
68. Hybritech, 802 F.2d 1367, 1380 note 4, 231 USPQ 81, 91 note 4 (emphasis in original).
69. Demaco Corp. v. F. Von Langsdorff Licensing Ltd., 851 F.2d 1387, 1390–91, 7 USPQ2d 1222, 1224–25 (Fed. Cir. 1988).
70. Custom Accessories, Inc. v. Jeffrey-Allan Industries, Inc., 807 F.2d 955, 960 note 12, 1 USPQ2d 1196, 1199 note 12 (Fed. Cir. 1986).
71. *See generally* A. Rollins, *PTO Practice: Spinning the Wheels of Evidence,* 70 J. PAT. OFF. SOC'Y 505 (1988).

72. *See In re* Margolis, 785 F.2d 1029, 228 USPQ 940, 941–42 (Fed. Cir. 1986) (comparative data in specific examples in the patent specification must be weighed along with the prior art in determining obviousness).
73. 37 C.F.R. § 1.132.
74. *In re* DeBlauwe, 736 F.2d 699, 705, 222 USPQ 191, 196 (Fed. Cir. 1984).
75. *In re* Lunsford, 357 F.2d 380, 148 USPQ 716 (C.C.P.A. 1966).
76. *See In re* Chupp, 816 F.2d 643, 2 USPQ2d 1437, 1439 (Fed. Cir. 1987); *but see In re* Eli Lilly & Co., 902 F.2d 943, 14 USPQ2d 1741, 1744–45 (Fed. Cir. 1990) (distinguishing *In re* Chupp).
77. *See In re* Merck, 800 F.2d 1091, 231 USPQ 375, 380–81 (Fed. Cir. 1986) (alleged unexpected sedative and anticholinergic properties of claimed amitriptyline were not so unexpectedly different from the properties of imipramine, the closest prior art); see also Merck & Co. v. Danbury Pharmacal Inc., 8 USPQ2d 1793, 1818–19 (D. Del. 1988) (distinguishing *In re* Merck); *Ex parte* Sugimoto, 14 USPQ2d 1312, 1314–15 (Bd. Pat. App. 1990) (alleged unexpected increase in production of human soluble immune response suppressor deemed suggested by prior art).
78. *Ex parte* Erlich, 22 USPQ2d 1463, 1468 (Bd. Pat. App. 1992).
79. *In re* Marosi, 710 F.2d 799, 218 USPQ 289, 292–93 (Fed. Cir. 1983).
80. *In re* Piasecki, 745 F.2d 1468, 1472, 223 USPQ 785, 787–88 (Fed. Cir. 1984) (ruling that *prima facie* obviousness had been established, but that rebuttal evidence was not evaluated properly in accordance with accepted evidentiary procedure).
81. *In re* Fine, 837 F.2d 1071, 1074, 5 USPQ2d 1596, 1598 (Fed. Cir. 1988) (ruling that *prima facie* obviousness had not been properly established).
82. ACS Hospital Systems, Inc. v. Montefiore Hospital, 732 F.2d 1572, 1577, 221 USPQ 929, 933 (Fed. Cir. 1984).
83. *In re* Nilssen, 851 F.2d 1401, 1403, 7 USPQ2d 1500, 1502 (Fed. Cir. 1988).
84. *In re* Wood, 599 F.2d 1032, 1037, 202 USPQ 171, 174 (C.C.P.A. 1979); *see also* EWP Corp. v. Reliance Universal, Inc., 755 F.2d 898, 906–07, 225 USPQ 20, 25 (Fed. Cir.), *cert. denied*, 474 U.S. 843 (1985); *In re* Sernaker, 702 F.2d 989, 995, 217 USPQ 1, 6 (Fed. Cir. 1983).
85. *Ex parte* Clapp, 227 USPQ 972, 973 (Bd. Pat. App. 1985).
86. *In re* Gorman, 933 F.2d 982, 18 USPQ2d 1885, 1888 (Fed. Cir. 1991).
87. Gorman, 18 USPQ2d at 1889 ("The large number of cited references does not negate the obviousness of the combination, for the prior art uses the various elements for the same purposes as they are used by appellants, making the claimed invention as a whole obvious in terms of 35 USC section 103.")
88. *Id.*
89. *In re* Lalu, 747 F.2d 703, 705, 223 USPQ 1257, 1258 (Fed. Cir. 1984) (ruling that *prima facie* obviousness had not been properly established).
90. *In re* Carleton, 599 F.2d 1021, 202 USPQ 165, 168 (C.C.P.A. 1979) (holding that the rebuttal evidence taken with all the evidence was sufficient to overcome the *prima facie* case of obviousness).
91. *See* 2 D. Chisum, PATENTS, § 5.06[1] (1992); H. Wegner, *Prima Facie Obviousness of Chemical Compounds*, 6 APLA QUART. J. 271 (1978).
92. *In re* Kerkhoven, 626 F.2d 846, 205 USPQ 1069, 1072 (CCPA 1980) (ruling that the process claim at issue would not have been *prima facie* obvious).
93. *In re* Oetiker, 977 F.2d 1443, 24 USPQ2d 1443, 1445 (Fed. Cir. 1992) (rejecting the appellant's argument that *prima facie* obviousness has no role outside of the chemical arts.)

94. *In re* Grabiak, 769 F.2d 729, 733, 226 USPQ 870, 873 (Fed. Cir. 1985).

95. *In re* Dillon, 919 F.2d 688, 16 USPQ2d 1897 (Fed. Cir. 1990).

96. *See, e.g.*, Brooks, *In re* Dillon in Banc, 32 Idea 299 (1992).

97. *In re* Dillon, 892 F.2d 1554, 1560, 13 USPQ2d 1337, 1341 (Fed. Cir. 1989) (". . . a *prima facie* case of obviousness is not deemed made unless both (1) the new compound or composition is structurally similar to the reference compound or composition and (2) there is some suggestion or expectation in the prior art that the new compound or composition will have the same or a similar utility as that discovered by the applicant.") (emphasis in original).

98. Dillon, 16 USPQ2d at 1901.

99. *In re* Wright, 848 F.2d 1216, 1219, 6 USPQ2d 1959, 1961 (Fed Cir. 1988).

100. Dillon, 16 USPQ2d at 1901 (footnote omitted) (emphasis in original).

101. Dillon, 16 USPQ2d at 1906 (emphasis in original).

102. Merck & Co. v. Danbury Pharmacal Inc., 694 F. Supp. 1, 8 USPQ2d 1793, 1794, 1815–21 (D. Del. 1988), *aff'd,* 873 F.2d 1418, 10 USPQ2d 1682 (Fed. Cir. 1989).

103. *In re* Grabiak, 769 F.2d 729, 226 USPQ 870 (Fed. Cir. 1985); *In re* Jones, 21 USPQ2d 1941 (Fed. Cir. 1992).

104. *See, e.g., In re* Fine, 837 F.2d 1596, 5 USPQ2d 1596, 1599 (Fed. Cir. 1988) ("But whether a particular combination might be 'obvious to try' is not a legitimate test of patentability."); *see generally* J. Badie, *"Motivation" or "Obvious to Try"—Is There a Difference? Is It a Proper Test of Obviousness?*, 75 J. PAT. OFF. SOC'Y 54 (1993); K. Piffat, *The "Obvious to Try" Doctrine and Biotechnology: A Comparison of Patent Cases in the United States and in the United Kingdom*, 72 J. PAT. OFF. SOC'Y 956 (1990).

105. *In re* O'Farrell, 853 F.2d 894, 7 USPQ2d 1673 (Fed. Cir. 1988); *see also* Ex parte Storrs, 13 USPQ2d 1390 (Bd. Pat. App. 1989) (reversing one obviousness rejection of method for solubilizing somatotropin and making new obviousness rejection under *In re O'Farrell*).

106. O'Farrell, 853 F.2d at 903, 7 USPQ2d at 1680–81.

107. Hybritech Inc. v. Monoclonal Antibodies, Inc., 802 F.2d 1367, 231 USPQ 81 (Fed. Cir. 1986), *cert. denied*, 107 S. Ct. 1606 (1987).

108. Hybritech, 231 USPQ at 90–91.

109. Hybritech, 231 USPQ at 91; *see also In re* Dow Chemical Co., 837 F.2d 469, 473, 5 USPQ2d 1529, 1532 (Fed. Cir. 1988) ("The PTO presents, in essence, an 'obvious to experiment' standard for obviousness. However, selective hindsight is no more applicable to the design of experiments than it is to the combination of prior art teachings. There must be a reason or suggestion in the art for selecting the procedure used, other than the knowledge learned from the applicant's disclosure [citation omitted]. Of the many scientific publications cited by both Dow and the PTO, none suggests that any process could be used successfully in this three-component system, to produce this product having the desired properties."); *In re* Tomlinson, 363 F.2d 928, 931, 150 USPQ 623, 626 (C.C.P.A. 1966) ("Our reply to this view is simply that it begs the question, which is obviousness under section 103 of compositions and methods, not of the direction to be taken in making efforts or attempts. Slight reflection suggests, we think, that there is usually an element of 'obviousness to try' in any research endeavor, that it is not undertaken with complete blindness but rather with some semblance of a chance of success, and that patentability determinations based on that as the test would not only be contrary to statute but result in a marked deterioration of the entire patent system as an incentive to invest in those efforts and attempts which go by the name of 'research.'").

110. *In re* Vaeck, 947 F.2d 488, 20 USPQ2d 1438 (Fed. Cir. 1991); *see also Ex parte* Kranz 19 USPQ2d 1216 (Bd. Pat. App. 1990) (reversing obviousness rejection for the process of making a targeted cell susceptible to lysis by a cytotoxic T lymphocyte where the art showed no technique necessary to carry out a required attaching step and making new rejection on enablement grounds).

111. Amgen, Inc. v. Chugai Pharmaceutical Co., 927 F.2d 1200, 18 USPQ2d 1016 (Fed. Cir.), *cert. denied*, 112 S. Ct. 119 (1991).

112. The Federal Circuit did not address the issue of whether the claimed genes would have been obvious aside from the alleged obviousness of a method of making them, even though the claims did not recite any process steps. It focused on the obviousness of the process in accordance with what the parties and the district court did at the trial. Amgen, 18 USPQ2d at 1022 note 3.

113. Amgen, 18 USPQ2d at 1023.

114. *Ex parte* Old, 229 USPQ 196 (Bd. Pat. App. 1986) (reversing the Examiner's Section 103 rejection of claims directed to monoclonal antibodies specific to malignant human renal cells since conclusion of "obvious to try" was contrary to the law set forth in *In re* Tomlinson).

115. *Ex parte* Erlich, 3 USPQ2d 1011 (Bd. Pat. App. 1986); *see also Ex parte* Sorg, 22 USPQ2d 1958 (Bd. Pat. App. 1992).

116. *Ex parte* Erlich, 22 USPQ2d 1463 (1992).

117. Erlich, 22 USPQ2d at 1466.

118. Piasecki, 223 USPQ at 788; *In re* Rinehart, 531 F.2d 1048, 1052, 189 USPQ 143, 147 (C.C.P.A. 1976).

119. *See* V. Vossius, *CAFC and EPO Technical Board of Appeal Decisions*, [1992] 11 EUROPEAN INTELLECTUAL PROPERTY REPORTS 412; *see also* R. Crespi, *Inventiveness in Biological Chemistry: an International Perspective*, 73 J. PAT. OFF. SOC'Y 351 (1991).

120. Genentech I/Polypeptide Expression, [1989] 1 EPOR 1.

121. *See* E. Marshall, *The Patent Game: Raising the Ante*, 253 SCIENCE 20 (July 5, 1991) (describing issuance of basic microprocessor patent 20 years after filing).

Special Issues in
Biotechnology Patents

8

Disclosure Requirements

Kenneth D. Sibley

A patent application must meet four deceptively simple disclosure requirements, which are listed in Section 112 of the patent statute. First, the application must contain a written description of the invention;[1] second, it must enable others to make and use the invention;[2] third, it must disclose the "best mode" known for carrying out the invention;[3] and fourth, it must conclude with claims "particularly pointing out and distinctly claiming" the invention.[4] The fourth requirement is technically a claim requirement rather than a disclosure requirement, nevertheless, it and the other three requirements are all contained in Section 112.

The enablement requirement, which relates primarily to the scope of a claim, and the best-mode requirement will be initially examined in the following section. This is followed by a discussion of the deposit requirement—a unique, nonstatutory requirement that arises because, for some biotechnology inventions, a deposit of living biological material may be the only way to satisfy the statutory enablement and best-mode requirements. The written-description requirement is discussed next, followed by a look at the definiteness requirement.

8.1 THE ENABLEMENT REQUIREMENT AND CLAIM SCOPE

Section 112 of the patent statute requires that a patent teach how to make and use the claimed invention. The make and use aspects together form what is known as the enablement requirement. Judicial decisions typically ask whether someone skilled in the art can make and use the claimed invention without "undue experimentation."[5]

Enablement issues are primarily issues of the scope of a claim. The underlying policy concern is that patent claims that are unduly limited in scope fail to promote progress in the art by failing to provide adequate economic incentives to inventors.[6] On the other hand, overly broad patent claims tend to defeat this goal by improperly dominating an area of research and discouraging further invention by others.[7] Indeed, Chief Judge Markey aptly summarized the issue by stating that questions of enablement "orbit around the more fundamental question: To what scope of protection is this applicant's particular contribution to the art entitled?"[8]

8.1.1 The Burden of Proving Enablement in the Patent and Trademark Office

A patent application must satisfy the enablement requirement as of the date that application is filed.[9] However, it is critical to note that when filed, an application need only "objectively" enable[10] the practice of the invention it claims. Enablement does not have to be accomplished in any specific way,[11] and the specification need not convince someone skilled in the art that the application's assertions are true.[12] When the PTO seeks to reject claims as nonenabled, it must state specific reasons for doubting[13] that the claimed invention can be practiced without undue experimentation—a requirement that often can be met by referring to literature that shows the known unpredictability of the particular biotechnology.[14] If a *prima facie* case of nonenablement is established by the PTO, then the burden shifts to the applicant to show that someone skilled in the art can practice the invention from the teaching provided in the specification without undue experimentation.[15] This is typically done by introducing additional evidence, such as experimental data or research papers done by other people. Providing additional evidence shows that specific aspects of the invention that are stated but not shown to be operable in the patent application are, in fact, operable. After the patent issues, those who contend that it does not satisfy the enablement requirement must use facts proven by clear and convincing evidence to show that the requirement has not been met.[16]

8.1.2 Facts Relevant to the Question of Enablement

Since the breadth of claims allowable in a particular case depends largely on the facts in that case, care should be taken when trying to derive general principles of claim breadth from prior cases.[17] Nevertheless, the question of enablement is a question of law. As such, prior cases are useful for guidance on how enablement questions might be decided in a new case. A number of factors relevant to enablement are reviewed in the following sections. All of the factors should be considered before a final decision is reached in any one case.

8.1.2.1 The Predictability of the Technology. Probably the most significant issue in deciding enablement is the predictability of the technology defined by the claims. The significance of this issue was emphasized in *In re Fisher*, where the court explained:

> In cases involving predictable factors . . . a single embodiment provides broad enablement in the sense that, once imagined, other embodiments can be made and their performance characteristics predicted by resort to known scientific laws. In cases involving unpredictable factors . . . the scope of enablement obviously varies inversely with the degree of unpredictability of the factors involved.[18]

In *Fisher*, claims to adrenocorticotrophic hormone preparations having a potency of one International Unit per milligram *or more* were held nonenabled when the specification did not teach how to make preparations having potencies greater than 2.3. The opinion implied that the inventor was not entitled to claims that encompassed compositions having potencies far greater than those disclosed when the inventor provided no suggestion of how such compositions might be made.

It is critical to note that the claim in *Fisher* was open-ended in that it encompassed compositions of a particular potency *or more*, with no upper limit. A similar situation arose in *Amgen Inc. v. Chugai Pharmaceutical Co.*[19] with respect to Claim 7 of Amgen's patent on DNA encoding erythropoietin. This claim read as follows:

> 7. A purified and isolated DNA sequence consisting essentially of a DNA sequence encoding a polypeptide having an amino acid sequence sufficiently duplicative of that of erythropoietin to allow possession of the biological property of causing bone marrow cells to increase production of reticulocytes and red blood cells, and to increase hemoglobin synthesis or iron uptake.

The District Court held the claim to be nonenabled. On appeal, the Federal Circuit affirmed the District Court's decision, commenting as follows:

> [D]espite extensive statements in the specification concerning all the analogs of the EPO gene that can be made, there is little enabling disclosure of particular analogs and how to make them. Details for preparing only a few EPO analog genes are disclosed. Amgen argues that this is sufficient to support its claims; we disagree. This "disclosure" might well justify a generic claim encompassing these and similar analogs, but it represents inadequate support for Amgen's desire to claim all EPO gene analogs.
>
> * * *
>
> [W]e do not intend to imply that generic claims to genetic sequences cannot be valid where they are of a scope appropriate to the invention disclosed by an applicant. That is not the case here, where Amgen has claimed every possible analog of a gene containing about 4,000 nucleotides, with a disclosure only of how to make EPO and a very few analogs.[20]

In *Scripps Clinic & Research Foundation v. Genentech Inc.*,[21] the Federal Circuit suggested (although it did not decide the issue) that open-ended claims are not always improper because the appropriateness of all claims depends on the facts of the specific case. The court commented that open-ended claims "may be supported if there is an inherent, albeit not precisely known, upper limit [in the claims] and the specification enables one of skill in the art to approach that limit."[22]

8.1.2.2   Facts Other Than Predictability: the State of the Art.   The significance of facts other than predictability to the question of enablement was made clear in *In re Angstadt*,[23] in which claims directed to the catalytic oxidation of alkylaromatic hydrocarbons encompassed thousands of potential catalysts, yet the specification disclosed only four examples of such catalysts and the process was found unpredictable. On these facts, the PTO concluded that the enablement requirement had not been met. On appeal, however, the CCPA stated:

> If [our prior decision stands] for the proposition that the disclosure must provide "guidance which will enable one skilled in the art to determine, <u>with reasonable certainty before performing the reaction,</u> whether the claimed product will be obtained . . . then <u>all</u> "experimentation" is "undue," since the term "experimentation" implies that the success of the particular activity is <u>uncertain</u>. Such a proposition is contrary to the basic policy of the patent act. . . .[24]

The court went on to observe that the claimed process was not complicated, that it required no special equipment or conditions to conduct, and that "[i]n this art the performance of trial runs . . . is 'reasonable,' even if the end result is uncertain. The court concluded its analysis as follows:

> We hold that the evidence <u>as a whole</u> . . . negates the PTO position that persons of ordinary skill in <u>this</u> art, <u>given its unpredictability,</u> must engage in <u>undue</u> experimentation to determine which complexes work. The key word is "undue," not "experimentation."[25]

The Federal Circuit elaborated at length on the factors to be considered in determining whether experimentation is "undue" in *In re Wands*.[26] In *Wands*, the PTO rejected as nonenabled an immunoassay method employing monoclonal antibodies where no deposit of hybridomas capable of producing the antibodies had been carried out. Claim 1, the broadest of the claims presented, read as follows:

> 1. An immunoassay method utilizing an antibody to assay for a substance comprising hepatitis B-surface antigen (HBsAg) determinants which comprises the steps of:
>
> contacting a test sample containing said substance comprising HBsAg determinants with said antibody; and
> determining the presence of said substance in said sample;
>
> wherein said antibody is a monoclonal high affinity IgM antibody having a binding affinity constant for said HBsAg determinants of at least 10^9 M^{-1}.

During prosecution of the application, Wands had introduced a Rule 132 declaration presenting evidence on the hybridomas he had produced prior to filing the patent application. The declaration showed that he had carried out four unsuccessful fusions, followed by six successful fusions. From the successful fusions, 143 hybridomas identified as "high-binders" were obtained. From the "high-binder" hybridomas, nine were tested for the production of IgM antibodies having affinities that met the requirements of the claims. Four were found. The position of the PTO was that these data only proved that 4 out of 143 hybridomas (2.8%) produced antibodies required by the claims. The PTO concluded that such a low level of success indicated undue experimentation was required to carry out the invention. On appeal, the Federal Circuit commented:

> Factors to be considered in determining whether a disclosure would require undue experimentation . . . include (1) the quantity of experimentation necessary, (2) the amount of direction or guidance presented, (3) the presence or absence of working examples, (4) the nature of the invention, (5) the state of the prior art, (6) the relative skill of those in the art, (7) the predictability or unpredictability of the art, and (8) the breadth of the claims.[27]

The court observed that Wands' disclosure provided considerable guidance on how to practice the invention, that the disclosure contained working examples, that there was a high level of skill in the art, that the methods needed to practice the invention were well known, and that the nature of monoclonal antibody technology is that it involves screening numerous hybridomas to determine which ones secreted antibodies with the desired characteristics. Based on these facts, the court found that "undue" experimentation was not required to practice the invention and reversed the enablement rejection.

8.1.2.3 The State of the Art After the Application Filing Date.

While it is common to submit additional information (for example, experimental data or subsequent publications) to show that the enablement requirement is satisfied after a patent application is filed, reference to a later *state of the art* cannot be used to support enablement. This would be contrary to the basic rule that the enablement requirement must be satisfied as of the effective filing date of the application. The difference between the two situations is that in the first case, new information is submitted to support the correctness of what the applicant said in the application, while in the second case, new information is submitted in an attempt to complete what the applicant left unsaid in the application.[28]

Likewise, a later state of the art cannot be used to negate enablement. This point was made clear in *In re Hogan*,[29] which involved claims to "a normally solid homopolymer of 4-methyl-1-pentene." In rejecting these claims, the PTO cited references that became available only after the effective filing date of Hogan's application. Among other things, these references showed that normally solid homopolymers of 4-methyl-1-pentene existed in both crystalline and amorphous form, while the application taught only how to make the crystalline form. On appeal, the CCPA held that the use of these references to test the sufficiency of the application's disclosure was erroneous. It reversed the rejections and remanded the case so that enablement could be determined in light of the state of the art existing on the application's filing date.

Hogan does not bar the use of later publications that pertain to the state of the art existing on the filing date of an application. In fact, the court noted numerous circumstances in which the use of such materials has been approved.[30] The difference, said the court, is "between the permissible application of later knowledge about art-related facts existing on the filing date and the impermissible application of later knowledge about later art-related facts . . . which did not exist on the filing date."[31]

The importance of considering *In re Hogan* in the area of biotechnology was underscored by the Federal Circuit in *Hormone Research Foundation Inc. v. Genentech Inc.*,[32] an infringement action in which Hormone Research Foundation sought to enforce its patent for synthetically produced human growth hormone (HGH) against Genentech's technology for the production of recombinant HGH. The district court summarily held Hormone Research Foundation's claims for synthetic HGH nonenabled because, among other things, it viewed Hormone Research Foundation's technique to be incapable of producing HGH in pure form or having the potency of natural HGH.

On appeal, the Federal Circuit observed that the district court had applied *In re Fisher* but had failed to apply *In re Hogan*. The court commented on *Hogan* and *Fisher* as follows:

> In *Fisher* this court set forth the basic considerations respecting enablement and the potential for domination of future developments, describing the effect of predictability factors upon those considerations. We adhere to what was there said concerning the high level of predictability in mechanical or electrical environments and the lower level of predictability expected in chemical reactions and physiological activity. With respect to the erroneous use of a later state of the art in determining enablement, however, we make no distinction between fields of invention.[33]

The Federal Circuit in *Hormone Research Foundation* went on to explain that merely because more pure and more potent forms of HGH might be produced using later-discovered technology, it did not mean that the foundation's patent was invalid for failing to satisfy the enablement requirement. The court accordingly remanded the case to the district court for a complete analysis of all the facts relevant to enablement and a decision based on that analysis.

While a later state of the art may not be used to show that a claim fails to satisfy the enablement requirement, it may be used to show that an accused product or process does not infringe that claim under the reverse doctrine of equivalents. The reverse doctrine of equivalents is discussed with the doctrine of equivalents in general in Chapter 13.

8.1.2.4 Combination Inventions. Historically, when inventions involve the combination of elements, patent applicants are granted greater latitude in describing each element of the combination in generic, open-ended terminology. The decisions emphasize that the invention resides in the combination and not the specific elements *per se*.[34] For example, in *In re Herschler*,[35] the CCPA stated that when the claims are drawn to the use of known compounds in a manner auxiliary to the invention, such as steroids carried through the skin by DMSO (the issue at hand), a functional recitation of those compounds in the claim may be a sufficient description.

The enablement requirement was applied to a combination invention in the biotechnology field by the Federal Circuit in *In re Vaeck*.[36] The invention claimed in *Vaeck* concerned the production of *Bacillus* proteins toxic to swamp-dwelling insects by expressing the proteins in cyanobacteria (blue-green algae). Claim 1, which illustrated the claims on appeal, read as follows:

1. A chimeric gene capable of being expressed in Cyanobacteria cells comprising:

    (a) a DNA fragment comprising a promoter region which is effective for expression of a DNA fragment in a Cyanobacterium; and
    (b) at least one DNA fragment coding for an insecticidally active protein produced by a *Bacillus* strain, or coding for an insecticidally active truncated form of the above protein or coding for a protein having substantial sequence homology to the active protein,

    the DNA fragments being linked so that the gene is expressed.

Note that both the Cyanobacterium and the *Bacillus* protein were broadly recited in Claim 1. Claim 47 was dependent on claim 1 and was directed to two *specific* genera of cyanobacteria but maintained the *generic* description of *Bacillus* proteins. All the claims were rejected by the PTO for failing to satisfy the enablement requirement, among other things.

The Federal Circuit agreed with the PTO that the term *cyanobacteria* was too broad, but disagreed with the PTO that the generic description of *Bacillus* proteins was too broad. The court noted that the cyanobacteria are a diverse and poorly studied group of organisms comprising approximately 150 genera, that heterologous gene expression therein is unpredictable, that only one species of cyanobacteria was disclosed in the working examples of the application, and that only nine genera of cyanobacteria were mentioned in the entire application. On the other hand, with respect to *Bacillus* proteins, the court noted that there was extensive understanding in the prior art of numerous *Bacillus* proteins having toxicity to various insects. Accordingly, the rejection of Claim 1 was affirmed but the rejection of Claim 47 (reciting *Bacillus* proteins in general but limited to two genera of cyanobacteria) was reversed. Note that an obviousness rejection by the PTO in *Vaeck* also was reversed by the Federal Circuit. Thus, while the applicants in *Vaeck* did not receive the broadest claims originally presented, they did receive protection that was both generic in scope and extended considerably beyond the specific experiments they had actually conducted.

8.1.2.5   Enablement Questions in the European Patent Office.   In appropriate cases, the EPO allows generic claims to biological inventions. The primary provisions governing claim scope under the EPC are articles 83 and 84. Article 83 of the EPC states:

The European patent application must disclose the invention in a manner sufficiently clear and complete for it to be carried out by a person skilled in the art.

This section is analogous to the enablement requirement of the U.S. patent statute. Its operation in the context of a biotechnology patent application was explored in detail in the *GENENTECH I/Polypeptide Expression* decision.[37] Claim 1 (as amended for appeal) read as follows:

> 1. A recombinant plasmid suited for transformation of a bacterial host wherein the plasmid comprises a homologous regulon, heterologous DNA, and one or more termination codon(s), the heterologous DNA encoding a desired functional heterologous polypeptide or intermediate therefor which is not degraded by endogenous proteolytic enzymes, said DNA being positioned in proper reading frame with said homologous regulon between said regulon and the termination codon(s), whereby on translation of the transcription product of the heterologous DNA in a suitable bacterium, the resulting expression product is said desired functional polypeptide or intermediate therefor in recoverable form.

This claim contains a number of generic and functional terms, such as *plasmid* and *regulon*. The EPO Examining Division found these terms objectionable under Article 83, among other things noting that they encompassed material that had not yet been made and were likely to encompass complex structures to be developed in the future. The Technical Board of Appeals, however, noted that the use of generic and functional terminology was well established in other technical areas, that the particular choice of "bacteria," "plasmid," and "regulon" was irrelevant to this invention, and that in a case such as this it was only possible to give "fair protection" by using functional terminology in the claims. The board explained its analysis as follows:

> Unless variants of components are also embraced in the claims, which are, now or later on, equally suitable to achieve the same effect in a manner which could not have been envisaged without the invention, the protection provided by the patent would be ineffectual. Thus it is the view of the Board that an invention is sufficiently disclosed <u>if at least one way is clearly indicated enabling the skilled person to carry out the invention</u>. Consequently, any non-availability of some particular variants of a functionally defined component feature of the invention is immaterial to sufficiency as long as there are suitable variants known to the skilled person through the disclosure or common general knowledge, which provide the same effect for the invention. The disclosure need not include specific instructions as to how all possible component variants within the functional definition should be obtained.[38]

The board's comment that it would consider the enablement requirement satisfied for generic terms in the case of a combination invention such as this when "at least one way is clearly indicated enabling" in the specification is noteworthy. If one way is not clearly indicated enabling, a different result would be reached.[39]

8.1.3 Timing the Filing of Applications in Light of the Enablement Requirement: Strategic Considerations

The constraints imposed by the enablement requirement often present a dilemma to a potential patent applicant: should he or she file an application early, risking rejection as unenabled, or should he or she file later, taking the risk that the intervening work of others might make the invention unpatentable? This is a complex question with a number of factors to be considered, some of which are discussed in the following sections. Note that these factors are a mix of concerns driven by the first-to-invent system of the United States, the first-to-file system of other countries, the practical constraints of the "treaty year" allowed for filing foreign counterparts of U.S. applications, and foreign definitions of what constitutes prior art that differ from U.S. law.

First, having the technology published directly by the inventor in the near future may force early filing. In such a case, the best course may be simply to insure that the publication does not speculate on future, distinct inventions (which frequently happens in the discussion section of scientific papers) so those future inventions can be pursued in subsequent applications without being disclosed by the publication. In addition, all the subject matter that might be considered either obvious or anticipated by the pending publication should be included in the application.

Second, if there is a concern that other competitors may publish a paper or file an application relating to the invention, an application can be filed early and optionally supplemented at a later date by submitting a subsequent "continuation-in-part" (CIP) application. A CIP is a "continuing application," an application that was filed during the pendency of the first application by at least one of the same inventors and specifically refers back to the first application to claim priority. If the continuing application adds nothing to (is identical to) the first application, it is called a "continuation" application; if it adds new matter, it is referred to as a continuation-in-part application. Continuing applications are entitled to the benefit of the earlier application filing date for determining what constitutes prior art against the original matter but not against the new matter.[40] If the concern is only that others may file applications first, the first filing can be kept narrow for defensive purposes only. As discussed in Chapter 10 on competitive research, to show first-to-invent, the priority of only a single species within a generic claim need be established. If, however, the concern is that others may publish articles first, it may be necessary to file the application with more generic disclosure so that the article will not count as prior art against the new matter added to the CIP application.

Third, when possible, care should be taken to consider the adverse effect an enablement rejection in a first application might have on a subsequent CIP application. If an enablement rejection is issued in the first case and a CIP application is then filed, it might be held that the CIP application is not entitled to the benefit of the original application filing date. The applicant may be said to have "acquiesced" in the enablement rejection.[41] If the CIP application does not get the benefit of the earlier filing date, then new "prior" art intervening between the first application and the CIP application might render the CIP application unpatentable. A solution is to introduce the new information in the form of a declaration or affidavit in the first case or a continuation case, rather than adding it in a CIP application.

If the applicant chooses to file multiple, closely related applications in the United States, it is important to consider the fact that the earlier-filed applications become prior art against the later-filed applications once the earlier applications are issued under Section 102(e).[42] This may necessitate combining closely related applications into one CIP claiming the benefit of both early application filing dates. If the patent office then issues a restriction requirement dictating that the different claims be pursued in separate "divisional" applications (a third type of continuing application), the applications that issue first are then prevented by statute from becoming 102(e) prior art against the applications that issue later.[43]

All of the procedural devices employed should be considered in light of the time limit for filing foreign applications. As discussed in Chapter 12, this usually means that the applicant has one year from the first filing to place the application in the proper form for foreign filing if the benefit of the early filing date is to be preserved for the foreign filings. Preserving the benefit of this filing date would be essential, for example, if the invention were described in a public talk or paper after the filing date.

Finally, the effect of the publication of the foreign application (typically 18 months from the *priority* date) as prior art in foreign countries against subsequent applications should be considered. This is discussed in Chapter 10, section 4, under "Priority Under the First-to-File System."

8.2   THE BEST-MODE REQUIREMENT

The U.S. patent statute, unlike the patent laws of most other countries and jurisdictions, requires patent applicants to disclose the "best mode" known for carrying out the invention at the time a patent application is filed. The policy behind this requirement was summarized by the Federal Circuit as follows:

> The best mode requirement thus is intended to ensure that a patent applicant plays "fair and square" with the patent system. It is a requirement that the *quid pro quo* of the patent grant be satisfied. One must not receive the right to exclude others unless at the time of filing he has provided an adequate disclosure of the best mode known to him of carrying out his invention. Our case law has interpreted the best mode requirement to mean that there must be no concealment of a mode known by the inventor to be better than that which is disclosed.[44]

The best-mode requirement is clearly distinct from the enablement requirement. It is entirely possible for someone to disclose a claimed invention in sufficient detail to enable others to carry out the invention, including numerous variations encompassed by a generic claim, yet withhold some trick or special feature that enables the invention to be carried out most successfully. Such concealment would cause a patent to be held invalid for failure to satisfy the best-mode requirement, even if the enablement requirement were satisfied.

The steps involved in determining whether the best-mode requirement has been satisfied were explored at length by the Federal Circuit in *Chemcast Corp. v. Arco Industries Corp.*[45] The court summarized these steps as follows:

> In short, a proper best mode analysis has two components. The first is whether, at the time the inventor filed his patent application, he knew of a mode of practicing his claimed invention that he considered to be better than any other. This part of the inquiry

is wholly subjective, and resolves whether the inventor must disclose any facts in addition to those sufficient for enablement. If the inventor in fact contemplated such a preferred mode, the second part of the analysis compares what he knew with what he disclosed—is the disclosure adequate to enable one skilled in the art to practice the best mode or, in other words, has the inventor "concealed" his preferred mode from the "public"?

Whether the best mode was satisfied in Amgen's patent for DNA encoding erythropoietin (EPO) was hotly contested in *Amgen Inc. v. Chugai Pharmaceutical Co.*[46] On appeal, defendants Chugai and Genetics Institute argued that the district court erred in holding that the inventor, Lin, had satisfactorily disclosed the best mammalian host cells known to him for producing EPO at the time his application was filed. The district court found that Lin knew a particular strain of Chinese Hamster Ovary (CHO) cell produced EPO at greater rates than other cells and disclosed this fact in Example 10 of his application. The district court also noted that Lin had not deposited the preferred CHO strain in a public depository, but concluded that a deposit of the preferred CHO cells was not necessary.

The Federal Circuit agreed with the conclusion reached by the district court. The court noted that Lin testified that "the isolation of the preferred strain was a 'routine limited dilution cloning procedure' well-known in the art," and that the defendant's own expert, Dr. Simonsen, testified that "I have no doubt that someone eventually could reproduce—well, could generate cell lines [*sic*, strains] making some level of EPO, and they could be better, they could be worse in terms of EPO production." In response to arguments that the best mode could not be duplicated exactly, the court emphasized that "[w]hat is required is an adequate disclosure of the best mode, not a guarantee that every aspect of the specification be precisely and universally reproducible."

The relation of the best-mode requirement to the claims is also illustrated in *Amgen*. Since the best-mode argument related to the disclosure of CHO cells, only those claims that were directed to a host cell were potentially affected. Other claims, such as those reciting isolated DNA or vectors, would not have been affected without a showing of inequitable conduct.[47]

Care should be taken in deducing general rules from *Amgen* because the decision clearly was close. It is easy to imagine facts (such as the withholding of a uniquely useful in-house host strain) that could lead to a different conclusion.[48]

8.3 THE DEPOSIT REQUIREMENT

The deposit requirement[49] evolved in the area of microbiology, since patent applications related to the uses and products of newly discovered micro-organisms often were rejected for failing to satisfy the enablement requirement (the micro-organisms themselves were not patentable subject matter at the time). An example is *Ex parte Kropp*,[50] in which claims to a method of producing an antibiotic with a newly discovered organism that was not considered readily available were held unpatentable. It was found that reproducing the invention would require "the initiation of a screening program similar to the screening programs followed in discovering antibiotics in the first instance" and that such a program had no assurance of ultimate success. The central issue of whether a deposit of biological materials should be required is stated in the PTO deposit regulations as follows:

> Biological material need not be deposited unless access to such material is necessary for the satisfaction of the statutory requirements for patentability under 35 U.S.C. 112. . . . Biological material need not be deposited, inter alia, if it is known and readily available to the public or can be made or isolated without undue experimentation.[51]

Thus, it is clear that deposits need not be carried out for every invention involving biological material. For example, claims to Chaim Weizmann's process of producing acetone with what is now known as *Clostridium acetobutylicum* were held enabled by the patent's written specification, even though there was no deposit of the bacteria. The court found that the procedure described for obtaining the bacteria was "unfailingly" operable in the hands of those who wished to succeed.[52] Another example, where the invention involved a process rather than new bacteria, is *Tabuchi v. Nubel*.[53] In this particular case, claims to a method of producing citric acid with a yeast selected from the genus *Candida* were held enabled where the only "experimentation" required was the selection of strains specifically mentioned in the application and screening them for efficacy in a "simple and straightforward" procedure. Still another example is *Merck & Co. v. Chase Chemical Co.*,[54] in which claims to vitamin B_{12} as a compound *per se*, along with claims for a process of producing this compound with a fungi selected from three different fungal classes, were held enabled because the patent listed a number of tests by which a microbiologist could select an organism capable of producing the vitamin.

Of course, there also are many cases that illustrate the need for a deposit. An example is *Ex parte Forman*,[55] in which claims to a genetic-hybrid, living, attenuated vaccine not limited to a specific deposit were held unenabled where there was "a lack of guidance leading to predictability" in determining which strains produced by genetic engineering procedures would be useful. A deposit may be necessary not only for enablement concerns, but because otherwise it might be difficult to provide an adequate written description of the deposited material.[56] Note that impermissible "new matter" may not be added to an application to incorporate a more complete written description of biological material referred to by a deposit in the specification.[57] Finally, it is important to carefully consider whether a deposit is required to satisfy the best-mode requirement in addition to the enablement requirement.

8.3.1 Deposit Procedures in the United States
As noted, the question of whether to deposit biological material varies considerably from case to case. If the deposit is made, the procedures for carrying out the deposit (at least for U.S. patent applications) have become straightforward. Regulations

governing the deposit of biological material in the United States have been in effect since January 1, 1990.[58] However, the situation is much more complex in many countries and jurisdictions outside the United States. Since securing patent protection outside the United States is often very important for biotechnology inventions, the procedures governing the deposit requirement in the European Patent Office are addressed separately in the following section.

Evolution of the current U.S. deposit regulations took place over a number of years. Before 1970, the PTO allowed applicants to deposit material in a public depository before filing a patent application so that the material would be publicly available as of the filing date of the patent application.[59] The requirement that the material be *publicly* available as of the filing date, which was inconsistent with the general rule that U.S. patent applications are confidential until they are issued, was addressed in *In re Argoudelis.*[60] In this, the CCPA held that a patent applicant could restrict access to the deposited material until a patent on that application actually issued. In 1975, the CCPA indicated in *Feldman v. Aunstrup*[61] that a deposit of biological material in a foreign depository (in *Feldman*, the Central Bureau for Mould Cultures in Baarn, Netherlands) was sufficient to satisfy Section 112 when it was clear that the material: (1) was available to the PTO during examination of the patent, and (2) would be available to the public when the patent issued. Finally, in 1985 the Federal Circuit indicated in *In re Lundak*[62] that a deposit need not even be carried out before filing the application and that the addition of reference to a deposit of the material described in the specification after the application is filed is not an impermissible addition of "new matter." In practice, when a reference to a deposit is added after the filing date, all that may be required is an affidavit establishing a chain of custody showing that the material deposited is the same material referred to in the application at the time of filing. Hence, in the United States there is considerable flexibility in how the deposit requirement can be met.

8.3.2   Deposit Procedures in the European Patent Office

Deposit procedures under the European Patent Convention (EPC) are much different from the United States deposit procedures. The general rule is set forth in Rule 28(1) of the EPC, which states that:

> If an invention concerns a microbiological process or the product thereof and involves the use of a micro-organism which is not available to the public and which cannot be described in the European patent application in such a manner as to enable the invention to be carried out by a person skilled in the art, the invention shall only be regarded as being disclosed [if an appropriate deposit has been completed].

The primary difference between the U.S. and the EPO deposit requirements is that for an EPO application, Rule 28 goes on to say that the deposit must be made in compliance with the Budapest Treaty by the date of filing the priority application (*e.g.,* the original U.S. application).[63] In contrast, if only a U.S. patent is desired, then the deposit of biological materials usually can be carried out after the application is filed.

Another important difference between U.S. and EPO practices is the availability of deposited biological material after the application is filed. Rule 28(3) under the EPC states in part that:

> The deposited culture shall be available upon request to any person from the date of publication of the European patent application. . . .

This is significantly different from U.S. practice, in which the applicant can withhold availability of the deposited material until a patent is issued.

Those who object to their deposited material being made freely available can reduce (but not eliminate) access by using the "expert solution" set forth in Rule 28(4). This rule provides that:

> Until the date on which the technical preparations for publication of the application are deemed to have been completed, the applicant may inform the European Patent Office that, <u>until the publication of the mention of the grant of the European patent or until the date on which the application has been refused or withdrawn or is deemed to be withdrawn</u>, the availability referred to in paragraph 3 shall be effected only by the issue of a sample to an expert nominated by the requester.

The "expert solution" limits access after publication, while the application is pending, to an approved expert only. Once the application is granted, refused, or withdrawn, the material becomes freely accessible. If only a U.S. patent application is filed and the application is rejected, the deposited biological material need never become publicly available.

8.4 THE WRITTEN-DESCRIPTION REQUIREMENT

In addition to providing an "enabling" disclosure of the invention, a patent application also must contain a "written description" of the invention. It may seem that there is little difference between these two requirements; in fact, some would argue that there should be no written description requirement separate from the enablement requirement.[64] However, the requirement is in fact well-founded and well established in patent law.[65]

The need for the written description requirement stems from the fact that science progresses after patent applications are filed. Although applicants try to anticipate and describe alternate forms of their basic invention when they file applications, sometimes the product or process that will become important is quite different from what was described in the application. Still, applicants always want to obtain claims that narrowly cover the commercially important aspects of their inventions because such claims are easier to enforce in court. It is possible to supplement an original application with new information as a "continuation-in-part" (CIP) application, but the new information is considered "new matter" and does *not* get the benefit of the filing date of the first application. If prior art or the patent applications of others *intervene* between the filing date of the first application and the filing date of the CIP application, the question of whether there is a "written description" in the *first* application of the invention now being claimed in the CIP application can become critical. The Federal Circuit recently summarized the written description requirement and how it relates to the invention being defined by the claims:

> The purpose of the "written description" requirement is broader than to merely explain how to "make and use"; the applicant must also convey with reasonable clarity to those skilled in the art that, as of the filing date sought, he or she was in possession of the invention. The invention is, for purposes of the "written description" inquiry, whatever is now claimed.[66]

In contrast to the enablement requirement (which is a question of law), the written-description requirement is a question of fact.[67]

Whether the written description requirement was satisfied was disputed in *Staehelin v. Secher*,[68] an interference proceeding in which the interfering subject matter was defined by the court as:

> A monoclonal antibody produced by a murine derived hybrid cell line wherein the antibody is capable of specifically binding to at least one antigenic determinant of interferon-α.

Secher's U.S. application was based on an earlier British application that corresponded exactly to an article on the invention appearing in *Nature*. This was a risky maneuver, since articles in refereed journals are written to serve a completely different purpose than patent applications and often do not contain a *generic* written description necessary to support *generic* claims. In this case, however, the board decided in favor of Secher. In noting that the priority application need not contain an *identical* recitation of what was claimed, the board provided the following explanation of the written description requirement:

> The function of the "written description" requirement of 35 USC 112, first paragraph, is to ensure that applicants had possession, as of the filing date of the application relied on, of the subject matter later claimed by them. The inquiry into satisfaction of the written description requirement is factual and depends on the nature of the invention and the amount of knowledge imparted to those skilled in the art by the disclosure. Satisfaction of the "written description" requirement does not require in haec verba antecedence in the originally filed application. The question is whether one following applicant's specification would necessarily select the later claimed subject matter. The question, therefore, is whether the originally filed application would have reasonably conveyed to a person of ordinary skill in the art that applicants invented the subject matter later claimed by them including the limitations in question.[69]

The Federal Circuit addressed what is required for a written description of a cloned gene in *Fiers v. Revel*,[70] a three-party interference in which the count defining the interfering subject matter was as follows:

> A DNA which consists essentially of a DNA which codes for a human fibroblast inter-feron-beta polypeptide.

Priority was awarded to Sugano by the PTO. One of the parties, Revel, argued that the PTO had improperly denied him of entitlement to the benefit of his earlier-filed Israeli patent application filing date. The board had held that Revel's Israeli application did not contain an adequate written description of a DNA coding for ß-IF because it did not describe the nucleotide sequence of a gene. Revel argued that because his Israeli application disclosed a method for isolating a fragment of the DNA coding for ß-IF and the language of the count referred to DNA generally rather than a specific sequence, only similar language need be included in the application.

The Federal Circuit disagreed with Revel, stating:

> An adequate written description of a DNA requires more than a mere statement that it is part of the invention and reference to a potential method for isolating it; what is required is a description of the DNA itself. Revel's specification does not do that.
>
> *   *   *
>
> As we stated in *Amgen* and reaffirmed above, such a disclosure just represents a wish, or arguably a plan, for obtaining the DNA. If a conception of a DNA requires a precise definition, such as by structure, formula, chemical name, or physical properties, as we have held, then a description also requires that degree of specificity. To paraphrase the Board, one cannot describe what one has not conceived.[71]

8.5   THE CLAIM DEFINITENESS REQUIREMENT

Section 112 of the patent statute includes, as its second paragraph, the following provision:

> The specification shall conclude with one or more claims particularly pointing out and distinctly claiming the subject matter which the applicant regards as his invention.[72]

Previously, this requirement had been combined with the enablement requirement now set forth in the first paragraph of Section 112 and previously discussed in this chapter. This led to considerable confusion and commingling of the requirements, and to the creation of a distinct paragraph concerning claims definiteness when the current patent statute was enacted in 1952.[73]

The purpose of the claim definiteness requirement is to make it possible for others to avoid infringing the patent, whether by keeping far outside the scope of the claims or by deliberately designing around the claims. The problem with indefinite claims, as explained by the Supreme Court in *United Carbon Co. v. Binney & Smith Co.*, is that a "zone of uncertainty which enterprise and experimentation may enter only at the risk of infringement [of] claims would discourage invention only a little less than unequivocal foreclosure of the field."[74] Of course, the limitation on claim scope posed by the claim definiteness requirement is frequently at odds with the expansion on claim scope provided by the doctrine of equivalents (discussed in Chapter 13). Complicating matters is the fact that, as Professor Chisum pointed out, judicial attitudes on which of these two concerns should predominate fluctuate over time.[75]

An instructive recent case is *Amgen, Inc. v. Chugai Pharmaceutical Co.*,[76] in which the Federal Circuit held claims 4 and 6 of Genetics Institute's patent on purified EPO invalid as indefinite. Claim 4 read as follows:

> 4. Homogeneous erythropoietin characterized by a molecular weight of about 34,000 daltons on SDS PAGE, movement as a single peak on reverse phase high performance liquid chromatography and a specific activity of at least about 160,000 IU per absorbance unit at 280 nanometers.

The standard of indefiniteness, the court noted, involved "a determination whether those skilled in the art would understand what is claimed." In this case, the problematic phrase was "at least about 160,000 IU." The court noted that this claim, as filed, included the phrase "at least 120,000 IU." A reference showing an EPO product with an activity of 128,620 IU had been used to reject this claim as anticipated during prosecution, and this rejection was overcome only when the claims were amended to recite "at least about 160,000." The word *about* seemed to the court to be an attempt to recapture some of what had been given up by the amendment without clearly specifying what the boundary was between infringement and noninfringement. Hence, the court concluded that "[w]hen the meaning of claims is in doubt, especially when, as is the case here, there is close prior art, they are properly declared invalid."[77] The court went on to caution that use of the word *about* in claims was not necessarily improper in other situations.

Biological inventions are sometimes less amenable to precise definition than other chemical inventions. If the claims necessarily involve elements that cannot be described with extremely rigorous precision, then it is sometimes said that the claims need only be as precise "as the subject matter permits."[78] Nevertheless, in light of the claims held invalid in *Amgen*, terms used in claims should be defined as precisely as possible.

REFERENCES

1. *See generally* Walterscheid, *Insufficient Disclosure Rejections (Part III)*, 62 J. PAT. & TRADEMARK OFF. SOC'Y 261 (1980).
2. *See generally* Walterscheid, *Insufficient Disclosure Rejections (Part V)*, 62 J. PAT. & TRADEMARK OFF. SOC'Y 387 (1980).

3. *See generally* Walterscheid, *Insufficient Disclosure Rejections (Part VI-Conclusion)*, 62 J. PAT. & TRADEMARK OFF. SOC'Y 546 (1980).
4. 35 U.S.C. § 112, second paragraph.
5. *See, e.g., In re* Metcalfe, 410 F.2d 1379, 1382, 161 USPQ 789, 792 (C.C.P.A. 1969).
6. *See In re* Hogan, 559 F.2d 595, 606, 194 USPQ 527, 537 (C.C.P.A. 1977).
7. *See, e.g.*, Franc-Strohmenger & Cowan, Inc. v. Arthur Siegman, Inc., 27 F.2d 785, 787 (2d. Cir. 1928) ("To allow this . . . would extend the patent [rights] beyond the discovery, and would discourage rather than promote invention.").
8. *In re* Hogan, 559 F.2d 595, 605–606, 194 USPQ 527, 537 (C.C.P.A. 1977).
9. *In re* Eynde, 480 F.2d 1364, 1370, 178 USPQ 470, 474 (C.C.P.A. 1973).
10. *In re* Vaeck, 947 F.2d 488, 20 USPQ2d 1438, 1445 note 23 (Fed. Cir. 1991).
11. *In re* Robins, 429 F.2d 452, 456, 166 USPQ 552, 555 (C.C.P.A. 1970).
12. *In re* Armbruster, 512 F.2d 676, 678, 185 USPQ 152, 153 (C.C.P.A. 1974); *see also* Staehelin v. Secher, 24 USPQ2d 1513, 1516 (Bd. Pat. App. 1992).
13. *In re* Bowen, 492 F.2d 859, 862, 181 USPQ 48, 51 (C.C.P.A. 1974).
14. *See, e.g., Ex parte* Humphreys, 24 USPQ2d 1255 (Bd. Pat. App. 1992).
15. *See In re* Strahilevitz, 668 F.2d 1229, 1232, 212 USPQ 561, 563 (C.C.P.A. 1982).
16. *See, e.g.*, Atlas Powder Co. v. E.I. DuPont de Nemours & Co., 750 F.2d 1569, 1577, 224 USPQ 409, 414 (Fed. Cir. 1984).
17. *See generally* Sibley, *Factual Inquiries in Deciding the Question of Enablement*, 70 J. PAT. & TRADEMARK OFF. SOC'Y 115 (1988).
18. *In re* Fisher, 427 F.2d 833, 839, 166 USPQ 18, 24 (C.C.P.A. 1974).
19. Amgen Inc. v. Chugai Pharmaceutical Co., 927 F.2d 1200, 18 USPQ2d 1016 (Fed. Cir. 1991), *cert. denied*, 112 S. Ct. 169 (1991).
20. Amgen, 18 USPQ2d at 1027.
21. Scripps Clinic & Research Foundation v. Genentech, Inc., 18 USPQ2d 1001 (Fed. Cir. 1991).
22. Scripps, 18 USPQ2d at 1006.
23. *In re* Angstadt, 537 F.2d 498, 190 USPQ 214 (C.C.P.A. 1976).
24. Angstadt, 537 F.2d at 503, 190 USPQ at 219.
25. Angstadt, 537 F.2d at 504, 190 USPQ at 219 (emphasis added and in original).
26. *In re* Wands, 858 F.2d 731, 8 USPQ2d 1400 (Fed. Cir. 1988).
27. Wands, 8 USPQ2d at 1404.
28. *See, e.g., Ex parte* Humphreys, 24 USPQ2d 1261 note 6, 1262 note 1 (Bd. Pat. App. 1992) (suggesting but not holding that the C.C.P.A. decision in *In re* Glass indicates subsequently published references cannot be used to support enablement); *but see In re* Hogan, 559 F.2d 595, 604, 194 USPQ 527 (C.C.P.A. 1977) (explaining when *In re* Glass is and is not applicable).
29. *In re* Hogan, 559 F.2d 595, 194 USPQ 527 (C.C.P.A. 1977).
30. Hogan, 559 F.2d at 605 note 17, 194 USPQ at 537 note 17.
31. Hogan, 559 F.2d at 605.
32. Hormone Research Foundation Inc. v. Genentech Inc., 904 F.2d 1558, 15 USPQ2d 1038 (Fed. Cir. 1990).
33. Hormone Research Foundation, 15 USPQ2d at 1048 (quoting *In re* Hogan).
34. *See In re* Anderson, 471 F.2d 1237, 176 USPQ 331 (C.C.P.A. 1973); *In re* Fuetterer, 319 F.2d 259, 138 USPQ 217 (C.C.P.A. 1963).
35. *In re* Herschler, 591 F.2d 693, 200 USPQ 711 (C.C.P.A. 1979).
36. *In re* Vaeck, 947 F.2d 488, 20 USPQ2d 1438 (Fed. Cir. 1991).
37. Genentech I/Polypeptide Expression [1989] 1 European Patent Office Reports 1.

38. Genentech I, [1989] 1 EPOR at 8 (emphasis added).
39. *See, e.g.*, Harvard/Fusion Proteins, [1992] EPOR 320, 328.
40. 35 U.S.C. § 120.
41. *See, e.g.*, Paperless Accounting, Inc. v. Bay Area Rapid Transit System, 804 F.2d 659, 662–65, 231 USPQ 649 (Fed. Cir. 1986) (discussing circumstances when a conclusion of acquiescence is appropriate).
42. *See* 35 U.S.C. § 102(e).
43. *See* 35 U.S.C. § 121.
44. Amgen Inc. v. Chugai Pharmaceutical Co., 927 F.2d 1200, 18 USPQ2d 1016, 1024 (Fed. Cir. 1991), *cert. denied*, 112 S. Ct. 169 (1991).
45. Chemcast Corp. v. Arco Industries Corp., 913 F.2d 923, 927, 16 USPQ2d 1033, 1036 (Fed. Cir. 1990).
46. Amgen Inc. v. Chugai Pharmaceutical Co., 927 F.2d 1200, 18 USPQ2d 1016 (Fed. Cir. 1991), *cert. denied*, 112 S. Ct. 169 (1991).
47. Amgen, 18 USPQ2d at 1023 note 5.
48. *See* Interview with Lawrence Tribe on Supreme Court Review of Amgen Inc. v. Chugai Pharmaceutical Co., PAT. TRADEMARK AND COPYRIGHT J. (BNA), vol. 42 at 466 (Sept. 12, 1991).
49. *See generally* Hampar, *Patenting of Recombinant DNA Technology: The Deposit Requirement*, 67 J. PAT. & TRADEMARK OFF. SOC'Y 569 (1985); Comment, *Microorganisms and the Patent Office: To Deposit or Not to Deposit, That Is the Question*, 52 FORDHAM L. REV. 592 (1984); Meyer, *Problems and Issues in Depositing Microorganisms for Patent Purposes*, 65 J. PAT. & TRADEMARK OFF. SOC'Y 455 (1983).
50. *Ex parte* Kropp, 143 USPQ 148 (Bd. Pat. App. 1959).
51. 37 C.F.R. § 1.802(b) (1991).
52. *See* Guaranty Trust Co. v. Union Solvents Corp., 54 F.2d 400, 403–06, 12 USPQ 47, 50–53, *aff'd*, 61 F.2d 1041, 15 USPQ 237 (3d Cir. 1932), *cert. denied*, 288 U.S. 614 (1933).
53. Tabuchi v. Nubel, 559 F.2d 1183, 1186–87, 194 USPQ 521, 525 (C.C.P.A. 1977).
54. Merck & Co. v. Chase Chemical Co., 273 F. Supp. 68, 77, 155 USPQ 139, 146 (D.N.J. 1967).
55. *Ex parte* Forman, 230 USPQ 546, 547–48 (Bd. Pat. App. 1986); *see also Ex parte* Humphries, 24 USPQ2d 1255 (Bd. Pat. App. 1992).
56. Cf. *In re* Jackson, 217 USPQ 804 (Bd. Pat. App. 1982).
57. *See Ex parte* Solomon, 201 USPQ 42 (Bd. Pat. App. 1978).
58. *See* 37 C.F.R. §§ 1.801–1.809 (1991).
59. *See, e.g.*, *In re* Interference A v. B. v. C., 159 USPQ 538 (Comm'r Pats. 1967).
60. *In re* Argoudelis, 434 F.2d 1390, 168 USPQ 99 (C.C.P.A. 1970).
61. Feldman v. Aunstrup, 517 F.2d 1351, 186 USPQ 108 (C.C.P.A. 1975), *cert. denied*, 424 U.S. 912 (1976).
62. *In re* Lundak, 773 F.2d 1216, 227 USPQ 90 (Fed. Cir. 1985).
63. *See generally* Keller, *European Patent Office Practice: Some Aspects of Interest for U.S. Applicants*, 71 J. PAT. & TRADEMARK OFF. SOC'Y 912 (1989).
64. K. Rhoades, *The Section 112 "Description Requirement"–A Misbegotten Provision Confirmed*, 74 J. PAT. & TRADEMARK OFF. SOC'Y 869 (1992) (including a detailed review of written description cases).
65. *See In re* Wilder, 736 F.2d 1516, 222 USPQ 369 (Fed. Cir. 1984).
66. Vas-Cath, Inc. v. Mahurkar, 935 F.2d 1555, 1563, 19 USPQ2d 1111, 1117 (Fed. Cir. 1991).

67. Wilder, 746 F.2d at 1520 (citing *In re* Wertheim, 541 F.2d 257, 262, 191 USPQ 90, 96 [C.C.P.A. 19760]).
68. Staehelin v. Secher, 24 USPQ2d 1513, 1519 note 6 (Bd. Pat. App. 1992).
69. Staehelin, 24 USPQ2d at 1519 (citations omitted; emphasis added and in original).
70. Fiers v. Revel, 984 F.2d 1164, 25USPQ2d 1601 (Fed. Cir. 1992).
71. Fiers, 984 F.2d at 1171.
72. 35 U.S.C. § 112.
73. P. Federico, Commentary on the New Patent Act, 75 J. PAT. & TRADEMARK OFF. SOC'Y 161 (1993).
74. United Carbon Co. v. Binney & Smith Co., 317 U.S. 228, 63 S. Ct. 165, 55 USPQ 381, 385 (1942).
75. 2 D. Chisum, PATENTS, § 8.02[3] (1992).
76. Amgen, Inc. v. Chugai Pharmaceutical Co., 927 F.2d 1200, 18 USPQ2d 1016, 1030–31 (Fed. Cir.), *cert. denied*, 112 S. Ct. 169 (1991).
77. Amgen, 18 USPQ2d at 1031.
78. Hybritech, Inc. v. Monoclonal Antibodies, Inc., 802 F.2d 1367, 1385, 231 USPQ 81 (Fed. Cir. 1986), *cert. denied*, 480 U.S. 947 (1987).

9

Collaborative Research

Kenneth D. Sibley

Very few inventions arise from a single researcher working in isolation. Most inventions, particularly in complex and expensive areas of research, involve at least some type of collaboration or interchange among people. The collaborative nature of research raises questions of who the inventors are for a particular invention and, sometimes, what prior art is applied when deciding whether the invention is nonobvious. Issues such as these, which typically arise in the context of collaborative research, are discussed in this chapter.

9.1 INVENTORSHIP ISSUES IN COLLABORATIVE RESEARCH

The requirement that patent applications be made in the name of the true, or "original," inventor is fundamental in U.S. patent law.[1] This requirement also is found in most first-to-file countries[2] and would, in all likelihood, be maintained in the United States even if a first-to-file priority system were adopted.[3]

Currently, the original inventor requirement is most notably enforced by Section 102(f) of the patent statute, which states:

A person shall be entitled to a patent unless . . .

(f) he did not himself invent the subject matter sought to be patented. . . .[4]

The requirement is not only that the correct person be named when the invention is by a sole inventor, but that the correct group of inventors be named when the invention is made by joint inventors. This follows from Section 116 of the patent statute, which states that:

> When an invention is made by two or more persons jointly, they shall apply for patent jointly and each make the required oath. . . .[5]

When inventions are the product of collaborative research, the question becomes who among the collaborative team is the inventor. The issue is a constant source of confusion and has generated considerable legal commentary.[6] It can present serious problems for the patent owner who may ultimately seek to enforce the patent. As the following discussion will show, inventorship determinations should be made carefully, based on an understanding of the potential ramifications if the intellectual property that develops from a collaborative research project is to receive thorough and effective patent protection.

9.1.1   Identifying the Inventors

A number of general rules of inventorship have been stated. Unfortunately, these rules seldom can be universally applied and easily can lead to error. Indeed, one district court judge has referred to the law of inventorship as "one of the muddiest concepts in the muddy metaphysics of patent law."[7] As will be seen in the following sections, however, the general rules can be helpful in explaining who is *not* automatically an inventor. Generally, inventors are considered to be those who contribute to or participate in the conception of the invention as claimed. The language of the patent claims plays a central role in determining who the inventors are.

9.1.1.1   One Who Suggests a Desired Goal Is Not Necessarily an Inventor.
Numerous legal decisions state that a person who merely suggests a desired goal is not an inventor just because the suggestion helps achieve the final goal.[8] The consequences of this rule and the complexity of its application in the area of biotechnology are illustrated by the litigation between Amgen and Genetics Institute over recombinant erythropoietin.

Amgen obtained an issued U.S. patent on isolated DNA encoding human erythropoietin (EPO), naming Lin as the sole inventor.[9] After Amgen's patent was filed but before it was issued, Genetics Institute (GI) filed a patent application that also was directed to isolated DNA encoding human EPO. GI's patent named Fritsch, Hewick, and Jacobs as the inventors. An interference was declared in the PTO, with GI as the junior party (placing the burden of proof on GI). Eventually, it was admitted that Amgen was the first to reduce the invention to practice. To prevail, GI had to show that it was the first to conceive of the invention and was diligent in its subsequent reduction to practice.[10]

Because of the inventors named on its application, this placed GI in a difficult position. Fritsch had contributed the overall strategy of isolating the gene by using two sets of fully degenerate probes to screen a genomic DNA library. His contribution to the claimed invention was much more than simply stating that the EPO gene should be isolated (in which case he might not have been an inventor at all). Indeed, this strategy ultimately led to the successful isolation of the gene and its reduction to practice. Moreover, Fritsch arguably made this contribution early enough to establish first conception. Hewick's contribution was to provide EPO amino-acid sequence information used by Fritsch to design degenerate probes, and Jacobs' contribution was in the procedures used to screen the genomic library.[11] The contributions of Hewick and Jacobs, however, were made at a later date; so, if their contributions were necessary to establish a complete conception, GI could not show first conception through Fritsch alone. Yet, Hewick and Jacobs had been named as inventors on the application by GI, indicating that they had contributed to the conception of the invention.

In an effort to overcome this problem, GI did two things: first, it argued that Fritsch's conception of isolated EPO DNA was complete; second, it sought to correct inventorship on the application by removing Hewick and Jacobs as inventors. The efforts were useless. With respect to the completeness of Fritsch's conception, the PTO noted that the Federal Circuit had already decided that for this case and at this time (1981 to 1983), conception could only occur simultaneously with reduction to practice.[12] Denial of GI's motion to correct inventorship followed from the decision on the lack of completeness of Fritsch's alleged conception.[13]

What would the outcome have been for GI if it had named Fritsch as the sole inventor when its application was filed, eliminating the need to correct inventorship to make its application consistent with its arguments on conception? This is not to say that such a minor change in the facts alone would have led to a different result. When GI argued prior conception in the infringement suit brought against it by Amgen on this patent in an effort to establish it as anticipatory prior art, its arguments were rejected.[14] Nevertheless, to fully appreciate how reasonable GI's arguments were, it is important to consider the outcome between GI and Amgen in an interference over a separate, related invention: producing recombinant human interferon in mammalian host cells capable of effecting glycosylation of those cells. This case is discussed in the following section.

9.1.1.2   Someone Who Merely Carries Out the Reduction to Practice Is Not Necessarily an Inventor.   Another often-stated general rule is that someone who merely works at the direction of another to reduce the invention to practice is not an inventor.[15] The litigation between Amgen and Genetics Institute (GI) over recombinant erythropoietin (EPO) again provides an illustration. Once again, the key question is which member of the collaborative team contributed to the conception of the invention as claimed.

Both GI and Amgen filed applications directed to methods of making recombinant human EPO in mammalian host cells capable of effecting post-translational glycosylation of the EPO. The Amgen application was in the name of Lin alone; the GI application was in the name of Fritsch, Hewick, and Jacobs. An interference was declared (this being a different interference from the interference over the isolation of the EPO gene itself).[16] In response to GI's argument that Lin was not the original inventor, the PTO noted:

> The record indicates that all the work at Amgen relating to expression of the EPO gene in mammalian host cells was directed and supervised by Dr. Browne, assisted by Ralph Smalling. Dr. Lin does not recall giving any instructions or suggestions as to how such expression should be carried out. The effort to isolate the EPO glycoprotein expression product was carried out by Dr. Strickland, and Dr. Lin gave no specific instructions for accomplishing that task. However, the expression of the EPO gene in mammalian host cells using the DNA sequence isolated by Dr. Lin was carried out at Lin's request and on his behalf.[17]

Lin, on the other hand, argued that "it is not essential for the inventor to be personally involved in carrying out process steps defined by the count where implementation of those steps does not require the exercise of inventive skill." The PTO stated "[w]e agree with Lin," deciding the case in favor of Amgen.

9.1.1.3 Someone Who Provides Background Information Is Not Necessarily an Inventor.
Still another often-repeated rule is that someone does not become an inventor merely by furnishing background information to the true inventor or inventors.[18] Distinguishing the suggestions that do not entitle someone to be named an inventor from those that do is not a simple matter. An important, but not decisive factor is whether the suggested elements are recited with specificity in the claims defining the invention.[19] When the suggested features are listed as elements in the claims, the importance of those elements in distinguishing the prior art and showing that the invention is nonobvious makes the suggested information particularly worthy of scrutiny. This is particularly true when, as Professor Chisum pointed out, such information must be considered prior art if it was contributed by a noninventor.[20]

9.1.1.4 The Coauthor of a Paper Reporting an Invention Is Not Necessarily an Inventor.
The fact that someone is the coauthor of a paper describing an invention in a scholarly journal has no relation to the question of whether that person is an inventor. This point is illustrated by *In re Katz*.[21]

In *Katz*, a patent application titled "Induction of Immunological Tolerance" was filed by Katz as sole inventor in February, 1977. The examiner rejected the application as anticipated by an article describing the invention and written by Chiorazzi, Eshhar, and Katz (N. Chiorazzi *et al.*, *Proc. Natl. Acad. Sci. USA* 73, 2091-95 [1976]). The article was published less than one year prior to the filing of the application. Katz submitted a declaration explaining that the other authors of the article were students working under his direction and supervision at the Harvard Medical School, and were not coinventors. Nevertheless, the PTO rejected Katz's application on the grounds that it was reasonable to infer that Chiorazzi and Eshhar were coinventors because they were coauthors, that the three were a different inventive entity from Katz alone, and that Katz's declaration alone was insufficient to negate this inference. The PTO ruled that Katz's application, therefore, was anticipated by the Chiorazzi *et al.* paper.[22]

Katz appealed, and the Court of Customs and Patent Appeals (CCPA) reversed the PTO in favor of Katz. The court characterized the issue as an evidentiary one: whether Katz had adequately established that the Chiorazzi *et al.* article reported his sole invention (in which case, it would be prior art against him only if he filed his application more than a year after its publication). As an initial matter, the court held that writing an article does *not* raise a *presumption* of inventorship. In this case, it merely created an ambiguity. The declaration offered by Katz provided a logical explanation that clarified this ambiguity. Since Katz was required only to clarify an ambiguity and not rebut a legal presumption, the court considered his explanation alone sufficient to establish his status as sole inventor and remove the Chiorazzi *et al.* article as a reference.[23]

9.1.1.5 An Inventor Contributes to the Conception of the Invention as Claimed.

To be an inventor, a person must contribute to the conception of the invention as it is defined by any one claim included in a patent or patent application.[24] A contribution to the reduction to practice of the invention is irrelevant[25] unless the technology is so unpredictable that conception can only occur simultaneously with the reduction to practice.

The definitions of "conception" and "reduction to practice" are discussed in detail in Chapter 10 on competitive research. In general, a common definition of conception is:

> the complete performance of the mental part of the inventive act. All that remains to be accomplished, in order to perfect the act or instrument, belongs to the department of construction, not invention. It is therefore the formation, in the mind of the inventor of a definite and permanent idea of the complete and operative invention, as it is thereafter to be applied in practice, that constitutes an available conception, within the patent law.[26]

For joint invention to occur, two or more individuals must work together in some way in its conception. The leading explanation of this aspect of joint invention is set forth in *Monsanto Co. v. Kamp*:

> A joint invention is the product of collaboration of the inventive endeavors of two or more persons working toward the same end and producing an invention by their aggregate efforts. To constitute a joint invention, it is necessary that each of the inventors work on the same subject matter and make some contribution to the inventive thought and to the final result. Each needs to perform but a part of the task if an invention emerges from all of the steps taken together. It is not necessary that the entire inventive concept should occur to each of the joint inventors, or that the two should physically

work on the project together. One may take a step at one time, the other an approach at different times. One may do more of the experimental work while the other makes suggestions from time to time. The fact that each of the inventors plays a different role and that the contribution of one may not be as great as that of another, does not detract from the fact that the invention is joint, if each makes some original contribution, though partial, to the final solution of the problem.[27]

The *Monsanto* decision presents a relatively liberal standard for finding joint invention. A key requirement is that joint inventors collaborate in some way. The Federal Circuit recently stated that for joint invention to occur, there must be some "element of joint behavior, such as collaboration or working under common direction."[28] How far the Federal Circuit might go in finding behavior sufficiently "joint" to establish joint invention in the absence of direct collaboration is still unclear.

9.1.2 Derivation of Invention

Derivation is the taking of an invention from the true original inventor by another. At its worst, derivation is simply the stealing of an invention. Fortunately, cases of intentional derivation are few. Derivation can occur inadvertently in chemical and biological technologies, however, when it is not fully appreciated that the inventor is the person who performs the mental acts of conception rather than the one who carries out the reduction to practice. Typically (and unfortunately) these cases present themselves as interference proceedings between ex-collaborators.

The attribution of inventorship to the person who carries out conception rather than the one who reduces it to practice is illustrated by *Applegate v. Scherer.*[29] Applegate had found that the compound 3-bromo-4-nitrophenol was useful for combatting lamprey eel infestations in bodies of water. Scherer wrote a letter to Applegate, suggesting that 3-trifluoromethyl-4-nitrophenol would also be effective and offering to send this compound to Applegate for testing. Applegate tested the compound, found it was effective, and filed a patent application on the use of Scherer's compound for combatting lamprey eels. Scherer also filed a patent application on the same invention, and an interference was declared. The PTO held Scherer to be the inventor, and the CCPA affirmed the PTO's decision.

The PTO stated that Scherer's suggestion was sufficient to "enable a person of ordinary skill in the art to practice the disclosure without extensive research or experimentation." Applegate argued on appeal that because of the unpredictable nature of this technology, Scherer could not have a complete conception of the invention without testing; that is, conception could occur simultaneously only with reduction to practice. In rejecting this argument, the CCPA stated that the rule proposed by Applegate may apply in a case where two *independently made* inventions interfered but it had no application to a case where the alleged conception was *communicated* to someone else. The court commented that:

> To adopt this proposition would mean, as a practical matter, that one could never communicate an invention thought up by him to another who is to try it out, for, when the

tester succeeds, the one who does no more than exercise ordinary skill would be rewarded and the innovator would not be.[30]

In *MacMillan v. Moffett*,[31] UpJohn and Procter & Gamble (P&G) entered into a program in which P&G would test anticholinergic compounds as antiperspirants. Moffett, an expert on anticholinergic compounds, selected 69 compounds for this program that were either known or prospective anticholinergic agents. MacMillan, an expert on topical antiperspirant testing, found 19 of the compounds to be inactive, 24 to be only slightly active, 11 fairly active, 4 moderately active, 2 highly active, and one compound (designated U-5008) outstandingly effective. MacMillan, followed by Moffett, filed patent applications concerning the method of controlling perspiration by topical application of this outstandingly active compound, and an interference was declared. The PTO found Moffett to be the first inventor, which the CCPA affirmed.

On appeal, MacMillan argued that Moffett's conception was incomplete because he did not appreciate that U-5008 would have unexpected properties that would render it patentable (namely, superior activity). The court replied:

We do not think that the conceiver must know the unexpected properties associated with the conceived invention. . . . These facts are of course relevant to patentability, but there is no requirement in the law that a conceiver be aware of the facts which render the conceived subject matter patentable.[32]

Finally, *GAF Corp. v. Amchem Products, Inc.*[33] provides a useful contrast to *MacMillan v. Moffett* and *Applegate v. Scherer* because in *GAF Corp.*, it was the screener of the compounds rather than the supplier of the compounds who was found to have invented a new use for a known compound.

GAF entered into a screening agreement with Amchem under which Amchem would test GAF compounds for biological activity in plants. The agreement provided that GAF would give Amchem lists of chemical compounds for possible screening and that Amchem then would select the chemicals it was willing to screen.

Among the compounds accepted by Amchem were 2-chloroethyl-phosphonic acid (the "acid") and the pyrocatechol ester of the acid (the "ester"). Initially the ester was found active and the acid was not, which puzzled the Amchem scientists because they believed the ester to be hydrolyzed to the acid *in vivo*. As a result, Amchem told GAF that the purity of the acid was in doubt. Amchem then indicated to GAF that it wished to obtain analogs of the ester, and Dr. Randall, a senior scientist at GAF, began synthesis of these analogs.

When Randall began preparation of the analogs, he made some notebook entries on the possible hydrolysis of the ester and speculated in his notebook that the ester could hydrolyze to the acid in plants. He then noted: "If the apical dominance is due to [the acid] the catechol ester would hydrolyze much easier than the aliphatic esters."

During the course of Randall's synthesis, he made the acid as an intermediate, found that the original sample was indeed impure, and personally delivered a pure sample of the acid to Amchem. Amchem found the acid was active and—because it was significantly less expensive to produce—concentrated on commercializing the acid.

Originally, it was unclear how the acid achieved its biological activity. Amchem scientists speculated that it was an ethylene response. Amchem also observed that the acid gave off gas when formulated into commercial batches and asked Randall to explain why this occurred. Randall confirmed the gas to be ethylene.

The screening agreement allowed each party to file patent applications on its respective inventions. A GAF patent attorney prepared an in-house memo stating that since GAF was submitting the chemicals with no expectation of a particular activity, this agreement essentially meant: (1) new chemical entities arising from the program would be the property of GAF, and (2) new uses of known chemicals would be the property of Amchem.

Amchem eventually filed patent applications on the use of the acid as a plant growth regulator and entered into negotiations with GAF to supply commercial quantities of the acid. When GAF was unable to negotiate an acceptable supply contract for the acid, it filed suit against Amchem, essentially arguing that Randall was the inventor and Amchem had derived the invention from Randall.

The trial court found in favor of Amchem. The issue, according to the court, was whether GAF could prove Randall to be the first inventor by clear and convincing evidence. The court concluded that it could not. It found that Randall's notebook entries were ambiguous and interpreted them to indicate that Randall continued to believe the ester was essential. In response to the argument that Randall told no one of his conception because he wanted proof of his theory, the court stated that his actions did not corroborate his alleged conception. In addition to illustrating the substantive law of conception, *GAF Corp.* illustrates the difficult standard of proof that must be met by someone who charges derivation of invention. This standard is discussed in greater detail in the following section.

9.1.2.1 Avoiding a Charge of Derivation Through Recordkeeping. *Lazo v. Tso*[34] illustrates the importance of recordkeeping to avoid a charge of derivation in a newly formed research collaboration. Tso, a U.S. Department of Agriculture employee, proposed testing compounds for their ability to inhibit sucker growth in tobacco plants. His proposal included, as material to be tested, "saturated and unsaturated long-chain aliphatic compounds, including primary, secondary, and tertiary alcohols, related ketones, acids, and esters." Later, in October of 1963, Tso submitted a written report in which he described a supplier willing to provide "other derivatives of C-9 fatty acids such as alcohol [derivatives in] . . . quantities for our evaluation in greenhouses as well as in the field." Two months later, Tso published an article describing sucker control with fatty acids and esters (but not alcohols), which was read by Lazo. Lazo then wrote to Tso, suggested that the alcohols might have activity, and offered to supply samples. Tso accepted the compounds, tested them, found they worked, and filed a patent application on the method of controlling suckers with C-3 to C-18 alcohols. Lazo filed an application shortly afterwards, and an interference was declared. The PTO held Tso to be first inventor, which the CCPA affirmed.

Lazo argued on appeal that the two documents used to prove conception were so generic that they could not establish conception of the narrow subject matter (or "species") claimed. On this the court disagreed, noting that "Tso not only had developed a master plan that contemplated future testing of such a compound but also had carried out research with related fatty acid derivatives and obtained encouraging results." The court specifically stated that the case was "readily distinguishable" from *Applegate v. Scherer*. Of course, if Tso had not kept corroborated records of his general research plan, enabling him to show conception prior to the communication from Lazo, then the case would have been very similar to *Applegate v. Scherer*. In all likelihood, inventorship would have been awarded to Lazo.

9.1.2.2 The Difficulty of Proving Derivation. When one party charges that an invention has been derived from another, the charge must be proven by "clear and convincing" evidence: a significantly higher standard than the usual "preponderance of evidence" or "more likely than not" standard usually found in civil litigation. The application of this standard and its underlying rationale are illustrated in *Amax Fly Ash Corp. v. United States.*[35] The *Amax* case involved a method of extinguishing underground fires in coal mine shafts by drilling holes into the mines and injecting a mixture of air and powdery fly ash to block the shafts. While not a biotechnology invention, the manner in which the invention arose parallels the way many biotechnology inventions arise: at a meeting between one of the inventors, an employee of Amax, and an official from the Bureau of Mines interested in finding solutions to mine fires. Amax filed a patent application after the meeting in the name of its employee. The Bureau of Mines argued that its own employee was the true inventor, with the Amax inventor having derived the invention from him at the meeting. The court summarized what the Bureau of Mines had to prove:

(a) a prior complete conception, properly corroborated; and
(b) communication of the conception to the party accused of derivation;
(c) with the elements being proved by clear and convincing evidence.

The court explained the reason for a "clear and convincing" standard of proof as follows:

> Since conception is an act of the mind . . . the temptation for even honest witnesses to reconstruct, in a manner favorable to their own position, what their state of mind may have been years earlier, is simply too great to permit a lower standard.[36]

After carefully reviewing all the evidence, including the personal diary of the Bureau of Mines official, the court concluded that the evidence did not show prior conception or communication of the conception by the Bureau of Mines official to the Amax employee. The court was careful to point out the candor of the Bureau of

Mines official.[37] Whether one side was not telling the truth was never an issue; it was simply a matter of deciding whether the Bureau of Mines could meet its standard of proof. The court concluded that it could not.

The *Amax* case suggests some practical considerations for those who meet with potential collaborators yet wish to insure that their inventions are properly attributed to them. First, they should make sure that all of their ideas are in writing and properly witnessed prior to the meeting. (This opportunity might even be taken by those who plan to meet with new collaborators or to brainstorm with their existing colleagues and reduce some of their new ideas to writing.) This step will at least establish conception. Second, the flow of information and the genesis of new ideas at the meeting should be documented either by formal minutes, informal notes, or a letter from one party to another after the meeting. Finally, if second thoughts or misgivings about the communication of information arise after the meeting, the rapid filing of a patent application should be considered. The first to file will be considered the senior party, and the burden will be on the other party to show derivation.

9.1.3   Joint Patent Applications and Joint Inventions Compared

Joint patent applications and joint inventions are completely different things. A patent might name multiple inventors without containing a single joint invention. This became evident in 1984 when Section 116 of the patent statute was amended to add the following paragraph:

> Inventors may apply for a patent jointly even though (1) they did not physically work together or at the same time, (2) each did not make the same type or amount of contribution, or (3) each did not make a contribution to the subject matter of every claim of the patent.[38]

The first two clauses of this section simply restate the law of joint invention. The third clause makes a completely different point—that inventorship in a patent application can differ from claim to claim. Thus, as already noted, inventorship in a patent application is based on claims and is determined on a claim-by-claim basis.

Amending or canceling claims in the course of patent prosecution can significantly change who should be named as an inventor on an application. To simplify dealing with this situation, the PTO rules provide as follows:

> If the correct inventors are named in the application when filed and the prosecution of the application results in the amendment or cancellation of claims so that less than all of the originally named inventors are the actual inventors of the invention being claimed in the application, an amendment shall be filed deleting the names of the person or persons who are not inventors of the invention being claimed. The amendment must be diligently made. . . .[39]

The ability to alter inventorship in response to the amendment or cancellation of claims during the ordinary course of prosecution is a logical necessity. This ability, however, can be especially important when a patent application is filed naming multiple inventors from different organizations that for some reason no longer wish to see their patent rights tied together. In this case, the claims can be sorted according to corporate ownership. All claims belonging to one corporation can be voluntarily canceled from the application and placed in a separate continuation application.

When inventorship differs among claims in an application, later misunderstandings by inventors can be avoided by having inventorship identified on a claim-by-claim basis at the time the application is filed. Where there are multiple owners assigned rights by multiple inventors in an application, identifying inventors on a claim-by-claim basis is essential to clearly define what each owner's intellectual property rights really are.

9.2 CORRECTING INVENTORSHIP

Honest mistakes can be made in identifying the correct inventors on a patent application. Sometimes mistakes in identifying inventors, such as naming the wrong sole inventor, can be corrected.[40] Corrections can be made with pending applications or issued patents. The following section briefly discusses each situation.

9.2.1 Correcting Inventorship in a Patent Application

When inventors are incorrectly identified in a pending patent application, the PTO rules provide for a solution:

> If the correct inventor or inventors are not named in an application for patent through error without any deceptive intention on the part of the actual inventor or inventors, the application may be amended to name only the actual inventor or inventors. Such amendment must be diligently made. . . .[41]

The key requirements are that the mistake occurred "through error without any deceptive intention" and that the correction of inventorship "be diligently made." The provision is remedial in nature, recognizes that honest errors can be made, and tends to be reasonably applied by the PTO.

9.2.2 Correcting Inventorship in an Issued Patent

Errors in inventorship should be corrected promptly, particularly while an application is pending. Nevertheless, an error may come to light only after the patent issues. In appropriate circumstances, the patent statute provides for the correction of inventorship on issued patents by the Commissioner of Patents under Section 256 of the patent statute as follows:

> Whenever through error a person is named in an issued patent as the inventor, or through error an inventor is not named in an issued patent and such error arose without any deceptive intention on his part, the Commissioner may, on application of all the

parties and assignees, with proof of the facts and such other requirements as may be imposed, issue a certificate correcting such error.[42]

An error in inventorship might come to light only after a patent is in litigation, with the opponent arguing that the patent is invalid for failing to name the proper inventors. Again, in certain situations, Section 256 provides a remedy:

> The error of omitting inventors or naming persons who are not inventors shall not invalidate the patent in which such error occurred if it can be corrected as provided in this section. The court before which such matter is called in question may order correction of the patent on notice and hearing of all parties concerned and the Commissioner shall issue a certificate accordingly.[43]

9.3   PRIOR ART ISSUES IN COLLABORATIVE RESEARCH

When potential inventors are in different organizations, proper determination of inventorship may be crucial to determining whether an invention is patentable under U.S. law. Indeed, U.S. law in this area is a trap for the unwary because it can dramatically affect the content of the "prior art" for determining nonobviousness in ways that are neither intuitive nor expected. The following section discusses these issues.

9.3.1   Prior Art Issues Under United States Law

Section 102 of the patent statute provides, in part, as follows:

> A person shall be entitled to a patent unless . . .
>
> (f) he did not himself invent the subject matter sought to be patented, or
> (g) before the applicant's invention thereof the invention was made in this country by another. . . .

These sections, which are the basis of the "first to invent" rule in the United States, also are essentially incorporated into Section 103 of the patent statute to define the content of the prior art when assessing the nonobviousness of an invention. Moreover, the phrase "he did not himself invent" in Section (f) and the phrase "by another" in Section (g) refer to inventions by different inventive entities. Thus, if one individual takes a project part way and then collaborates with another in completing the invention, the prior work of the first inventor is considered prior art for obviousness purposes against the subsequent joint invention.

The incorporation of sections 102(f) and 102(g) into a prior-art analysis creates serious problems for corporate inventions, which usually arise from ongoing projects involving multiple researchers.[44] To solve this problem, Section 103 of the patent statute was amended in 1984 to add the following exclusion:

> Subject matter developed by another person, which qualifies as prior art only under subsection (f) or (g) of section 102 of this title, shall not preclude patentability under this section where the subject matter and the claimed invention were, at the time the invention was made, owned by the same person or subject to an obligation of assignment to the same person. . . .[45]

The 1984 amendment to Section 103 only solves the prior art problems created by sections 102(f) and 102(g) when the inventors have a common obligation to assign, such as when they are employed by the same company. Thus, instructions from a patent examiner in a first official action on a patent application naming joint inventors may read as follows:

> This application currently names joint inventors. In considering patentability of the claims under 35 U.S.C. § 103, the Examiner presumes that the subject matter of the various claims was commonly owned at the time any inventions covered therein were made absent any evidence to the contrary. Applicant is advised of the obligation under 37 C.F.R. section 1.56 to point out the inventor and invention dates of each claim that was not commonly owned at the time a later invention was made in order for the Examiner to consider the applicability of potential 35 U.S.C. § 102(f) or (g) prior art under 35 U.S.C. § 103.[46]

This is a stern warning because it couples a reminder of the operation of sections 102 and 103 with a reminder of the duty to disclose material information (the knowing violation of which can result in a patent being held unenforceable for inequitable conduct).

The operation of sections 102(f) and (g) in combination with Section 103 can be illustrated by an example. Suppose person A isolates a protein, advises person B of his work under a confidential disclosure agreement, and A and B together develop a new use for that protein. Assume the protein itself is obvious but the new use is not. Also assume, however, that the new use would be obvious if the protein itself were part of the prior art. If A and B work at the same company, the new use is nonobvious under U.S. law. If, however, A and B do not share a common obligation to assign the invention when the new use is invented, A's work will be treated as prior art against the subsequent "new use" invention made by A and B together, even though B is the only person who knows of A's prior work.

This way, U.S. law creates a peculiar penalty for collaborative research when the collaborators are not located at the same company. The problem is most acute when collaborations are first initiated or when an ongoing stream of inventions arise from the collaboration. The problem is ameliorated somewhat by the fact that U.S. law clearly makes the first person to conceive of an invention the inventor. Thus, one party to a collaboration can share his or her ideas with another who is to carry the work out without creating prior art problems. If the collaboration were to extend the original ideas to new ideas, however, constant attention to inventorship would be required to insure the duty of disclosing prior art to the patent office. Failure to attend to these rather complex issues could jeopardize the validity of the entire patent if later it was found that relevant prior art, even though completely secret and available only to those within the collaboration, was not brought to the attention of the patent office during prosecution of the application.

When collaborations occur between different corporate entities, several steps can be taken to maximize patent protection for inventions arising from that collaboration. The most simple step, at least for patent purposes, would be to work out an agreement that inventions made in the course of the collaboration would be assigned to a single entity, such as one or the other of the two corporations, or a separate corporate entity set up for the collaboration. If this is not possible, inventions might be assigned to one or the other of the companies involved in the collaboration according to the subject matter of the invention, rather than by simply determining who is the employer of the particular inventor. This course would seem to provide a solution only where the collaboration involved multiple and distinct fields of work. If no agreement can be reached that addresses the prior art problems created for collaborative research by U.S. patent law, at least the research should be carefully managed to avoid creating unnecessary prior art problems and potential inventors should be encouraged to keep thorough, properly witnessed laboratory notebooks (including ideas for future work). This should facilitate the proper identification of inventors and the accurate, expeditious clarification of prior art issues. Finally, even if the peculiarities of U.S. law result in a collaborative invention being unpatentable in the United States, the outcome may well be different in other countries and regions, as illustrated by the following discussion of the European Patent Convention.

9.3.2 Prior Art Issues Under the European Patent Convention

Under the European Patent Convention, the novelty requirement and the "state of the art" are defined as follows:

(1) An invention shall be considered to be new if it does not form part of the state of the art.

(2) The state of the art shall be held to comprise everything made available to the public by means of a written or oral description, by use, or in any other way, before the date of filing of the European patent application.[47]

What is most relevant for inventions arising from collaborative research is what the EPC does not say, rather than what it does say. There is nothing that makes the prior, secret work of one party prior art against another party—whether that other party is a second individual alone, or the first and second individual in collaboration (of course, the derivation of a complete invention from one party by another is still improper). There is nothing to create the difficult prior art problems posed for collaborative research in the United States, and developments that may be unpatentable in the United States, nevertheless, may be patentable under the EPC. Most other countries are more like the EPC than the United States in this respect, making patent protection outside the United States particularly important for collaborative research.

REFERENCES

1. *See, e.g.*, 35 U.S.C. § 101 ("Whoever invents . . ."); 35 U.S.C. § 111 ("Application for patent shall be made, or authorized to be made, by the inventor . . ."); 35 U.S.C. § 115 ("The applicant shall make oath that he believes himself to be the original and first inventor . . .").

2. *See, e.g.*, The Paris Convention for the Protection of Industrial Property, Article 4.

3. *See generally* C. Gholtz, *How the United States Currently Handles the Interference Issues That Will Remain in a First-to-File World*, 18 AIPLA QUART. J. 1 (1990); R. Wilkes, *The Canadian Viewpoint: A New Perspective Bridging the First-To-Invent and First-to-File Worlds*, 18 AIPLA QUART. J. 18 (1990); B. Fisher, *A European View Relating to Interference Issues in a First-to-File World*, 18 AIPLA QUART. J. 52 (1990); D. Harrison, *Interference Issues in Europe*, 18 AIPLA QUART. J. 65 (1990); J. Kakinuki, *How the Japanese Handle Interference Issues in Their First-to-File World*, 18 AIPLA QUART. J. 80 (1990).

4. 35 U.S.C. § 102(f).

5. 35 U.S.C. § 116.

6. *See generally* J. Tresansky, *Joint Inventorship*, 7 AIPLA QUART. J. 96 (1979); *see also* B. Collins, *The Significance of Inventorship Determinations for Foreign and Domestic Inventors*, 7 AIPLA QUART. J. 117 (1979); K. Jorda, *Inventorship Discrepancies Between Foreign Priority and U.S. Applications*, 7 AIPLA QUART. J. 145 (1979).

7. Mueller Brass Co. v. Reading Industries, 352 F. Supp. 1357, 1372, 176 USPQ 361, 372 (E.D. Pa. 1972), *aff'd*, 487 F.2d 1395, 180 USPQ 547 (3d. Cir. 1973).

8. *See, e.g.*, Morgan v. Hirsch, 728 F.2d 1449, 1452, 221 USPQ 193, 195 (Fed. Cir. 1984) ("[A]sking someone to produce something without saying just what it is to be or how to do it is not what patent law recognizes as inventing.").

9. U.S. Patent No. 4,703,008.

10. Fritsch v. Lin, 21 USPQ2d 1731, 1734 (Bd. Pat. App. 1991).

11. Fritsch, 21 USPQ2d at 1736.

12. Fritsch, 21 USPQ2d at 1734.

13. Fritsch, 21 USPQ2d at 1736.

14. Amgen Inc. v. Chugai Pharmaceutical Co., 13 USPQ2d 1737, 1759–61 (D. Mass. 1989), *aff'd*, 927 F.2d 1200, 18 USPQ2d 1016 (Fed. Cir.), *cert. denied*, 112 S. Ct. 169 (1991).

15. *See* Mineral Separations, Ltd. v. Hyde, 242 U.S. 261, 270 (1916) ("The claim that the patentees of the patent in suit are not the original discoverers of the process patented because an employee of theirs happened to make the analyses and observations which resulted immediately in the discovery, cannot be allowed. The record shows very clearly that the patentees planned the experiments in progress when the discovery was made; that they directed the investigations day by day, conducting them in large part personally and that they interpreted the results."); Mueller Brass Co. v. Reading Industries, Inc., 352 F. Supp. 1357, 1372, 176 USPQ 361, 372 (E.D. Pa. 1972) (a person who has mere-

ly followed the instructions of others has not contributed to the conception and hence is not an inventor); Mattor v. Coolegem, 530 F.2d 1391, 1395, 189 USPQ 201, 204 (C.C.P.A. 1976) (a technician who followed another's instructions is not a coinventor).

16. Fritsch v. Lin, 21 USPQ2d 1737 (Bd. Pat. App. 1991).
17. Fritsch, 21 USPQ2d at 1739.
18. *See, e.g.*, Hobbs v. United States, 451 F.2d 849, 171 USPQ 713, 724–25 (Ct. Cl. 1971).
19. *See generally* Harris, *Conceptual Specificity as a Factor in Determination of Inventorship*, 67 J. PAT. & TRADEMARK OFF. SOC'Y 315 (1985).
20. 1 D. Chisum, PATENTS, § 2.02[4] (1991).
21. *In re* Katz, 687 F.2d 450, 215 USPQ 14 (C.C.P.A. 1982).
22. Katz, 687 F.2d at 452–53, 215 USPQ at 15–16.
23. Katz, 687 F.2d at 455, 215 USPQ at 18.
24. *See In re* Hardee, 223 USPQ 1122, 1123 (Comm'r Pats. 1984); *see also* Rodgard Corp. v. Miner Enterprises Inc., 12 USPQ2d 1353, 1356 (W.D.N.Y. 1989).
25. *In re* Hardee, 223 USPQ 1122, 1123 (Comm'r Pats. 1984).
26. Coleman v. Dines, 754 F.2d 353, 359, 224 USPQ 857, 862 (Fed. Cir. 1985).
27. Monsanto Co. v. Kamp, 269 F. Supp. 818, 824, 154 USPQ 259, 262 (D.D.C. 1967) (cited with approval in Kimberly-Clark Corp. v. Procter & Gamble Distributing Co., 973 F.2d 911, 23 USPQ2d 1921 (Fed. Cir. 1992).
28. *See* Kimberly-Clark Corp. v. Procter & Gamble Distributing Co., 973 F.2d 911, 917, 23 USPQ2d 1921, 1926 (Fed. Cir. 1992); *see generally* D. Carstens, *Joint Inventorship Under 35 U.S.C. §116*, 73 J. PAT. & TRADEMARK OFF. SOC'Y 616 (1991).
29. Applegate v. Scherer, 332 F.2d 571, 141 USPQ 796 (C.C.P.A. 1963).
30. Applegate, 141 USPQ at 799.
31. MacMillan v. Moffett, 432 F.2d 1237, 167 USPQ 550 (C.C.P.A. 1970).
32. MacMillan, 167 USPQ at 552.
33. GAF Corp. v. Amchem Products, Inc., 514 F. Supp. 943, 211 USPQ 172 (E.D. Pa. 1981).
34. Lazo v. Tso, 480 F.2d 908, 178 USPQ 361 (C.C.P.A. 1973).
35. Amax Fly Ash Corp. v. United States, 182 USPQ 210 (Ct. Cl. 1974).
36. Amax, 182 USPQ at 215.
37. Amax, 182 USPQ 215 note 8.
38. 35 U.S.C. § 116; *see also* 37 C.F.R. § 1.45.
39. 37 CFR section 1.48(b).
40. *See, e.g.*, F. Sherling, *Correction of Inventorship in Patent Applications*, 7 AIPLA QUART. J. 126 (1979); D. Daus, *A.F. Stoddard & Co. v. Dann: A Doctrine of Innocence*, 7 AIPLA QUART. J. 130 (1979).
41. 37 CFR § 1.48(a).
42. 35 U.S.C. § 256 paragraph 1.
43. 35 U.S.C. § 256 paragraph 2.
44. *See, e.g.*, Kimberly-Clark Corp. v. Johnson & Johnson, 745 F.2d 1437, 223 USPQ 603 (Fed. Cir. 1984).
45. 35 U.S.C. § 103 paragraph 2.
46. How the PTO handles the issue of prior art under sections 102(f) and 102(g) is discussed in the MANUAL OF PATENT EXAMINING PROCEDURE, sections 2185–89 (Rev. 6, Oct. 1987) (U.S. Government Printing Office).
47. European Patent Convention, Article 54.

CHAPTER
10

Competitive Research

Kenneth D. Sibley

It is common for two or more separate groups to work independently and very competitively toward the same goal. Even two separate groups in different fields that are not deliberately working towards the same goal can independently make the same invention. In such a case, priority of invention (who is entitled to the patent) must be determined.

As you already know, the United States uses a first-to-invent system to determine priority of inventorship. Under this system, even if someone has filed a patent application, someone else can file a patent application later and try to prove that he or she was the first to invent. Almost all other countries use a first-to-file system in which the first to file a patent application is considered the first inventor. There is no other opportunity for litigation on the issue of who invented first (as long as the invention was not derived from another inventor).

The following sections discuss both the first-to-invent and the first-to-file systems, with particular emphasis on the first-to-invent system in the U.S. Although the United States may amend its patent statute to adopt a first-to-file system in the near future,[1] at least a portion of the law established in this area will continue to be viable on issues such as determining correct inventorship. In any case, because preserving patent rights outside of the United States is particularly important for biotechnology inventions, research programs carried out in the United States usually adopt a patent strategy based, at least in part, on the first-to-file system.

A situation that frequently goes along with priority of invention occurs when one inventor allegedly learns of, or "derives," an invention from someone else.

153

Under both the first-to-file and first-to-invent systems, someone who derives an invention is not considered an inventor and is not entitled to a patent. The issue of derivation was treated in Chapter 9, since derivation issues often inadvertently arise in the course of collaborative research.

10.1 PRIORITY OF INVENTION UNDER THE FIRST-TO-INVENT SYSTEM

The rules for determining who was the first to invent are based on Section 102(g) of the patent statute and are relatively simple. The first to reduce an invention to practice is the first to invent, unless a second inventor can prove that he or she (or they) was the first to conceive of the invention and was continuously diligent from a time just before the other inventor's reduction to practice through to his or her own reduction to practice later on. In some circumstances, a second inventor can establish that he or she is the first to invent by showing that the first inventor abandoned, suppressed, or concealed the invention.

While the substantive laws of the U.S. first-to-invent system are fairly easy to summarize, they can be difficult to apply in practice. Each of the substantive issues just raised is discussed in greater detail in the following sections. Particular attention is given to the law concerning conception, since this is a common area of misconception. The procedural aspects of determining priority are discussed only briefly and in terms of how interferences are actually initiated, since interference procedure is a separate area of specialty outside the scope of this book.

10.1.1 Conception of Invention

Precisely what a "conception" is and when it is complete can be difficult to determine in practice. The basic definition is quite simple, however. In *Hybritech Inc. v. Monoclonal Antibodies, Inc.*, the Federal Circuit explained that conception is the "formation in the mind of the inventor, of a definite and permanent idea of the complete and operative invention, as it is hereafter to be applied in practice."[2] This is essentially the same as the classic definition stated nearly 100 years ago in *Mergenthaler v. Scudder*, in which the court explained that "[t]he conception of the invention consists in the complete performance of the mental part of the inventive act. All that remains to be accomplished in order to perfect the act or instrument belongs to the department of construction, not invention."[3] Where there are joint inventors, evidence of conception by one of the inventors works to the benefit of all.[4]

10.1.1.1 Conception and Recognition. Perhaps the most fundamental element of a complete conception is the simple recognition that an invention has been made. This is consistent with the rule (discussed in Chapter 6 in connection with the novelty requirement) that an accidental or unappreciated duplication of an invention does not constitute an anticipation of that invention. However, inventions often come about unexpectedly, and when this occurs the invention may not actually be recognized until well after it was first produced.

The recognition requirement is illustrated by *Silvestri v. Grant*,[5] which involved a new, anhydrous, and storage-stable crystalline form of ampicillin. The patent office had awarded priority of invention to Grant (employed by American Home Products Corp.). The patent office contended that Silvestri (employed by Bristol-Myers Co.) had failed to establish a prior conception of the new crystalline form because he had not established a recognition of the new form at the time of its preparation. On reviewing the evidence, the Court of Customs and Patent Appeals noted records such as an infrared spectrograph log entry that described the product of one of the recorded runs as a "different xyl [crystal] form." While the evidence did not show Silvestri had recognized all the features of the new form, the court emphasized that all that was required was that Silvestri recognize it *as* a new form. Ultimately, the patent office was reversed and priority was awarded to Silvestri.

10.1.1.2 Conception and Enablement. For a conception to be complete, it must be developed to the point that it is a routine matter to reduce the invention to practice; in other words, the invention must be "enabled." The enablement requirement was discussed in detail in Chapter 8, and essentially the same principles apply here.

When an alleged conception does not satisfy the enablement requirement, it is sometimes said that the conception is "simultaneous" with the reduction to practice. For example, in *Smith v. Bosquet*,[6] a case involving phenothiazine-containing insecticides, both sides sought to prove a conception date prior to their actual reductions to practice. The examiner, noting the unpredictability of the relationship between chemical structure and insecticidal action, commented that:

> In the experimental sciences of chemistry and biology this element of unpredictability frequently prevents a conception separated from actual experiment and test. Here the work of conception and reduction to practice goes forward in such a way that no date can be fixed as subsequent to conception but prior to reduction to practice.[7]

The Court of Customs and Patent Appeals agreed with the examiner. This case was decided in 1940, however. If techniques such as computer modeling had been available at the time, conception prior to actual reduction to practice might have been more tangible.

The "rule" of simultaneous conception and reduction to practice is only a guideline and often a trap. It is important to note that the conception and simultaneous reduction-to-practice argument is in great disfavor when it is made by someone who reduced the invention to practice only after learning of its conception by another. This scenario, which can arise in the course of collaborative research, was discussed in Chapter 9.

10.1.1.3 Conception of a Cloned Gene. How the conception requirement is applied when the invention is a cloned gene was discussed at length by the

Federal Circuit in *Amgen Inc. v. Chugai Pharmaceutical Co.*[8] and reiterated in *Fiers v. Sugano.*[9]

In *Amgen*, Chugai argued that Amgen's erythropoietin (EPO) patent (U.S. Patent No. 4,703,008 for DNA sequences encoding erythropoietin) was invalid under Section 102(g) over the prior work of Dr. Fritsch at Genetics Institute. Claim 2 of this patent, which is representative of the claims in this case, read as follows:

> 2. A purified and isolated DNA sequence consisting essentially of a DNA sequence encoding human erythropoietin.

Dr. Fritsch, it was argued, had conceived the strategy of using two sets of fully degenerate cDNA probes to two different regions of the EPO gene to screen a genomic DNA library in 1981 and had diligently pursued this strategy until his reduction to practice in May, 1984. Accordingly, it was argued that he should be treated as the first inventor over Amgen's inventor, Dr. Fu-Kuen Lin, who reduced the invention to practice in September, 1983. The district court rejected this argument by concluding that conception occurred simultaneously with reduction to practice, and Chugai appealed.

The district court's decision was upheld by the Federal Circuit on appeal. The court noted the following facts:

> The structure of this DNA sequence was unknown until 1983, when the gene was cloned by Lin; Fritsch was unaware of it until 1984. As Dr. Sadler, an expert for GI, testified in his deposition: "You have to clone it first to get the sequence." In order to design a set of degenerate probes, one of which will hybridize with a particular gene, the amino acid sequence, or a portion thereof, of the protein of interest must be known. Prior to 1983, the amino acid sequence for EPO was uncertain, and in some positions the sequence envisioned was incorrect. Thus, until Fritsch had a complete mental conception of a purified and isolated DNA sequence encoding EPO and a method for its preparation, in which the precise identity of the sequence is envisioned, or in terms of other characteristics sufficient to distinguish it from other genes, all he had was an objective to make an invention which he could not then adequately describe or define.[10]

In light of these facts, the Federal Circuit went on to decide as follows:

> We hold that when an inventor is unable to envision the detailed constitution of a gene so as to distinguish it from other materials, as well as a method for obtaining it, conception has not been achieved until reduction to practice has occurred, i.e., until after the gene has been isolated.[11]

The *Amgen* decision was decided in light of a set of facts involving a gene that, arguably, had been particularly difficult to clone. The standard that would be applied in other cases remained unclear until *Amgen* was reaffirmed in *Fiers v. Sugano*, a three-party interference in which the interfering subject matter was defined as:

> A DNA which consists essentially of a DNA which codes for a human fibroblast interferon-beta polypeptide.

Priority was awarded to Sugano because he had the benefit of his Japanese priority application, which was filed March 19, 1980 and disclosed both a complete nucleotide sequence for a DNA encoding ß-IF and a method for isolating that DNA.[12] Fiers had filed a patent application in England shortly after Sugano, on April 3, 1980. However, this was not enough for Fiers to win unless, among other things, he established conception in the United States before Sugano did. Accordingly, Fiers argued that he indeed established prior conception when two scientists he had told of his method for isolating the DNA arrived in the United States. Further, Fiers's patent attorney brought a draft patent application back to the United States on February 26, 1980 that described Fiers's method but not the nucleotide sequence.

On appeal, Fiers argued that the *Amgen* case was limited to the isolation of a DNA in which serious difficulties confronted the scientists attempting to isolate that DNA. He also argued that "the standard for proving conception of a DNA by its method of preparation is essentially the same as that for proving that the method is enabling."[13] The Federal Circuit disagreed with Fiers and reaffirmed *Amgen* as follows:

> The present count is to a product, a DNA which codes for ß-IF; it is a claim to a product having a particular biological activity or function, and in *Amgen,* we held that such a product is not conceived until one can define it other than by its biological activity or function. The difficulty that would arise if we were to hold that a conception occurs when one has only the idea of a compound, defining it by its hoped-for function, is that would-be inventors would file patent applications before they had made their inventions and before they could describe them. That is not consistent with the statute or the policy behind the statute, which is to promote disclosure of inventions, not of research plans. While one does not need to have carried out one's invention before filing a patent application, one does need to be able to describe that invention with particularity.[14]

10.1.1.4   Conception and the Utility Requirement.   The question of whether the conception of a new chemical compound (for example, a cloned gene) requires a conception of a practical utility for that compound has been characterized as "open" by the Court of Customs and Patent Appeals.[15] The position of the Patent and Trademark Office is that for a conception to be complete, the conception must include a practical utility.[16] Of course, conception is entirely a mental construct, and if practical utility is required for a complete conception, it need only be a belief of a practical utility. For example, in *Rey-Bellet v. Englehardt*, the Court of Customs and Patent Appeals held a conception of the chemical compound nortriptyline (an antidepressant) to be complete when Englehardt testified, in essence, that he believed nortriptyline would be useful as an antidepressant simply because of its structural similarity to the known antidepressant amitriptyline.[17]

Rey-Bellet was the case where the question of whether a conception must include a conception of practical utility was characterized as "open."[18] The court treated it as required only because Englehardt had not argued to the contrary. When an inventor admits that a particular activity was expected because of its similarity to a known compound, the danger is that his or her testimony might be used by an opponent to argue that the new compound was obvious over the known compound. Consider *In re Merck*,[19] in which a claim for a method of treating depression with amitriptyline was held obvious by the Federal Circuit over, among other things, the known usefulness as an antidepressant of the structurally similar compound imipramine.

10.1.1.5   Conception of Genus and Species.   The requirements for a complete conception can be somewhat confusing when considering genus and species relationships. Take, for example, a claim for recombinant plants in general carrying one member of a broad family of genes versus a claim for a particular species of plant in recombinant form carrying a specific gene for a specific purpose. Generally, in a priority contest, conception of a single species within a broad genus may establish conception of the genus.[20] Hence, for an important invention, some applicants will file a narrow patent application describing a few species at an early date and file a broader continuation-in-part application describing the complete genus at a later date. The idea is to quickly establish, for defensive purposes, an early and concrete date of conception and reduction to practice for at least one species.[21] The broader application is filed later because a broad genus may not be patentable to an applicant unless that applicant has broad enabling support for it[22] and does not wish to lose time in establishing a filing date to either conduct additional experiments or prepare a lengthy patent disclosure.

The opposite is *not* true: conception of a genus does not necessarily establish conception of a species.[23] Such a rule would fly in the face of the written description requirement discussed in Chapter 8, which allows later researchers to make narrower "improvement" or "selection" inventions within a broadly known class. Thus, if a generic patent application is filed but does not specifically disclose what later emerges as a particularly valuable specific embodiment of the invention, either a continuation-in-part application or a new application describing that embodiment should be filed; otherwise, it might be successfully patented by another party.

10.1.1.6   Conception and Inventorship.   Aside from determinations of priority of inventorship, the law concerning conception is important in determining inventorship. In general, to be an inventor, a person must contribute to the conception of the invention. A contribution to reduction to practice is irrelevant.[24] Of course, a person's contribution to reduction to practice may become important if, because of either luck or technical complexity, there can be no conception prior to reduction to practice.

Even if the United States adopts a first-to-file system, the law on conception established under the current first-to-invent system most likely will continue to be important to inventorship determinations.

10.1.2   Reduction to Practice

A reduction to practice may be either actual or constructive. The former involves actually making and practicing the invention; the latter involves simply filing a patent application.

It is important to note that the standard for achieving an actual reduction to practice can be so high in a competitive field that it is essential to secure a constructive reduction to practice by filing a patent application. While such a high standard may seem unfair at first, it is consistent with the court policy of encouraging early filing for patent applications.

10.1.2.1   Constructive Reduction to Practice.

As noted, the filing of a patent application is a constructive reduction to practice.[25] The application must satisfy the enablement requirement set forth in the first paragraph of Section 112 of the patent statute[26] and also the written description requirement of the same section.[27] There is no requirement that actual testing be carried out or persuasive proof be presented— only that the statutory requirements for patentability be met.

An example of the requirement that an application be enabling to establish a constructive reduction to practice is provided by *Staehelin v. Secher*,[28] in which the sole interference count defining the conflicting subject matter was:

> A monoclonal antibody produced by a murine derived hybrid cell line wherein the antibody is capable of specifically binding to at least one antigenic determinant of interferon-α.

Staehelin tried to attack Secher's case by arguing, among other things, that Secher's application did not provide an enabling disclosure of the count. The Patent Office Board of Appeals noted that:

> It has been consistently held that the first paragraph of 35 USC 112 requires nothing more than objective enablement [citation omitted]. In satisfying the enablement requirement, an application need not teach, and preferably omits, that which is well-known in the art [citations omitted]. How such a teaching is set forth, whether by the use of illustrative examples or by broad descriptive terminology, is of no importance. . . .[29]

The board noted that Staehelin, who bore the burden of proof, had failed to present any evidence that *undue* experimentation would have been required to practice the invention. Secher, on the other hand, produced declaration testimony from Caesar Milstein indicating that he (Milstein) found Secher's disclosure enabling and Staehelin's position founded on a "misunderstanding of the science involved."[30] The Board decided in favor of Secher.

10.1.2.2   Actual Reduction to Practice.

As with conception, a basic requirement for an actual reduction to practice is that it must be recognized and appreci-

ated.[31] Every element of the claimed invention must exist in the invention when reduced to practice. It also must be proven that the invention performed as intended in
order to establish actual reduction to practice.[32] The requirement that the elements of
the invention must work as intended can be quite stringent. In *Medtronic, Inc. v.
Daig Corp.*, for example, the district court held that there was no actual reduction to
practice of a pacemaker lead without actual human tests. Animal tests alone were
held insufficient to show that it would operate in the human heart. The district
court's decision was affirmed by the Federal Circuit.[33] The testing requirement may
be dispensed with in the case of very simple technology, but it may be that few situations in the area of biotechnology are sufficiently simple.[34]

For new compounds, testing must show the utility of the compound to establish
an actual reduction to practice.[35] New compounds can be reduced to practice by
showing their operability for any practical utility, however. So, if an *in vitro* utility
is sufficient, then *in vitro* testing alone would be enough to establish an actual reduction to practice.[36] The situation would be different for new therapeutic uses of
known compounds, which presumably would have to be used *in vivo* to show an actual reduction to practice. In general, no such data needs to be presented in a patent
application to establish a constructive reduction to practice.

10.1.3 Diligence

A showing of conception must be coupled to a showing of reduction to practice (actual or constructive) by a showing of diligence. The period of diligence must begin
just before a second party enters the field[37] and it must be continuous from that time
up to the later reduction to practice. Once a reduction to practice is established, diligence need no longer be shown. A second party might attempt to show the inventor
has abandoned, suppressed, or concealed the invention, but he or she bears the burden of proof. As with the requirement for showing actual reduction to practice, the
diligence requirement is stringently applied. Once again, this stringency stems from
the policy favoring early disclosure of inventions.[38] Diligence need only be reasonable, and there are many court decisions that seem to place the diligence requirement in a favorable light. In *Hybritech Inc. v. Abbott Laboratories,*[39] for example,
Abbott challenged Hybritech's diligence in reducing its monoclonal sandwich assay
invention to practice by arguing that there were many days in Hybritech's records
that did not show work being done on the invention. The court responded:

> The question of diligence is considered in light of all the circumstances. For example,
> people may be sick or even take vacations (thereby creating gaps in activity) while still
> being diligent [citation omitted]. The question is whether they were pursuing their goal
> in a reasonable fashion. If they were doing the things reasonably necessary to reduce
> the idea to practice, then they were diligent even if they did not actually work on the
> invention each day.[40]

The court noted that a start-up company such as Hybritech "had to establish an office, obtain laboratory equipment, get financing and so on." Under these particular
circumstances, the court held that the diligence requirement was met.

The *Hybritech* decision should be considered with caution because what is "reasonable" diligence varies from case to case, and, generally, the diligence requirement continues to be stringently applied. For example, in *Griffith v. Kanamaru*[41] the Federal Circuit reviewed the "reasonable diligence" requirement in detail. The court decided that the diligence requirement had not been met when gaps in diligence for research carried out at Cornell University were attributable only to Professor Griffith's effort to obtain outside funding for the research and his desire to assign the project to a new graduate student to whom it had been promised, but who had not yet arrived. Comparing the result reached in this case with the result in *Hybritech* makes it clear that there is no precise definition of "reasonable" gaps in diligence.

10.1.4 Corroboration of Inventive Acts

One of the most troublesome aspects of proving prior inventorship is that the inventive acts (conception, reduction to practice, and diligence) must be corroborated by someone who is not an inventor. Corroboration is typically in the form of detailed record-keeping but also may be in other forms, such as sworn testimony. Without corroboration these acts are legally irrelevant and of no help in establishing priority.

It is often said that the amount of corroboration required is determined by a "rule of reason" that makes the corroboration requirement less burdensome. Of course, inadequate corroboration cannot be cured by the "rule of reason." As explained by the Federal Circuit in *Coleman v. Dines*:[42]

> This "rule of reason," which was developed over the years in order to ease the requirement of corroboration, usually is applied when establishing actual reduction to practice [citations omitted]. Even so, Coleman's attempt to apply the rule to establish conception fails in this present case. The rule suggests a reasoned examination, analysis and evaluation of all pertinent evidence so that a sound determination of the credibility of the inventor's story may be reached [citations omitted]. The rule of reason, however, does not dispense with the requirement for some evidence of independent corroboration. Coleman has not presented any evidence of an independent nature to support his testimony. . . .

The corroboration requirement can be more easily satisfied when the invention arose from an organized research program and the facts concerning that organization are properly presented. An illustration is *Nashef v. Pollock*,[43] a priority contest between Baxter Travenol (Nashef) and Extracorporeal Medical Specialties (Pollock) concerning a method for inhibiting the mineralization of fixed natural tissue after implantation in a living body. Pollock was able to corroborate her actual reduction to practice (treatment of tissue samples by the claimed method) by introducing research notebook pages that were internally consistent, and by introducing the testimony of a research technician stating she had prepared samples for Dr. Pollock for testing and transferred them to Dr. Pollock by February 5, 1982. She also introduced her own testimony that the treatments were set up and carried out on February 9, 1982 and introduced the testimony of the director of research at Ethicon Research Foundation confirming that treated samples had been received on or about February

23, 1982 for implantation. In light of this evidence and testimony, the Board of Patent Appeals stated:

> The notion that each individual act necessary for an actual reduction to practice must be proved in detail by an unbroken chain of evidence has been rejected [citation omitted]. Over-the-shoulder observation of every step is not necessary to satisfy the corroboration rule where there is independent circumstantial evidence of a reduction to practice [citations omitted]. This is especially true where, as here, the activities in question were apparently part of an organized research program [citation omitted].
>
> Viewing the evidence as a whole, we find it reasonable to conclude that Dr. Pollock carried out the method of the count on February 9, 1982.[44]

Obviously, considerable care had been devoted to establishing the proper procedures for documenting and corroborating inventive acts by Pollock's employer, Extracorporeal Medical Specialties.

The *Nashef v. Pollock* decision does not mean that the corroboration requirement is easy to meet or simple to prove. The issue in *Hahn v. Wong*,[45] for example, concerned laboratory notebook pages allegedly showing the preparation and cross-linking of the contested polymer, complete with reduced photocopies of infrared spectroscopy and nuclear magnetic resonance results. The pages, along with separate affidavit testimony of coworkers stating that they had "read and understood" those pages, was held insufficient to establish an actual reduction to practice. The court noted that the infrared and NMR data required separate evidence to interpret and that no such evidence had been presented.

Perhaps the best-known interpretation of the corroboration requirement in biotechnology is found in the dispute over monoclonal sandwich assays in *Hybritech Inc. v. Monoclonal Antibodies, Inc.*[46] The inventors, David and Greene, had kept laboratory notebooks recording their work but had not had them independently witnessed by someone who was not an inventor until Tom Adams joined Hybritech and advised them to do so. The trial court found the David and Greene patent invalid, noting, among other things, that "there was no credible evidence of conception before May 1980." The Federal Circuit reversed the trial court and upheld the patent, commenting on this point as follows:

> The laboratory notebooks, alone, are enough to show clear error in the findings that underlie the holding that the invention was not conceived before May 1980. That some of the notebooks were not witnessed until a few months to one year after their writing does not make them incredible or necessarily of little corroborative value. Admittedly, Hybritech was a young, growing company in 1979 that failed to have witnesses sign the inventors' notebooks contemporaneously with their writing. Under a reasoned analysis and evaluation of all pertinent evidence, however, we cannot ignore that Hybritech, within a reasonable time thereafter, prudently had researchers other than those who performed the particular experiments witness the notebooks in response to Tom Adams' advice.[47]

The prudent course is to get someone who will not be an inventor to witness (read, understand, sign, and date) laboratory notebook pages at the same time they are being recorded, signed, and dated by the laboratory worker. The *Hybritech* decision indicates that witnessing need only be as concurrent as is reasonably possible. The decision is unclear on whether the lengthy period of time considered reasonable in *Hybritech* would be considered reasonable in other circumstances.

10.1.5   Abandonment, Suppression, and Concealment

The law concerning abandonment, suppression, and concealment was summarized by the Federal Circuit in *Lutzker v. Plet*[48] as follows:

> Generally, the party who establishes that he is the first to conceive and the first to reduce an invention to practice is entitled to a patent thereon. However, the second party to conceive and reduce the same invention to practice will be awarded priority of invention if he can show that the first party to reduce to practice abandoned, suppressed or concealed the invention.

It is not clear that there is any difference, in practice, between abandonment, suppression, and concealment. It is clear that the right to priority is lost when evidence establishes that the invention was actively concealed. Evidence that the first inventor was spurred back into activity on learning that a second party had entered the field is often particularly persuasive evidence that the invention was concealed.[49]

In addition to active concealment, concealment may be inferred from a long, unexplained delay in the filing of a patent application. This principle was reviewed in detail by the Federal Circuit in *Paulik v. Rizkalla*,[50] in which the court stated:

> From the earliest decisions, a distinction has been drawn between deliberate suppression or concealment of an invention, and the legal inference of suppression or concealment based on "too long" a delay in filing the patent application. Both types of situations were considered by the courts before the 1952 Patent Act, and both are encompassed in 35 U.S.C. § 102(g).[51]

Precisely what constitutes "too long" a delay varies from case to case depending on the circumstances. In the numerous decisions summarized in *Paulik*, delays as long as seven years were excused while delays of as little as 27 months were held to be too long. A particularly important factor in determining whether the delay was too long was whether the second inventor had entered the field during the period of inactivity.

A delay is not fatal if the party that delayed "too long" would be entitled to the patent otherwise under the usual first-to-invent principles—even if all the work prior to the delay had never occurred. This was the situation in *Paulik*, in which the Federal Circuit concluded:

> [W]e hold that the first inventor will not be barred from relying on later, resumed activity antedating an opponent's entry into the field, merely because the work done before the [later] work occurred was sufficient to amount to a reduction to practice.[52]

The court went on to comment that it saw no reason to discourage inventors who had once worked on a project, and set it aside, from renewing their work on that project by creating a rule making it impossible for them to rely even on their renewed work to establish reduction to practice in a priority contest.

10.2 APPLYING THE FIRST-TO-INVENT SYSTEM TO INVENTIONS MADE OUTSIDE THE UNITED STATES

Inventors who work outside the United States face a substantial disadvantage over those working in the U.S. in establishing that they are the first to invent. Section 104 of the patent statute states that a patent applicant "may not establish a date of invention by reference to knowledge or use thereof" in a foreign country, *except* as provided in Section 119 (and subject to certain other exceptions). Section 119 of the patent statute seems to place foreign applicants on common ground with U.S. applicants. Section 119 sets forth the "right to priority," granted under the Paris Convention, which gives foreign patent applications filed within 12 months in the United States the "same effect as the same application would have if filed in this country. . . ." Section 102(g), however, states that prior invention must be shown "in this country," and the Court of Customs and Patent Appeals has clearly stated that the "same effect" language of Section 119 "does not remove the limitation of Section 102(g) found in the phrase 'in this country.' "[53] Accordingly, inventors outside the United States sometimes at least seek to establish evidence of conception in the United States by shipping documents such as invention disclosures and draft patent applications into the United States.[54]

10.3 INTERFERENCE PROCEDURE: INITIATION OF INTERFERENCES

The rules governing interference proceedings in the United States Patent and Trademark Office are complex and are substantially different from the rules governing patent litigation in the district courts.[55] Interferences can be easily won or lost on procedural issues alone, and should not be initiated without a full appreciation of the process being undertaken. The initial steps in initiating an interference are explained briefly in the following section; for a discussion of the procedures involved in the major phases of an interference proceeding, refer to materials specializing on that subject.[56]

10.3.1 Interferences Involving at Least One Pending Application

For an interference to be declared in the patent and trademark office, at least one pending application must be involved.[57] All that is required is for an examiner to believe that there are overlapping claims in separate applications that do not belong to the same party:[58]

> An interference may be declared between two or more pending applications naming different inventors when, in the opinion of an examiner, the applications contain claims for the same patentable invention. An interference may be declared between one or more pending applications and one or more unexpired patents naming different inventors when, in the opinion of an examiner, any application and any unexpired patent contain claims for the same patentable invention.[59]

In a case involving an issued patent, a subsequent application must be filed at least one year before the date that patent was granted or there can be no interference between the two.[60] The subsequent application is barred on the principle that the subject matter was described in a printed publication more than one year prior to the filing date.

10.3.1.1 Interference Counts.

The subject matter of an interference is defined by one or more interference "counts."[61] Interference counts read like patent claims but only serve to decide who was the first to invent. Multiple counts are used in an interference only when each count defines a "separate patentable invention" (one party can win on one count and lose on another count). If it is necessary to artificially create a count that is broader than the claim of any party to bring interfering yet different claims together in an interference proceeding, that count is referred to as a "phantom count." Once the interference is declared, all the interfering claims in the applications and patents considered to define "the same patentable invention"[62] are designated to the count. Obviously, subsequent motions to present new counts and reformulate old counts in the way most favorable to a party later becomes an important part of the overall interference strategy.[63]

10.3.1.2 Initiating the Interference at the Applicant's Request.

An interference with either another application or another patent can be initiated at the request of the applicant. In the case of another application, the applicant proceeds by:

> (1) suggesting a proposed count and presenting a claim corresponding to the proposed count, (2) identifying the other application and, if known, a claim in the other application which corresponds to the proposed count, and (3) explaining why an interference should be declared.[64]

In the case of another application, the applicant proceeds similarly by:

> (1) presenting a proposed count and a claim corresponding to the proposed count and, if any claim of the patent or application does not correspond exactly to the proposed count, explaining why an interference should be declared, (2) identifying the patent and

indicating which claim in the application and which claim or claims of the patent correspond to the proposed count, and (3) applying the terms of the application claim corresponding to the count to the disclosure of the application.[65]

In either case, if the applicant presents claims corresponding to those found in a patent or application, the applicant is *obligated* to identify that patent or application to the examiner.[66]

10.3.1.3 Initiating the Interference at the Examiner's Request. When a patent examiner is aware of a pending patent application or an issued patent containing claims that he or she believes interfere with the claims of a pending application, the examiner can suggest that an applicant present claims for the purpose of initiating an interference. Following such a suggestion, the applicant must proceed as follows:

> The applicant to whom the claim is suggested shall amend the application by presenting the suggested claim within a time specified by the examiner, not less than one month. Failure or refusal of an applicant to timely present the suggested claim shall be taken without further action as a disclaimer by the applicant of the invention defined by the suggested claim.[67]

10.3.2 Interferences Between Issued Patents

There must be at least one patent application pending that contains interfering subject matter for the patent and trademark office to have jurisdiction to act. If two or more patents actually issue that contain interfering claims, the patent owner can bring a civil action in U.S. District Court to resolve the interference.[68]

10.4 PRIORITY UNDER THE FIRST-TO-FILE SYSTEM

The first-to-file system appears deceptively simple: the person who files a patent application first, wins. This is not the end of the process, however. Almost all inventions are capable of improvement (both obvious and nonobvious), and the way such improvement inventions are treated differs drastically between the United States and first-to-file jurisdictions such as the European Patent Convention. Failing to consider these distinctions can lead to forfeiting significant patent rights in a number of jurisdictions, even for someone who is neither the first to file nor the first to invent.

In the United States, so-called "secret prior art" creates consistent problems. These are U.S. patent applications that are filed before, but not made publicly available as issued patents until after, a later application is filed. Such patents are effective as prior art references as of their filing date[69] but are held in confidence by the patent office until they issue.[70] In the United States, secret prior art can be used as either an anticipatory reference or in combination with other references to show obviousness.

A significantly different view applies in the European Patent Office. Article 54 (the novelty section) of the European Patent Convention provides as follows:

(3) Additionally, the content of European patent applications as filed, of which the dates of filing are prior to the date referred to in paragraph 2 and which were published under Article 93 on or after that date, shall be considered as comprised in the state of the art.

Article 56 (the inventive step section) of the EPC further states:

If the state of the art also includes documents within the meaning of Article 54, paragraph 3, these documents are not to be considered in deciding whether there has been an inventive step.

Hence, while secret prior art can be used in the EPO to show an invention lacks novelty, it cannot be used to show that the invention lacks an inventive step. This provides a significant opportunity for obtaining patent protection in Europe and other jurisdictions that apply a similar approach, even when it is unavailable in the United States. In summary, a first-to-file system does not only mean patent applications should be filed early, it also means that in an important field, patent applications should be filed frequently and on all aspects of a particular invention. Then, even if the basic patent rights are lost, the patent rights to at least the significant improvement inventions may be secured.

REFERENCES

1. *See, generally*, THE ADVISORY COMMISSION ON PATENT LAW REFORM, A REPORT TO THE SECRETARY OF COMMERCE (August 1992).
2. Hybritech Inc. v. Monoclonal Antibodies, Inc. 802 F.2d 1367, 231 USPQ 81, 87 (Fed. Cir. 1986), *cert. denied*, 480 U.S. 947 (1987).
3. Mergenthaler v. Scudder, 11 App. D.C. 264, 1897 C.D. 724 (D.C. Cir. 1897).
4. Haskell v. Colebourne, 671 F.2d 1362, 213 USPQ 192, 195 (C.C.P.A. 1982).
5. Silvestri v. Grant, 496 F.2d 593, 181 USPQ 706 (C.C.P.A. 1974), *cert. denied*, 420 U.S. 928 (1975).
6. Smith v. Bosquet, 111 F.2d 157, 45 USPQ 347 (C.C.P.A. 1940).
7. Smith, 45 USPQ at 348.
8. Amgen Inc. v. Chugai Pharmaceutical Co., 927 F.2d 1200, 18 USPQ2d 1016 (Fed. Cir. 1991), *cert. denied*, 112 S. Ct. 169 (1991).
9. Fiers v. Revel, 984 F.2d 1164, 25 USPQ2d 1601 (Fed. Cir. 1993).
10. Amgen, 927 F.2d at 1206.
11. Amgen, 927 F.2d at 1206.
12. Fiers, 984 F.2d at 1166–68.
13. Fiers, 984 F.2d at 1168.
14. Fiers, 984 F.2d at 1169.
15. Rey-Bellet v. Engelhardt, 493 F.2d 1380, 181 USPQ 453 (C.C.P.A. 1974); *see also* Fay, *Conception of a Chemical Compound—Is a Mental Formation of Utility Required?*, 56 J. PAT. OFF. SOC'Y 482 (1974).

16. *See* D'Amico v. Brown, 155 USPQ 534 (Bd. Pat. Int'f 1967); Bey v. Kollonitsch, 215 USPQ 454 (Bd. Pat. Int'f 1981).
17. Rey-Bellet v. Engelhardt, 493 F.2d 1380, 181 USPQ 453 (C.C.P.A. 1974).
18. *See also* Suh v. Hoefle, 23 USPQ2d 1321, 1329 (Bd. Pat. App. 1991) ("Conception requires (1) the idea of the structure of the chemical compound, and (2) possession of an operative method of making it.").
19. *In re* Merck, 800 F.2d 1091, 231 USPQ 375 (Fed. Cir. 1986).
20. *See* Oka v. Youssefyeh, 849 F.2d 581, 7 USPQ2d 1169 (Fed. Cir. 1988).
21. *See, e.g.*, Suh v. Hoefle, 23 USPQ2d 1321 (Bd. Pat. App. 1991).
22. *See In re* Zletz, 893 F.2d 319, 13 USPQ2d 1320 (Fed. Cir. 1989).
23. *See* Ganguly v. Sunagawa, 5 USPQ2d 1970 (Bd. Pat. App. 1987).
24. *See generally* 1 D. Chisum, PATENTS, § 2.02 (1991).
25. Hazeltine Corp. v. United States, 820 F.2d 1190, 2 USPQ2d 1744 (Fed. Cir. 1987).
26. *See* Feldman v. Aunstrup, 517 F.2d 1351, 186 USPQ 108 (C.C.P.A. 1975), *cert. denied*, 424 U.S. 912 (1976).
27. Bigham v. Godtfredsen, 857 F.2d 1415, 8 USPQ2d 1266 (Fed. Cir. 1988).
28. Staehelin v. Secher, 24 USPQ2d 1513, 1515 (Bd. Pat. App. 1992).
29. Staehelin, 24 USPQ2d at 1516.
30. Staehelin, 24 USPQ2d at 1517.
31. *See* Thomas v. Eicken, 219 USPQ 900 (Bd. Pat. Int'f 1983).
32. Newkirk v. Lulejian, 825 F.2d 1581, 3 USPQ2d 1793 (Fed. Cir. 1987).
33. *See* Medtronic, Inc. v. Daig Corp., 611 F. Supp. 1498, 227 USPQ 509 (D. Minn. 1985), *aff'd*, 789 F.2d 903, 229 USPQ 664 (Fed. Cir. 1986), *cert. denied*, 479 U.S. 931 (1986).
34. *See* P. Morris, *Actual Reduction to Practice in Biotechnology*, 71 J. PAT. & TRADEMARK OFF. SOC'Y 311 (1989).
35. *See* Hoffman v. Klaus, 9 USPQ2d 1657, 1660 (Bd. Pat. App. 1988); Fisher v. Bouzard, 3 USPQ2d 1677 (Bd. Pat. App. 1987).
36. *See* Cross v. Iizuka, 753 F.2d 1040, 224 USPQ 739 (Fed. Cir. 1985).
37. Brown v. Barton, 102 F.2d 193, 41 USPQ 99 (C.C.P.A. 1939).
38. *See* Hunter v. Beissbarth, 230 USPQ 365 (Bd. Pat. App. 1986).
39. Hybritech Inc. v. Abbott Laboratories, 4 USPQ2d 1001 (C.D. Cal. 1987), *aff'd*, 849 F.2d 1446, 7 USPQ2d 1191 (Fed. Cir. 1988).
40. Hybritech, 4 USPQ2d at 1006.
41. Griffith v. Kanamaru, 816 F.2d 624, 2 USPQ2d 1361 (Fed. Cir. 1987).
42. Coleman v. Dines, 754 F.2d 353, 224 USPQ2d 857 (Fed. Cir. 1985).
43. Nashef v. Pollock, 4 USPQ2d 1631 (Bd. Pat. App. 1987).
44. Pollock, 4 USPQ2d at 1636.
45. Hahn v. Wong, 892 F.2d 1028, 13 USPQ2d 1313 (Fed. Cir. 1989).
46. Hybritech Inc. v. Monoclonal Antibodies, Inc., 802 F.2d 1367, 231 USPQ 81 (Fed. Cir. 1986), *cert. denied*, 480 U.S. 947 (1987).
47. Hybritech, 802 F.2d at 1378.
48. Lutzker v. Plet, 843 F.2d 1364, 1366, 6 USPQ2d 1370 (Fed. Cir. 1988).
49. *See, e.g.*, Palmer v. Dudzik, 481 F.2d 1377, 178 USPQ 608 (C.C.P.A. 1973).
50. Paulik v. Rizkalla, 760 F.2d 1270, 226 USPQ 224 (Fed. Cir. 1985).
51. Paulik, 760 F.2d at 1273.
52. Paulik, 760 F.2d at 1275–76.
53. *In re* Hilmer, 424 F.2d 1108, 165 USPQ 225 (C.C.P.A. 1970).
54. *See, e.g.*, Clevinger v. Kooi, 190 USPQ 379 (Bd. Pat. Int'f 1974); Staehelin v. Secher, 24 USPQ2d 1513, 1521–22 (Bd. Pat. App. 1992).

55. *See generally* 37 CFR §§ 1.601–1.688.
56. *See, e.g.*, B. Collins, CURRENT PATENT INTERFERENCE PRACTICE (1987) (Prentice Hall Law and Business).
57. *See* 35 U.S.C § 135.
58. 37 C.F.R § 1.602.
59. 37 C.F.R § 1.601(i).
60. 35 U.S.C § 135(b).
61. 37 C.F.R § 1.601(f).
62. 37 C.F.R §§ 1.603 and 1.606.
63. *See, e.g.*, 37 C.F.R § 1.633(c).
64. 37 C.F.R § 1.604(a).
65. 37 C.F.R § 1.607(a).
66. *See* 37 C.F.R §§ 1.604(b) and 1.607(c).
67. 37 C.F.R § 1.605(a) (emphasis added).
68. 35 U.S.C. § 291.
69. 35 U.S.C. § 102(e).
70. 35 U.S.C. § 122.

11

Plant Biotechnology

Virginia C. Bennett

Patent protection for plants was not available in the United States before 1930. The courts reasoned that since plants were products of nature, they did not fall within Constitutional patenting powers.[1] The increasing economic importance of plant breeders in the booming agricultural industry of the 1900s, however, created pressure for some sort of intellectual property protection for new and useful plant varieties.

11.1 PLANT PATENTS

In the United States, ownership rights in plants now are conferred specifically by two different and not necessarily exclusive statutory systems: the Plant Patent Act[2] (PPA) and the Plant Variety Protection Act[3] (PVPA). These provisions were developed before the growth of genetic engineering, however, and are not designed to protect transgenic plants or the methods of producing them. Since 1985, utility patents have been available to protect transgenic plants. Utility patents also may be used to protect new plant varieties that could be protected under the PPA or PVPA as well. Each system has different application procedures and varies in the nature and extent of rights granted. In certain cases, forgoing formal protection and keeping a plant as a trade secret may be the preferred strategy. Plants and cell lines, as tangible property, also may be protected against misappropriation by the common law of conversion. The most useful approach in any one case ultimately depends on

171

the specifics of the plant or plant part for which protection is sought, its economic use, and the needs and resources of the owner.

International protection of plant varieties is available through the International Union for the Protection of New Varieties of Plants (UPOV, an acronym taken from the group's French name). Protection also may be available through the European Patent Convention for plants produced using recombinant technology.

The following section outlines the extent of plant protection available in the United States through plant patents, the Plant Variety Protection Act (PVPA), and utility patents. Trade secrets will be discussed briefly, as will the concept of plants as tangible property and the protection of plants in the international market.

11.1.1   The Plant Patent Act of 1930

Before 1930, plants were denied patent protection because plant breeding techniques were not considered sufficiently inventive to warrant patent protection. More pragmatically, it was assumed that plant breeders were unable to create true-to-type varieties and that plants could not be described with the detail needed to distinctly claim a specific variety. As a result, profits on a newly developed plant were limited to first sales. Once a plant or seed was sold, any subsequent owner could legally propagate and sell the variety—clearly an economic disadvantage to developing improved plants.

The Plant Patent Act (PPA) of 1930 provided that:

> Whoever invents or discovers and <u>asexually reproduces</u> any distinct and new variety of plant, including cultivated sports, mutants, hybrids, and newly found seedlings, other than a tuber propagated plant or a plant found in an uncultivated state, may obtain a patent therefor, subject to the conditions and requirements of this title.[4]

The PPA was integrated into the larger framework of general patent law contained in Title 35 of the United States Code, which means that applications for plant patents now are made to the patent and trademark office.

Only asexually reproduced plants are eligible for plant patents. Asexual reproduction is that achieved by means other than using seeds and includes rooting of cuttings, layering, budding, grafting, inarching, and so on. The breeder's work is seen as an "aid to nature" worthy of patent protection. The term *plant* as used in the act refers only to plants in the ordinary sense of the word and does not include bacteria or parts of plants, or tissue cultures.[5] There is no protection for varieties reproduced from seeds, tubers (Irish potatoes and Jerusalem artichokes),[6] or wild varieties found in nature but not asexually reproduced.

A plant patent grants protection for a specific variety of plant and not for a group of varieties with a single trait. Thus, the first plant patent to issue on a yellow African violet would encompass only that particular variety. A subsequently developed variety of yellow African Violet also could be patented. Despite sharing the commercially valuable characteristic of color, it would not be covered by the previous plant patent if otherwise distinct.

Infringement of a plant patent occurs when the patented plant is asexually reproduced without permission. A plant patent grants the patent owner a 17-year period during which he or she can prevent others from asexually reproducing the plant, or selling or using a plant asexually reproduced.[7] A patent holder *cannot* prevent another from reproducing the patented variety sexually. Protection is limited to the plant as a whole, so patent holders cannot prevent the sale of the flowers or fruit of illegally grown, patented varieties. In addition, the sports or mutants of a patented plant are not protected, and if asexual reproduction of a sport or mutant leads to a new variety, it is patentable. Unlike a utility patent, a plant patent will not necessarily prevent all copying. A competitor is free to independently develop a variety with all the characteristics of the patented plant, if otherwise distinct.

11.1.2   Patentability

The invention of a plant has been defined as the discovery of new traits plus the "foresight and appreciation to take the step of asexual reproduction."[8] A sport or mutant newly discovered in a cultivated field and asexually reproduced can be patented under the PPA. In *Ex parte Foster*, however, the patent office stated that there is no inventive step for a plant variety newly discovered in the wild, even if it is subsequently cultivated and asexually reproduced.[9] The PTO reasoned that it could not give a different interpretation to the statutory words "invents or discovers"[10] when the item sought to be patented was a plant. The accepted interpretation was that an invention or discovery must be of something that did not exist before, rather than something that was merely unknown or overlooked. In *Foster,* the board noted that the legislative history behind the Plant Patent Act indicated Congress wished to specifically exclude plants existing in nature. However, an isolated stand of such plants, a collection of seeds from them, an accumulation of parts of such plants, and so on might be protectable under the Utility Patent Act, which will be discussed in the following section.

The Plant Patent Act was incorporated into the existing patent statutes. Unless a specific exception is made, the applicable law is the same for both plant patents and utility patents. Novelty, utility, and nonobviousness are required in plant patents just as in utility patents.

In a plant patent, utility is considered to be equal to distinctness (the totality of the plant's distinguishing characteristics). Novelty also is required, with the same conditions that render an invention non-novel under Section 102 applying to plants. Thus, public use or sale may prevent patenting a plant variety.[11] However, the mere existence of the plant prior to asexual reproduction and patenting is not, in itself, conclusive evidence of prior use and knowledge by others.[12]

The obviousness of a newly derived plant has been examined on the basis of "the underlying Constitutional standard that it codifies, namely, invention."[13] In *Yoder Brothers*, the court said:

> If the plant is a source of food, the ultimate question might be its nutritive content or its
> prolificacy. A medicinal plant might be judged by its increased or changed therapeutic

value. Similarly, an ornamental plant would be judged by its increased beauty and desirability in relation to other plants of its type, its usefulness in the industry, and how much of an improvement it represents over prior ornamental plants, taking all of its characteristics together.[14]

As pointed out by Iver Cooper, the analysis of obviousness set forth in *Yoder Brothers* is severely flawed. For practical purposes, the PTO usually takes the position that a variety that is "distinct" under Section 161 is also nonobvious.[15]

The description requirement of Section 112 has been statutorily altered for plants by Section 161, which states that "[n]o plant patent shall be declared invalid for noncompliance with section 112 of this title if the description is as complete as is reasonably possible." A clear and complete description according to standard botanical methods is required.[16] This creates a double standard because, if published, a description sufficient for the application might not be an enabling publication that would bar a patent.[17] A complete published description would not by itself be enabling if access to the plant material were required to reproduce the variety. Under Section 161, however, the same description would be sufficient for the application if it were as complete as possible.

Because plant patents issue on the whole plant, only a single claim is permitted.[18] No method claims are allowed. For example, the patent for Rose Plant Jacinal, Plant Patent 5,734, granted May 6, 1986 claims:

> A new and distinct variety of rose plant of the floribunda class, substantially as herein shown and described, characterized particularly as to novelty by the unique combination of abundant production of medium length stems bearing deep pink buds comparable to R.H.S. Colour Chart Red 51A, opening to lighter pink blooms, of very little fragrance.

The specification of the application must contain as full and complete a disclosure as possible of the plant and the characteristics that distinguish it from related varieties and its antecedents.[19] Drawings or photographs are required. The application may be rejected if the examiner is unable to make a meaningful comparison of the claimed characteristics with the characteristics of known varieties. In *Application of Greer*,[20] rejection of a plant application was upheld when the applicant described the allegedly superior qualities of the claimed plant but did not offer any data on comparative studies of the claimed plant and existing varieties.

The specification also must point out where and in what manner the variety of plant was asexually reproduced or, in the case of a plant newly found in a cultivated state, the location and character of the area where the plant was discovered.[21]

Plant patent applications are submitted to the Patent and Trademark Office, which in turn submits the applications to the Agricultural Research Service (ARS) of the U.S. Department of Agriculture for review. An advisory report is prepared by the ARS regarding whether the claimed plant is distinct over known varieties, although the official PTO action may or may not quote the ARS report. While the PTO examiner may show the ARS report to the inventor or the inventor's attorney, this is not required. If the ARS report states that its specialists are unable to determine whether the claimed variety is new and distinct, the PTO may require the applicant to submit affidavits or declarations from recognized plant experts regarding novelty.[22] Similarly, when rejection is based on an ARS report stating that the variety is not new, affidavits of the applicant and others may be used to contradict or further explain the ARS report.[23]

11.2   THE PLANT VARIETY PROTECTION ACT OF 1970

Plant patents grant protection to asexually reproduced plants, but until the Plant Variety Protection Act[24] (PVPA) of 1970 was passed, no protection was available for sexually reproduced varieties. The impetus for the passage of the PVPA was, in part, the protection granted to sexually reproduced plants in the international market by the UPOV, passed in 1961 and discussed in detail in the following section. The PVPA is administered by the U.S. Department of Agriculture and is distinct from the patent system as a whole; it is a registration system and issues Plant Variety Protection Certificates (PVPCs). Application procedures are contained in Title 7 of the United States Code, starting at Section 2422. Issued PVPCs are published in the *Plant Variety Protection Office Official Journal.*

The PVPA provides to sexually reproduced plants much of the protection available to asexually reproduced plants through plant patents. Sexually reproducing plants are defined as nonhybrids that breed true-to-type. Specifically excluded from PVPA protection are fungi, bacteria, tuber-propagated or uncultivated plants, and first-generation hybrids. The rights granted by the PVPA are limited to the variety claimed and do not encompass a group of varieties sharing a common trait.

Certificates are issued for novel varieties that are: (1) distinctive, (2) uniform, and (3) stable when sexually reproduced.[25] These three points are often called the "DUS" criteria. A variety is distinctive if it "clearly differs by one or more identifiable morphological, physiological, or other characteristics."[26] For example, the distinctive characteristics of Soybean 9251 (Certificate No. 8600121) are that, while it is most similar to soybean variety DSR 227, it is resistant to "races 1 and 2 of Phytophthora, and has a low seed protein peroxidase activity; whereas DSR 227 is susceptible to Phytophthora (races 1 and 2) and has high peroxidase activity." The chrysanthemum "Santana" (Certificate No. 8600076) is distinguished from its nearest cultivar by being smaller and more compact, and day-length neutral. Distinctive characteristics include those that are important only in the ultimate product, such as baking or fiber characteristics. A common reason for rejecting PVPC applications is that the applicant is unable to sufficiently describe and identify the distinguishing characteristics of the variety claimed.

A PVPC grants an owner the right to exclude others from importing or exporting the variety; selling or offering the variety for sale; sexually or asexually reproducing the variety; and from distributing, without proper notice of the PVPC, the variety to others in a form that can be propagated.[27] The owner also has the right to exclude others from producing a hybrid or different variety using the protected variety, although there is an exemption for *developing* a hybrid using the protected variety. These rights last for 18 years.[28] Infringement also may occur *prior* to the issuance of a certificate; novel varieties marked "propagation prohibited" may be distributed without losing protection as long as the variety is under testing or a PVPC application has been filed. This is in sharp contrast to the Utility Patent Act, where no protection exists until the patent actually issues.

A series of statutory bars exist that will defeat a PVPC application.[29] For example, public use or sale for more than a year prior to filing is a bar. While a publication describing the variety is not necessarily a bar under the Plant Patent Act, under the PVPA a publication describing the distinguishing characteristics and indicating a source from which the variety could be purchased, or teaching how to produce the variety from available material, will bar a PVPC.[30]

11.2.1 Exemptions in the PVPA

There are two important exemptions to PVPC protection. Breeders can use a protected variety to develop new varieties under the research exemption;[31] under the crop exemption[32] farmers can save seed for crop production or for sale to other farmers for crop production.

11.2.1.1 The Research Exemption. The research exemption mandates that a breeder cannot keep others from using the protected variety to *develop* a new variety or hybrid. This is distinguished from using a protected variety to *produce* a new variety or hybrid, which is prohibited. For example, a breeder who crossed protected variety X with variety Y to develop new variety Z would violate the PVPA's ban on production if this method were used in producing variety Z plants for sale. However, if Z were capable of inbreeding and production involved only Z plants, no violation would occur because the protected variety was used only in *developing Z*. The research exemption for PVPCs thus would seem significantly broader and more tangible than the court-created "experimental use" exemption for utility patents.

11.2.1.2 The Crop Exemption. Under the crop exemption, once the initial crop is grown, an individual whose primary occupation is growing crops for food (rather than growing plants for their seed) does not infringe a PVPC by saving seed from that crop to produce another crop. And while the unauthorized sale of seed harvested from protected varieties is infringing under Section 2541, Title 7 of the United States Code, the crop exemption provides a limited exemption from Section 2541. Thus, farmers may save and sell seed harvested from crops grown with PVPA-protected seed under certain conditions. These sales are commonly termed "brown-bag" sales to distinguish them from sales made by the PVPC holder.

The Federal Circuit Court recently clarified the rights provided by the crop exemption in *Asgrow Seed Company v. Winterboer*.[33] The court noted that the PVPA clearly states that an individual can save the seed of a protected variety only if the parent seed was obtained "by authority of the owner of the variety."[34] Thus, a farmer who purchases the seed of a protected variety in a brown-bag sale cannot save any seed from the resulting crop because he or she did not obtain the parent seed from the PVPC holder. However, a farmer who purchases seed from the PVPC holder can save seed from the resulting crop.

The pivotal issue in *Asgrow Seed Company* was how much of a given crop could be sold in brown-bag seed sales. The act clearly states that both buyer and seller must be farmers whose "primary farming occupation" is growing the crop for food. However, "primary" is not defined, and it is unclear how much of the original crop must be sold as food before the crop exemption will apply. The Federal Circuit Court interpreted "primary" to mean that a majority of the crop must be used for food. A farmer who purchases protected seed from the PVPC holder and sells or uses the majority of the resulting crop for food, therefore, can sell the remaining seed in brown-bag sales to other farmers. The sale must be between farmers and cannot involve a third party who provides marketing assistance.[35] The farmer who purchases seed in brown-bag sales can neither save nor sell the seed of the resulting crop.

In addition to these two exemptions, the U.S. Secretary of Agriculture has the power to mandate that a protected variety is open for use upon payment of a reasonable royalty to the plant owner. This compulsory licensing power can be exercised only when necessary to insure an adequate supply of "fiber, food, or feed" in the United States at a fair price.[36] No such compulsory licensing power exists under the Utility Patent Act.

11.3   TRADE SECRETS

Trade secrets are governed by state laws, which vary across the country. In general, a trade secret is any device, formula, pattern, or compilation of information that provides a competitive business advantage to the possessor and is guarded by the possessor. More simply put, a trade secret relates to business and is kept a secret. State courts vary on the extent of security required to confer "secret" status and on the specific forms of misappropriation that are prohibited.

Trade secrets have limited applicability to plants. In most situations, the sale of the plant or seed effectively discloses any secret. In addition, the security measures required to keep a plant grown in the open a trade secret can be too burdensome to maintain. Where two inbred parent plants are used to produce hybrid seed for sale, however, relying on trade-secret law is often preferred over obtaining a plant patent or PVPC. The primary advantage is that trade-secret protection can theoretically last indefinitely, or as long as the secret is maintained.

Protecting the identity and seed of inbred parents to a hybrid is a common practice, especially for corn varieties. The hybrid seed produces plants that are larger and more vigorous than either parent but seed from these hybrids will not reproduce plants as desirable as the initial hybrid generation or as valuable in the marketplace. The inbred parent corn plants must be grown outdoors. While open fields contrast with the usual locked doors of trade secrets, a recent district court decision (discussed below) held that the "genetic message" of such a parent corn plant can be given trade-secret status.[37]

11.4 PLANTS AS TANGIBLE PROPERTY

New plant varieties and genetically engineered plant cell lines require access to the original invention material in order to practice the invention. This situation contrasts with other forms of patented intellectual property, where anyone with knowledge of the invention can readily practice it. With many plants, of course, commercialization requires that the plants be sold, and once plants are sold tangible property rights in those materials are generally exhausted. An emerging line of thought argues that due to the physical aspect of the invention, a protectable property right exists in the genetic message of a cell line or plant variety.

In *Pioneer Hi-Bred v. Holden Foundation Seeds*, the Southern District Court of Iowa stated that the plaintiff had a property interest in the "genetic message" of an inbred parent corn plant that was protected by the common law of conversion. However, the *Pioneer Hi-Bred* discussion of property rights is non-binding dicta because the actual case was decided under trade secret law. It remains to be seen how far this line of protection might be extended under state law before being considered pre-empted by federal law.

11.5 UTILITY PATENTS

What is commonly referred to as a patent is more correctly called a utility patent. Utility patents are issued for any "new and useful process, machine, manufacture, or composition of matter, or any new and useful improvement thereof."[38] While utility patents have long been granted for processes involving living organisms, not until *Diamond v. Chakrabarty* was authority provided for a utility patent claiming a living thing *per se*.[39] However, the *Chakrabarty* decision did not answer the question of whether plants could be claimed in utility patents because the additional issue of statutory exemption existed. Because the PPA and PVPA statutory schemes already provided marketplace protection to plant breeders, it was argued that plants had been specifically removed (statutorily preempted) from utility patent protection. In *Ex parte Hibberd*,[40] however, the Board of Appeals and Interferences in the PTO ruled that there was no conflict between existing statutory protection for plants and utility patent protection. While no *court* has ruled on the question yet, many utility patents have issued since then on new varieties of plants and on genetically altered plants.

A utility patent may claim a new plant variety that may be propagated either asexually or sexually. A variety is claimed simply by reciting its designation. First-generation hybrid plants and seeds also may be claimed by designation. A utility patent provides a 17-year period of protection during which the patent owner can prevent others from making, using, and selling the plant.

A utility patent also can provide generic protection, covering not only the variety developed but also subsequently developed plants with all of the characteristics of the claimed plant. For example, U.S. Patent No. 5,124,505 claims a celery plant "having all of the characteristics of a plant produced by seed deposited with the American Type Culture Collection and assigned accession number 40621, and progeny, clones, and somaclones having all of said characteristics thereof."

Claims may be directed to distinct phenotypic characteristics or to a combination of phenotypic and genotypic characteristics; genetic characteristics can be claimed whether they arise through selective breeding or through recombinant technologies. U.S. Patent No. 5,082,993 claims "a corn plant of the line WIL500 wherein said plant produces corn kernels containing at least 10.5% crude protein and 0.31% lysine based on 12% kernel moisture." U.S. Patent No. 5,107,064 lists genetic and phenotypic characteristics, claiming seed with:

> a homozygous allelic pair of dwarf genes . . . conditioning for reduced internode length, which seed will, upon cultivation, produce a fully fertile plant which is characterized by reduced internode length and which exhibits no increase in internode elongation upon the application of an aqueous solution having a concentration of 100 to 1,000 mg gibberellic acid per liter of water.

Plant products such as seeds, fruit, and flowers, as well as plant genes, gene transfer vectors, transgenic plants, tissue culture techniques, processes for producing plants, and hybrid plants also have been successfully claimed.

11.5.1 Requirements

The requirements for obtaining a utility patent for a plant are the same as for any other invention: novelty, utility, nonobviousness, and enablement. The enablement requirement can be met for biological inventions by making a deposit of biological materials exemplifying the claimed invention in a suitable manner. The deposit allows others to obtain propagatable material after the patent issues and ensures an enabling disclosure. However, only stable and storable materials such as seeds are accepted by depositories.

Published descriptions printed more than one year prior to filing the patent application may be a statutory bar under Section 102(b) if the publication is enabling. While it was held that a mere description and photograph of a new rose variety was *not* an enabling publication in *In re Le Grice*,[41] in *Ex Parte Thomson*[42] the Board of Patent Appeals and Interferences found that a printed description of a new cotton cultivar was enabling because the seed of the cultivar was available commercially in a foreign country at the time of publication. Given the description in the publication and the availability of the seed, the board reasoned that someone skilled in cotton cultivation could have practiced the claimed invention.

11.6 THE STRATEGY OF PROTECTING PLANTS

In deciding whether to obtain a plant patent, PVPC, or a utility patent for a particular plant, the method of production, the potential use, and the needs and resources of the

TABLE 11–1   **Plant Patent Act—35 U.S.C. § 161 *et seq.***

Protects:	• Asexually reproduced plants, including cultivated sports, mutants, and hybrids
Excludes:	• Uncultivated or tuber-propagated plants
Requires:	• Novelty
	• Distinctness
	• Stability
Disclosure:	• As complete as reasonably possible
	• Photographs or drawings required
	• No deposit of material required
Claims:	• Single varietal claim
Rights:	• Prevents others from asexually reproducing, selling, or using claimed plant
	• Does *not* protect sexual reproduction of claimed plant
	• Does *not* protect plant products

breeder must be considered. The choice of PPA or PVPA depends on whether the plant is produced sexually or asexually; a plant capable of propagating either way may be protected by both a plant patent and a PVPC. If the plant is simply one newly isolated from nature, utility patent protection or the PVPA may be the only means of protection available. The primary advantage of utility patents is the possibility of generic claims and claims to plant parts or genetic components, although a utility patent also may claim a single variety of plant. Other advantages of utility patents are the lack of exemptions, such as the crop and research exemptions. Two disadvantages of the utility patent act are its complexity and expense. Finally, as the following section discusses, international factors may lead to the strengthening of protection under the PVPA—particularly if the concept of an "essentially derived variety" being explored under the Union for the Protection of New Varieties of Plants is incorporated into U.S. law.

Tables 11-1, 11-2, and 11-3 summarize the requirements and benefits of plant patents, PVPCs, and utility patents.

11.7   INTERNATIONAL CONSIDERATIONS IN PLANT PROTECTION

The Union for the Protection of New Varieties of Plants (UPOV) was created in 1961 to provide international protection to the plant-breeding industry. Each member country agrees to grant the same rights to plant breeders from other member-countries as it provides to its own nationals. The United States became a signatory

TABLE 11–2   Plant Variety Protection Act—7 U.S.C. § 2321 *et seq.*

Protects:	• Sexually reproduced plants
Excludes:	• Bacteria and fungi, first-generation hybrids, uncultivated plants
Requires:	• Distinctness
	• Uniformity
	• Stability
Disclosure:	• Description of novel characteristics and genealogy
	• Seed deposit required
Claims:	• Single varietal claim
Rights:	• Prevents others from importing or selling, sexually or asexually reproducing, distributing without proper notice
	• Prevents others from producing a hybrid or new variety using the claimed plant
	• Exemptions for developing a new hybrid or variety and for farmers' saving and sale of seed; compulsory license provision

TABLE 11–3   Utility Patents—35 U.S.C. § 101 *et seq.*

Protects:	• Plant genotypes not found in nature
Requires:	• Novelty
	• Utility
	• Nonobviousness
	• Enablement
Disclosure:	• Enabling disclosure required
	• Best-mode disclosure required
	• Deposit of novel material required
Claims:	• Varietal claim, generic claims
	• Claims to plant genes, gene transfer vectors, processes for producing plants, and so on
Rights:	• Prevents others from making, using, selling claimed invention
	• Prevents others from selling a component of the claimed invention

country in 1978, and the PVPA was amended in 1980 to conform to UPOV standards. Both the PPA and the PVPA are used in the U.S. to confer rights recognized by UPOV Convention countries. The UPOV Convention was most recently revised on March 19, 1991. As of September 1993, 24 countries were members.[43]

While Section 2 of the original UPOV convention proscribed dual protection for a single variety, Section 37(1) qualified this proscription by allowing the continuance of any forms of protection in use at the time a country became a member. Since the PPA and PVPA had been enacted by the time the United States became a member, a single plant variety capable of being propagated asexually and sexually still could receive both a plant patent for asexually reproduced forms and a PVPC for sexually reproduced forms. While grants of utility patents for plants initially appeared to violate this UPOV ban, the March, 1991 revised UPOV Convention eliminated the ban on double protection.

UPOV protection in any member-country is granted for varieties that are new, distinct, uniform, and stable, whether the plant's origin is natural or artificial. Distinctness is shown if the variety is "distinguishable from any other variety whose existence is a matter of common knowledge" at the time of filing.[44] Common knowledge can be established by showing cultivation or marketing in progress, entry into an official register of varieties, inclusion in a reference collection, or precise description in a publication. Certain time bars exist. Novelty is destroyed if the variety is sold by the breeder or with the breeder's consent in the country where the application is filed more than one year before the date of filing. Sale or distribution in a country other than the one of filing will bar the application if the sale occurred more than four years prior to filing (six years for trees and vines).

The plant breeder chooses in which country the initial application is made. Additional applications in other countries may be made before the first application is granted. Each country is required to make an independent assessment of an application and cannot refuse an application simply because it was not granted or had expired in another country. Subsequent applications made within 12 months after the first application are granted the priority date of the first application.

Under the UPOV Convention, the breeder does not have the right to prevent acts done privately for noncommercial purposes, acts done for experimental purposes, or acts done for the purpose of breeding other varieties. In addition, countries may choose to allow farmers to use the seed obtained from planting the variety on their own land to repropagate the variety on their own land.

11.7.1 Essentially Derived Varieties
Under UPOV

The 1991 revision of the UPOV Convention extended protection to "essentially derived varieties" (EDVs) in an attempt to strengthen protection for plant breeders who initially develop a new and distinct variety against others who merely make derivations from that initial work.[45] The concept of EDVs focuses on the genotype of a protected variety rather than its phenotype.

Under the EDV provision, the breeder's rights granted for a certain variety extend to all "essentially derived varieties." A second variety that contains and expresses the essential part of the initial variety's genotype is an EDV despite any morphological or physiological differences. To be termed an EDV, a plant must contain virtually the totality of the genome of the initial variety and must retain the expression of the essential characteristics that result from the genotype. How much genetic identity is "too much" remains to be decided and may vary from species to species. Factors to be considered may include the breeding technology and the species involved. The concept and limits of the EDV provision will, no doubt, be refined and focused.

It is up to the breeder of the initial variety to enforce his or her rights regarding an EDV. The fact that a plant is an EDV is not to be considered in granting protection under the UPOV Convention; if a new variety meets the requirements it is protectable. However, a breeder of a protected initial variety may prove that a second variety is an EDV by showing genetic conformity, predominant derivation, and the fact that the second variety retains the expression of the initial variety's essential characteristics while being distinct in the sense of Article 7 of UPOV. The second breeder then must prove no genetic conformity or no predominant derivation to avoid the EDV label.

11.7.2   The European Patent Convention

Article 53(b) of the European Patent Convention specifically excludes patent protection for "plant . . . varieties or essentially biological processes for the production of plants or animals." (This exclusion does not extend to microbiological processes or products.) A broad interpretation would leave some plant inventions completely unprotected in European markets. For example, a group of transgenic plants created by inserting a foreign gene into a number of different plant types would be ineligible for varietal protection under the UPOV Convention and ineligible for patent protection under a strict reading of Article 53(b). However, the European Patent Office uses a narrow interpretation of patentability exclusions and will provide generic patent protection for plants if the plant is *not* a "new variety" under the UPOV definition and if the process for producing that plant is not "essentially biological."[46] Under this reasoning many transgenic plants would be patentable, but it appears to be difficult to obtain a European patent for a plant produced by traditional breeding techniques.

REFERENCES

1. *See, e.g., Ex parte* Latimer, Comm'n Dec 123 (1899) (fiber from the needle of an evergreen tree as unpatentable product of nature).
2. 35 U.S.C. §§ 161–64.
3. 7 U.S.C. §§ 2321 *et seq.*
4. 35 U.S.C. § 161 (emphasis added).
5. *In re* Arzberger, 112 F.2d 834, 46 USPQ 32 (C.C.P.A. 1940); *see also* I. Cooper, *Arzberger Under the Microscope*, 78 PATENT AND TRADEMARK REV. 59 (1980).
6. The rationale for the tuber-propagated exception is that in asexually reproduced plants, the same part of the plant that is sold for food is used for propagation.

7. The March, 1991 UPOV Convention has extended the minimum period of protection to 20 years from the date of the grant of breeder's rights (25 years for trees and vines). To comply with the UPOV convention, the PPA will have to be similarly revised.
8. Yoder Bros., Inc. v. California-Florida Plant Corp., 537 F.2d 1347, 193 USPQ 264 (5th Cir.), *cert. denied,* 429 U.S. 1094, 200 USPQ 128 (1977).
9. *Ex parte* Foster, 90 USPQ 16 (Bd. Pat. App. 1951).
10. 35 U.S.C. § 101.
11. Plant patents covering sugarcane varieties were found invalid due to public use two years prior to the plant patent application in Bourne v. Jones, 114 F.Supp. 413, 98 USPQ 206 (D. Fla. 1951), *aff'd,* 207 F.2d 173, 98 USPQ 205 (5th Cir.), *cert. denied,* 346 U.S. 897, 99 USPQ 490 (1953).
12. Nicholson v. Bailey, 182 F.Supp. 509, 125 USPQ 157 (S.D. Fla. 1960).
13. Yoder Bros., Inc. v. California-Florida Plant Corp., 537 F.2d 1347, 193 USPQ 264 (5th Cir. 1976), *cert. denied* 429 U.S. 1094, 200 USPQ 128 (1976).
14. *Id.* at 1379.
15. I. Cooper, BIOTECHNOLOGY AND THE LAW, § 8.06 (1991).
16. "The specification should include a complete detailed description of the plant and the characteristics thereof that distinguish the same over related known varieties, and its antecedents, expressed in botanical terms in the general form followed in standard botanical text books or publications dealing with the varieties of the kind of plant involved (evergreen tree, dahlia plant, rose plant, apple tree, etc.), rather than a mere broad nonbotanical characterization such as commonly found in nursery or seed catalogs. The specification should also include the origin or parentage of the plant variety sought to be patented and must particularly point out where and in what manner the variety of plant has been asexually reproduced. Where color is a distinctive feature of the plant the color should be positively identified in the specification by reference to a designated color as given by a recognized color dictionary." MANUAL OF PATENT EXAMINING PROCEDURES, Ch. 1605.
17. *In re* LeGrice, 301 F.2d 929, 133 USPQ 365 (C.C.P.A. 1962) (Before publication can amount to a statutory bar, the disclosure must be such that a skilled artisan could take the publication's teachings in combination with his or her own knowledge of the particular art and reproduce the invention. Thus, a published picture of a rose in bloom, with a brief description of its color and characteristics, was not enabling and not a bar to a patent.); *but see Ex Parte* Thomson, 24 USPQ2d 1618 (Bd. Pat. App. 1992).
18. 37 C.F.R. 1.164.
19. 37 C.F.R. 1.163(a).
20. *See In re* Greer, 484 F.2d 488, 179 USPQ 301 (C.C.P.A. 1973) (Comparative data was needed to substantiate the claim that the plant had different characteristics than known varieties; it is applicant's duty to provide information so that a meaningful comparison with existing varieties can be made; merely reciting that characteristics differ is insufficient).
21. 37 C.F.R. 1.163(a).
22. 37 C.F.R. 1.167(b).
23. 37 C.F.R. 1.107(b); *See Ex parte* Rosenberg, 46 USPQ 393 (Bd. Pat. App. 1940).
24. 7 U.S.C. § 2321 *et seq.*
25. 7 U.S.C. § 2402.
26. 7 U.S.C. § 2401.
27. 7 U.S.C. § 2541.
28. 7 U.S.C. § 2483. However, the March, 1991 UPOV Convention has extended the minimum period to 20 years from the date of the grant of breeder's rights (25 years for trees

and vines). To comply with the UPOV convention, the PVPA will have to be similarly revised.

29. 7 U.S.C. § 2402.

30. 7 U.S.C. § 2402(a).

31. 7 U.S.C. § 2544.

32. 7 U.S.C. § 2543.

33. Asgrow Seed Co. v. Winterboer, 982 F.2d 486, 25 USPQ2d 1202 (Fed. Cir. 1992).

34. 7 U.S.C. § 2543.

35. Delta and Pine Land Co. v. Peoples' Gin Co., 694 F.2d 1012 (5th Cir. 1983), *aff'd*, 546 F.Supp. 939 (N.D. Miss. 1982).

36. 7 U.S.C. § 2404.

37. Pioneer Hi-Bred International, Inc. v. Holden Foundation Seeds, Inc., No. 81-60-E, slip op. (S.D. Iowa, Oct. 29, 1987).

38. 35 U.S.C. § 101.

39. Diamond v. Chakrabarty, 447 U.S. 303, 206 USPQ 193 (1980).

40. *Ex parte* Hibberd, 227 USPQ 443 (Bd. Pat. App. 1985).

41. *In re* Lebrice, 301 F.2d 929, 133 USPQ 365 (C.C.P.A. 1962).

42. *Ex Parte* Thomson, 24 USPQ2d 1618 (Bd. Pat. App. 1992).

43. As of September 1993, 24 nations belonged to the UPOV Union. They were: Australia, Belgium, Canada, Czech Republic, Denmark, Finland, France, Germany, Hungary, Ireland, Israel, Italy, Japan, the Netherlands, New Zealand, Norway, Poland, Slovakia, South Africa, Spain, Sweden, Switzerland, the United Kingdom, and the United States.

44. UPOV Article 7.

45. UPOV Article 14(5).

46. Lubrizol patent EP122791 (the modification of plant cells with plasmids and production of plants from those cells was allowed by the EPO board of appeals, thus granting patent protection to a method of genetically altering plant cells *and* to the generic group of plants produced. The reasoning was that the plants were not new varieties suitable for UPOV protection and the process was not "essentially biological" due to the amount of human intervention required. Hybrid plants/LUBRIZOL (November 10, 1988; T 320/87, OJ 1990, 71).

12

Foreign Patents

Kenneth D. Sibley

Inventors often consider filing foreign patents only after they have filed a national patent application. This is unfortunate. Treating foreign patents as an afterthought to a U.S. patent often leads to the sacrifice of valuable foreign rights—a sacrifice that few companies can afford in today's competitive climate.

Given the high costs and risks associated with developing biotechnology and the intense, worldwide competition in this area, few companies can afford to forego competing on a global scale. Indeed, even start-up companies now commonly pursue foreign markets.[1] If a company is interested in foreign markets, foreign patents will significantly enhance its chances of success.

Foreign patents have been filed for inventions in biotechnology for more than 100 years.[2] Nevertheless, obtaining foreign patents can be an extremely expensive undertaking—so expensive that some will dismiss pursuing them as a poor investment. This choice limits the markets in which proprietary technology can be successfully introduced, however, and often makes it difficult to bring new technology to market at all. Much of the expense of foreign filings can be controlled through advance planning. In addition, treaty revisions continue to make the pursuit of foreign patents significantly more cost-effective than it was even a few years ago.[3] Established corporations are already successfully using these revisions,[4] with start-up corporations and university research offices close behind.

The following section will address the primary considerations involved in pursuing foreign patents. It will review the long-established "right of priority," which makes the regular pursuit of foreign patents feasible, and then will focus on recent treaty provisions that have made the process more cost-effective. Attention will be given to the tension between obtaining patent protection and publishing research—a frequent issue for those conducting university research. The section will conclude with one suggested approach for pursuing foreign patents.

Substantive patent law provisions vary from country to country. The United States has several provisions that are unique among the major industrial nations, the most notable being that the United States is a first-to-invent rather than a first-to-file country. As a result, different issues arise depending on whether the research on which foreign patents are to be based occurs within or outside the United States. In this book, the term *foreign* applies to countries outside the United States. This term was chosen to more clearly present the legal and procedural issues under current law and is not intended to suggest that the substantive patent law of the United States is superior to that of any other country (a doubtful proposition at best). Nevertheless, many of the general principles in the following section apply equally to research carried on both in and outside of the United States, depending on the national laws and treaty memberships of the country in which that research is conducted.

12.1 AVOIDING FORFEITURE OF FOREIGN PATENT RIGHTS

12.1.1 The Absolute Novelty Requirement

The rules concerning the forfeiture of foreign patent rights are much stricter than the rules concerning the forfeiture of U.S. patent rights. In the United States, a patent application must be filed within one year of certain critical events, such as the publication of an invention, or the right to a patent is lost. (See Chapter 5 for a detailed discussion of the novelty requirement.) For most industrial countries other than the United States, however, there is no one-year grace period: a patent application must be filed before the invention is made public (divulged) or the right to a patent is lost. These are referred to as "absolute novelty" countries. The United Kingdom and Germany, two of the three major pharmaceutical markets outside the United States, are both absolute novelty countries.[5] The third major pharmaceutical market, Japan, is not a strict absolute novelty country but, nevertheless, applies a more rigorous forfeiture standard than the United States does.[6]

The divulgence that results in forfeiture of patent rights in absolute novelty countries need not be a "printed publication," a "public use," or an "offer for sale," all of which are issues under U.S. law. A mere speech or slide presentation at a scientific meeting or trade show usually will be sufficient to forfeit foreign rights, as long as it *enables* others to practice the invention (the following sections will discuss this in greater detail). Under Japanese law, generally speaking, the divulgence must be in Japan to result in forfeiture; divulgence outside of Japan will result in forfeiture only if it rises to the level of a publication.

12.1.2   The Requirement of an Enabling Disclosure

When trying to resurrect rights that have been placed in jeopardy through a divulgence prior to filing a patent application, it is frequently argued that the divulgence did not "enable" others to practice the invention and, therefore, should not result in forfeiture. This often is a losing argument. The enablement issue arises in two distinct contexts in patent law: first, when deciding whether a particular invention is entitled to broad patent protection, and second, when deciding whether a prior divulgence or the like actually bars a patent for the invention.[7] In the first case, the argument usually is that the invention as broadly claimed would be routine for other skilled people to practice. In the second case, the usual argument is that the general disclosure of the invention is *insufficient* to teach these same skilled people how to carry out the claimed invention. These arguments are usually inconsistent. When these two arguments are used, often the best that can be achieved is foreign protection that is substantially more limited than the protection obtained in the United States.

12.1.3   The Right of Priority

Applications do not have to be filed in every country in which patent protection is desired before the invention is divulged. By treaty or agreement in most foreign countries, filing a *utility* patent application in country *A* has the same effect as filing an application in country *B* if an application is actually filed in country *B* within one year (design patents are handled differently). Thus, filing a patent application in the United States will preserve foreign rights in many countries for a full year. Divulgence can take place immediately after the U.S. application is filed, and rights in these countries will not be lost as long as applications for these countries are filed within one year. The right to assert the U.S. filing date as the filing date in these countries is called the *right of priority*. The filing date of the original application is referred to as the *priority date*, and the one-year deadline for filing foreign applications is called the *treaty year*. The most prominent treaty providing this right is the Paris Convention, which includes the United States and more than 90 other countries. Most industrialized countries in the world provide a right to priority but there are a few notable exceptions, some of which are presented in Table 12-1.

TABLE 12–1   **Principal Countries that Are Not Members of the Paris Convention**

(Do NOT Provide a Right of Priority)
Taiwan
India
Venezuela
Thailand

12.1.4   Reconciling the Publication of Articles with the Filing of Patent Applications

The absolute novelty requirement can be troublesome for those carrying out research in a university, where publishing and disseminating information are important goals. The requirement also can be troublesome for start-up companies attempting to build a business around university technology. If steps have not been taken in advance to preserve foreign rights, these companies face the difficult task of sorting through and separating technology for which foreign rights are available from technology for which foreign rights have been lost.

The goals of publishing and disseminating information on the one hand and avoiding forfeiture of foreign patent rights on the other often can be reconciled. Much of the pressure for an early publication date stems from concern over being "scooped" in competitive areas of research. If nothing else, an early patent filing date goes a long way towards establishing who was the first to invent[8] and—through the right of priority—can establish absolute rights to the invention in first-to-file countries. Once priority is established, some find the pressure for early publication alleviated and are able to pursue both publications and further patent filings at a more methodical pace. While patent and publication considerations may not always be reconcilable, well-planned efforts to harmonize these goals before divulgence has occurred are much more successful than attempts to resurrect foreign rights after premature divulgence.[9]

12.2   CHOOSING WHERE TO FILE FOREIGN APPLICATIONS

Without planning, the pursuit of foreign patents can be exceedingly expensive. Simply filing foreign applications can involve translating documents, hiring foreign patent counsel, and paying fees in foreign patent offices. Obtaining and maintaining issued foreign patents is substantially more expensive. Clearly, foreign patent applications should be filed only in those countries where the expense is worthwhile.

Choosing where to file foreign applications involves balancing, country by country, the likely cost of pursuing a patent against the likely benefit of obtaining that patent. A number of factors enter into this equation. The first consideration should be the substantive patent law of a particular country. The subject matter for which patent protection is sought may not be patentable in that country and the working requirements for maintaining exclusivity in that country may be difficult to meet. In addition, annuities for maintaining an issued patent there may be high and patent enforcement may be untenable. Of equal importance are the business considerations involved in pursuing the patent. The country may represent a very important market; there even may be a potential business partner there willing to absorb expenses. Even if no patent is pursued, it may be economically unfeasible for a competitor to commercialize the technology in that country if patent protection is obtained in one or more neighboring countries. Finally, the procedural costs of pursuing a patent in that country should be considered. It may be necessary to retain foreign legal counsel and to pay for the translation of the patent application. It also is possible that a patent can be inexpensively secured in that country without the need for a formal examination procedure.

The speculative nature of patent rights makes deciding where to file foreign applications more difficult. One prominent federal judge has likened the pursuit of patents to betting on horses, observing that "not every horse places in a race but those which do make the race very attractive."[10] Pursuing a patent that ultimately has no value may be part of the expense of building an effective patent portfolio, but needlessly pursuing such patents worldwide is an undue drain on resources.

12.3 STRATEGY: PRESERVE FOREIGN RIGHTS AND DEFER FOREIGN COSTS

The high costs of foreign filings and the speculative nature of patent rights lead to a simple rule for pursuing foreign patents: *preserve foreign rights and defer foreign costs*. Once rights are preserved, a foreign filing program can be narrowed by dropping applications if it later appears that the patent either has little value or has been filed in more countries than necessary for protection. As the following section discusses, modern treaty provisions make it possible to significantly narrow a foreign filing program before many expenses need be incurred.

12.3.1 Integrated Pursuit of European Patents: The European Patent Convention

Under the European Patent Convention (EPC), a single patent application can be filed for a European patent in the European Patent Office (EPO). The object of the EPC is to make the protection of an invention in member countries simpler, cheaper, and more reliable by creating a single European procedure for the granting of patents on the basis of a uniform body of substantive patent law.[11] While not all European countries are members of the EPC, the current membership includes Germany, the United Kingdom, and France (see Table 12-2). Currently, the granting of a European patent leads to a bundle of national patents, each of which must be validated and each of which is enforced under the same provisions of national law that govern patents issued from the national patent office for that country. Further adaptation and consolidation of patent laws within the European Economic Community (EEC) is planned.

For searching and examination, an EPO application may be filed in either French, German, or English, deferring the expense of translations until after the patent is granted. After being granted it must be validated in those member countries of the EPC that were designated when the application was filed and where protection is desired. Any translations necessary must be submitted only at the time of validation.

A European patent need not be validated in every country that belongs to the EPC. Instead, it can be validated only in those countries where protection is desired

TABLE 12–2 Member Countries of the European Economic Community (EEC) and the European Patent Convention (EPC)

Country	EEC Member	EPC Member
Austria	No	Yes
Belgium	Yes	Yes
Denmark	Yes	Yes
France	Yes	Yes
Germany	Yes	Yes
Greece[1,2]	Yes	Yes
Ireland[1]	Yes	Yes
Italy	Yes	Yes
Liechtenstein[4]	Yes	Yes
Luxembourg[1]	Yes	Yes
Monaco[1]	No	Yes
Netherlands	Yes	Yes
Portugal[1]	Yes	Yes
Spain[2]	Yes	Yes
Sweden	No	Yes
Switzerland[2,4]	No	Yes
United Kingdom	Yes	Yes

[1] Not a member of the Budapest Treaty.
[2] Not bound by Chapter II of the Patent Cooperation Treaty.
[3] Not a member of the Patent Cooperation Treaty.
[4] Protected under a Swiss or Swiss/EPO patent.

once the examination process is completed—providing an opportunity for narrowing a patent program well after the filing date but before significant additional expenses are incurred. Of course, if patents are only desired in one or two European countries, the procedures of the EPO may not need to be pursued. As progress is made towards a unified Europe under the EEC, however, it may be a serious blunder to forgo patent protection in *any* EEC country if protection within the EEC as a whole is desired. While a discussion of free trade principles under the EEC is beyond the scope of this work, it should be clear that the pursuit of patent protection in Europe should consider European law as a whole, not simply EPC patent law.

A common concern with seeking a European patent is that all of your eggs are in one basket. In practice, however, the European Patent Office appears very careful to be fair to patent applicants—perhaps because it must compete with the national patent offices in Europe for business. There are a number of practical considerations weighing in favor of pursuing a European patent. For example, if a U.S. patent must be enforced in court, it is common practice for an opponent to demand from the patent holder all correspondence that concerns related foreign patents. Statements made in this correspondence often are turned back against the patent holder, making enforcement of the U.S. patent more difficult. The consolidation of European patent proceedings in a single patent office can streamline enforcement of the corresponding U.S. patent.

12.3.2   Integrated Pursuit of Worldwide Patents: The Patent Cooperation Treaty

The Patent Cooperation Treaty (PCT) provides an integrated scheme for pursuing patents in approximately 50 countries worldwide, including most members of the EPC, Japan, Canada, and China (see Table 12-3).[12]

Under the PCT, a single application can be filed, a search report secured, and a preliminary examination obtained before the application must be filed in the national patent offices of the PCT member countries (before the national stage is entered). Foreign rights are preserved in all countries or regions designated at the time the PCT application is filed. As discussed in the following section, most EPO members can be designated under the PCT so the advantages of the PCT generally add to the advantages of the EPC. One of the most significant advantages of the PCT is that a PCT application can be filed and considerable foreign rights preserved simply by mailing it to the U.S. Patent and Trademark Office.

The PCT provides two separate procedures: a search of the invention and an optional, preliminary examination of the invention. Search procedures are set forth in Chapter I of the PCT,[13] with this phase of the proceeding referred to as "PCT Chapter I." Procedures for the optional examination phase are set forth in Chapter II,[14] so this examination phase is called "PCT Chapter II." In general, a PCT application is filed within 12 months of the priority date established by the filing of an original national patent application, is searched within 18 months of the priority

---

TABLE 12–3   Patent Cooperation Treaty (PCT) Member Countries as of March 1994

Europe	Austria, Belarus, Belgium, Bulgaria, the Czech Republic, Denmark, Finland, France, Germany, Greece, Hungary, Ireland, Italy, Latvia, Liechtenstein, Luxembourg, Monaco, the Netherlands, Norway, Poland, Portugal, Romania, the Russian Federation, the Slovak Republic, Slovenia, Spain, Sweden, Switzerland, Ukraine, and the United Kingdom
Asia and the Pacific Rim	Australia, China, Japan, Kazakhstan, Mongolia, New Zealand, North Korea, South Korea, Sri Lanka, Uzbekistan, and Viet Nam
The Americas	Barbados, Brazil, Canada, Trinidad and Tobago, and the United States
Africa	Benin, Burkina Faso, Cameroon, Central African Republic, Chad, Congo, Côte d'Ivoire, Gabon, Guinea, Madagascar, Malawi, Mali, Mauritania, Niger, Senegal, Sudan, and Togo.

date, preliminary examination is requested within 19 months of the priority date,[15] and the preliminary examination is completed within 28 months of the priority date. Therefore, the filing of applications in foreign patent offices (entry into the national stage), with all the attendant costs, is deferred for most PCT countries until 30 months from the priority date.

The PCT sometimes can provide a special benefit for biotechnology inventions. Because of the backlog of cases in the U.S. Patent Office, biotechnology applications often are not searched by the time the treaty year expires. A patent examiner's search, however, provides at least some additional reassurance that foreign filing is justified; that is, that the invention will ultimately be found patentable. If foreign filing through the PCT is chosen, a search report is assured before the national stage is entered.

12.3.3   Using the PCT and the EPC in Combination

All members of the EPC currently belong to the PCT and can be pursued together under the PCT. The EPC is simply designated when the PCT application is filed, and when the PCT proceedings are completed, an EPC application is filed.

Switzerland and Spain belong to the EPC and to PCT Chapter I, but not to PCT Chapter II. This does not present any special problems for those wishing to take advantage of both PCT Chapter II and the EPC. Both Switzerland and Spain will defer the time limit that ordinarily would require entry of their national stage following completion of PCT Chapter I *if* they are designated for a European patent along with other members of the EPC in the PCT application. This allows completion of PCT Chapter II prior to the filing of the European patent application.[16] Thus, the only way to obtain the time-deferral benefit of PCT Chapter II for Switzerland and Spain is to pursue these countries through a European patent.

A final noteworthy advantage of using the PCT and the EPC in combination is that both preliminary searching under PCT Chapter I and preliminary examination under PCT Chapter II may be carried out in the European Patent Office.[17] While these options require the payment of additional fees, there is a strong presumption that a favorable search report and preliminary examination in the EPO for a PCT application will result in the expeditious allowance of a subsequently filed European patent application.

12.4   AN APPROACH TO SECURING FOREIGN PATENTS

This section will present a hypothetical foreign-filing program to point out a cost-effective approach to foreign filing that maximizes the advantages available through the use of PCT Chapter II and the EPC. Of course, an actual foreign patent program would be based on a more detailed analysis of foreign substantive patent law and market considerations than our discussion suggests.

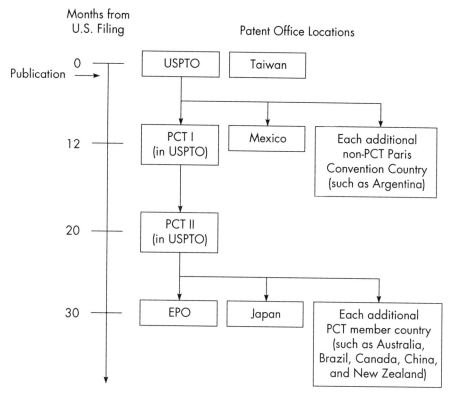

Months from
U.S. Filing   Patent Office Locations

FIGURE 12–1   Illustrative Foreign Filing Program

To understand the program, refer to Figure 12-1, which has a time line down the left margin and represents the various patent offices in which applications must be pursued or maintained in the flow chart. The elements of the flow chart are explained in the following section. The program assumes that filing starts with the filing of a patent application in the United States Patent and Trademark Office (USPTO in Figure 12-1).

12.4.1   Limit Filings in Countries that Do Not Provide a Right to Priority

The first step is to decide whether foreign patent protection will be sought in any country that is not a "right of priority" country, such as Taiwan (see Table 12-1). If this path is chosen, patent applications in these countries must be filed before the invention is divulged regardless of the filing of any U.S. application. In general, this shortens the time frame for filings in that country. For our purposes, we will assume that no special market considerations justify the extra expense and complexity of pursuing foreign applications in countries that do not provide a right to priority.

12.4.2 Preserving Rights in Europe and Japan: Using the PCT and the EPC in Combination

Most U.S. patent applicants also choose to file applications in Europe and Japan. The first issue regarding filing in Europe is whether the cost of a European patent is justified when an applicant could simply file directly in a few selected European countries. Assume that at least three of the countries in Table 12-2 represent attractive markets for the invention, which warrants pursuing these countries through a single European patent application. At this point, the only foreign patent office that must be used to place a foreign application on file is the EPO.[18]

The need for protection in Japan can require filing an application in the Japanese patent office, involving the expense of translating the application into Japanese and retaining a Japanese associate to transact business in the Japanese patent office. However, Japan is a member of both Chapters I and II of the PCT. The strategy, therefore, will be to pursue Japan and the EPC through a single PCT application—a choice that provides still further advantages.

12.4.3 Broaden Options by Preserving Rights in Other PCT Member Countries

Since filing a PCT application has been added to our foreign filing strategy, it is relatively inexpensive to at least preserve rights in other PCT member countries. Table 12-3 shows that Australia, Brazil, New Zealand, Canada, and China are members of the PCT. Thus, substantial additional options in North America and the Pacific rim can be preserved by simply designating additional countries under the PCT. Assume that these countries are designated in our hypothetical PCT application.

12.4.4 Take a Conservative Approach to Filing in Non-PCT Member Countries

A number of countries are not members of the PCT, including most of South America, Mexico, Israel, and the Philippines. All of these countries must be pursued by direct foreign filings within the treaty year. A detailed review of substantive considerations in pursuing patent protection in individual foreign countries is beyond the scope of this book.[19] Briefly, before undertaking such an expense, the following points should be considered: (1) the substantive patent law of the country in which a filing is contemplated, (2) the importance of the market in each of these countries, (3) the enforceability of patents that issue in these countries, and (4) the economic feasibility of a third party practicing the invention in these countries while being blocked from pursuing it in countries where you have patent protection. For our purpose, assume that the only non-PCT country in which patent protection is sought is Mexico.

12.4.5 Drop Less Promising Applications Before Incurring Additional Expenses

Our strategy so far represents a moderately aggressive foreign patent program for a university, a small-to-moderate-sized corporation, and even some large corporations. So far, countries targeted by our program include all EPC member countries, Brazil, Mexico, Canada, Japan, Australia, China, and New Zealand. The hypothetical program is biased towards use of the PCT—a logical consequence of the cost deferrals available through the PCT. The only foreign country in which patent protection will be sought outside the PCT is Mexico.

Figure 12-1 illustrates that the proposed filing program advantageously defers the majority of expenses until about 28 to 30 months from the U.S. filing date, when the majority of individual patent applications are filed in the national patent offices. Initially, only one application has to be filed in the USPTO. At the 12-month point (the end of the treaty year), additional applications are filed in the PCT Receiving Office of the U.S. patent office (PCT I in Figure 12-1) and in Mexico. The PCT application most likely will be assigned to the same U.S. examiner assigned to search the U.S. application. Assume that all PCT proceedings are conducted in the USPTO and not the EPO.

Eighteen months from the U.S. filing date, the PCT application should have been searched. At this point, for PCT Chapter II member countries the application can be either: (1) filed directly in the remaining countries, or (2) preliminarily examined under PCT Chapter II (PCT II in Figure 12-1). If preliminary examination is demanded, entry into the national phase will be deferred an additional year, or until 30 months from the U.S. filing date. To complete our hypothetical strategy, assume that preliminary examination under PCT Chapter II is chosen for all PCT-member countries. Note that preliminary examination of the PCT application in the USPTO is the least-expensive option for pursuing this application.

After preliminary examination is completed but before the 30-month filing level is reached in the flow chart of Figure 12-1 (before the expense of entering the national phase in the EPO, Brazil, Canada, Japan, New Zealand, China, and Australia), the applicant should make a thorough and critical review of the following:

1. The technical status of the invention. Is the technology still considered as significant a contribution to the company's portfolio at this point as it was 30 months earlier when the application was first filed?
2. The current commercial situation in each of these countries. Is there an industrial partner for a country? Does protection in neighboring countries make the need for a patent in that country unnecessary?
3. Other applications that are being foreign-filed. Would it be more worthwhile to devote resources towards adding other patents to the foreign patent portfolio rather than this one?
4. The treatment received by other, related patent applications the company has previously filed in the patent office of that country. Has it been unduly burdensome to secure protection in that country in the past?
5. The treatment the application has received during preliminary examination. Has the invention been characterized as unpatentable, narrowly patentable, or broadly patentable?

When viewed in hindsight, the expense of continuing with some or all of these countries may or may not be justified. In a foreign-filing program such as the hypothetical one just outlined, hindsight can be used before the bulk of foreign patent expenses is incurred. If necessary, the effort can be directed towards other, more significant filings.

12.5 CONCLUSION

The effective pursuit of foreign patents requires planning, which must occur before an original national patent application is filed. Three significant treaties provide procedures for developing a cost-effective foreign filing program: the Right of Priority under the Paris Convention preserves foreign rights for up to a year after the priority date in most foreign countries; the Patent Cooperation Treaty extends options for up to 30 months from the priority date in a number of countries and regions; the European Patent Convention greatly simplifies the pursuit of patent protection in Europe. These procedures can be used together, logically and cost-effectively. Of course, the ultimate structure of the foreign-filing strategy depends on the needs of the organization attempting to build a foreign patent portfolio. The program just presented illustrates one such strategy, but there are others. Regardless of the particular approach, if a well-planned program is followed for each patent application, an organization should develop over time a reasonably cost-effective patent portfolio that gives it a significant competitive edge in global markets.

REFERENCES

1. *See, e.g.*, U. Gupta, *Small Firms Aren't Waiting to Grow Up to Go Global*, WALL STREET JOURNAL, Dec. 5, 1989, at B2.
2. *See, e.g.*, U.S. Patent No. 141,072, awarded to Louis Pasteur in 1873.
3. The United States removed its reservation to Chapter II of the Patent Cooperation Treaty effective July 1, 1987.
4. R. Armitage, *Chemical Patent Practice—Drafting the Patent Application*, in AMERICAN INTELLECTUAL PROPERTY LAW ASSOCIATION, BASIC CHEMICAL PRACTICE, A1 (1986), provides an excellent discussion of the use of the Patent Cooperation Treaty in conjunction with the pursuit of U.S. patent applications.
5. *See generally* 1 MANUAL OF INDUSTRIAL PROPERTY B.V., MANUAL FOR THE HANDLING OF APPLICATIONS FOR PATENTS, DESIGNS AND TRADE MARKS THROUGHOUT THE WORLD (Suppl. August 1989) (hereafter MANUAL OF INDUSTRIAL PROPERTY); *see also International Chemical Practice*, 13 AIPLA QUART. J. 1 *et seq.* (1985).
6. Japan grants a six-month grace period from an inventor's own publication. Prior to July 1, 1980, West Germany granted a similar six-month grace period, but this was abolished on ratification of the Strasbourg Convention on the Unification of Certain Points of Substantive Law on Patents of November 27, 1963. *See generally* MANUAL OF INDUSTRIAL PROPERTY.
7. The classic example is *In re* LeGrice, 301 F.2d 929, 939 (C.C.P.A. 1962), in which a description of a new variety of rose in a printed publication was held to not bar a patent application for that variety because it was not an enabling publication.

8. Patent priority often is significant in determining the contribution of particular individuals to an area of research. A recent example is in the field of high-temperature superconductors. *See, e.g.*, R. Pool, *IBM Wins a Patent for Thallium Superconductor*, 246 SCIENCE 320 (1989).

9. The problem of harmonizing the goals of basic research with the goals of industry has been the subject of considerable discussion. *See* S. Bondurant, *Establishing Relationship with a University (The Academy in the Marketplace: Prostitute or Hero?)*, 24 LES NOUVELLES 45 (1989) (contending that the university can beneficially participate in industrial relationships while maintaining its traditional role as a university); *see also* H. Rubin, *Biomedical Research as Philosophy*, 25 LES NOUVELLES 44, 46 (1990) (commenting that "[t]o develop together in an orderly fashion and still achieve individual goals, the components of an embryonic cooperative [academic and industrial] research environment must find the shared historical, institutional, perceptual and philosophical frameworks. This can be accomplished by placing biomedical research squarely in the framework of practical philosophy.").

10. *In re* Kirk, 376 F.2d 936, 963 (C.C.P.A. 1967).

11. *See generally* European Patent Office, HOW TO GET A EUROPEAN PATENT (6th ed. 1983) (available from the European Patent Office, Munich, Germany); *see also* MANUAL OF INDUSTRIAL PROPERTY PART III: THE EUROPEAN PATENT SYSTEM.

12. *See generally* WORLD INTELLECTUAL PROPERTY ORGANIZATION PCT APPLICANT'S GUIDE (1985) (available from the International Bureau, World Intellectual Property Organization, CH 1211 Geneva 20, Switzerland).

13. *See generally* PCT articles 15–18; PCT Regulations rules 33–43.

14. *See* PCT articles 31–42; PCT Regulations rules 53–78.

15. If preliminary examination is desired, a demand for preliminary examination must be filed within 19 months of the priority date. *See* PCT Article 39.

16. *See* 4 PCT APPLICANT'S GUIDE, Annex B1 (Information on Contracting States).

17. *See* 1022 OFFICIAL GAZETTE OF THE UNITED STATES PATENT AND TRADEMARK OFFICE 53 (Sept. 28, 1982) (hereafter OFFICIAL GAZETTE); 1091 OFFICIAL GAZETTE 3 (June 7, 1988).

18. There is a designation fee for each country designated under the PCT for the preservation of rights. Note that only one PCT designation fee is due whether an EPO patent is sought for one, several, or all EPC member countries. See PCT Regulations Rule 15.1(ii).

19. *See generally* U.S. Congress, Office of Technology Assessment, *New Developments in Biotechnology* 5: PATENTING LIFE (U.S. Government Printing Office, April 1989); *see also* MANUAL OF INDUSTRIAL PROPERTY.

PART

IV

Patent Litigation

13

Substantive Aspects
of Patent Litigation

James D. Myers, Brian P. O'Shaughnessy,
and Robert W. Glatz

For a business dealing in innovative products, it can be a disaster when a competitor copies those products. Even the simplest products, particularly in the pharmaceutical and biotechnology industries, often require many years and millions of dollars invested in research, development, product approval, and marketing. If a highly innovative product is successful, others will attempt to enter the market with competing products.

A company that pursues patent protection on an innovative product must protect its investment in the research that led to that product. The company introducing a new product must seek the broadest possible patent protection available for that product because competitors will explore all possible weaknesses in that patent position. If a competitor believes the patent position on the innovative product is strong, it may seek to introduce a completely different competitive product. If the competitor believes the patent position on the innovative product is weak, it may try to introduce a similar or identical product. Finally, in extremely lucrative markets, competitors may view the cost of an infringement suit as justified simply on the odds that the patent might be held invalid or significantly narrowed as a result of the lawsuit. Thus, patents on commercially significant products are frequently litigated.

The following section discusses the nature of the rights granted by a patent. The rest of this chapter focuses on the two major substantive issues in a patent suit: patent infringement and patent validity.

13.1 THE PATENT GRANT

An issued U.S. patent entitles the holder to exclude others from making, using, or selling the invention in the United States for a period of 17 years from the date of grant.[1] To violate the exclusive right of the patent holder without permission is an infringement of the patent. The statutory standard for infringement is set forth in Section 271 of the patent act, which provides that "[E]xcept as otherwise provided in this title, whoever without authority makes, uses or sells any patented invention, within the United States during the term of the patent therefor, infringes the patent."[2]

13.1.1 The Central Role of Patent Claims

To understand what infringement is and how it must be proven first requires discussing the patent document itself. The patent act requires that "[A]n application for patent shall be made, or authorized to be made, by the inventor, and shall include, among other things, a specification."[3] The patent statute goes on to state that "[t]he specification shall conclude with one or more claims particularly pointing out and distinctly claiming the subject matter which the applicant regards as his invention."[4]

The relationship between the specification and the claims of the patent document recently has been restated by the U.S. Court of Appeals for the Federal Circuit. In *General Foods Corporation v. Studiengesellschaft Kohle mbH*, the Federal Circuit said:

> The patent document which grants the patentee the right to exclude others and hence bestows on the owner the right to license, consists of two primary parts: (1) a written description of the invention, which may and here does include drawings, called the "specification," enabling those skilled in the art to practice the invention, and (2) claims which define or delimit the scope of the legal protection which the government grant gives the patent owner, the patent "monopoly." As stated by Judge Lane, who served on both of our predecessor courts, [citation omitted] "A claim is a group of words defining only the *boundary* of the patent monopoly." (emphasis ours) The Supreme Court has likened patent claims to the description of real property in a deed "which sets the bounds to the grant which it contains. It is to the claims of every patent, therefore, that we must turn when we are seeking to *determine what the invention is, the exclusive use of which is given to the inventor by the grant* provided for in the statute, — 'He can claim nothing beyond them.'" [citation omitted] (emphasis ours).[5]

Thus the claims of an issued patent define the scope of the exclusive right granted by the patent. Interpreting precisely what the claims mean is a complex matter, however, and is discussed in greater detail in following sections.

13.1.2 Remedies for Infringement

In the event of infringement, a patent holder may bring a civil action in federal court against the infringer.[6] A patent holder who establishes that infringement has occurred is entitled to injunctive relief[7] preventing the infringer from practicing the invention in the United States[8] and to a monetary award "adequate to compensate for the infringement but in no event less than a reasonable royalty for the use made of the invention by the infringer."[9] If the patent holder has proven willful or intentional infringement or that there are other circumstances suggesting bad faith or intentional misconduct, the patent holder is entitled to an increased monetary award equal to three times the calculated damages, the costs of the action, and reimbursement of its attorney fees.[10]

Corporate officers and directors may, in some situations, be held individually liable for the infringing acts of their company.[11]

13.1.3 Infringement Opinions and the Duty to Avoid Infringement

To avoid the serious consequences of willful infringement, any company seeking to develop a new product or process that is similar to a patented one should work closely with their counsel. In *Minnesota Mining and Manufacturing Co. v. Johnson & Johnson Orthopaedics*, the Federal Circuit observed "[I]t is well settled that a potential infringer having actual notice of another's patent has an affirmative duty of due care that normally requires the potential infringer to obtain competent legal advice before infringing or continuing to infringe."[12] Failing to attend to this duty obviously can be extremely expensive.

13.2 PATENT INFRINGEMENT

An issued patent typically contains numerous claims. In an infringement trial, some of the claims may be held valid while others are held invalid; some of the claims may be held infringed[13] while others are held noninfringed. If at least one claim is both valid and infringed, patent infringement has occurred.

Deciding the question of infringement requires multiple steps involving claim interpretation and literal infringement, the doctrine of equivalents, file wrapper estoppel, and the reverse doctrine of equivalents. Each step is discussed in the following sections, followed by a case study illustrating its application in practice.

13.2.1 Literal Infringement and Claim Interpretation

Since claims define the scope of the exclusive right, a question of patent infringement must start with an analysis of the claims.[14] "In determining whether an accused device or composition infringes a valid patent, resort must be had in the first instance to the words of the claim. If accused matter falls within the claim, infringement is made out and that is the end of it."[15] A finding of infringement depends on whether the accused device falls within the scope of the asserted claims as properly interpreted by the court.[16] This suggests two inquiries: first, what is the proper interpretation of the asserted claim or claims; and second, does the accused matter come within that interpretation.[17] As summarized by the Federal Circuit, the "patented invention as indicated by the language of the claims must first be defined (a question of law), and then the trier must judge whether the claims cover the accused device (a question of fact)."[18] If the accused matter falls clearly within the terms of the claim, infringement is normally made out.[19] Put another way, the question is often asked as to whether the claims "read on" the accused product or process.[20]

It is important to note that the exclusive rights granted by the patent are not limited to the specific examples shown in the specification. The sole duty of the claims is to define the invention and, thus, what will constitute an infringement. Accordingly, where a claim does not require a limitation, a limitation should not be read from the specification into the claims.[21] Failing to appreciate the central role of the claims in defining the scope of patent protection creates constant confusion.

Properly interpreting claims is fundamental to deciding literal infringement. Words in a claim are given their ordinary and accustomed meaning unless it appears that the inventor used them differently.[22] As is often the case, where terms of art are employed the claims must be interpreted as they would be understood by someone of ordinary skill in the art at the time the patent application was filed.[23] However, in some cases the ordinary or art-recognized meaning of claim terms may not be sufficiently clear. In this case, it is appropriate to look to the patent specification and its prosecution history to learn if the inventor defined the disputed terms differently than their accepted meaning.[24]

It often is necessary for the inventor to describe elements of the invention for which there are no commonly accepted terms. For this reason it has long been established that a patent holder can be his or her own lexicographer. When inventors are inclined or obliged to define their own terms, they must do so unambiguously within the specification or within the claims themselves.[25] Subsequent interpretation of the claim must use that definition. Thus, it often is necessary to reach back into the specification or the prosecution history of the application to properly interpret the claims.

Once a claim has been properly interpreted, it must be asked whether the disputed product falls within that claim. For a properly interpreted claim to read on a disputed product, the product must possess all the elements recited in the asserted claim.[26] That is, since every element listed in the claim is a limitation that defines the scope of the invention, it necessarily follows that all of those elements must be found in the disputed product. This is the so-called "all-elements" rule. The rule is most frequently applied in the analysis of method or combination claims. Thus, to directly infringe a patent claim, the disputed product must include all of the elements recited in the claim.[27]

Another way of expressing the principle of the all-elements rule is that the "claim is an <u>entity</u> which must be considered as a whole."[28] That is to say, no single element is claimed in and of itself, but each element of the claim is an essential part of the claim as a whole. For the sake of convenience many claims are broken down into enumerated steps or elements. Thus, where a claim recites elements *A*, *B*, and *C*, it is the *combination* of the three elements that is claimed; there are no rights granted in any of elements *A* or *B* or *C* separately or in subcombination. In *General Foods*, the Federal Circuit explained the principle as follows:

> Another way of stating the legal truism is that patent claims, being definitions which must be read <u>as a whole</u>, do not "claim" or cover or protect all that their words may <u>disclose</u>. Even though the claim to the A-B-C combination of steps contains a detailed description of step A, that does not give the patentee any patent right in step A and it is legally incorrect to say that step A is "patented."[29]

If the claim as a whole has been properly interpreted and it is clear that the disputed product falls within that claim, then literal infringement is established and that is usually the end of the infringement analysis.[30] If literal infringement cannot be clearly established, however, the analysis must consider the doctrine of equivalents.

13.2.1.1   A Case Study of Literal Infringement: *North American Vaccine v. American Cyanamid.* An example of how claim interpretation affects whether an accused product will be held to literally infringe a patent is provided by the district court's analysis in *North American Vaccine Inc. v. American Cyanamid Co.*,[31] in which North American brought an infringement action against American Cyanamid and Praxis Biologics alleging the HibTITER™ infant meningitis vaccine infringed its patent on polysaccharide-protein conjugate vaccines (U.S. Patent No. 4,356,170). The disputed claims read as follows:

> 11. An antigenic-polysaccharide:protein conjugate wherein the polysaccharide and protein are covalently linked through a CH_2-HN-protein linkage to a terminal portion of the polysaccharide without significant crosslinking, said antigenic polysaccharide having a MW above about 2,000.
> 12. The conjugate of claim 11 wherein the antigenic polysaccharide is selected from the group derived from meningococci, Haemophilus influenza, pneumococci, B-hemolytic streptococci, and E. coli.
> 25. A human infant vaccine comprising the conjugate of claim 11 wherein the polysaccharide comprises at least one of meningococcal polysaccharide and Haemophilus influenza polysaccharide.

The central issue was the interpretation of the phrase "a CH_2-HN-protein linkage to a terminal portion" in Claim 11. The HibTITER™ vaccine had a protein linkage at each end of the polysaccharide; the specific experiments described in the North American patent concerned monofunctional conjugates. North American argued that the phrase "a terminal portion" was a generic term that should not be limited to a single terminal; American Cyanamid argued that the phrase should be interpreted as limited to a single terminal linkage.

In deciding which interpretation was correct, Judge Griesa initially noted:

> In order to solve the problem, we need to look at some of the other evidence that can be considered properly under the law on the question of interpretation. We, of course, need

to look at the other portions of the patent; the summary of the invention; the description of the experiments; other claims besides 11, 12 and 25. In other words, the whole patent.[32]

Judge Griesa first noted that the inventor, Dr. Jennings, had written an article that served as the basis of the patent where the monofunctionality of his vaccines was given special emphasis. While the word *monofunctional* had not been carried over into the patent and Dr. Jennings testified that he did not intend his patent to be limited to monofunctionality, other language from the paper that Judge Griesa considered "inexorably linked" to the concept of monofunctionality was carried into the patent. The judge concluded:

> Now, the question naturally presents itself. If Dr. Jennings sought to broaden his patent beyond what was contained in the article and the speech, why did he not express this intention? If his intention was to have a patent on the production of aldehydes at both terminal ends, this is something that can be easily expressed in the English language, and clearly expressed. If he desired to depart from the objectives that he so clearly had in his experimentation described in his article and his speech, if that was his purpose, surely that was something that he thought about, it wasn't just chance, and he would want to think about how to express it.
>
> He did not express it. And that is the basic reason why I am holding in favor of the defendants on the question of interpretation.[33]

Other prior art may or may not have permitted the North American patent to be written in a manner more explicitly encompassing dual protein conjugates. While other evidence, including the prior art and the patent prosecution history, could have been more extensively considered on the question of claim interpretation, the *North American* decision quite properly places special emphasis on the text of the patent itself. Although the trial court's focus on the scientific papers was considered error (albeit harmless error) on appeal, the case dramatically illustrates that patents are quite different documents from scientific papers.

13.2.2 The Doctrine of Equivalents

In certain instances where the accused device or process does not literally infringe the claims, infringement still may be found under the doctrine of equivalents.[34] In general, the doctrine of equivalents provides that when the accused product performs substantially the same function in substantially the same way to achieve substantially the same result as a patented product, infringement may be found.[35] Professor Chisum, viewing the doctrine as an aid to claim construction, characterizes it as "a prescription against sterile literalism in construction and application of claim language."[36]

While this section generally reviews the doctrine of equivalents, it is important to note that how the doctrine is applied will vary considerably, depending on the facts of the case. Moreover, the law of the doctrine of equivalents is the subject of rapid evolution and active debate.[37] As a result, any analysis of how the doctrine may be applied in a particular case should be approached with caution.

The basic theory and rationale underlying the doctrine of equivalents was stated by the U.S. Supreme Court in *Graver Tank & Mfg. Co. v. Linde Air Products Co.*[38] In *Graver Tank*, the court first explained the tenets of literal infringement and went on to say:

> [B]ut courts have also recognized that to permit imitation of a patented invention which does not copy every literal detail would be to convert the protection of the patent grant into a hollow and useless thing. Such a limitation would leave room for—indeed encourage—the unscrupulous copyist to make unimportant and insubstantial changes and substitutions in the patent which, though adding nothing, would be enough to take the copied matter outside the claim, and hence outside the reach of the law. One who seeks to pirate an invention, like one who seeks to pirate a copyrighted book or play, may be expected to introduce minor variations to conceal and shelter the piracy. Outright and forthright duplication is a dull and very rare type of infringement. To prohibit no other would place the inventor at the mercy of verbalism and would be subordinating substance to form. It would deprive him of the benefit of his invention and would foster concealment rather than disclosure of inventions, which is one of the primary purposes of the patent system.
>
> The doctrine of equivalents evolved in response to this experience. . . . The theory on which it is founded is that "if two devices do the same work in substantially the same way, and accomplish substantially the same result, they are the same, even though they differ in name, form or shape."[39]

In short, the "doctrine of equivalents is designed to protect inventors from unscrupulous copyists . . . and unanticipated equivalents."[40]

In *Pennwalt v. Durand Wayland*, the Federal Circuit ruled that a doctrine of equivalents analysis should determine, in order, whether the accused device achieves substantially the same result, performs substantially the same work, and operates in substantially the same manner as the claimed invention. In so doing, each element of the claim must be compared with the accused device to determine whether the accused device contains each element or its substantial equivalent.[41] Note, however, that a determination of equivalency is, as in the case of literal infringement, made against the claim *as a whole*.[42]

By looking beyond the precise language of the claims, the doctrine creates a tension between the requirements of the statute and the principles of equity. In *Laitram Corp. v. Cambridge Wire Cloth Co.*,[43] the Federal Circuit expressed the dilemma as follows:

> On one side rests the very important, statutorily-created necessity of employing the clearest possible wording in preparing the specification and claims of a patent, one of "the most difficult legal instruments to draw with accuracy." . . . On the other lies the equally important, judicially-created necessity of determining infringement without the risk of injustice that may result from a blinded focus on words alone. The former, set out in 35 U.S.C. Section 112, recognizes a competitor's need for precise wording as an

aid in avoiding infringement. The latter is called the "doctrine of equivalents." While requiring a look at all the words while resisting their tyranny, and requiring, because the claims measure the invention, a look at all claim limitations, the doctrine, in a proper case, "temper[s] unsparing logic and prevent[s] an infringer from stealing the benefits of an invention." . . . In that sense, the doctrine recognizes a fact of the real business world: words are not misappropriated; claimed inventions are.

The tension between the doctrine of equivalents and countervailing legal considerations is one of the factors that makes the application of this doctrine so difficult.

Thus, the doctrine grants the patent holder the right to exclude others from making, using, or selling the equivalents of the claimed inventions. The doctrine of equivalents is limited by two factors, which are discussed in the following sections.

13.2.2.1   The Prior Art.   The prior art defines the boundary of the doctrine of equivalents. The doctrine cannot be used to expand the patent holder's rights so that the patent prevents the public from using technology already disclosed in the art.[44]

It follows that the extent to which the doctrine can be used to expand the scope of the patent is fundamentally tied to the understanding within the art as to what constitutes "equivalents." Thus, the Court in *Graver Tank* said "[T]he doctrine operates not only in favor of a pioneer or primary invention, but also for the patentee of a secondary invention consisting of a combination of old ingredients which produce new and useful results, although the area of equivalents may vary under the circumstances."[45]

By implication, *Graver* recognized that so-called pioneering inventions are generally entitled to a broader scope of equivalents. This is apparently in recognition of both the significance of the patent holder's contribution and the pragmatic realization that there is a lesser degree of teaching and understanding within the art as to what is an "equivalent" substitution. Conversely, in the case of a nonpioneering invention the art is relatively well-defined, giving the patent holder and the public a well-developed idea as to what is known in the art, how the claimed subject matter differs, and, therefore, what is infringing subject matter, whether literally or by equivalents.

13.2.2.2   File Wrapper Estoppel.   Actions taken by an applicant during the processing of the application can later be held against the applicant. This principle, known as "file wrapper estoppel," is an equitable doctrine designed to limit a patent applicant's use of the doctrine of equivalents. It prevents a patent applicant from using the doctrine of equivalents to expand the scope of the claims to recover subject matter he or she surrendered during examination of the patent application.

A brief review of the examination process may be helpful. First, the patent applicant submits the specification and claims for examination. After going over the application, the examiner presents the applicant with an analysis, most often in the form of a rejection based upon prior art references. The applicant is entitled to respond with amendments to the claims and arguments explaining why the amended claims deserve a patent. If the applicant's response includes amendments that alter the claims to avoid the art and that amendment is found to have been an essential reason for allowing the application, the courts may view the applicant's amendments as an admission that the claims prior to amendment were not patentable over the cited prior art. Accordingly, the applicant or patent holder will not be entitled to any "equivalents" corresponding to the original claim.

As the Federal Circuit stated in *Hughes Aircraft Co. v. United States*:

> Having chosen specific words of limitation to avoid the McLean disclosure, Hughes is estopped by the prosecution history of the application ("file wrapper estoppel"), from obtaining a claim interpretation so broad as to encompass the McLean structure. . . . The doctrine of prosecution history estoppel precludes a patent owner from obtaining a claim construction that would resurrect subject matter surrendered during prosecution of his patent application. The estoppel applies to claim amendments to overcome rejections based on prior art, and to arguments submitted to obtain the patent.[46]

Some courts have adopted the view that any amendment of the claims creates a "file wrapper estoppel" effective to bar any resort to the doctrine of equivalents and to confine the patent holder strictly to the letter of the limited claims granted. Both the Federal Circuit in *Hughes* and the Supreme Court in *Graver* have rejected such a view, however. Not every amendment of a patent application will serve as the basis for file wrapper estoppel.

Specifically, estoppel is not found where a patent applicant's amendments were not required in response to an examiner's rejection or were not critical to the allowance of the claim. Further, estoppel is not generally created by an amendment designed to overcome a rejection such as indefiniteness under 35 U.S.C. Section 112 or double patenting.[47]

When an applicant amends claims or cancels them specifically to distinguish the claimed invention over the prior art, he or she cannot later ignore those concessions to bring disputed subject matter within the scope of the claims under the doctrine of equivalents.[48]

13.2.3   A Case Study of the Doctrine of Equivalents:
Genentech v. The Wellcome Foundation

In *Genentech Inc. v. The Wellcome Foundation Ltd.*,[49] Genentech brought suit against Wellcome, Genetics Institute, and others alleging infringement of its patents on tissue plasminogen activator (t-PA). Two compounds were accused of infringement: met t-PA (human t-PA modified by the substitution of a methionine for valine at position 245) and FE1X (met t-PA further modified by the deletion of the protein F and E regions). Summary judgment in favor of Wellcome was issued on the question of literal infringement, but the question of infringement under the doctrine of equivalents was allowed to proceed to a trial before a jury.[50]

After the case was presented, the trial court judge instructed the jury on the doctrine of equivalents. What was read to this jury provides a practical summary of the law in this area:

Doctrine of Equivalents

The doctrine of equivalents exists in order to hinder the "unscrupulous copyist" who could otherwise imitate a patented invention as long as he was careful to avoid some inconsequential detail, or to make some unimportant and insubstantial change. While the doctrine of equivalents extends the claims beyond their literal words, it does not prevent the manufacture, use or sale by others of a product just because it is generally similar to the patented invention.

In applying the doctrine of equivalents, you must determine, for each individual element in the claim, whether the accused product or process meets the following criteria: (1) works in substantially the same way; (2) has substantially the same function; and (3) produces substantially the same result.

If the way, function, or result is not met, then there is no equivalency. Therefore to find infringement under the doctrine of equivalents, you must make separate findings as to each of the three criteria.

Further, in order to find infringement under the doctrine of equivalents, you cannot merely view the potential invention as a whole. Rather, you must make an element-by-element analysis of the patent claims and must find that each element of each claim, or its substantial equivalent, is found in the accused product. . . .

Pioneer Patent

A pioneer patent is one which is of such novelty and importance as to mark a distinct step in the progress of the art which it serves. If you determine that any of the patents in suit is such a pioneer patent, the claims of that patent are entitled to a broader range of equivalent elements.

Unpredictability

In applying the doctrine of equivalents, one factor you may consider is the degree of unpredictability of the effect that a particular change in the claimed invention might have. The greater the degree of unpredictability, the narrower the range of equivalents.

"File Wrapper" Defined

During the course of the trial and in some of the interrogatories that will be submitted to you are references to a "file wrapper." A file wrapper is a copy of everything pertaining to the patent application that was filed with the PTO or mailed from the PTO during the prosecution of the application for patent.

Prosecution History Estoppel

It is a general rule that in applying the doctrine of equivalents, one cannot impart a scope so broad as to cover that which the prior art as a whole already disclosed at the time the invention was made.

If the prosecution history reveals that a patent owner has surrendered or amended claims in response to a rejection by the PTO based on prior art, then what was surrendered or given up by amendment cannot be recaptured. When the holder of a patent has narrowed a claim in order to avoid prior art cited by the PTO and thus obtains the issuance of a patent, the holder is precluded from attempting to enforce the claim in a manner that ignores the effect of the narrowing language.

Arguments made during the prosecution of a patent application can also surrender subject matter from the scope to be given a particular claim. During prosecution, it is common for patent applicants, through their attorneys, to argue a particular interpretation for a claim in order to avoid prior art. If such arguments are made, the claim cannot be given an interpretation or a range of equivalents which would recapture that which was surrendered by the arguments of the attorney.[51]

The jury decided that both met t-PA and FE1X infringed Genentech's patents under the doctrine of equivalents. Interestingly, when asked what damages would compensate Genentech for the infringement, the jury answered "none."[52] After the jury's verdict, The Wellcome Foundation and Genetics Institute filed motions for a judgment notwithstanding the verdict or, in the alternative, for a new trial. Both motions were denied.[53]

13.2.4 The Reverse Doctrine of Equivalents

Taking the claim construction process to yet another level of abstraction is a concept known as the "reverse doctrine of equivalents."[54] The reverse doctrine is a rarely applied principle that says that even though claims are literally infringed, the accused subject matter does so in a way so fundamentally different from the claimed subject matter that there is no infringement.

The reverse doctrine of equivalents was given life in the Supreme Court's commentary in *Graver Tank*. There, the court stated:

> [T]he wholesome realism of [the doctrine of equivalents] is not always applied in favor of a patentee but is sometimes used against him. Thus, where a device is so far changed in principle from a patented article that it performs the same or similar function in a substantially different way, but nevertheless falls within the literal language of the claim, the doctrine of equivalents may be used to restrict the claim and defeat the patentee's action for infringement.[55]

The Federal Circuit has noted that the doctrine is rarely used successfully because products that literally infringe a claim are usually the same in substance as the claimed invention. As a result, the defense of the reverse doctrine of equivalents is seldom raised. A defendant who relies on the doctrine has the burden of establishing a *prima facie* case of noninfringement. If the defendant meets this burden, the patent holder, who always retains the burden of persuasion on infringement, must rebut the *prima facie* showing.[56]

However, in *Scripps v. Genentech*, the Federal Circuit reversed a district court's grant of summary judgment on the issue of infringement based upon Genentech's assertion of the reverse doctrine of equivalents.[57] In *Scripps*, Genentech stood accused of infringing Scripps's patent for blood-clotting factor VIII:C, which had been derived from chromatographic purification of blood. Genentech was producing factor VIII:C by recombinant technology. Genentech argued that its product should be seen as changed "in principle," particularly when viewed in the context of the prior art, and that the specific activities and purity obtained by recombinant technology exceeded those of the Scripps process. The Federal Circuit found that the district court neglected to adequately address the issue and, noting that "the issues raised by new technologies require considered analysis," held that "consideration of extrinsic evidence is required, and summary judgment is inappropriate."[58]

13.2.5 Contributory Infringement

The patent statute imposes liability on anyone who aids or abets direct infringement by others. Section 271 imposes liability for inducement of infringement and contributory infringement, respectively, as follows:

> (b) Whoever actively induces infringement of a patent shall be liable as an infringer.

> (c) Whoever sells a component of a patented machine, manufacture, combination or composition, or a material or apparatus for use in practicing a patented process, constituting a material part of the invention, knowing the same to be especially made or especially adapted for use in an infringement of such patent, and not a staple article or commodity of commerce suitable for substantial noninfringing use, shall be liable as a contributory infringer.[59]

Thus, someone may incur liability as an infringer not only by directly infringing; that is, by making, using, or selling patented subject matter, but also by encouraging others to do so or purposely providing them with the means to do so.

The manufacture or sale of an apparatus, *per se*, does not constitute direct infringement of a *method* claim because direct infringement of a method claim requires execution of the method by a user of the apparatus. Depending on the circumstances, however, the manufacture, promotion, or sale of such an apparatus can infringe method claims either by inducement of infringement or contributory infringement.

If a vender promotes an instrument on its usefulness in performing patented methods and the vender does not have the authority to confer rights on the buyer to practice that method, that promotion and sale may be either or both inducement or contributory infringement. To avoid such liability a vender must avoid inducing others to practice the methods claimed, namely, avoid promotional and instructional materials that advertise the apparatus as useful in the claimed methods. Similarly, to avoid contributory infringement, a vender must not sell an apparatus that has as its only commercially reasonable use the performance of the patented method. In the latter case, however, if the instrument has substantial noninfringing use, there is no contributory infringement.

13.2.6 The Process Patent Amendment Act of 1988

In response to a long-felt perception that process patents could be easily circumvented by manufacturing products with the patented process outside the United

States and then importing those products into the country, the Process Patent Amendment Act of 1988 added the following section to the patent statute:

> Whoever without authority imports into the United States or sells or uses within the United States a product which is made by a process patented in the United States shall be liable as an infringer, if the importation, sale, or use of the product occurs during the term of such process patent. In an action for infringement of a process patent, no remedy may be granted for infringement on account of the non-commercial use or retail sale of a product unless there is no adequate remedy under this title for infringement on account of the importation or other use or sale of that product. A product which is made by a patented process will, for purposes of this title, not be considered to be so made after—
>
> (1) it is materially changed by subsequent processes; or
> (2) it becomes a trivial and nonessential component of another product.[60]

In addition to providing meaningful extension of the reach of process patents, the Process Patent Amendment Act provides the holder of a process patent with some extremely useful procedural tools for learning of a potential infringer's extraterritorial process.[61] As discussed in the following section, however, obtaining patent protection that can make meaningful use of this section may be difficult for at least some types of biotechnology inventions.

13.2.7.1 Process Patents in Biotechnology and *In re Durden*. Some people in the biotechnology industry believe that the Process Patent Amendment Act contains loopholes prejudicial to their industry. This belief stems from the Federal Circuit's decision in *Amgen Inc. v. I.T.C.*, in which it was decided that Amgen's U.S. Patent No. 4,703,008, which contained claims directed to host cells used to produce recombinant erythropoietin, was not infringed by Chugai Pharmaceutical's importation of recombinant EPO made from host cells covered by those claims. The Federal Circuit found there was no infringement under the provisions of the Process Patent Amendment Act because Amgen's claims simply were not process claims.[62]

The reason Amgen did not have process claims in the patent was explained by the Federal Circuit as follows:

> The application which matured into the '008 patent originally contained claims to the process of producing rEPO [from the recombinant host cells]. The Patent and Trademark Office (PTO) Examiner rejected these claims, at least in part, because he considered the claims to be to the application of an old process to new starting materials and thus not patentable on the authority of <u>In re Durden</u>, 763 F.2d 1406, 226 USPQ 359 (Fed. Cir. 1985). The process claims were canceled prior to issuance of the '008 patent.[63]

The law relating to the nonobviousness of process inventions under *In re Durden* was discussed in detail in Chapter 8. The confusion over this law and its application to biotechnology inventions continues to limit the availability of the Process Patent Amendment Act to some biotechnology inventions.

13.2.7.2 Boucher-Type Legislation. The perceived constraints created by the law of nonobviousness under *In re Durden* and the limits of the Process Patent Amendment Act have led to continued support for legislative action.[64] Referred to as Boucher-type legislation because the first bills were introduced by Congressman Boucher,[65] this type of legislation basically proposes to: (1) amend the provisions added by the Process Patent Amendment Act so the use of a patented material, such as a host cell, to make another product that is then imported into the United States will constitute infringement, and (2) amend Section 103 of the patent statute so that a process of using a patentable product, such as a host cell, becomes patentable itself.[66] Debate over Boucher-type legislation is ongoing, with some parts of the biotechnology industry, universities, and the patent and trademark office itself supporting the legislation, while the American Intellectual Property Law Association, the American Bar Association, and the Intellectual Property Owners Inc. oppose the legislation.[67] Remedies supported by some groups have consequences outside of the biotechnology industry that are opposed by still other groups. Until the proposed legislative solutions are satisfactory, it seems unlikely legislative action will be taken.

13.2.7 Exceptions to Patent Infringement

There are two instances where activity that is otherwise infringing is not: the judicially created experimental use exception and the statutory experimental use exception (created in conjunction with the Patent Term Extension Act).

13.2.7.1 Experimental Use. The experimental use exception to infringement has a long history of uncertain significance. In several articles reviewing the history of the experimental use exception, Feit[68] remarks that Bee[69] and Hantman[70] demonstrate "how able writers can interpret the same facts to reach very different conclusions."

The doctrine has its origins in two 1813 opinions by Supreme Court Justice Joseph Story. In *Whittemore v. Cutter*[71] Justice Story approved the lower court's jury instructions that an intent to use a patented machine *for profit* was a requirement for a finding of infringement. Justice Story elaborated in *Swain v. Guild*[72] by saying:

> [T]his Court has already had occasion to consider the clause in question, and upon mature deliberation, it has held that the making of a patented machine to be an offence within the purview of it, must be the making with an intent to use for profit, and not for the mere purpose of philosophical experiment, or to ascertain the verity and exactness of the specification.

Recent cases suggest that in the commercial world, the exception is narrowly construed. In *Pfizer, Inc. v. International Rectifier Corp.*[73] the court had previously held Pfizer's patent for doxycycline valid and infringed by International's sales in the U.S. and enjoined International from further infringement. Nevertheless, International continued to manufacture doxycycline for bioequivalency tests and so on. The court found International had performed the tests to enable it to compete with Pfizer after the expiration of Pfizer's patent. International claimed that its uses were solely experimental and that none of its doxycycline had been sold in the United States. The court found International's position without merit and held that "the underlying rule of permissible experimental use demands that there must be no intended commercial use of the patented article, none whatsoever, if the exception is to be recognized at all."

Since the mid-1980s concern has been expressed that the experimental use exception does not provide the protection it should.[74] This is of particular concern to the biotechnology industry, where the line between commercial research and basic research is often fuzzy and a great deal of research is conducted at nonprofit institutions. To date, little has occurred to clarify the situation. Hence, all potential infringement situations should be approached with care, and a potential experimental use defense should be explored carefully before it is relied on.

13.2.7.2 Statutory Experimental Use. In 1984 the patent statute was amended to include a narrow statutory experimental use provision.[75] Section 271(e)(1) provides that:

> It shall not be an act of infringement to make, use, or sell a patented invention (other than a new animal drug or veterinary biological product (as those terms are used in the Federal Food, Drug and Cosmetic Act and the Act of March 4, 1913) which is primarily manufactured using recombinant DNA, recombinant RNA, hybridoma technology, or other processes involving site specific genetic manipulation techniques) solely for uses reasonably related to the development and submission of information under a Federal law which regulates the manufacture, use, or sale of drugs or veterinary biological products.

It is important to note that certain biotechnology products are excluded from the experimental use exception contained in this section.

Section 271(e)(2) of the patent statute goes on to provide that it *shall* be an act of infringement to submit new drug applications or amended new drug applications for patented products not within the bounds of Section 271(e)(1). Remedies include injunctions to delay approval under such applications and to prevent commercial manufacture, use, or sale of an approved drug or veterinary product until after the expiration of the patent. Similarly, damages may be awarded, but only if there has been commercial manufacture, use, or sale of the product.[76] Despite few applications, it appears that the exemption from infringement will be narrowly construed to those instances where the challenged use is limited strictly to development and submission of information to a federal regulatory agency.[77]

13.3   PATENT VALIDITY IN THE COURTS

Validity and infringement are separate issues. A patent is issued only after the patent office has made a determination of validity.[78] This determination of validity is not, however, binding on accused infringers or the federal courts. The accused infringer in almost every case will raise invalidity of the patent as a defense to liability for infringement.[79] Numerous grounds of invalidity may be advanced, as summarized in Table 13-1.[80] Each claim in a patent must be separately evaluated for validity, as well as infringement.[81] If only invalid claims are found infringed, then there can be no liability for patent infringement.

The substantive law underlying each of these grounds for invalidity is generally the same for both the litigation of issued patents before the courts and the prosecution of pending patent applications before the patent office. While this substantive law has been the subject of preceding chapters, those chapters focused primarily on patent prosecution, and these issues can take on a different perspective in court. These differences, along with issues that do not usually arise before the patent office, are discussed in the following section.

13.3.1   Claim Interpretation for the Validity Analysis

As with infringement, claim interpretation for assessing validity is a two-step process. First, the claims must be interpreted to define the invention. Proper claim interpretation was described previously in this chapter, but it is important to note that the claims must be interpreted *identically* for purposes of validity and infringement.[82] Where more than one interpretation is possible, courts will interpret the claims to uphold their validity.[83] In litigation, in contrast with prosecution, a patent holder is able to advance his or her own interpretation of the claims but is not allowed to amend the claims to overcome an invalidating reference.[84] Therefore, the patent holder must balance the benefits of arguing a broad interpretation of the

TABLE 13–1   Grounds for Patent Invalidity

Grounds for Invalidity	Statutory Basis
Anticipation	35 U.S.C. § 102
Obviousness	35 U.S.C. § 103
Inventorship—derivation	35 U.S.C. § 102(f)
Inventorship—deception	35 U.S.C. §§ 101, 111, 256
Enablement	35 U.S.C. § 112
Best mode	35 U.S.C. § 112
Written description	35 U.S.C. § 112
Indefiniteness	35 U.S.C. § 112
Patentable subject matter	35 U.S.C. § 101

claims to facilitate a finding of infringement with the risk of having the claims read so broadly that they encompass an invalidating prior art reference that later comes to light.[85] The patent holder is, of course, limited in what scope can be argued based on the choices made during prosecution, as explained previously.

13.3.2 The Presumption of Validity

Issued patents are granted a statutory presumption of validity during litigation, and the patent statute provides that "the burden of establishing invalidity of a patent or any claim thereof shall rest on the party asserting such invalidity."[86] The party challenging the validity of the patent must prove the invalidity of each claim alleged to be infringed by clear and convincing evidence.[87] This is true even if the party challenging validity is able to prove the existence of prior art that was not cited to the patent office.[88] As stated by the Court of Appeals for the Federal Circuit, when the prior art being relied on by the party challenging validity adds nothing material to that considered by the patent office, the challenger faces the

> added burden of overcoming the deference that is due to a qualified governmental agency presumed to have properly done its job, which includes one or more examiners who are assumed to have some expertise in interpreting the references and to be familiar from their work with the level of skill in the art and whose duty it is to issue only valid patents.[89]

Therefore, if an accused infringer is unable to identify prior art that is more pertinent than what was considered by the patent office during the prosecution of the patent, the accused infringer must show that the patent office erred in order to meet the burden of proving invalidity.[90] In practice, accused infringers will almost always argue that they have discovered prior art that was more relevant than that considered by the examiner.

13.3.3 Assessing Novelty and Defining the Prior Art in the Courts

The validity analysis under both Section 102 for anticipation and Section 103 for obviousness requires a preliminary legal determination of what is prior art.[91] If a reference does not fit within any of the categories of prior art established by Section 102, that reference may not be considered as prior art for purposes of anticipation or obviousness.[92] The accused infringer alleging anticipation or obviousness must as a preliminary matter establish the facts necessary to qualify each and every reference relied on as prior art under Section 102.[93]

While the recognized statutory categories of prior art were discussed previously, prior public use or knowledge by others takes on an added importance in litigation. Because patent prosecution before the patent office is an *ex parte* process with the application maintained in secrecy, there is little or no opportunity for third parties to come forward with evidence of having practiced the claimed invention before the applicant's invention of it. In contrast, during litigation, which is typically brought against a direct competitor of the patent holder, the accused infringer may claim to have practiced the invention first or argue that others in the industry knew of or practiced the claimed invention prior to the patent holder. These types of prior art are regarded with disfavor by the courts in patent infringement disputes, especially when they are supported solely by oral testimony. Consequently, the accused infringer bears a heavy evidentiary burden in establishing the facts supporting an alleged prior use.

To be a statutory (and relevant) public use, the alleged use must be a successful reduction to practice of the claimed invention. Whether the alleged prior knowledge or use is advanced under sections 102(a) or 102(b), the party claiming it is prior art must establish that such a use was of a complete, reduced-to-practice invention.[94] The alleged prior use also must be public, not a secret.[95] While it is sufficient to show that the prior use was not intentionally hidden from the public, regardless of whether anyone actually knew of the use, prior-process activities of another that are maintained in confidence will not be considered prior art if they are shown to be truly secret.[96] Even a use for commercial purposes may be secret—as long as the prior use is by a third party and not the patent holder.[97]

Given the heavy burden on the defendant to establish a prior use and the ease with which oral testimony can be fabricated after the fact, it is not surprising that the U.S. Supreme Court long ago recognized limitations on the use of such testimony to establish a prior use. In discussing the probative value of oral testimony on prior invention, the Supreme Court has said:

> The very fact, which courts as well as the public have not failed to recognize, that almost every important patent, from the cotton gin of Whitney to the one under consideration has been attacked by the testimony of witnesses who imagined they had made similar discoveries long before the patentee had claimed to have invented his device, has tended to throw a certain amount of discredit upon all that class of evidence, and to demand that it be subjected to the closest scrutiny. Indeed, the frequency with which testimony is tortured, or fabricated outright, to build up the defence of a prior use of the thing patented, goes far to justify the popular impression that the inventor may be treated as the lawful prey of the infringer.[98]

The limited value of oral testimony on prior use has been recognized by the Federal Circuit.[99] Such claims are especially suspect in cases in which the patent holder introduces evidence of significant commercial success for a product or process that the alleged infringer claims—after the fact—was known or in use all along.[100]

While the benefits of the presumption of validity and the limited probative value of oral testimony of prior use aid the patent holder in litigation, they raise problems for an accused infringer who may legitimately have practiced the invention before the patent holder. Therefore, it is critical that properly corroborated records of in-house activities be maintained in writing to prove later claims of prior knowledge or use.

13.3.4 Assessing Nonobviousness in the Courts

As discussed in Chapter 7, once the prior art is defined the next difficulty in determining nonobviousness is to avoid the temptation to find an invention obvious based on hindsight.[101] While patent examiners are well aware of the impropriety of a hindsight analysis of nonobviousness, judges and jurors who rarely deal with such issues are more prone to reach an improper conclusion on nonobviousness. Accordingly, the Supreme Court and the Federal Circuit have laid out factual, objective criteria that must be considered in assessing nonobviousness. While these criteria apply both to prosecution before the patent office and to litigation, they are most commonly found in litigation. These objective criteria, commonly referred to as "secondary" or "objective" considerations, include, among other things:

1. The commercial success of the patented invention
2. The long-felt need for the patented invention
3. Copying the patented invention
4. The failure of others to develop the patented invention
5. Unexpected results obtained
6. Trade acceptance through licensing[102]

For all practical purposes, this mode of analysis is quite different from the analysis of nonobviousness carried out in the patent office. As noted in Chapter 8, arguing nonobviousness in the patent office tends to emphasize scientific evidence and arguments on "motivation to try" and "reasonable expectation of success." In contrast, objective considerations often prove to be the most substantiating evidence of nonobviousness in a trial.[103] Thus, even if the prior art were to make the invention appear obvious on a subjective basis, the objective indications of nonobviousness or secondary considerations may be sufficiently persuasive to compel the opposite.[104]

Probably the most substantiating secondary consideration in the courts is evidence of commercial success. For example, in the dispute between Hybritech and Monoclonal Antibodies, Inc. over Hybritech's monoclonal sandwich assay patent, the commercial success enjoyed by Hybritech's products was given special emphasis by the Federal Circuit in concluding that the invention was nonobvious.[105] In fact, evidence of commercial success sometimes is considered too great an influence on the ultimate question of nonobviousness.[106]

13.4 PATENT ENFORCEABILITY IN THE COURTS

Even if a patent is found to be valid and infringed, the patent holder will not be able to obtain any relief if the patent is found to be unenforceable under any of a number of judicially created defenses to patent infringement. The most commonly alleged ground of unenforceability is inequitable conduct by the patent holder that, if proven, makes every claim of the patent unenforceable. Patent misuse is another reason for finding a patent unenforceable. Unlike inequitable conduct, however, once the misuse ceases the patent once again becomes enforceable. Additional equitable defenses to enforceability of a patent include laches and equitable estoppel, which may stop the patent holder from enforcing the patent or collecting damages for past infringing acts from a defendant.

13.4.1 Inequitable Conduct

A patent applicant is held to a high standard of candor and good faith in all dealings with the patent office, particularly with respect to his or her obligation to bring relevant prior art to the patent office's attention.[107] Failing to meet this standard can result in an otherwise valid patent being held unenforceable for inequitable conduct.

Inequitable conduct has become an increasingly common defense in all patent infringement actions. As stated by the Federal Circuit, however, "'inequitable conduct' is not, or should not be, a magic incantation to be asserted against every patentee."[108] To establish inequitable conduct, the accused infringer must prove either a failure to disclose information or the submission of false information; in either case, both the materiality of the information and intent to deceive must be proven by clear and convincing evidence.[109] An allegation of inequitable conduct cannot be established simply by showing that prior art or information having some degree of materiality was not disclosed to the patent and trademark office. While the case law on materiality is somewhat unclear, the standard does not require the reference to be so material that the patent would not have issued if the reference had been presented during prosecution.[110] On the other hand, a reference that does not qualify as prior art under any category, or merely is an accumulation of what was already before the patent office, cannot be the basis for a finding of inequitable conduct.[111]

To establish inequitable conduct based on a material misrepresentation, an accused infringer must show: (1) that the applicant made a false representation of a material fact, and (2) that the representation was made with the intent to deceive the PTO and improperly secure the issuance of a patent.[112] An accused infringer asserting a "failure to disclose" form of inequitable conduct must offer clear and convincing proof of: (1) prior art or information that is material, (2) knowledge chargeable to the applicant of that prior art or information and of its materiality, and (3) failure of the applicant to disclose the art or information resulting from an intent to mislead the PTO.[113]

Both forms of inequitable conduct require an intent to deceive. The question of intent to deceive must be based on all the evidence, including that showing good faith.[114] Mere nondisclosure alone is not enough to establish intent.[115] Negligence alone, even gross negligence, also is insufficient for a finding of inequitable conduct.[116] This does not mean that direct evidence of intent to deceive is required, however. It is enough if circumstantial evidence sufficient to support an inference of deceptive intent is presented.[117]

Inequitable conduct is an equitable defense. Therefore, the inquiry does not end with establishing materiality and intent. When the deceptive intent of the applicants and the materiality of the reference are first made by the party alleging inequitable conduct, the court must balance the materiality of the reference and the culpability of the applicants to reach an equitable decision on the enforceability of the patent.[118]

The necessity for candor can create a dilemma for patent applicants. Realistically speaking, it is impossible for a patent applicant to refer to every conceivable piece of information that arguably deals with the subject of the patent application. In fact, patent applicants can be found guilty of inequitable conduct if too much information is cited during the prosecution of the application.[119] Accordingly, all charges of inequitable conduct must be considered in light of the problems faced by the patent applicant in deciding which materials to cite and which to ignore. While there is no fixed rule on what should be disclosed, at the very least an applicant is well-advised to put all related publications before the patent office during prosecution of the application.

13.4.2 Patent Misuse and Antitrust Implications

A complete consideration of the application of the antitrust laws to patents in the courts or in evaluating licensing agreements is beyond the scope of this chapter.[120] Antitrust issues frequently arise in patent litigation, however. A counterclaim for antitrust violations may allow the accused infringer to both escape liability and to obtain damages from the patent holder. On the other hand, patent misuse is an equitable defense making the patent unenforceable without providing grounds for claiming monetary damages from the patent holder. Under the patent misuse defense, however, once the misuse ceases the patent again will be enforceable.[121]

Allegations of antitrust violations against patent holders are often directed at illegal tying arrangements (e.g., requiring the purchaser to take a second product in order to obtain a first product), or anticompetitive pricing or marketing situations that go beyond the scope of the monopoly rights provided by the patent. These allegations may be aided in the patent context by a presumption that monopoly market power exists based on the existence of the patent.[122] Otherwise, all of the elements of the alleged antitrust violation must be established in the patent context as in any other antitrust case. The viability of such allegations, as with other areas of antitrust law, is suspect in light of the recent trend away from the strict enforcement of antitrust laws based on *per se* rules and towards a rule-of-reason approach and high requirements for showing economic market power and competitive impact.[123]

In a counterclaim to a patent infringement suit, the accused infringer often alleges that the patent holder is guilty of patent misuse and antitrust violations for bringing that suit in "bad faith." Typical grounds for the bad-faith contention are that the patent was obtained fraudulently, or that the patent holder knew the patent was invalid or not infringed before bringing suit.[124] The patent holder is presumed to have brought the suit in good faith, however. This presumption may be rebutted only by clear and convincing evidence.[125]

13.4.3 Laches and Estoppel

Laches and equitable estoppel are two additional equitable defenses available to an accused infringer that may limit a patent holder's ability to enforce a valid patent. Each has separate elements that must be established by the accused infringer. Unlike inequitable conduct and invalidity, these defenses may be satisfied by a preponderance of the evidence rather than clear and convincing evidence. As equitable defenses, the court rather than the jury determines, first, whether the accused infringer has established the elements of the defense and second, the extent to which the patent holder's claim should be barred.

Laches is an equitable doctrine analogous to a statute of limitations. To establish laches, the accused infringer must show that the "patentee's delay in bringing suit was unreasonable and inexcusable" and that the accused infringer suffered "material prejudice attributable to the delay."[126] The defense depends on the personal circumstances of each particular party and, unlike a finding of invalidity, does not stop a patent holder from enforcing the patent against others who are unable to establish a laches defense.

The period for determining delay runs from "the time the [patent holder] knew or reasonably should have known of its claim against" the accused infringer.[127] The prejudice against the accused infringer may be either economic or evidentiary. Evidentiary prejudice "may arise by reason of a defendant's inability to present a full and fair defense on the merits due to the loss of records, the death of a witness, or the unreliability of memories of long-past events, thereby undermining the court's ability to judge the facts."[128] Economic prejudice requires a showing of more than the expected damages flowing from infringement. The accused infringer must show some change in economic position by the accused infringer during the delay that resulted in damages that could have been prevented if suit was brought earlier.[129]

If the delay in bringing suit is more than six years, a presumption of laches arises that establishes in favor of the accused infringer both the unreasonable delay and the prejudice elements.[130] This presumption requires the patent holder to present rebuttal evidence showing that the delay either was reasonable or that no prejudice was suffered. If the patent holder can produce this rebuttal evidence, then the presumption of laches disappears.[131]

Once the two elements of laches are established—by presumption or otherwise—the court must determine if the particular circumstances between the parties justify the application of the laches defense. The court will consider all the facts, including justifications for the patent holder's delay such as other litigation, negotiations with the accused infringer, and negotiations over settlement.[132] If the laches defense is found to apply, the patent holder will be barred from recovering damages for the period prior to filing suit, but he or she still may bring suit for damages that occur after filing the suit, or for an injunction blocking further infringing conduct.[133]

Three elements must be established by an accused infringer asserting the doctrine of equitable estoppel. First, the patent holder must have engaged in misleading conduct that led the accused infringer to believe that the patent holder would not enforce the patent against the accused infringer. Second, the accused infringer must have relied on the patent holder's misleading conduct. Finally, the accused infringer must be materially prejudiced due to its reliance on the patent holder's misleading conduct.[134] While delay may be evidence of misleading conduct, it is not an element under equitable estoppel. Furthermore, there is no presumption available to aid the accused infringer under equitable estoppel.

As with laches, even if all three elements are established, the court still must look at all the circumstances to reach the proper decision (that is, must "balance the equities").[135] While equitable estoppel is generally harder to establish than laches, it allows the accused infringer not only to avoid damages for activities prior to filing suit but may bar all relief, including both monetary damages and injunctive relief.[136]

13.5 ESTOPPEL APPLIED TO THE ACCUSED INFRINGER

Concepts of estoppel may be applied to accused infringers as well as to those who seek to enforce the patent, and may prevent certain parties from ever contesting the validity of an issued patent. This is distinct from general principles of law that prevent losing parties from relitigating issues that were previously raised and decided in court.

13.5.1 Licensee Estoppel and *Lear v. Adkins*
One party that might already have admitted a patent's validity is a licensee of the patent. However, this argument was expressly rejected by the Supreme Court in *Lear, Inc. v. Adkins*.[137] The Supreme Court in *Lear* determined that public policy favoring free competition in ideas that are part of the public domain outweighed any argument that a licensee should be prevented from contesting validity against its licensor after entering into a binding license agreement.

13.5.2 Assignor Estoppel and *Diamond v. Ambico*
Despite the Supreme Court's rejection of licensee estoppel, the Court of Appeals for the Federal Circuit recognized the doctrine of assignor estoppel in *Diamond Scientific Co. v. Ambico, Inc.*[138] Under this doctrine, anyone who has assigned the rights to a patent, including the inventor or anyone in a close relationship with the assignor, is prohibited from later disputing the validity of the patent. Assignor estoppel is one of the rare circumstances where an invalid patent can be enforced against an accused infringer.

REFERENCES

1. 35 U.S.C. § 154.
2. 35 U.S.C. § 271.
3. 35 U.S.C. § 111.
4. 35 U.S.C. § 112, second paragraph.
5. General Foods Corporation v. Studiengesellschaft Kohle mbH, 972 F.2d 1272, 1274, 23 USPQ2d 1839, 1840 (Fed. Cir. 1992).
6. 35 U.S.C. § 271; 28 U.S.C. § 1338.

7. 35 U.S.C. § 283 provides: "The several courts having jurisdiction of cases under this title may grant injunctions in accordance with the principles of equity to prevent the violation of any right secured by patent, on such terms as the court deems reasonable."

8. Compare this with 35 U.S.C. § 295, which provides for infringement by the importation, sale, or use of a product that is made from a process patented in the United States.

9. 35 U.S.C. § 284.

10. 35 U.S.C. §§ 284, 285.

11. *See generally* R. Cooley, *Personal Liability of Corporate Officers and Directors for Infringement of Intellectual Property*, 68 J. PAT. & TRADEMARK OFF. SOC'Y 228 (1986).

12. Minnesota Mining and Manufacturing Co. v. Johnson & Johnson Orthopaedics, Inc., 976 F.2d 1559, 24 USPQ2d 1321 (Fed Cir. 1992).

13. *See, e.g.*, R. Hantman, *Patent Infringement*, 72 J. PAT. & TRADEMARK OFF. SOC'Y 454 (1990).

14. A complete discussion of claim interpretation is beyond the scope of this chapter. For a thorough treatment of the subject see 4 D. Chisum, PATENTS, § 18 (1992).

15. Graver Tank & Mfg. Co. v. Linde Air Products Co., 339 U.S. 605, 607, 85 USPQ 328, 330 (1950).

16. Kalman v. Kimberly-Clark Corp., 713 F.2d 760, 770, 218 USPQ 781, 788 (Fed Cir. 1983).

17. *See generally* 4 D. Chisum, PATENTS, § 18.03. For thorough discussions of claim interpretation, *see* Autogiro Co. of America v. United States, 384 F.2d 391, 155 USPQ 697 (Ct.Cl. 1967); and SRI International v. Matsushita Electric Corp. of America, 775 F.2d 1107, 227 USPQ 577 (Fed. Cir. 1985).

18. Envirotech Corp. v. Al George, Inc., 730 F.2d 753, 758, 221 USPQ 473, 477 (Fed. Cir. 1984).

19. Envirotech, 730 F.2d at 759, 221 USPQ at 477.

20. *See, e.g.*, Black & Decker Inc. v. Hoover Service Center, 886 F.2d 1285, 1293, 12 USPQ2d 1250, 1257 (Fed. Cir. 1989) ("The limitation in the claim to a 'front wall and a snout extending forward of said front wall' does not 'read on' Hoover's cleaner. There therefore can be no literal infringement."); LaSalle v. Carlton's Laydown Service, Inc., 680 F.2d 432, 216 USPQ 276 (5th Cir. 1982).

21. *See, e.g.*, Smith v. Snow, 294 U.S. 1, 11, 55 S. Ct. 279, 283 (1935); E.I. du Pont de Nemours & Co. v. Phillips Petroleum Co., 849 F.2d 1430, 1433, 7 USPQ2d 1129, 1131 (Fed. Cir. 1988); Lemelson v. United States, 752 F.2d 1538, 1552, 224 USPQ 526, 534 (Fed. Cir. 1985).

22. *See, e.g.*, Envirotech, 730 F.2d at 759, 221 USPQ at 477.

23. *See generally* 4 D. Chisum, PATENTS, § 18.03 note 1.

24. *See, e.g.*, ZMI Corp. v. Cardiac Resuscitator Corp., 844 F.2d 1576, 1579–1580, 6 USPQ2d 1557, 1560 (Fed. Cir. 1988) *on remand* 11 USPQ2d 1634 (D. Ore. 1989) ("The ordinary meaning of claim language, however, is not dispositive and resort must still be had to the specification and prosecution history to determine if the inventor used the disputed terms differently than their ordinary accustomed meaning."). *Compare* General Battery Corp. v. Gould, Inc., 545 F.Supp. 731, 760, 215 USPQ 1007, 1030 (D. Del. 1982) ("Before turning to the specifications to determine the meaning of an ambiguous term, '[a] Court should consider how ambiguous the claimed ambiguity really is, and how difficult a task it would have been to make the claim read literally what it is urged to mean by reference to the specification.'" [citation omitted]); *and* Black & Decker Inc. v. Hoover Service Center, 887 F.2d 1285, 1294, 12 USPQ2d 1250,

1257 (Fed. Cir. 1989) (When a district court unnecessarily considered prior art, prosecution history, and operation of device it did not detract from the finding of literal infringement.).

25. For a discussion of various canons of claim construction *see generally* 4 D. Chisum, PATENTS, § 18.03[2]. *See esp.* at n. 3, citing, among others, Dennis v. Pitner, 106 F.2d 142, 148 (7th Cir. 1939).

26. Consolidated Aluminum v. Foseco International, 10 USPQ2d 1143 (N.D. Ill. 1988).

27. *See* Consolidated Aluminum, 10 USPQ2d at 1158.

28. General Foods Corp., 972 F.2d at 1274, 23 USPQ2d at 1840.

29. General Foods Corp., 972 F.2d at 1274–75, 23 USPQ2d at 1840.

30. *See, e.g.*, General Battery, 545 F. Supp. at 760, 215 USPQ at 1030 (citing Graver Tank and Mfg. Co. v. Linde Air Products Co., 339 U.S. 605, 607, 85 USPQ 328, 330 [1950]).

31. North American Vaccine Inc. v. American Cyanamid Co. 24 USPQ2d 1898 (S.D.N.Y. 1992), *aff'd in pertinent part,* 7 F.3d 1571(Fed. Cir. 1993).

32. North American Vaccine, 24 USPQ2d at 1900.

33. North American Vaccine, 24 USPQ2d at 1902.

34. *See generally* R. Hantman, *Doctrine of Equivalents*, 70 J. PAT. & TRADEMARK OFF. SOC'Y 511 (1988); J. Kushan, *Protein Patents and the Doctrine of Equivalents: Limits on the Expansion of Patent Rights*, 6 HIGH TECHNOLOGY LAW JOURNAL 109 (1991).

35. Pennwalt, Inc. v. Durand Wayland, 833 F.2d 931, 4 USPQ2d 1737 (Fed. Cir. 1987), *cert. denied,* 485 U.S. 961 (1988); *see also* Wilson Sporting Goods Co. v. David Geoffrey and Assocs., 904 F.2d 677, 14 USPQ2d 1942 (Fed. Cir.), *cert. denied,* 111 S. Ct. 537 (1990); Malta v. Schulmerich Carillons, Inc., 952 F.2d 1320, 21 USPQ2d 1161 (Fed. Cir. 1991), *reh'g denied,* 959 F.2d 923, 21 USPQ2d 2039 (Fed. Cir. 1992), *cert. denied,* 112 S.Ct. 2942 (1992).

36. 4 D. Chisum, PATENTS § 18.04[1], pp. 18–74 *et seq.*

37. *See, e.g.*, A. Preston and D. Elderkin, *Malta v. Schulmerich: The Federal Circuit at a Crossroads in its Search to Harmonize Substantive Patent Law with Jury Trial Procedure and Review*, 20 AIPLA QUART. J. 49 (1992); H. Wegner, *The Doctrine of Equivalents After London*, 74 J. PAT. & TRADEMARK OFF. SOC'Y 67 (1992); H. Parker, *Doctrine of Equivalents Analysis After Wilson Sporting Goods: The Hypothetical Claim Hydra*, 18 AIPLA QUART. J. 262 (1990); M. Adelman and G. Francione, *The Doctrine of Equivalents in Patent Law: Questions that Pennwalt Did Not Answer*, 137 U. PA. L. REV. 673 (1989).

38. Graver Tank & Mfg. Co. v. Linde Air Products Co., 339 U.S. 605, 70 S. Ct. 854 (1950).

39. Graver, 339 U.S. at 607–08, 70 S. Ct. at 856 (citing Union Paper-Bag Machine Co. v. Murphy, 97 U.S. 120, 125, 24 L.Ed. 935).

40. Kinzenbaw v. Deere & Co., 741 F.2d 383, 222 USPQ 929 (Fed. Cir. 1984). *See also In re* Certain Double Sided Floppy Disk Drives, 229 USPQ 968, 974 (U.S.I.T.C. 1986) ("The doctrine is judicially created to do equity and is designed to protect inventors from unscrupulous copyists.").

41. Pennwalt v. Durand Wayland, 833 F.2d 931, 4 USPQ2d 1737 (Fed. Cir. 1987), *cert. denied*, 485 U.S. 961 (1988).

42. *See* 4 D. Chisum, PATENTS, § 18.04[1] note 3, pp. 18–76.

43. Laitram Corp. v. Cambridge Wire Cloth Co., 863 F.2d 855, 856–57, 9 USPQ2d 1289, 1291 (Fed Cir. 1988).

44. *See, e.g.*, Loctite Corporation v. Ultraseal Ltd., 781 F.2d 861, 228 USPQ 90 (Fed. Cir. 1985).

45. Graver Tank, 339 U.S. at 608, 70 S. Ct. at 856 (citations omitted).
46. Hughes Aircraft Co. v. United States, 717 F.2d 1351, 1362, 219 USPQ 473, 481 (Fed. Cir. 1983) (citations omitted).
47. Phillips Petroleum Co. v. U.S. Steel Corp., 673 F.Supp. 1278, 1349, 6 USPQ2d 1065, 1122 (D. Del. 1987).
48. *See, e.g.,* Loctite Corporation v. Ultraseal Ltd., 781 F.2d 861, 870, 228 USPQ 90, 96 (Fed. Cir. 1985); Exhibit Supply Co. v. Ace Patents Corp., 315 U.S. 126 (1942); Hughes Aircraft, 717 F.2d at 1361, 219 USPQ at 480.
49. Genentech Inc. v. The Wellcome Foundation Ltd., 798 F. Supp. 213, 24 USPQ2d 1782 (D. Del. 1992).
50. Genentech Inc. v. The Wellcome Foundation Ltd., 14 USPQ2d 1363 (D. Del. 1990).
51. Charge to the Jury at 30–34, Genentech Inc. v. The Wellcome Foundation Ltd., Civ. A. No. 88-330/89-407-JJF (consolidated) (D. Del.).
52. BNA's Patent, TRADEMARK & COPYRIGHT JOURNAL, April 19, 1990 at 503.
53. Genentech, 798 F. Supp. at 219, 24 USPQ2d at 1787.
54. *See generally* Westinghouse v. Boyden Power Brake Co., 170 U.S. 537 (1896); SRI International v. Matsushita Electric Corp., 227 USPQ 577, 775 F.2d 1107 (Fed. Cir. 1985); see also K. Bozicevic, *The "Reverse Doctrine of Equivalents" in the World of Reverse Transcriptase*, 71 J. PAT. & TRADEMARK OFF. SOC'Y 353 (1989); C. Pigott, *Equivalents in Reverse*, 48 J. PAT. OFF. SOC'Y 291 (1966).
55. Graver Tank, 339 U.S. 608–09, 70 S. Ct. 856.
56. Phillips Petroleum, 673 F.Supp. at 1350, 6 USPQ2d at 1123 (citations omitted).
57. Scripps Clinic & Research Fdn. v. Genentech, Inc., 927 F.2d 1565, 1581, 18 USPQ2d 1001, 1011 (Fed. Cir. 1991).
58. *Id.; see also* R. Merges, *A Brief Note on Blocking Patents and Reverse Equivalents: Biotechnology as an Example*, 73 J. PAT. & TRADEMARK OFF. SOC'Y 878 (1991).
59. 35 U.S.C. § 271.
60. 35 U.S.C. § 271(g). *See also* Comment, *The Process Patent Amendments Act of 1988: Solving an Old Problem, But Creating New Ones*, 1989 B.Y.U. L. REV. 567.
61. *See generally* 35 U.S.C. § 287(b).
62. Amgen Inc. v. ITC, 902 F.2d 1532, 1540, 14 USPQ2d 1734, 1741 (Fed. Cir. 1990).
63. Amgen, 902 F.2d at 1534 note 1, 14 USPQ2d at 1736 note 1.
64. *See generally* I. McAndrews, *Removing the Burden of Durden Through Legislation: HR 3957 and HR 5664*, 72 J. PAT. & TRADEMARK OFF. SOC'Y 1188 (1990).
65. *See Bill Seeks Stronger Protection Against Foreign Infringement of Biotech Patents*, PAT. TRADEMARK & COPYRIGHT J. (BNA), Vol. 39 at 262 (Feb. 8, 1990).
66. *See, e.g., Amended Biotech Process Patent Bill Is Cleared by Senate Subcommittee*, PAT. TRADEMARK & COPYRIGHT J. (BNA), Vol. 42 at 313 (Aug. 1, 1991).
67. *See, e.g., Biotech Process Patent Bill Is Debated Before House Panel*, PAT. TRADEMARK & COPYRIGHT J. (BNA), Vol. 43 at 63 (Nov. 28, 1991).
68. I. Feit, *Biotechnology Research and the Experimental Use Exception to Patent Infringement*, 71 J. PAT. & TRADEMARK OFF. SOC'Y 819 (1989).
69. R. Bee, *Experimental Use as an Act of Patent Infringement*, 39 J. PAT. OFF. SOC'Y 357 (1957).
70. R. Hantman, *Experimental Use as an Exception to Infringement*, 67 J. PAT. & TRADEMARK OFF. SOC'Y 617 (1985).
71. Whittemore v. Cutter, 29 Fed. Cas. 1120, No. 17,600 (CCD Mass. 1813).
72. Sawin v. Guild, 21 Fed. Cas. 554, No. 12,391 (CCD Mass. 1813).
73. Pfizer, Inc. v. International Rectifier Corp., 217 USPQ 157 (C.D. Cal. 1982).
74. *See, e.g.,* J. Fox, *Patents Encroaching on Research Freedom*, 224 SCIENCE 1080 (1984).

75. 35 U.S.C. § 271(e).
76. 35 U.S.C. § 271(e)(4).
77. *See, e.g.*, Scripps Clinic & Research Fdn. v. Genentech, Inc., 666 F.Supp. 1379, 3 USPQ2d 1481 (N.D. Cal. 1987), *rev'd and remanded on other grounds*, 927 F.2d 1565, 18 USPQ2d 1001 (Fed. Cir. 1991).
78. 37 C.F.R. § 1.311.
79. 35 U.S.C. § 282.
80. The ultimate question of validity is classified as a question of law, not fact. However, anticipation is classified as a question of fact, while obviousness is classified as a question of law. These distinctions are primarily relevant to the propriety of granting judgment as a matter of law and the scope of appellate review as discussed in Chapter 2 of this book.
81. 35 U.S.C. § 282 ("Each claim of a patent . . . shall be presumed valid independently of the validity of other claims.").
82. Smithkline Diagnostics, Inc. v. Helena Laboratories Corp., 859 F.2d 878, 882, 8 USPQ2d 1468, 1471 (Fed. Cir. 1988); *see also* White v. Dunbar, 119 U.S. 47, 51 (1886).
83. ACS Hospital Systems, Inc. v. Montefiore Hospital, 732 F.2d 1572, 1578, 221 USPQ 929, 933 (Fed. Cir. 1984).
84. *In re* Etter, 756 F.2d 852, 225 USPQ 1 (Fed. Cir. 1985) (in banc).
85. This tradeoff extends beyond the litigation at hand to future lawsuits against other infringers as the patent holder will be estopped from arguing an inconsistent construction in all subsequent litigation. Hybritech, Inc. v. Abbott Labs., 849 F.2d 1446, 7 USPQ2d 1191 (Fed. Cir. 1988).
86. 35 U.S.C. § 282.
87. Alco Standard Corp. v. Tennessee Valley Auth., 808 F.2d 1490, 1498, 1 USPQ2d 1337, 1342 (Fed. Cir. 1986), *cert. dismissed*, 483 U.S. 1052, 108 S. Ct. 26 (1987).
88. Alco, 808 F.2d at 1497–98, 1 USPQ2d at 1342.
89. American Hoist & Derrick Co. v. Sowa & Sons, Inc., 725 F.2d 1350, 1359, 220 USPQ 763, 770 (Fed. Cir.), *cert. denied*, 469 U.S. 821, 105 S. Ct. 95 (1984).
90. Syntex Pharmaceuticals International, Ltd. v. K-Line Pharmaceuticals, Ltd., 721 F. Supp. 653, 658, 12 USPQ2d 1710, 1714 (D.N.J. 1989).
91. Panduit Corp. v. Dennison Mfg. Co., 810 F.2d 1561, 1568, 1 USPQ2d 1593, 1597 (Fed. Cir.), *cert. denied*, 481 U.S. 1052, 107 S. Ct. 2187 (1987).
92. *Id.*; Preemption Devices, Inc. v. Minnesota Mining and Mfg. Co., 732 F.2d 903, 906, 221 USPQ 841, 843 (Fed. Cir. 1984). While a reference not qualifying as prior art under any of the statutory categories may not be considered as a prior art reference, it may be admissible in court as evidence of the level of ordinary skill in the pertinent art. Thomas & Betts Corp. v. Litton Systems, Inc., 720 F.2d 1572, 1581, 220 USPQ 1, 7 (Fed. Cir. 1983).
93. Panduit, 810 F.2d at 1568, 1 USPQ2d at 1597.
94. Medtronic, Inc. v. Daig Corp., 611 F. Supp. 1498, 1508, 227 USPQ 509 (D. Minn. 1985), *aff'd*, 789 F.2d 903, 229 USPQ 664 (Fed. Cir.), *cert. denied*, 479 U.S. 931, 107 S. Ct. 402 (1986); *see also* Coffin v. Ogden, 85 U.S. (18 Wall.) 120, 124 (1873).
95. *Compare* Gillman v. Stern, 114 F.2d 28, 31, 46 USPQ 430, 433–34 (2d Cir.), *cert. denied*, 311 U.S. 718, 61 S. Ct. 411 (1940) *with* Electric Storage Battery Co. v. Shimadzu, 307 U.S. 5, 59 S. Ct. 675, 41 USPQ 155 (1939).
96. W.L. Gore & Associates, Inc. v. Garlock, Inc., 721 F.2d 1540, 1550–54, 220 USPQ 303 (Fed. Cir. 1983), *cert. denied*, 469 U.S. 851, 105 S. Ct. 172 (1984); Electric Storage, 307 U.S. at 5 (1939).

97. *Id.*; Jacobson v. Cox Paving Co., 19 USPQ2d 1641, 1648 (D. Ariz. 1991).
98. The Barbed Wire Patent, 143 U.S. 275, 284–5 (1892).
99. *See, e.g.*, Intra Corp. v. Hamar Laser Instruments, Inc., 662 F.Supp. 1420, 1439, 4 USPQ2d 1337, 1351 (E.D. Mich. 1987) ("Testimony of anticipation, without contemporaneous documentary or physical evidence showing reduction to practice and prior public use, is insufficient."), *aff'd*, 862 F.2d 320 (Fed. Cir. 1988), *cert. denied*, 490 U.S. 1021 (1989); Rolls-Royce, Ltd. v. GTE Valeron Corp., 625 F. Supp. 343, 353–54, 228 USPQ 489, 495 (E.D. Mich. 1985)(same), *aff'd*, 800 F.2d 1101, 231 USPQ 185 (Fed. Cir. 1986); Shields v. Halliburton Co., 493 F. Supp. 1376, 1388, 207 USPQ 304, 315 (W.D. La. 1980) ("This Court will not invalidate an otherwise valid patent on the basis of oral testimony alone."), *aff'd*, 667 F.2d 1232 (5th Cir. 1982); Carboline Co. v. Mobil Oil Corp., 301 F. Supp. 141, 146, 163 USPQ 273, 277–78 (N.D. Ill. 1969) ("More is required than the uncorroborated, self-serving statements of an alleged prior user or inventor.").
100. Pentech Int'l Inc. v. Hayduchok, 18 USPQ2d 1337, 1342 (S.D.N.Y. 1990).
101. *In re* Dow Chemical Co., 837 F.2d 469, 473 (Fed. Cir. 1988); Gore, 721 F.2d at 1553, 220 USPQ at 313.
102. Graham v. John Deere Co., 383 U.S. 1, 17–18 (1966); Panduit Corp., 810 F.2d at 1566.
103. Alco, 808 F.2d at 1500, 1 USPQ2d at 1344.
104. Alco, 808 F.2d at 1501; Continental Can Co. v. Monsanto Co., 948 F.2d 1264 (Fed. Cir. 1991); *In re* Piasecki, 745 F.2d 1468, 1475, 223 USPQ 785, 790 (Fed. Cir. 1984). *But see* Ryko Mfg. Co. v. Nu-Star, Inc., 950 F.2d 714, 719–20, 21 USPQ2d 1053, 1058 (Fed. Cir. 1991) (upholding a summary judgment of obviousness despite secondary considerations indicating nonobvious).
105. Hybritech Inc. v. Monoclonal Antibodies, Inc., 802 F.2d 1367, 1381–82, 231 USPQ 81, 92 (Fed. Cir. 1986).
106. *See generally* R. Merges, *Commercial Success and Patent Standards: Economic Perspectives on Innovation*, 76 CALIF. L. REV. 803 (1988).
107. 37 C.F.R. § 1.56; Norton v. Curtiss, 433 F.2d 779, 794, 167 USPQ 532, 534 (C.C.P.A. 1970).
108. FMC Corp. v. Manitowoc Co., 835 F.2d 1411, 1415, 5 USPQ2d 1112, 1115 (Fed. Cir. 1987).
109. Kingsdown Medical Consultants v. Hollister, Inc., 863 F.2d 867, 872, 9 USPQ2d 1384, 1389 (Fed. Cir. 1988), *cert. denied*, 490 U.S. 1067 (1989); Halliburton Co. v. Schlumberger Technology Corp., 952 F.2d 1435, 1442, 17 USPQ2d 1834, 1838 (Fed. Cir. 1991).
110. The current test would appear to be a "reasonable examiner" standard, meaning that a reasonable examiner would have considered the information important. Specialty Composites v. Cabot Corp., 845 F.2d 981, 992, 6 USPQ2d 1601, 1608 (Fed. Cir. 1988). However, the patent office recently amended Rule 1.56, and the potential impact of this rule change in the courts is not yet clear. *See generally* J. Lee, *Introduction*, 20 AIPLA QUART. J. 131 (1992) (Special issue entitled *Evolution and Future of New Rule 56 and the Duty of Candor*).
111. Northern Telecom, Inc. v. Datapoint Corp., 908 F.2d 931, 940, 15 USPQ2d 1321, 1328 (Fed. Cir.), *cert. denied*, 111 S. Ct. 296 (1990); Specialty Composites v. Cabot Corp., 845 F.2d at 992, 6 USPQ2d at 1609; Halliburton, 925 F.2d at 1440, 17 USPQ2d at 1.
112. Kingsdown Medical, 863 F.2d at 872, 9 USPQ2d at 1389.

113. FMC v. Manitowoc, 835 F.2d at 1415, 5 USPQ2d at 1115.
114. Kingsdown Medical, 863 F.2d at 876, 9 USPQ2d at 1392.
115. Halliburton, 925 F.2d at 1442, 17 USPQ2d at 1.
116. Halliburton, 925 F.2d at 1443.
117. Hewlett-Packard Co. v. Bausch & Lomb, Inc., 882 F.2d 1556, 1562, 11 USPQ2d 1750, 1755 (Fed. Cir. 1989).
118. Halliburton, 925 F.2d at 1439.
119. Penn Yan Boats, Inc. v. Sea Lark Boats, Inc., 359 F. Supp. 948, 965, 175 USPQ 260, 272 (S.D. Fla. 1972), *aff'd*, 479 F.2d 1328, 178 USPQ 577 (5th Cir. 1973).
120. *See generally* I. Millstein, *The Role of Antitrust in an Age of Technology*, 9 CARDOZO L. REV. 1175 (1988).
121. *See* Allen Archery, Inc. v. Browning Mfg. Co., 819 F.2d 1087, 1097, 2 USPQ2d 1490, 1498 (Fed. Cir. 1987).
122. *Compare* United States v. Loew's Inc., 371 U.S. 38, 46, 135 USPQ 201, 204–05 (1962) *with* Abbott Laboratories v. Brennan, 952 F.2d 1346, 1354–55, 21 USPQ2d 1192, 1199 (Fed. Cir. 1991) (the mere existence of a patent does not establish market power for a Sherman Act section 2 claim) *and* 35 U.S.C. § 271(d) (listing acts not sufficient to constitute misuse).
123. *See, e.g.*, Continental TV v. GTE Sylvania, 443 U.S. 36, 97 S. Ct. 2549 (1977).
124. Fraudulent procurement may itself be a basis for alleging antitrust violations. *See* American Hoist & Derrick Co. v. Sowa & Sons, Inc., 725 F.2d 1350, 220 USPQ 763 (Fed. Cir.), *cert. denied*, 469 U.S. 821 (1984); Albert v. Kevex Corp., 729 F.2d 757, 221 USPQ 202 (Fed. Cir. 1984).
125. *See* Loctite Corp. v. Ultraseal, Ltd., 781 F.2d 861, 877, 228 USPQ 90, 101 (Fed. Cir. 1985).
126. A.C. Aukerman Co. v. R.L. Chaides Construction Co., 960 F.2d 1020, 1028, 22 USPQ2d 1321, 1324–25 (Fed. Cir. 1992).
127. Aukerman, 960 F.2d at 1032, 22 USPQ2d at 1328.
128. Aukerman, 960 F.2d at 1033, 22 USPQ2d at 1328.
129. Aukerman, 960 F.2d at 1033, 22 USPQ2d at 1329.
130. The six-year period is loosely related to the six-year limit on recovery of damages in 35 U.S.C. § 286.
131. Aukerman, 960 F.2d at 1037–38, 22 USPQ2d at 1332.
132. Aukerman, 960 F.2d at 1033, 22 USPQ2d at 1329.
133. Aukerman, 960 F.2d at 1041, 22 USPQ2d at 1335.
134. Aukerman, 960 F.2d at 1028, 22 USPQ2d at 1325.
135. Aukerman, 960 F.2d at 1043, 22 USPQ2d at 1337.
136. Aukerman, 960 F.2d at 1028, 22 USPQ2d at 1325.
137. Lear, Inc. v. Adkins, 395 U.S. 653, 162 USPQ 1 (1969).
138. Diamond Scientific Co. v. Ambico, Inc., 848 F.2d 1220, 6 USPQ2d 2028 (Fed. Cir. 1988).

14

Procedural Aspects
of Patent Litigation

James D. Myers and Robert W. Glatz

Patent infringement suits are among the most complex and expensive types of litigation. Attorneys' fees and other expenses incurred in a hotly contested case can run well over $1 million.[1] Regardless of the substantive merits of a case, for all practical purposes a lawsuit can be won or lost on matters of procedure. This chapter accordingly reviews the procedural issues that arise in the course of a patent infringement suit, from the first steps in initiating the suit through appeal.[2] All the parties involved in patent litigation, no matter what side they are on, should have a basic understanding of the procedural rules well before taking any steps even remotely related to a potential lawsuit. Otherwise, they may find they are hurting their own cause.

14.1 STEPS TAKEN PRIOR TO A LAWSUIT

Legal counsel should be consulted as soon as the possibility of a lawsuit (either for or against a patent) arises. Attorneys' fees at this stage are by far the most cost-effective expenditures that can be made in the course of a lawsuit. Rushing into a lawsuit in an overly aggressive manner can be disastrous.

Before a lawsuit is filed, typical steps include reviewing and confirming the scope and validity of the patent, performing a factual investigation of the potentially infringing conduct, obtaining the opinion of counsel on the position to be taken when the suit is initiated (to avoid court sanctions at a later date), and, possibly, approaching the other side in an effort to settle the matter without the need for a lawsuit. (If the effort to settle is done improperly, however, this could provide the other side with exactly what it needs to bring a declaratory judgment action against the patent and gain significant procedural advantages.) Retaining counsel at this point helps to insure that the proper background steps are taken, begins the process for attaching the attorney work-product privilege to make confidential documents that otherwise might be accessible to the opponent, and helps set the stage for bringing the suit in the most advantageous way.

14.2   INITIATING THE SUIT

How, where, and when a lawsuit is initiated can have a lasting influence on the cost and convenience of carrying it out, among other things. The party on the side of the patent typically brings a patent infringement suit, while the party opposed to the patent may initiate a declaratory judgment action. Each party wants the suit carried out in the forum it prefers. For example, in the dispute over recombinant erythropoietin, Amgen first brought an action against Genetics Institute and Chugai in Boston for infringement of its recombinant DNA patent; the next day Genetics Institute and Chugai brought suit against Amgen and Kirin-Amgen in Los Angeles for infringement of their purified erythropoietin patent.[3]

14.2.1   The Patent Infringement Action

Patent disputes most commonly are brought into court by a patent holder who is filing a patent infringement suit. In this situation, the first question to determine is which court is the proper location for filing the suit. Three requirements determine what court will (or can) hear an action: (1) subject-matter jurisdiction, (2) personal jurisdiction, and (3) venue. Each of these requirements will be addressed in the following sections.

A federal court has subject-matter jurisdiction over only those matters Congress has given it the authority to decide. On all other matters, the court is powerless. In the case of patent law, the Federal District courts have been given exclusive jurisdiction by Congress.[4] No state court may even consider an action for patent infringement because the federal courts' jurisdiction is exclusive.[5]

In addition to subject-matter jurisdiction, a court must also have personal jurisdiction over the person[6] or entity being sued. As discussed in Chapter 2, the federal court system is based on a number of separate geographic districts. Many states have several districts. To establish personal jurisdiction, the defendant must have certain "minimum contacts" with the district. When a party is a corporation engaged in interstate commerce, this requirement usually is not difficult to meet. Even when the defendant is a foreigner, establishing personal jurisdiction in an appropriate district is not a problem as long as the defendant has been doing business or has established contact in the district. Even if the defendant's only activity in the district is soliciting sales, this may be sufficient to establish the minimum contacts required for personal jurisdiction.

Once the group of Federal District courts that have both subject-matter and personal jurisdiction for a patent dispute is established, the next step is to determine which court among that group is the proper location, or "venue," for the suit. Patent infringement actions have a separate statutory provision defining the proper bases for venue.[7] Venue is proper in a patent case when either of two tests is met: (1) the defendant resides in the district, or (2) the defendant has committed acts of infringement and has a regular and established place of business in the district. The scope of these two tests is broader than first may appear: 1988 revisions to the definition of where a corporation resides for general-venue purposes have been held to apply to the patent venue statute.[8] Based on these revisions, the first test for venue, the defendant's residence, now reaches beyond the corporate defendant's state of incorporation to any district in which personal jurisdiction exists over the defendant at the time the action is brought.[9] Consequently, the plaintiff in a patent infringement lawsuit now may bring suit against a corporate defendant in any district where that defendant has the minimum contacts necessary to establish personal jurisdiction.

This broad interpretation of venue for patent suits provides an advantage to the astute plaintiff by allowing suit to be brought in the district that is most convenient to the plaintiff. This convenience may benefit the plaintiff (choosing the district where the plaintiff's offices are located) and counsel (choosing a "home" district where the judges and local rules of court are familiar). A defendant can request a change of venue, which can be granted at the discretion of the district court judge "for the convenience of the parties" or "in the interest of justice."[10] However, a plaintiff is rarely deprived of its chosen forum unless all of the parties are located elsewhere and all of the events in dispute occurred elsewhere.

14.2.2 The Declaratory Judgment Action

Under some circumstances, infringement litigation may be initiated by an accused infringer rather than by the patent holder. Such an action is known as a *declaratory judgment action*.[11] For example, in the dispute over the polymerase chain reaction patents, DuPont brought a declaratory judgment action against Cetus rather than await suit against it by Cetus.[12]

A potential defendant in a patent dispute may sue for a declaratory judgment that it does not infringe the patent at issue or that the patent is invalid or unenforceable. The only jurisdictional requirement for bringing such an action is that an "actual controversy" exist between the potential defendant and the patent holder.[13] The most common circumstance triggering a declaratory judgment suit is when the patent holder sends a letter alleging infringement and demanding that the infringing activities cease and an accounting for damages be made. The actual controversy requirement also can be satisfied when a patent holder has been aggressive in suing other competitors and a new competitor wishes to invest in starting production of a potentially infringing product.

When a potential defendant has a reasonable concern about being sued, enough to satisfy the "actual controversy" requirement, bringing a declaratory judgment action rather than waiting to be sued for patent infringement provides numerous advantages. As the plaintiff, the potential infringer gains all the associated benefits of being able to choose a preferred forum. Typically, this means the action is brought in the district in which the potential infringer is located rather than in the patent holder's preferred district. The potential infringer also is able to choose the time of filing the suit, which provides the opportunity to resolve possible infringement disputes before investing large sums in new products or processes. Furthermore, the potential infringer, as the plaintiff, will likely be able to present its case first at the trial, then have the opportunity to rebut the patent holder's case.

Finally, once a lawsuit is brought, any discussions about a license or royalties with the patent holder are clearly settlement negotiations and are inadmissible during the trial.[14] If the potential infringer attempts to negotiate a license before a lawsuit is filed and is unsuccessful, these facts may be admissible later and ultimately held against the potential infringer as indicating that: (1) products made after the failed license negotiations are infringing, and (2) the potential infringer is a willful infringer subject to paying triple damages and the patent holder's attorneys' fees.[15] The disadvantage of a declaratory judgment suit is that it almost always triggers a counterclaim by the patent holder for patent infringement. It also launches a legal battle that may well have been resolved without any suit being filed by the patent holder in the first place.

14.2.3 The Complaint, Answer, Counterclaim, and Rules 11 and 12 of the Federal Rules of Civil Procedure

Once the appropriate forum is selected, a lawsuit starts when a complaint is filed in the court and the complaint and a summons are served on the named defendants.[16] Very little factual detail needs to be included in the complaint. It is enough to state the basis of the court's jurisdiction, the facts sufficient to support a claim for relief if true, and a demand for relief.[17] As a result, extensive investigations are not required prior to filing suit—so long as enough information is obtained that the claim "to the best of the [party's] knowledge, information, and belief formed after reasonable inquiry . . . is well grounded in fact and is warranted by existing law [and] . . . is not interposed for any improper purpose."[18] In a patent suit, this requires a reasonable belief that the patent is valid and enforceable and that based on a reasonable investigation, the defendant is infringing the patent. Failing to meet this requirement can result in sanctions against the plaintiff and plaintiff's counsel, including payment of the defendant's attorneys' fees in defending the action.[19]

A single complaint can name multiple defendants. For example, both the manufacturer and any seller of the manufacturer's products may be named as defendants.[20] In some circumstances not only may the corporation be sued, but controlling officers or shareholders may be sued individually.[21] Naming individuals along with the corporation may facilitate recovery of damages in a successful action by making the controlling individuals in small and closely held corporations personally liable. This personal liability allows recovery from individual assets as well as corporate assets.

Once the complaint is filed, the defendant is allowed to answer, raise counterclaims against the plaintiff, and make various motions to enhance its position.[22] In most cases the defendant will contend that the patent is invalid and that the defendant is not infringing the patent even if it were valid. It also is common for defendants to allege inequitable conduct on the part of the inventors, which would render the patent unenforceable. Common counterclaims include patent misuse, antitrust violations, and the violation of state unfair-competition statutes.[23] A defendant also may move to have the complaint dismissed for lack of jurisdiction or for failure to allege facts that support the relief demanded by plaintiff.[24] All of these maneuvers can rapidly increase the complexity of the case.

14.2.4. The Preliminary Injunction

Any time after the suit is initiated, the patent holder can ask the trial court to issue a preliminary injunction blocking accused infringing conduct. While the standard for issuing a preliminary injunction can be quite high, its effect can be disastrous on the enjoined party. If sufficient evidence is not available at the time the suit is initiated, it may become available as time passes. Thus, obtaining a preliminary injunction during an infringement suit (or having the opponent obtain a preliminary injunction) is always a possibility.[25]

14.3 THE DISCOVERY PHASE

During the discovery phase each side obtains information from the other and from third parties that can be used in the trial. Seemingly innocuous, the discovery phase (at least as it is carried out in the United States) can be extremely expensive and difficult—even degenerating into a war of attrition between the parties. It has been consistently criticized as a source of abuse. To make the discovery phase as effective and efficient as possible, potential litigants should be familiar with the basic tools of discovery and how they work.

14.3.1 Overview of the Objectives of Discovery

The Federal Rules of Civil Procedure allow broad and extensive discovery, and provide numerous methods for obtaining that discovery. Companies sometimes are amazed at the vast amount of sensitive technical and business information that the court can force them to provide to their opponent. This is especially problematic in patent litigation where the opposing party usually is a fierce competitor. Nevertheless, any discovery request that may lead to information relevant to the lawsuit is considered proper.[26] For the defendant, this means full discovery of all development activities leading up to the allegedly infringing product or process. For the patent holder, this means the complete revelation of tests and activities leading to the invention, as well as the technical details of any products or processes the patent holder alleges are covered by the patent.[27]

The scope of discovery goes beyond technical matters to business matters as well. A patent holder is entitled to damages measured in lost profits or at least a reasonable royalty, depending on the circumstances of the infringement.[28] To establish damages, information related to sales in units or dollars, costs, profits, and marketing, including customer lists and distribution channels, is relevant. Therefore, all of this sensitive information is open to the opposing party. This discovery may even extend beyond information related to the patented product or process to related products or processes. Information on these collateral issues may be used to show the relative success of the invention as evidence of nonobviousness; relative profit margins may be evidence of a reasonable royalty. As will be discussed later in this chapter, the federal rules can be used by the careful litigant to prevent abuse of this broad discovery process and to protect sensitive business and technical information.

14.3.2 The Tools of Discovery

The federal rules of evidence not only allow a very broad scope of discovery, they also define the tools of discovery available to the parties. The basic methods of discovery used in patent suits are: (1) interrogatories, (2) production or inspection of documents or things, (3) depositions, and (4) requests for admissions.[29] Each of these methods is discussed in the following sections, along with the options available to a party to resist discovery.

14.3.2.1 Interrogatories. Interrogatories are written questions that may be served on any party.[30] The party receiving the interrogatories must answer each one fully or provide a reason for objecting to it. Typical interrogatories submitted by a patent holder inquire about the business structure of the defendant, sales volume in units and dollars, and the names of individuals involved or familiar with the development of the accused product or process. They also ask for a description of the allegedly infringing products or processes used by defendant, the identification of all documents related to the accused product or process, and the identification of all documents in the possession of the defendant referring to the patent holder. The patent holder also may use interrogatories to uncover the basis of the defendant's contentions regarding noninfringement, invalidity, and unenforceability. Finally, interrogatories allow the patent holder to require the defendant to identify specifically what prior art he or she will rely on and what claim language defendant will contend is not present in its product or process.

For the defendant, interrogatories provide an opportunity to gain more information about the basis of the patent holder's contentions regarding infringement and the sources of information he or she relied on to determine that the defendant was infringing. A defendant also may use interrogatories to discover details related to the prosecution of the U.S. patent, any foreign prosecution of counterpart patents, any prior art references known by the patent holder, and activities such as first sale or use of the invention by the patent holder. Questions related to sales and profit margins also are pursued by defendants to determine potential damages and objective evidence of nonobviousness such as commercial success. A defendant also should try to determine who else the patent holder considers to be infringing and who else the patent holder has sued. Many of these questions may require the patent holder to provide opinions or contentions that require an application of law to the facts, but they are proper nonetheless.[31]

While interrogatories would appear to be among the most cost-effective ways to gain information from other parties, in practice they rarely live up to this expectation. The adversarial nature of the legal system extends to the discovery phase just as much as to the courtroom itself.[32] As a result, rather than being a truth-seeking process, discovery can easily turn into a battle between adversaries.[33] Interrogatories are liberally objected to and interpreted as narrowly as possible to avoid providing more than a minimal amount of information to the adversary. Furthermore, although an interrogatory response may be used as evidence at a trial, the parties generally are not bound by interrogatory responses and may supplement answers or present proof at the trial contradicting interrogatory responses.[34] The parties may abuse interrogatories by posing excessive requests in order to burden the opposing side with the obligation to respond, and as a result most district courts have local rules limiting the number of interrogatories allowed.[35] Consequently, interrogatories generally are used to support other discovery activities, such as identifying appropriate individuals to depose or documents to request.

14.3.2.2 Requests for the Production of Documents. A much more probing discovery tool is titled the request for "production of documents and things and entry upon land for inspection or other purposes."[36] Recorded documents are a far more reliable source of information than an attorney's response to an interrogatory request after litigation has started. Like interrogatories, production requests technically may be served only on the other parties in the litigation. However, third parties are subject to subpoena and may be compelled to produce documents for inspection.[37] Document requests targeting damages may request copies of invoices, purchase orders, and other documents reflecting sales and costs; those targeting technical liability may request test results and manufacturing specifications and standards.

A patent holder also always requests all documents referring to the patent or the patent holder in the hope of finding the "smoking gun" memo, which in a patent suit is an admission of infringement proving both infringement and willfulness on the defendant's part. For the defendant, the "smoking gun" document is one indicating that the defendant's product or process is not covered by the claims of the patent, a sale of the invention prior to the statutory bar date, or proof that the inventors intentionally withheld known, material prior art from the patent office during prosecution of the patent.

Requests for entry upon land (or plant facilities) for inspection also are important in patent cases, especially where the defendant is accused of infringing a method claim by use of a process in the defendant's plant. While infringement of product-type claims generally can be detected from sales of the product, identifying infringement of process claims often is more difficult. An inspection of defendant's facility in order to observe and take measurements while the process is in operation is far more reliable and beneficial than an interrogatory requesting a description of defendant's process. The patent holder should be aware that in most cases, the defendant also will have the right to inspect the patent holder's facility to examine the work the patent holder is doing under the patent.

Like interrogatories, requests for production or inspection are subject to abuse and contribute to the expense of discovery. Given the liberal scope of discovery under U.S. law, huge volumes of documents may be produced in any patent litigation. The attorney's role here is to be an advocate; no effort is made to help the opposing side acquire documents that would be to their benefit. Huge volumes of documents frequently are requested, and often the court must intervene and order an obstructive party to produce them. The documents obtained then must be reviewed to find the few helpful documents that will ultimately be used at the trial to prove a party's case. Producing the documents can be time-consuming. An attorney must oversee a review of extensive records to determine their relevance, whether they fall within the scope of any discovery request, and whether any basis is available for refusing to produce them.

14.3.2.3 Depositions. While discovery of documents is an invaluable tool to obtain evidence for use at the trial, documents alone rarely uncover the whole story of a case. Given the limitations on interrogatories discussed previously, depositions, particularly oral depositions, have become the principal discovery mechanism for building a case. The Federal Rules of Civil Procedure provide for depositions based on oral examination and written questions.[38] There also are provisions for videotaping oral depositions and taking them by phone.

Depositions based on written questions are much more inflexible than oral depositions because the questioning cannot be adapted in response to answers provided during the deposition. New variants of questions cannot be posed to force answers from an evasive or nonresponsive witness. With depositions based on written questions, furthermore, the attorney has no opportunity to meet and observe how potential witnesses act and appear under questioning, which is critical to trial preparation. Because of these limitations, depositions based on written questions are only used when the costs of an oral deposition cannot be justified or a witness cannot be compelled to attend an oral deposition.

Understanding the process of an oral deposition (and why they can be so expensive) requires some understanding of the Federal Rules of Evidence. A background premise of the rules is that oral statements are more suspect than documents unless the opposing party has an opportunity to test the witness's basis of knowledge and the witness's credibility. This concept lies at the heart of the rules relating to excluding evidence as hearsay.[39] Since one of the primary objectives of depositions is to develop evidence for use at a trial, deposition procedures provide for full cross-examination by the opposing party. The deposition also must be given under oath and recorded by a stenographer.[40]

Depositions may be taken from both parties and from third parties on proper notice.[41] Rule 30(b)(6) of The Federal Rules of Civil Procedure provides for deposing a corporation or other organization or association rather than a named individual.[42] When the deposition of such an organization is requested, it is the responsibility of the organization to produce the individual or individuals most knowledgeable with respect to the issues the deposition will cover. Consequently, it is important that the notice of deposition state "with reasonable particularity the matters on which examination is requested."[43] The designated individual will testify for the organization "as to matters known or reasonably available to the organization," not as an individual.[44]

Third parties also may be interviewed without notice to opposing parties and without the formalities of a deposition. This process, however, does not provide for putting the witness under oath, compelling answers to questions by court order, or preserving testimony for trial.[45]

Given the costs of taking oral depositions, other methods of discovery are often used to determine who should be deposed and what areas of questioning should be pursued. For example, interrogatories directed to identifying who developed the infringing product or process can identify key technical individuals. If these individuals are not produced pursuant to a Rule 30(b)(6) notice, their depositions may be requested by name.[46] Documents produced in response to requests for production also should be reviewed to determine the names of individuals involved with the facts of the case, including both employees of the party and third parties such as suppliers and customers.

Once the individuals to be deposed and the matters on which Rule 30(b)(6) depositions will be taken are determined, the proper procedures for insuring the deponents attend must be followed. Parties are under an obligation to appear and need only be provided a notice of deposition (be "noticed"). A notice of deposition also may include a demand for production of documents and other tangible items at the deposition, allowing for discovery of documents without a separate request.[47]

To depose a third party, a subpoena must be served on the deponent that, besides providing notice to the other parties in the lawsuit, compels his or her attendance. While it is possible to obtain a third party's voluntary agreement to attend a deposition without serving a subpoena, there is no legal obligation for the third party to attend. If the third-party deponent does not appear and no subpoena has been served, not only have the costs for the attorneys and a court reporter been wasted, but the party failing to ask for the subpoena is liable to pay the opposing parties' costs of attending the deposition, including attorneys' fees.[48] The subpoena also may include a demand for the production of documents and tangible items at the deposition. In addition, a subpoena may be used to obtain documents from either party or from third parties without requiring anyone to appear for a deposition.[49] It also can be used to compel witnesses to attend and give testimony at a trial.

Additional problems arise when witnesses are located outside of the United States. A subpoena issued by a U.S. court has no power of extraterritorial enforcement without adoption by the proper authority in the foreign state. The Federal Rules of Civil Procedure recognize depositions taken in a foreign country when they are taken: (1) before someone authorized to administer oaths in the United States or the country where it is taken, (2) before a person commissioned by the court, and (3) pursuant to letters rogatory.[50]

The most common method is through the use of letters rogatory, which are letters from the U.S. district court issuing the subpoena to a foreign court requesting that the foreign court enforce the subpoena pursuant to principles of reciprocity.[51] The letters rogatory may be transmitted through the U.S. State Department or, where allowed by foreign law, directly to the court in the foreign country.[52] It is important to remember that foreign law governs any discovery activity outside of the United States, and many countries can be extremely hostile to discovery activities within their borders.[53] Hence, great caution is warranted in pursuing extraterritorial discovery.

14.3.2.4   Requests for Admissions.   The Federal Rules of Civil Procedure also provide for requests for admissions.[54] These are a series of statements served on one party by another with the request that they be admitted or denied. Such requests are not a discovery method, strictly speaking, but they are a powerful tool for narrowing the issues for trial. Requests for admission sometimes are coupled to interrogatories, launching a series of questions if a particular request is denied. Requests may extend to any matter within the scope of discovery, including requests requiring the application of law to the facts. For example, a defendant could ask a patent holder to admit that certain publications, or prior use or sales activities, are prior art to the patent. The patent holder could ask the defendant to admit that different elements of the claims of the patent are present in the defendant's product or process. Once a request for admission is received, the party must: (1) admit the request, (2) raise a specific objection to the request that the court will uphold, or (3) "specifically deny the matter or set forth in detail the reasons why the answering party cannot truthfully admit or deny the matter."[55] Failing to properly respond to a request for admission in a timely fashion is considered an admission.[56] Once admitted, the matter is "conclusively established unless the court on motion permits withdrawal or amendment of the admission."[57]

14.3.3   Resisting Discovery

As will be readily apparent, the diverse tools of discovery provide a means for an unscrupulous or overly zealous party to place an incredible burden on the opposing party. Even if the legal fees associated with discovery do not become burdensome, the time required of a company's employees to repeatedly resist improper requests, answer questions, sort through documents, conduct tours and the like can quickly turn the discovery process into a war of attrition. Fortunately, mechanisms are available that (sometimes) alleviate this burden.

14.3.3.1   Objections and Protective Orders.   It is a very rare patent case where all discovery requests are fully and promptly honored. Two broad categories where discovery is often refused are privileged or protected information and unduly burdensome requests.

Certain documents and information are protected from discovery.[58] If a document reflects an attorney-client communication, it is not discoverable by the opposing side unless the party asserting the privilege somehow waives the privilege.[59] A patent attorney working with an inventor in preparing a patent application is considered to be acting as an attorney, and the inventor is entitled to claim the attorney-client privilege for related communications.[60] The exception to this rule is that a communication from an inventor to a patent attorney solely to pass that information on to the patent office, in the application or otherwise, is not considered privileged.[61] To maintain the privilege, the communication must be treated as confidential by the attorney and patent holder, and it must be related to obtaining the legal advice of the patent attorney.[62] Furthermore, if a privileged communication is used or produced by a party, the privilege is usually waived as to the subject matter of that communication, and inquiry into the basis for statements made in the communication is allowed.[63]

Materials prepared in anticipation of litigation also are protected from discovery, although to a more limited extent.[64] For example, if a technical person at a company performs a test on a competitor's product to aid in determining if the product infringes before filing suit, those test results are protected by the work-product doctrine.[65] However, work-product materials may be discovered where the opposing party has a substantial need for the information and is otherwise unable to obtain the information.[66]

Any person from whom discovery is sought may request a protective order from the court with respect to specific information, even if it is not privileged.[67] For example, discovery of confidential business information and trade secrets may be limited. One commonly used protective order in patent cases limits disclosure of such confidential information to the opposing party's attorneys, who are obligated not to reveal the information to their client. Discovery also may be limited by the court to "protect a party or person from annoyance, embarrassment, oppression, or undue burden or expense."[68]

14.3.3.2   Motions to Compel Responses to Discovery Requests.   When a discovery request has been improperly or incompletely answered, the party seeking discovery may make a motion to compel the discovery. Both sides present their positions to the court on the motion, after which the court may order a party to comply with discovery requests. Failing to comply with such a court order carries severe sanctions, including being prohibited from presenting evidence on the disputed issue at the trial.[69] In some circumstances, such an order can determine the outcome of the trial.

14.3.4   Stays of Discovery

Under certain circumstances, discovery may be suspended in a lawsuit. For example, if a related suit is under way in a different district court, proceedings may be stayed pending the outcome of that dispute in the interests of judicial economy and efficiency.[70] One unique circumstance in patent lawsuits in which stays are commonly granted is when the patent is brought back before the patent office. This can occur either on a request for reexamination or on a reissue application (discussed in Chapter 2). Stays are commonly granted under these circumstances until a final decision is reached in the patent office action.[71]

14.4   DETERMINATION OF THE ISSUES

Because of the numerous issues raised in a patent suit, patent trials tend to be detail-oriented, requiring careful preparation and presentation of the facts and issues. How a properly prepared patent case is perceived by the person who is trying the facts in the case was summarized by Magistrate Judge Saris in *Amgen Inc. v. Chugai Pharmaceutical Co.*:

> As the late Judge Charles Wyzanski so aptly wrote, patent cases are "so satisfactory to try" because "[t]he patent lawyer understands better than most of us that the mystery of the universe lies in the detail. And to make his lesson clearer the patent lawyer gives me the benefit of the instruction of the topnotch professors from the finest technological institutes." [citation omitted] After trying this case, where the quality of the lawyering has been so high and the expertise of the leading scientists in the fields of protein chemistry and recombinant DNA technology so remarkable, the court is in full agreement with Judge Wyzanski's assessment.[72]

The actual presentation of the case at trial is an art and science of its own and is beyond the scope of this chapter.[73] The purpose of this section is to explain the decision-making process during and after the trial.

14.4.1   Findings of Fact and Trial

After discovery is completed, the next major phase of litigation is the trial. Any party has the right to demand a trial by jury.[74] However, to obtain a jury trial a demand must be included by the party desiring a jury trial in its initial pleadings. If no jury is demanded, all issues will be tried by the judge.[75]

The choice of trial before a jury or judge only affects who decides the factual issues: legal issues are always the province of the judge.[76] As a general rule, both liability and damages are considered in a single trial. However, the judge has the discretion to order the separation of the issues of liability and damages.[77] If during the liability phase no party is found liable on any count, the damages phase is avoided.

Trial begins with each party making an opening statement, after which the plaintiff presents its evidence. After the plaintiff has presented its case, the defendant presents its evidence. The plaintiff then is given the opportunity to rebut the defendant's case. The plaintiff's rebuttal is limited to presenting evidence on new issues raised during the defendant's case and to challenging the credibility of the defendant's witnesses. Each side then presents its closing argument to the jury (when there is one), following the same order of presentation as used for the presentation of the evidence.

After the closing arguments it is the judge's responsibility to instruct the jury on the applicable law.[78] The jury instructions, which in a patent case can easily run more than 50 pages, also include what the judge determines to be the legal issues in the case. For example, the jury instructions might include the judge's interpretation of the claims at issue and instructions on what facts are required to find the claim to be infringed. Usually, both sides propose instructions to the judge, with the judge selecting and modifying the proposed instructions to produce the final instructions. The jury then retires to consider the case and comes back with a verdict, which may be very general, such as finding a patent valid and infringed. Alternatively, the parties may request that specific interrogatories be submitted to the jury requiring yes or no answers to questions related to specific claims and even underlying factual issues.[79]

14.4.2 Expert Witnesses in Patent Litigation

Patent litigation, particularly in biotechnology, brings complex factual issues before judges and jurors who rarely have relevant technical training. As a result, the testimony of experts during the trial becomes particularly important. Often the only evidence of the existence of claim limitations in the accused structure or process is the testimony of such experts (who are paid by the party that retains them). As with other types of litigation that use expert testimony, almost every patent case involves testimony from experts for both sides, often presenting directly contradictory views. While this may indicate a lack of technical honesty on the part of the experts, in most cases the conflicting testimony simply reflects the fact that the English language, particularly as it is used in drafting patent claims, generally is susceptible to more than one interpretation. Even in technically centered litigation, the gray areas of language and competing viewpoints inevitably defy one right answer: there are simply some things on which honest experts will disagree, and it is these difficult situations that must be brought before a court for a final answer. In response to this complexity, judges are beginning to make greater use of their authority to call their own independent technical experts.[80]

14.4.3 Summary Disposition of the Issues in Dispute

The Federal Rules of Civil Procedure provide for the final decision of issues by the judge even where the issues would normally be submitted to a jury. Such "summary" rulings may occur before a trial, during a trial, and even after a jury verdict is returned. Before a trial, summary disposition provides an opportunity to avoid unnecessary litigation and its related costs (to both parties and the court). During and after a trial, summary disposition provides a way to prevent the jury from imposing a verdict that is clearly contrary to the law.

14.4.3.1 Motions to Dismiss.   A party's first opportunity to request summary disposition arises immediately on receipt of a complaint from the opposing party. If the complaint fails to state a logical basis for the suit, the party receiving the pleading may make a motion to dismiss.[81] The motion to dismiss may be on procedural grounds, such as lack of jurisdiction or improper venue, or on substantive grounds, such as when the complaint fails to state a claim that would support the remedy demanded. Of course, when the error is correctable, the court generally will allow the pleading party to amend its pleadings to correct the defect.[82] Motions to dismiss play an important role in keeping clearly frivolous cases out of court, but they seldom play a role in keeping biotechnology patent litigation out of court.

14.4.3.2 Motions for Summary Judgment.   A far more important mechanism for simplifying patent litigation, particularly biotechnology patent litigation, is the motion for summary judgment.[83] For example, numerous issues in the dispute between Scripps Clinic and Genentech over purified factor VIII:C were decided at the trial-court level by summary judgment, although in this case, the trial court's use of summary judgment was substantially curtailed by the appeals court, and many of the issues were returned to the trial court for a full trial.[84]

Summary judgment is appropriate whenever there is no material factual dispute because in this situation there is no reason to submit the issue to the jury.[85] A factual dispute must be shown by evidence—summary judgment cannot be avoided by an attorney's argument alleging disputed factual issues unless the evidence shows an actual dispute exists.[86] Even if a factual issue is disputed, a party seeking summary judgment who does not bear the burden of proof at the trial is entitled to summary judgment if the party *with* the burden has insufficient evidence to support a jury verdict.[87]

The party who is not making the motion does have certain presumptions in its favor, regardless of whether it will bear the burden of proof at the trial.[88] Specifically, all disputed facts must be viewed in the light most favorable to the party who is not making the motion. Furthermore, all reasonable factual inferences that can be drawn from those facts must be inferred in favor of the party who is not making the motion.

To demonstrate how these standards apply in a patent suit, summary judgment will be explained by applying it to the specific issue of infringement. It is the patent holder's burden to prove infringement at the trial by a preponderance of the evidence showing that each limitation of a claim in the patent is met (either literally or equivalently) by the accused product or process. In other words, for a jury to return a verdict of infringement, the evidence as a whole must make it more likely than not that the accused product or process infringes the claim. If the evidence is such that no reasonable juror could conclude that the accused product or process infringes the claim, any jury verdict of infringement would be contrary to the law and would have to be set aside by the judge.

Regardless of who moves for summary judgment as to infringement, if it is an undisputed fact that a limitation of the claim is not met by the accused structure, then summary judgment of noninfringement is appropriate. If the undisputed facts show all the limitations are present, then summary judgment of infringement is appropriate. If the accused infringer moves for summary judgment of noninfringement, its motion also should be granted if the evidence relating to any one limitation of the claim, viewed in the light most favorable to the patent holder, is insufficient for a reasonable juror to find the limitation is present.

14.4.3.3   Judgment as a Matter of Law.   A court also may enter judgment as a matter of law during or after the trial.[89] For example, at the close of the plaintiff's case in a patent infringement lawsuit, the defendant may move for judgment as a matter of law if the plaintiff has failed to present evidence to meet its burden of proof on any one limitation of the claim at issue. The standards for determining such a motion are identical to those discussed for summary judgment. The defendant also may raise or renew its motion for judgment as a matter of law at the close of all the evidence and before the jury retires to consider its verdict.

Even after a jury verdict is returned, any party having raised a motion for judgment as a matter of law at the close of all the evidence may renew that motion. This situation typically arises where the judge initially believed that judgment as a matter of law was appropriate but chose to let the issue go to the jury anyway. If the jury finds in favor of the party requesting judgment as a matter of law, then the issue is moot. If the jury finds against that party, the judge still may enter judgment as a matter of law. However, if his or her decision is overturned on appeal, the jury verdict will stand and it will be unnecessary to retry the case. The standard for granting judgment as a matter of law is the same as for summary judgment regardless of whether a jury verdict has been given.

14.4.3.4   Motions for a New Trial.   As an alternative to asking for judgment as a matter of law, a party losing a jury verdict may move for a new trial. A trial court judge has much more discretion in granting a new trial than in granting judgment as a matter of law.[90] Typical grounds for a new trial include a damages award that is clearly inconsistent with the evidence or a finding of liability based on evidence sufficient to avoid judgment as a matter of law but contrary to the clear weight of the evidence.[91]

14.4.4   The Appeals Process

An appeal is not an opportunity for a new trial of all the issues. The role of the appeals court in reviewing a final judgment is limited to addressing specific errors raised by the party appealing the decision. Such errors include improper admission of evidence by the judge in violation of the Federal Rules of Evidence and an improper statement of the law in the jury instructions, among numerous others. If no specific error can be identified there is no proper basis for appeal. No new evidence can be introduced during the appeal that was not offered into evidence at the trial.[92]

The appeals court can freely review legal issues for correctness, but it cannot review and reverse factual determinations unless a glaring mistake was made; that is, it was "clearly erroneous."[93] Decisions of appeals courts on legal issues are precedents that bind other district courts in the future. An appeals court such as the CAFC will quickly reverse a trial court that does not adhere to the precedent it has established. On the other hand, the Supreme Court has repeatedly demonstrated that it will reverse an appeals court decision if it thinks the appeals court has encroached on the factfinder's domain. Consequently, appeals based on legal errors supported by CAFC precedent are clearly more justified than appeals pursuing a potentially futile argument that the factual determinations were clearly erroneous, especially when the factual issues have been decided by a jury.[94] Of course, this analysis is complicated by the numerous issues in patent cases that are mixed questions of fact and law, such as nonobviousness and enablement (often two critical issues in biotechnology patent litigation). On these types of issues, the appeals court has broad leeway to inject itself into the role of fact-finder when the judges on the panel are uncomfortable with the verdict reached in the trial court.[95] Nonetheless, the general rule is that the appeals court will not second-guess the fact-finder when no legal error is present.

14.4.1   A Case Study: *Amgen v. Chugai* and the Deposit of Host Cells

In *Amgen v. Chugai*, one of the numerous points argued by Chugai and Genetics Institute during the trial was that Amgen's patent should be held invalid because it failed to satisfy the best mode requirement. The argument was based on the fact that Amgen had not deposited the best host cell line described in the patent so that the cell line itself would be available to the public on issuance of the patent. Noting the question to be "extremely close," the trial court nevertheless decided the question in favor of Amgen.[96] The best mode question is classified as a question of fact for purposes of appeal.

Chugai and Genetics Institute appealed this holding to the Federal Circuit. After reviewing the law in this area, the Federal Circuit noted trial testimony of Genetics Institute's own expert indicating he had no doubt that someone eventually would reproduce cell lines that made EPO that could be better—or worse—than Amgen's. The Federal Circuit noted that "[t]he district court relied on this testimony, and, upon review, we agree with its determination."[97] If it reversed the district court, it would have had to find the district court's decision to be "clearly erroneous."

Chugai and Genetics Institute petitioned the U.S. Supreme Court to review the Federal Circuit's best-mode decision, arguing the merits of its position.[98] The Supreme Court denied this request.[99] Note that even though the trial court magistrate had referred to the issue as being "extremely close," best mode is a question of fact, and "extremely close" questions of fact are precisely the type that are to be decided by the trial court rather than the appeals court. The failure to give proper deference to the findings of trial courts on questions of fact is one of the few things for which the Federal Circuit has been chastised by the Supreme Court.[100]

14.5 ALTERNATIVE DISPUTE RESOLUTION AND SETTLEMENT

As a result of the long delays and high costs associated with resolving disputes through traditional trial mechanisms, there is an increasing emphasis on negotiating settlement or employing alternative methods of dispute resolution.[101] Numerous organizations are available for carrying out these types of proceedings, one of which is The Private Adjudication Center, Inc.,[102] affiliated with the Duke University School of Law. Such proceedings can be binding, in which case the determination will be enforceable by the parties in a court of law, or nonbinding, in which case the "verdict" is advisory and provides a basis for settlement by the parties. Recent legislation orders each Federal District Court to implement a plan for reducing the expense and delays of civil litigation.[103] Partly in response to this impetus, many district courts are requiring litigants to participate in alternative dispute resolution.[104] Furthermore, many major corporations have gone beyond the traditional approach of including arbitration agreements in contracts and are now entering into general agreements with other large competitors to submit all future disputes to alternative dispute resolution.

Numerous methods fall under the general label of alternative dispute resolution. One approach is arbitration. The arbitrator, whether selected by agreement of the parties or otherwise, oversees the discovery process and determines the award. Another approach is mediation. The mediator facilitates discussion between the parties to encourage settlement but does not act as the "judge" and does not decide a winner or make an award. The mediator is free to meet with each side separately and to obtain information that will be maintained as confidential and will not be provided to the opposing side. Numerous other approaches exist, such as mini-trials, trial before a privately hired judge, and summary jury trials. Hybrid types of dispute resolution combine the features of these approaches or use the alternative approach in cooperation with traditional court resolution. For example, a mediator could be appointed by the judge to confer with all the parties involved and provide a report on his or her conclusions. With the increasingly high costs and delays of traditional litigation, alternative dispute resolution is certain to play an increasingly important role in patent litigation in the future.

REFERENCES

1. Read Corp. v. Portec, Inc., 970 F.2d 816, 821, 23 USPQ2d 1426, 1430 (Fed. Cir. 1992); American Medical Sys., Inc., v. Medical Eng'g Corp., 794 F. Supp. 1370 (E.D. Wis. 1992).
2. *See generally* E. Horwitz and L. Horwitz, PATENT LITIGATION: PROCEDURE AND TACTICS (1991).
3. Amgen Inc. v. Chugai Pharmaceutical Co., 13 USPQ2d 1737, 1738 (D. Mass. 1989).
4. 28 U.S.C. § 1338(a) (1988).
5. The issues of patent validity and infringement do occasionally arise in state court such as in actions involving enforcement of a patent license agreement or in actions alleging defamation or unfair competition when a party alleges a competitor has made false

statements about either the validity of a patent or the infringement of a patent to customers. The truth of those statements may be put at issue. *See* Albright v. Teas, 106 U.S. 613, 15 S. Ct. 550 (1883).

6. Throughout this chapter, the term *person* refers not only to individuals but also to corporations, partnerships, or any other entity capable of being sued.

7. 28 U.S.C. § 1400(b) (1988).

8. VE Holding Corp. v. Johnson Gas Appliance Co., 917 F.2d 1574, 1575, 16 USPQ2d 1614 (Fed. Cir. 1990), *cert. denied*, 111 S. Ct. 1315 (1991); 28 U.S.C. § 1391 (Supp. II 1990).

9. VE Holding Corp., 917 F.2d at 1583, 16 USPQ2d at 1617.

10. 28 U.S.C. § 1404(a) (1988); Skill-Craft Enterprises, Inc. v. Astro Mfg., Inc., 18 USPQ2d 1555 (N.D. Ind. 1990).

11. 28 U.S.C. § 2201 (1988); *see generally* J. Voight, *Declaratory Judgment Actions in Patent Cases Where There Has Been No Act of Infringement*, 72 J. PAT. & TRADEMARK OFF. SOC'Y 1136 (1990).

12. E.I. DuPont de Nemours & Co. v. Cetus Corp., 19 USPQ2d 1174, 1176 (N.D. Cal. 1990).

13. West Interactive Corp. v. First Data Resources, Inc., 972 F.2d 1295, 23 USPQ2d 1927 (Fed. Cir. 1992).

14. Fed. R. Evid. 408.

15. 35 U.S.C. § 284–85, 289 (1988).

16. Fed. R. Civ. Pro. 3–4. While it is beyond the scope of this chapter, extraterritorial service raises difficulties not encountered in the United States as well as questions of foreign law. These problems generally may be avoided in lawsuits against corporations doing business in the United States, because most states require a foreign corporation (both from another state and outside the United States) to register to do business in the state and also to appoint a domestic agent for service. *See, e.g.*, Model Business Corporation Act § 15 (1992).

17. Fed. R. Civ. P. 8(a). To obtain a jury trial a party must demand a jury trial in the pleadings and the plaintiff should normally do so in the complaint. Fed. R. Civ. P. 38(b).

18. Fed. R. Civ. P. 11.

19. *Id.* In a patent suit, failure to meet this requirement is also evidence of patent misuse. This is a defense for any charge of infringement and may provide the basis for a charge that the patent holder has violated the antitrust laws. Atari Games Corp. v. Nintendo of Am., Inc., 897 F.2d 1572, 14 USPQ2d 1034 (Fed. Cir. 1990), *reh'g denied*, nos. 89–1396, 89–1426, 1990 U.S. App. LEXIS 5205 (Fed. Cir. Apr. 4, 1990).

20. A patent confers the right to exclude others from making, using, or selling the patented invention. 35 U.S.C. § 154 (1988); Standard Oil Co. v. American Cyanamid Co., 774 F.2d 448, 227 USPQ 293 (Fed. Cir. 1985).

21. 35 U.S.C. § 271 (1988); Preemption Devices, Inc. v. Minnesota Mining & Mfg. Co., 803 F.2d 1170, 231 USPQ 297 (Fed. Cir. 1986); Power Lift, Inc. v. Lang Tools, Inc., 774 F.2d 478, 227 USPQ 435 (Fed. Cir. 1985).

22. Fed. R. Civ. P. 8, 13; *see also* K. Adamo, *Basic Motion Practice for the Accused Infringer*, 15 AIPLA QUART. J. 124 (1987).

23. *See* J. Barnhardt, *Counterclaiming in Patent Infringement Litigation*, 15 AIPLA QUART. J. 175 (1987).

24. Fed. R. Civ. P. 12.

25. *See generally* J. Foster, *The Preliminary Injunction—A "New" and Potent Weapon in Patent Litigation*, 68 J. PAT. & TRADEMARK OFF. SOC'Y 281 (1986).

26. Fed. R. Civ. P. 26(b)(1).

27. Any patent holder generally will allege that he or she is practicing the invention, since this provides a basis for sales and profit-margin data on products that can be used in determining the measure of damages and to show the commercial success of the invention in support of nonobviousness. Akzo N.V. v. United States ITC, 808 F.2d 1471, 1 USPQ2d 1241 (Fed. Cir. 1986), *cert. denied*, 482 U.S. 909 (1987); Afros S.P.A. v. Krauss-Maffei Corp., 671 F. Supp. 1402, 5 USPQ2d 1145 (D. Del.), *reh'g denied*, 671 F. Supp. 1458 (D. Del. 1987), *aff'd*, 848 F.2d 1244 (Fed. Cir. 1988).

28. In general, if there is no acceptable noninfringing substitute for the patented invention used or sold by the patent holder and if the patent holder would have been able to meet all of the demand, the patent holder is entitled to its lost profits on all of the defendant's sales. Water Technologies Corp. v. Calco, Ltd., 850 F.2d 660, 7 USPQ2d 1097 (Fed. Cir.), *cert. denied*, 488 U.S. 968 (1988). Otherwise, the patent holder is entitled to a reasonable royalty on the defendant's sales of infringing goods or use of an infringing process. Trans-World Mfg. Corp. v. Al Nyman & Sons, Inc., 750 F.2d 1552, 224 USPQ 259 (Fed. Cir. 1984).

29. Fed. R. Civ. P. 26(a).

30. Fed. R. Civ. P. 33.

31. *Id.*

32. In fact, failure to do so is a violation of ethical rules for attorneys, potentially subjecting them to severe penalties, including disbarment. Model Code of Professional Responsibility Canon 7 (1980).

33. This does not mean either party has a right to refuse to provide factual information without asserting a privilege or seeking a protective order. What it does mean is that no party has any obligation to help the other side obtain information that is relevant without a specific request from the other party.

34. Fed. R. Civ. P. 33. This is not true for averments in complaints or answers that are binding on a party and can only be contradicted if the court allows the party to amend the pleading. Amendments to pleadings generally are liberally allowed unless the other party is prejudiced. Fed. R. Civ. P. 15. Responses to Requests for Admissions also are considered to be "conclusively established" unless the court permits withdrawal of the response. Fed. R. Civ. P. 36(b).

35. *See, e.g.,* U.S. Dist. Ct. D.S.C. R. 9.00; U.S. Dist. Ct. M.D.N.C. C.R. 205; U.S. Dist. Ct. N.D. Ga. C.R. 225-2.

36. Fed. R. Civ. P. 34.

37. *Id.* Obtaining documents from third parties will be discussed later in this chapter in the section on subpoenas and Rule 45 of the Federal Rules of Civil Procedure.

38. Fed. R. Civ. P. 30-32.

39. Fed. R. Evid. 801–06. Hearsay "is a statement, other than one made by the declarant while testifying at the trial or hearing, offered in evidence to prove the truth of the matter asserted." Fed. R. Evid. 801. While the general rule is that hearsay is not admissible, the exceptions to the rule generally overwhelm the rule itself.

40. Fed. R. Civ. P. 30(c).

41. Fed. R. Civ. P. 30.

42. Fed. R. Civ. P. 30(b)(6); *see generally* J. Barnhardt and J. Whittle, *Use of Rule 30(b)(6) Depositions in Intellectual Property Litigation*, 74 J. PAT. & TRADEMARK OFF. SOC'Y 683 (1992).

43. Fed. R. Civ. P. 30(b)(6).

44. This distinction often raises disputes over questions of the scope of the deposition. For example, a technical manager designated to testify regarding a defendant's product design may have worked previously for other companies in the industry. When ques-

tioned on his experiences at the previous employer or the previous employer's opinions on the patent, the attorney representing the deponent may object that the question goes beyond the scope of the Rule 30(b)(6) notice and into the deponent's personal capacity. In practice, however, most attorneys are liberal in allowing a broad scope of questioning once a deposition has commenced unless the party taking the deposition is clearly abusing the process.

45. In the case of parties, while it is permissible for one party to contact another directly after litigation has commenced, it is improper for an attorney to contact an opposing party without going through that party's attorney. Model Rules of Professional Conduct Rule 4.2 (1992).

46. If the named individuals are low-level employees they are arguably not subject to a Rule 30(b)(6) deposition and will need to be subpoenaed to compel their attendance like any third party. However, in practice, most employers are in a position to insure such employees' attendance at a deposition and will routinely do so.

47. Fed. R. Civ. P. 30(b)(5).

48. Fed. R. Civ. P. 30(g)(2).

49. Fed. R. Civ. P. 45(a)(1)(C).

50. Fed. R. Civ. P. 28(b).

51. In simple terms, the United States court is saying that if the foreign court recognizes and enforces the subpoena we will do the same for them in the future.

52. *See* 28 U.S.C. § 1781 (1988). If the person noticed is a United States national or resident, the subpoena may be served directly and, if ignored, sanctions may be imposed against that person's property in the United States. 28 U.S.C. §§ 1783–84 (1988).

53. *See generally* H. Maier, *Extraterritorial Discovery: Cooperation, Coercion and the Hague Evidence Convention*, 19 VAND. J. TRANSNAT'L L. 239 (1986).

54. Fed. R. Civ. P. 36.

55. Fed. R. Civ. P. 36(a).

56. *Id.*

57. Fed. R. Civ. P. 36(b).

58. *See generally* L. Pretty, *The Boundaries of Discovery in Patent Litigation: Privilege, Work Product and Other Limits*, 18 AIPLA QUART. J. 101 (1990).

59. Zenith Radio Corp. v. United States, 764 F.2d 1577 (Fed. Cir. 1985), *aff'd*, 823 F.2d 518 (Fed. Cir. 1987).

60. American Standard, Inc. v. Pfizer, Inc., 828 F.2d 734, 3 USPQ2d 1817 (Fed. Cir. 1987).

61. Hewlett-Packard Co. v. Bausch & Lomb, Inc., 116 F.R.D. 533, 542, 4 USPQ2d 1676 (N.D. Cal. 1987); Burroughs Wellcome Co. v. Barr Lab., 25 USPQ2d 1274 (E.D.N.C. 1992).

62. American Standard, Inc. v. Pfizer, Inc., 828 F.2d 734, 3 USPQ2d 1817 (Fed. Cir. 1987).

63. Carter v. Gibbs, 909 F.2d 1452 (Fed. Cir. 1990).

64. Fed. R. Civ. P. 26(b).

65. Obviously, if a party intends to rely on the results as evidence at the trial, they will have to be produced.

66. Fed. R. Civ. P. 26(b)(3).

67. Fed. R. Civ. P. 26(c).

68. Fed. R. Civ. P. 26(c). Such abusive uses of the discovery process also subject a party and that party's attorneys to monetary sanctions pursuant to Rule 11 of the Federal Rules of Civil Procedure.

69. Fed. R. Civ. P. 37(b)(2).

70. Katz v. Lear Siegler, Inc., 909 F.2d 1459, 15 USPQ2d 1554 (Fed. Cir. 1990); Kahn v. General Motors Corp., 889 F.2d 1078, 12 USPQ2d 1997 (Fed. Cir. 1989).

71. Ethicon, Inc. v. Quigg, 849 F.2d 1422, 7 USPQ2d 1152 (Fed. Cir. 1988).

72. Amgen Inc. v. Chugai Pharmaceutical Co., 13 USPQ2d 1737, 1738–39 (D. Mass. 1989).

73. *See, e.g.*, THE LITIGATION MANUAL: A PRIMER FOR TRIAL LAWYERS (J. Koeltl, Ed., 2d ed. 1989) (published by the American Bar Association Section of Litigation); T. Mauet, FUNDAMENTALS OF TRIAL TECHNIQUES (1980).

74. Fed. R. Civ. P. 38.

75. Fed. R. Civ. P. 39. A judge has the discretion to order a jury trial of some issues even if neither party demanded jury trial of the issue. *Id.* The Federal Rules provide for local rule procedures allowing trial by a magistrate with the consent of the parties. Fed. R. Civ. P. 73. This provision generally provides the parties with an opportunity for a speedier trial with a more predictable start date because magistrates, unlike judges, generally are not subject to the priority demands of a criminal docket. Magistrates also are frequently used by a judge to handle procedural issues throughout the discovery and pretrial process. Fed. R. Civ. P. 72.

76. The distinction between legal issues and factual issues is discussed in Chapter 2. Of course, it is not a reversible error for a judge to submit a legal question to the jury for advisory purposes so long as the judge makes the ultimate determination of the legal issue. Richardson v. Suzuki Motor Co., 868 F.2d 1226, 9 USPQ2d 1913 (Fed. Cir.), *cert. denied*, 493 U.S. 853, 110 S. Ct. 154 (1989); Connell v. Sears, Roebuck & Co., 722 F.2d 1542, 220 USPQ 193 (Fed. Cir. 1983).

77. Fed. R. Civ. P. 42 (b). This determination may be made early in the discovery process to allow discovery on damages issues to be delayed until after liability is determined.

78. Fed. R. Civ. P. 51.

79. Fed. R. Civ. P. 49. Such special interrogatories often are in conflict with the jury's ultimate conclusions on liability or damages, creating a challenge for the trial court judge and appeals court on review. Beckman Instruments, Inc. v. LKB Produkter AB, 892 F.2d 1547, 13 USPQ2d 1301 (Fed. Cir. 1989); Richardson v. Suzuki, 868 F.2d 1226, 9 USPQ2d 1913. If the jury's answers cannot be reconciled with its verdict, a new trial or resubmission to the jury generally is required. Fed. R. Civ. P. 49(b).

80. Fed. R. Evid. 706. *See generally* J. Moses, *Judges Are Calling in Their Own Experts*, WALL STREET JOURNAL, July 2, 1992 at B11.

81. Fed. R. Civ. P. 12.

82. Fed. R. Civ. P. 15(b).

83. C.R. Bard, Inc. v. Advanced Cardiovascular Sys., Inc., 911 F.2d 670, 15 USPQ2d 1540 (Fed. Cir. 1990).

84. *See* Scripps Clinic & Research Foundation v. Genentech, Inc., 927 F.2d 1565, 18 USPQ2d 1001 (Fed. Cir. 1991).

85. A.B. Chance Co. v. RTE Corp., 854 F.2d 1307, 7 USPQ2d 1881 (Fed. Cir. 1988).

86. The evidence relied on must be admissible evidence under the Federal Rules of Evidence. The only distinction from trial is that a party may rely on affidavits of witnesses rather than testimony to present evidence related to the summary judgment motion. Fed. R. Civ. P. 56(e).

87. Celotex Corp. v. Catrett, 477 U.S. 317, 106 S. Ct. 2548 (1986).

88. A.B. Chance Co. v. RTE Corp., 854 F.2d 1307, 7 USPQ2d 1881 (Fed. Cir. 1988).

89. Fed. R. Civ. P. 50.

90. This relates to the type of review on appeal. Since judgment as a matter of law is by definition a legal determination, it is subject to full review by the appeals court. The grant of a new trial will be overturned on appeal only when the district court judge has abused his or her discretion. Orthokinetics, Inc. v. Safety Travel Chairs, Inc., 806 F.2d 1565, 1 USPQ2d 1081 (Fed. Cir. 1986).

91. Shatterproof Glass Corp. v. Libbey-Owens Ford Co., 758 F.2d 613, 225 USPQ 634 (Fed. Cir.), *cert. dismissed*, 474 U.S. 976 (1985).

92. Evidence not *admitted* into evidence at a trial may be considered when the alleged error was an improper exclusion of the evidence by the trial court judge. The evidence must have been *offered* at the trial, however.

93. P. Carrington, *The Power of District Judges and the Responsibility of Courts of Appeals*, 3 GA. L. REV. 507, 520 (1969); 9 C. Wright & A. Miller, FEDERAL PRACTICE AND PROCEDURE § 2588 at 750 note 44 (1971 & Supp. 1992).

94. Railroad Dynamics, Inc. v. A. Stucki Co., 727 F.2d 1506, 220 USPQ 929 (Fed. Cir.), *cert. denied*, 469 U.S. 871 (1984); Connell v. Sears, Roebuck & Co., 722 F.2d 1542, 220 USPQ 193 (Fed. Cir. 1983).

95. Connell v. Sears, Roebuck & Co., 722 F.2d 1542, 220 USPQ 193 (Fed. Cir. 1983).

96. Amgen, Inc. v. Chugai Pharmaceutical Co., 13 USPQ2d 1771, 1773 (D. Mass 1989).

97. Amgen, Inc. v. Chugai, 927 F.2d 1200, 18 USPQ2d 1016, 1025 (Fed. Cir. 1991).

98. *See, e.g., Interview with Laurence Tribe on Supreme Court Review of Amgen Inc. v. Chugai Pharmaceutical Co.*, PAT. TRADEMARK & COPYRIGHT J. (BNA), Vol. 42 at 466 (Sept. 12, 1991).

99. 112 S. Ct. 169 (1991).

100. *See* Dennison Mfg. Co. v. Panduit Corp., 475 U.S. 809, 106 S. Ct. 1578, 229 USPQ 478 (1986).

101. *See* T. Arnold, PATENT ALTERNATIVE DISPUTE RESOLUTION HANDBOOK (1991); S. Szczepanski, *Licensing or Settlement: Deferring the Fight to Another Day*, 15 AIPLA QUART. J. 298 (1987); W. Heinze, *Patent Mediation: The Forgotten Alternative in Dispute Resolution*, 18 AIPLA QUART. J. 333 (1991).

102. The Private Adjudication Center, Inc., 3101 Petty Road, Suite 207, Durham, NC 27707.

103. 28 U.S.C.A. § 471 (West Supp. 1992). Additional provisions are directed to management of lawsuits in which the government is a party. 28 U.S.C. § 519 (Supp. II 1990).

104. U.S. Dist. Ct. D.N.J. R. 15, 47.

Abandonment, 163–164
Absolute novelty requirement, 188
Accidental anticipation doctrine, 79, 154
Acetone, production of, 3, 6–9, 65, 128
Adams, Tom, 162
Admissions, requests for, 240
Adrenocorticotrophic hormone preparations, 119
Agriculture, U.S. Department of, 144, 175
Agricultural Research Service (ARS) of, 174–175
AIDS, 71
Alcohol
  amyl, 7
  butyl, 7, 62–63, 65
  ethyl, 63
  isopropyl, 62–63
Alkylaromatic hydrocarbons, 120
All-elements rule, 204–205
Alternaria euphorbiicola, 23
Alternative dispute resolution and settlement, 247
Amax Fly Ash Corp. v. United States, 145–146
Amchem, 143–144
American Bar Association, 214
American Cyanamid Co., 205
American Home Products Corp., 155
American Intellectual Property Law Association, 214
American Type Culture Collection (ATCC), 17, 179
Amgen, 17, 232
Amgen, Inc. v. Chugai Pharmaceutical Co., 64, 108–109, 132, 133, 138–140, 242
  and best-mode requirement, 127
  and conception of cloned gene, 155–157
  and deposit of host cells, 246
  and enablement requirement, 119
  and *In re Durden,* 99
Amgen Inc. v. I.T.C., 213
Ampicillin, 155
Animal patent, first, 22, 68
Animal science, 21–22
Answer, 235
Anticholinergic compounds, 143
Anticipatory prior art, *see* Prior art
Antidepressants, 157–158

Antitrust laws, application of, to patents, 221
Appeals, 32, 40–41
  to Federal Circuit, 33–34
  process, 245–246
Applegate v. Scherer, 142–143, 145
Application of Greer, 174
Application process, patent, 27–28
  examination process, 29–34
  patent examiners, 28–29
  patent filings, 29
  post-examination processes, 34–36
Arbitration, 247
Aronson v. Quick Point Pencil Corp., 50
Asgrow Seed Company v. Winterboer, 176–177
Assignor estoppel, 223
Atkinson, William M., 27
Australia, 196, 197
Automated Patent System (APS), 30–31

Bacillus protein, 107–108, 123
Bailments
  defined, 52
  use of, to transfer biological material, 52–53
Basic claims, 13–14, 15
Baxter Travenol, 161
Bee, R., 214
Bennett, Virginia C., 171
Best-mode requirement, 11, 117, 126–127, 246
Biogen, 22
Biological materials
  derivatives of, 51–52
  use of bailments to transfer, 52–53
Biological Patents Directive, 69
Black's Law Dictionary, 52
Blocking patent, 4
Board of Patent Appeals and Interferences, 29, 30, 32, 37, 83, 162
Boucher-type legislation, 99, 214
Boyer, H., 17, 18
Brazil, 196, 197
Brenner v. Manson, 69
Bristol-Myers Co., 155
Broome, David E., Jr., 49
Brown-bag sales, 176–177
Brown v. Guild, 85

Budapest Treaty, 129
Bureau of Mines, 145–146
Bureau of National Affairs, Inc., 34

Calgene, 21
California, University of, 51
California Supreme Court, 51
Canada, 196, 197
Candida, 128
Cannon, James R., 75
Cech, Thomas, 19
Cell lines, 49–50, 51, 53
Chakrabarty, Ananda, 66
Chakrabarty case, *see Diamond v. Chakrabarty*
Chemcast Corp. v. Arco Industries Corp., 126–127
Chemical Abstracts, 77–78
Chemical compositions, 104–105
China, 196, 197
Chinese Hamster Ovary (CHO) cell, 127
Chiorazzi, N., 140–141
Chisum, D., 2, 133, 140, 206
Cholera, vaccines for, 23
Chrysanthemums, 175
Chugai Pharmaceutical Company, 127, 213, 232, 246. *See also Amgen Inc. v. Chugai Pharmaceutical Co.*
Churchill, Winston, 6
Civil suits, 32–33
Claim(s), patent, 11
    central role of, 11–12, 202
    elements of, included in reference, 76–77
    examples of, in biotechnology, 16–23
    genus vs. species, 76–77
    interpretation
        general rules of, 12–14
        literal infringement and, 203–206
        for validity analysis, 216–217
    practical interpretation of, 14–16
    proper application of prior art to, 80–86
    scope, enablement requirement and, 117–126
Claim definiteness requirement, 117, 132–133
Claims Court, U.S., *see* Court of Federal Claims, U.S.
Close-ended claims, 13, 15–16
Clostridium acetobutylicum, 6–9, 128
Coauthors/coinventors, 140–141
Code, U.S. (U.S.C.), 3, 5, 30, 75, 172, 175–176

Cohen, S., 17, 18
Coleman v. Dines, 161
Collaborative research, 137, 154
    inventorship issues in, 137–147
    prior art issues in, 148–151
Combination inventions, 122–123
Commerce, U.S. Department of, 27
Commercial Solvents Corp., 8–9
Commissioner of Patents, 32, 33, 34, 37, 42, 147–148
Competitive research, 153. *See also* First-to-file system; First-to-invent system; Interference proceedings
Complaint, 234–235
Compositions, therapeutic, 22–23
Compounds, therapeutic, 22–23
Concealment, 163–164
Conception of invention, 141, 154
    of cloned gene, 155–157
    and enablement, 155
    of genus and species, 158
    and inventorship, 158
    and recognition, 154–155
    and utility requirement, 157–158
Conferences, 81–82
Confidential documents, 83–84
Confidential relationships, 56
Confidentiality agreement, 54
Constitution, U.S., 62, 67
    Seventh Amendment to, 39
Continuation-in-part (CIP) application, 125–126, 131
Contracts
    to assign intellectual property rights, 55
    express, vs. employment manuals, 55–56
Conversion, common law of, 171
Cooper, Iver, 174
Cordite, 6, 7
Corn plants, 177–178, 179
Cornell University, 19, 161
Corporate research facilities, trade secrets at, 54
Correcting inventorship, 147
    in issued patent, 147–148
    in patent application, 147
Corroboration of inventive acts, 161–163
Cotton cultivar, 77, 179
Counterclaims, 235
Court of Customs and Patent Appeals (CCPA), 62, 64, 65, 69–70, 97, 120
    on conception of invention, 155, 157

on derivation of invention, 142–143, 145

on first-to-invent system outside United States, 164

and *In re Herschler,* 122

and *In re Hogan,* 121–122

and *In re Katz,* 141

Court of Federal Claims, U.S., 37, 41

Crassotrea gigus, 67

Crop exemption, in PVPA, 176–177, 182

Cross-license, 4

Cross v. Iizuka, 70–71

Cyanobacteria, 107–108, 123

Daunorubicin, 65

David and Greene, 162

Declaratory judgment action, 233–234

Dependent claims, 13–14, 15

Depositions, 238–240

Deposit requirement, 117, 127–128

in European Patent Office, 129–130

in United States, 128–129

Deputy Assistant Commissioner for Patents, 34

Derivation of invention, 142–144, 153–154

avoiding charge of, through recordkeeping, 144–145

difficulty of proving, 145–146

Diamond Scientific Co. v. Ambico, Inc., 223

Diamond v. Chakrabarty, 1, 4, 50, 53, 65–67, 178

Diligence, 160–161

Disclosure requirements, 117. *See also* Best-mode requirement; Claim definiteness requirement; Deposit requirement; Enablement requirement; Written-description requirement

Discovery, 235

overview of objectives of, 235–236

resisting, 240–241

stays of, 242

tools of, 236–240

Dismiss, motions to, 244

District Court, U.S. (District of Columbia), 32, 33, 36, 37, 41, 247

and enablement requirement, 119

and interference proceedings, 166

and patent infringement action, 232, 233

DNA, 20, 106, 107, 110, 123, 132

and erythropoietin, 17, 64, 108–109, 119, 127, 138–139, 156

and *Fiers v. Revel,* 156–157

recombinant, 17–18

sequences, 21, 22, 69

Documents

confidential, 83–84

requests for production of, 237–238

Doxycycline, 215

Duke University School of Law, 247

DuPont v. Cetus, 84, 233

"DUS" criteria, 175

Employees, ownership of inventions of, 54–56

Employers, shop rights of, 56

Enablement requirement, 11, 12, 13, 117–118, 179

burden of proving, in PTO, 118

conception and, 155

facts relevant to question of, 118–124

timing of filing of applications in light of, 124–126

Enabling

disclosure, requirement of, 189

of prior art, 77–78

Enforceability, patent, in the courts, 219–223

Equitable estoppel, 221–223

Equivalents, doctrine of, 12, 133, 206–208

case study of, 209–211

and file wrapper estoppel, 208–209

and prior art, 208

reverse, 211–212

Erythropoietin (EPO), 17, 156, 232

and *Amgen v. Chugai,* 64, 108–109, 119, 127, 133, 138–140

Escherichia coli, 23, 108

Eshhar, 140, 141

Essentially derived varieties (EDVs), 182–183

Estoppel

applied to accused infringer, 223

assignor, 223

equitable, 221–223

file wrapper, 208–209

licensee, 223

Ethicon Research Foundation, 161

European Economic Community (EEC), 191, 192

European Patent Convention (EPC), 68, 78, 123–124, 129, 166–167, 172

integrated pursuit of European patents with, 191–193, 198

membership in, 191, 192, 197

and Patent Cooperation Treaty, 193, 194, 196

and plant patents, 183

European Patent Convention *(continued)*
    prior art issues under, 150–151
European Patent Office (EPO), 110, 167,
    183, 191–193, 197
    deposit procedures in, 129–130
    enablement questions in, 123–124
    Examining Division, 124
    Technical Board of Appeals, 68, 77–78,
        110, 124
    and use of PCT and EPC in combina-
        tion, 194, 196
Examination process, 29–34
Examiners, patent, 28–29
Exclude, right to, 3–4
Ex parte Albert, 81
Ex parte Allen, 67, 94
Ex parte Balzarini, 71–72
Ex parte Erlich, 103, 109, 111
Ex parte Forman, 128
Ex parte Foster, 173
Ex parte Harris, 83
Ex parte Hibberd, 66–67, 178
Ex parte Kropp, 127–128
Ex parte Prescott, 62–63
Ex parte proceedings, 35, 36, 37, 42, 104
Ex parte Thomson, 77, 179
Experimental use, 86, 214–215
    statutory, 215
Experimentation, undue, 120–121
Extracorporeal Medical Specialties,
    161–162

Fact and law, questions of, 37–39, 131
Falkow, S., 20
Federal Circuit, 2, 32, 33, 36, 95, 97
    on abandonment, suppression, and con-
        cealment, 163–164
    and *Amgen v. Chugai,* 108–109, 119,
        127, 133, 139, 155–157, 246
    appeals to, 33–34, 41
    and best-mode requirement, 126–127
    Court of Appeals for, 1, 4, 30, 41, 99,
        108, 202, 217, 223, 246
    on diligence, 161
    on doctrine of equivalents, 207–208,
        211–212
    on experimental use, 86
    on file wrapper estoppel, 209
    and *Hormone Research Foundation,*
        122
    and *Hybritech, Inc. v. Monoclonal Anti-
        bodies, Inc.,* 76, 98, 107, 154,
        162–163
    on inequitable conduct, 220
    on infringement, 204, 205, 213
    and *In re Dillon in banc,* 104–105
    and *In re Durden,* 98–99, 101
    and *In re Merck,* 102–103, 158
    and *In re O'Farrell,* 106, 107, 110–111
    and *In re Pleuddemann,* 99–101
    and *In re Vaeck,* 107–108, 123
    and *In re Wands,* 120–121
    on joint invention, 142
    and jury trials, 39
    on known inventions, 85
    on nonobviousness, 93–94
    on obviousness, 219
    and patent grant, 202, 203
    on person with ordinary skill, 95–96
    on plant patents, 176–177
    and *Polisky et al.,* 106–107
    on practical utility, 70–71
    on prior use, 85, 218
    on reduction to practice, 160
    on skepticism of experts, 102
    and written-description requirement,
        131–132
Federal Reporter, 34
Federal Rules of Civil Procedure
        (Fed.R.Civ.P.), 35, 39, 235,
        238–240, 243
Federal Rules of Evidence, 238, 245
Federal vs. state
    court, 36–37
    patent law rights, 50
"Federico's Commentary," 3
Feit, I., 214
Fernbach, Professor, 7
Fiers v. Revel, 132, 156–157
File wrapper estoppel, 208–209
Filings, patent, 29
First-to-file system, 153–154, 188
    priority under, 166–167
First-to-invent system, 148, 153–154, 188
    applying, to inventions made outside
        United States, 164
    priority of invention under, 154–164
Foley, Shawn P., 93
Foreign patent(s), 187–188, 198
    applications, 126, 164
        choosing where to file, 190–191
    approach to securing, 194–198
    preserving foreign rights and deferring
        foreign costs, 191–194
    rights, avoiding forfeiture of, 188–190
France, 191
Freedom of Information Act (FOIA), 83–84
Fritsch, Dr., 138–139, 140, 156

Full signatory authority program, 28

GAF Corp. v. Amchem Products, Inc.,
        143–144
Gene, conception of cloned, 155–157
Genentech, 18, 122, 211, 244
Genentech Inc. v. The Wellcome Founda-
        tion Ltd., 209–211
GENENTECH I/Polypeptide Expression
        decision, 110–111, 124
General Foods Corporation v. Studien-
        gesellschaft Kohle mbH, 202, 205
Generic claim elements, 13, 15
Genetics Institute, 17, 127, 138–140, 156,
        232, 246
    and claim definiteness requirement,
        133
    and doctrine of equivalents, 209–211
Genus and species, 76–77
    conception of, 158
Germany, 188, 191
Glatz, Robert W., 201, 231
Graham v. John Deere Co., 4–5, 93, 103,
        109–110
Grant, patent, 202–203
Graver Tank & Mfg Co. v. Linde Air Prod-
        ucts Co., 207, 208, 209, 211
Griesa, Judge, 205–206
Griffith v. Kanamaru, 161
Guaranty Trust Co. of New York v. Union
        Solvents Co., 65

Hahn v. Wong, 162
Hantman, R., 214
Harmon, R., 2, 95
Harvard Medical School, 140
"Harvard mouse" patent, 22, 68
Hewick, 138–139, 140
HibTITER™ vaccine, 205
Homopolymers, 121
Hormone Research Foundation Inc. v.
        Genentech Inc., 122
Houghton v. U.S., 57
Hughes Aircraft Co. v. United States, 209
Human donors, materials derived from, 51
Human fibroblast interferon, 109
Human growth hormone (HGH), 122
Human hematopoietic stem cells, 17
Human leucocyte interferon, 109
Hybridomas, 14–16, 49–50, 120–121
Hybritech, 20
Hybritech Inc. v. Abbott Laboratories,
        160–161

Hybritech, Inc. v. Monoclonal Antibodies,
        Inc., 76, 98, 103, 107, 154,
        162–163,219

Indexing, of single manuscripts, 82–83
Inequitable conduct, 220–221
Infringement, 11, 12, 16, 201, 203, 216
    actions, patent, brought into court,
        232–233
    contributory, 212
    and doctrine of equivalents, 206–212
    duty to avoid, 203
    exceptions to, 214–215
    liability for, 14
    literal, and claim interpretation,
        203–206
    opinions, 203
    and Process Patent Amendment Act of
        1988, 212–214
    remedies for, 202–203
    standards of proof for, 39–40
Inherency, doctrine of, 79
In re Angstadt, 120
In re Bayer, 83
In re Bergy, 4, 61
In re Cronyn, 83
In re Dillon in banc, 104–105
In re Durden, 98–99, 100–101, 213–214
In re Eltgroth, 71
In re Fisher, 119, 122
In re Grasselli, 101
In re Hafner, 78–79
In re Hall, 83
In re Herschler, 122
In re Hogan, 121–122
In re Joliot, 62
In re Katz, 140–141
In re Kirk, 69–70
In re LeGrice, 77, 179
In re Mancy, 65–66
In re Merck, 102–103, 158
In re O'Farrell, 95, 96, 106–111
In re Papesch, 93, 97–98, 100
In re Pleuddemann, 99–101
In re Smith, 86
In re Tenney, 82, 83
In re Vaeck, 107–108, 123
In re Wands, 120–121
In re Wilder, 79
In re Wright, 105
Insecticidal carbonates, 98
Intangible property, see Tangible vs. intan-
        gible property

Intellectual property, ownership of, 50, 54
employees' inventions, 54–56
joint ventures (confidential relation-
ships), 56
universities, 57–58
Intellectual Property Owners Inc., 214
Interference counts, 165
Interference proceedings, 35–36, 164–166
International Rectifier Corp., 215
International Union for the Protection of
New Varieties of Plants (UPOV), 172,
175, 180, 181
Convention, 181–183
essentially derived varieties under,
182–183
and European Patent Convention, 183
Inter parties, 35
Interrogatories, 236–237
Invention, claims covering subsequent, 14
Inventive step and nonobviousness com-
pared, 110–111
"Invention as a whole" requirement,
97–101
Inventors, identifying, 138–142
Inventorship, 11
conception and, 158
correcting, 147–148
removing prior art by showing, 86–88
Iowa, Southern District Court of, 178
Israel, 7, 196
Issued patents, proceedings on, 36
patent litigation, 36–41

Jacobs, 138–139, 140
Japan, 188, 196, 197
Jennings, Dr., 206
Joint inventions, 141–142
and joint patent applications compared,
146–147
Joint ventures, 56
Judgment, as matter of law, 245
Jury trials, 39, 242, 243, 247

Kane, 7, 8
Kayton, I., 2
Kirin–Amgen, 232
Kligman, Albert, 57
Known inventions, 85
Kohler, G., 14, 107, 109

Laches, 221–223
Lactobacilli strains, 16–17
*Laitram Corp. v. Cambridge Wire Cloth
Co.,* 207–208

Law
and fact, questions of, 37–39, 131
prior art issues under United States,
148–150
Lawsuit
alternative dispute resolution and settle-
ment, 247
determination of issues, 242–246
discovery phase, 235–242
initiating, 232–235
steps taken prior to, 231–232
Lazo v. Tso, 144–145
Lear, Inc. v. Adkins, 223
Leder, P., 68
Leukemia, 51
Lewmar Marine Inc. v. Barient, Inc., 76
Licensee estoppel, 223
Life span, patent, 50, 53, 202
Lin, Fu-Kuen, 127, 138, 140, 156
Litigation, patent, 36–41. *See also* Lawsuit
Living things
European experience with patenting of,
68–69
patentability of, 65–69
Long-felt need, 101–102
Lubrizol Genetics, 21, 68
Lutzker v. Plet, 163

MacMillan v. Moffett, 143
Maize, production of acetone from, 3, 6–9
Manchester University, 7
Manual of Patent Examining Procedure
(MPEP), 27, 62, 88
Manuscripts, collections of single, 82–83
Markey, Chief Judge, 118
Materials transfer agreements (MTAs), 52
Mediation, 247
Medtronic, Inc. v. Daig Corp., 160
Merck & Co. v. Chase Chemical Co., 128
Merck & Co. v. Danbury Pharmacal Inc.,
105–106
*Merck & Co. v. Olin Mathieson Chemical
Corp.,* 63–64
Mergenthaler v. Scudder, 154
Methods, therapeutic, 22–23
Methylomonas decision, 77–78
Mexico, 196, 197
Microbiology, 127
Milk, production of recombinant proteins in
animal, 22
Milstein, C., 14, 107, 109, 159
*Minnesota Mining and Manufacturing
Company v. Johnson & Johnson
Orthopaedics,* 203

Misuse, patent, 221
Moffett, 143
Monoclonal Antibodies, Inc., 210. *See also Hybritech, Inc. v. Monoclonal Antibodies, Inc.*
Monoclonal antibodies (Mabs), 14–16, 49–50, 98, 107, 109
Monoclonal sandwich assays, 20, 162
Monsanto Co. v. Kamp, 141–142
Moore v. Regents of the University of California, 51–52
Moseley, S., 20
Motions to compel discovery, 241
Mullis, Kary, 19
Mycogen, 23
Mycoherbicide compositions, 23
Myers, James D., 201, 231

Nashef v. Pollock, 161–162
National Institutes of Health, 52, 69, 84
National Rose Society, 77
National Science Foundation, 84
National Semiconductor v. Linear Technology, Inc., 82
Nature
    materials isolated from, 16–17
    patentability of products of, 62–65
Nature, 131
Near-simultaneous invention, 102–103
Nelson v. Bowler, 70
New England Medical Center, 16
New Zealand, 196, 197
Nexus, 101
Nobel's Explosive Company, 7–8
Nonobviousness, 4–6, 11–12, 13, 93–94, 111, 179
    assessing, in the courts, 219
    basic test of, 94
    inventive step and, compared, 110–111
    objective evidence of, 101–103
    and *prima facie* obviousness, 104–110
Nonprecedential opinions, 33, 34
North American Vaccine v. American Cyanamid Co., 205–206
North Carolina State University, 57
North Carolina Supreme Court, 57
Novelty, 5, 11–12, 61, 75, 179, 188
    assessing, in the courts, 217–218

Objections, 241
"Obvious to try," 106–109
O'Farrell, see *In re O'Farrell*
Offer to sell, 85, 188
Office Action, 30, 31

On sale, 85–86
Open–ended claims, 13, 15
Operability, 61, 71–72
Organosilane coupling agents, 99–100
O'Shaugnessy, Brian P., 61, 201

Paris Convention, 164, 189, 198
Parke–Davis v. H.K. Mulford Co., 63
Partial signatory authority program, 28
Pasteur, Louis, 16, 66
Patentability
    plant, 173–175
    requirements for, 4–6
Patent Act of 1952, 2, 117, 164, 202
    brief overview of, 3–6
    on claim definiteness requirement, 132
    on collaborative research, 137–138, 146, 148–149
    enablement requirement of, 159
    on nonobviousness, 93–94, 95, 104, 106
    on novelty requirement, 61, 75–76
    on prior art, 80, 95
Patent and Trademark Office, U.S. (USPTO), 1, 12, 42, 67–68, 70, 77, 108
    Allowed Files Division, 34
    and *Amgen v. Chugai,* 138–140
    Application Division, 29
    and Boucher-type legislation, 214
    burden of proving enablement in, 118, 120–121, 123
    on conception of invention, 157
    on correcting inventorship, 147
    on derivation of invention, 142, 143, 145
    Examining Group, 28, 29, 30
    and *Fiers v. Revel,* 132
    and foreign patents, 193, 195, 197
    Group Art Unit, 29–30, 31
    Group 180, 29
    and inequitable conduct, 220
    and *In re Durden,* 100, 101
    and *In re Katz,* 140–141
    on interference procedure, 164
    on joint inventions, 146
    and monoclonal antibodies, 109
    and nonobviousness, 93–94
    and patent application process, 27–34
    and Patent Cooperation Treaty, 193
    and patent litigation, 37–41
    on plant patents, 173, 174–175, 178
    Security Group (Group 220), 29
Patent Cooperation Treaty (PCT), 193–194, 197, 198

Patent Cooperation Treaty *(continued)*
  Chapter I, 193, 194, 196
  Chapter II, 193, 194, 196, 197
  and European Patent Convention, 193,
    194, 196
  membership in, 193, 196
Patent Office, U.S., 70, 95, 99, 111, 194
  Board of Appeals, 62, 66, 69–70, 71–72,
    98, 159
Patent Term Extension Act, 214
Paulik v. Rizkalla, 163
Pennsylvania, University of, 57
Pennwalt v. Durand Wayland, 207
Perkin, Professor, 7
Pertinent art, 94
Pfizer, Inc. v. International Rectifier Corp.,
    215
Phantom count, 165
Philippines, 196
Philips Electric & Pharmaceutical Indus-
    tries Corp. v. Thermal & Electric
    Industries, 83
Phytophthora, 175
Pioneer Hi-Bred, 21
Pioneer Hi-Bred v. Holden Foundation
    Seeds, 178
Plant(s)
  international considerations in protect-
    ing, 181–183
  patents, 171–175
  strategy of protecting, 179–180
  as tangible property, 178
Plant Patent Act (PPA) of 1930, 66–67,
    171, 172–173, 176, 178, 180
  and international considerations in plant
    protection, 181–182
Plant science, 20–21
Plant Variety Protection Act (PVPA) of
    1970, 66–67, 171, 172, 175–176,
    178, 180
  exemptions in, 176–177
  and international considerations in plant
    protection, 181–182
Plant Variety Protection Certificate
    (PVPC), 175–177, 179
Plant Variety Protection Office Official
    Journal, 175
Plasmids, 124
  genetically engineered, 49–50, 53
Polisky et al., 106–107, 110
Pollock, Dr., 161–162
Polygalacturonase gene, 21
Polymerase chain reaction (PCR), 19, 84,
    233

Polyploid oysters, 67, 94
Postal Service, U.S., 81
Post-examination processes, 34–36
Practical utility, 61, 69–71
Precedential opinions, 33, 34
Preliminary injunction, 235
Prima facie case, 40
Prima facie obviousness, 104
  rebutting, 109–110
  significance of, 105–109
  and structural obviousness, 104–105
Primary examiners, 28
Printed publications, 80, 188
  publication date of, 81
  types of, 81–84
Prior art
  anticipatory, qualifications for, 76–79
  defining, in the courts, 217–218
  differences between claimed invention
    and, 97–101
  and doctrine of equivalents, 208
  issues in collaborative research,
    148–151
  product, 12, 15
  proper application of, to claims, 80–86
  removing, by showing prior inventor-
    ship, 86–88
  scope and content of, 94–95
  secret, 166–167
Prior failure, 101–102
Prior use, 84–85
Priority
  date, 189
  right of, 189, 195, 198
Priority of invention, 153
  under first-to-invent system, 154–164
Private Adjudication Center, Inc., 247
Procaryotae, 108
Processes, claims directed to, 12
Process Patent Amendment Act of 1988,
    212–214
Procter & Gamble (P&G), 143
Production of documents, requests for,
    237–238
Products, claims directed to, 12
Prostaglandins, 70
Protective orders, 241
Public use, 84–85, 188
Publication of articles, reconciling, with fil-
    ing of foreign patent applications,
    190

Randall, Dr., 143–144
Reagents, biological, 49–50

Recognition, conception and, 154–155
Reduction to practice, 141, 155, 159
 actual, 159–160
 constructive, 159
Reexamination proceedings, 42
*Regents of the University of California v.
    Howmedica,* 82
Regulon, 124
Reissue proceedings, 41–42
Rejection, final, 31–32
Research. *See also* Collaborative research;
    Competitive research
 agreement, 57
 facilities, corporate, trade secrets at, 54
 outside funding of university, 58
Research Corporation, 23
Research exemption, in PVPA, 176
Res judicata, 35
Retin-A, 57
Retroviruses, 23
Revel, 132
Rey-Bellet v. Englehardt, 157
Ribozymes, 19
Rich, Giles, 4, 61, 70, 93, 107
Right of priority, 189, 195, 198
Rintoul, Dr., 7–8
RNA, 19, 106
"Rosa floribunda plant," 77
Rose Plant Jacinal, 174
"Rule of reason," 161
Rule 131 Declaration, 86
 content of, 87–88
 use of, 87

Saco-Lowell Shops v. Reynolds, 56
Saris, Judge, 242
*Scripps Clinic & Research Foundation v.
    Genentech Inc.,* 119, 211–212,
    244
Secret prior art, 166–167
Seminars, 81–82
"Shoes," 30
Shop rights, 56
Sibley, Kenneth D., 1, 11, 117, 137, 153,
    187
Silvestri v. Grant, 155
Simonsen, Dr., 127
Skepticism, 102
Skill, person having ordinary, in the art,
    95–96
Smith v. Bosquet, 155
"Smoking gun" memo or document, 237
South America, 196
Soybeans, 175

Spain, 194
Specific claim elements, 13, 15
Speck v. N.C. Dairy Foundation, Inc., 57
Staehelin v. Secher, 131, 159
Standards of proof, 39–40
Stanford University, 17
State court, 36–37
State Department, U.S., 240
State of the art, enablement requirement
    and, 120–122
Statute, patent, *see* Patent Act of 1952
Statutory subject matter, 61–62
 defining "useful arts," 62
 living things, 65–69
 products of nature, 62–65
Stealing, *see* Derivation of invention
Steroids, 69, 122
Stewart, T., 68
Story, Joseph, 214
Strange & Graham Ltd., 7
Streptomyces bifurcus, 65–66
 griseus, 63
Structural obviousness, 104–105
Subject matter, patentable, 11
Summary disposition of issues in dispute,
    243–245
Summary judgment, motions for, 244–245
Supervisory primary examiner (SPE), 28
Suppression, 163–164
Supreme Court, U.S., 4, 30, 36, 41, 67, 102
 on *Amgen v. Chugai,* 246
 and appeals process, 246
 on *Brenner v. Manson,* 69
 on *Diamond v. Chakrabarty,* 1, 65, 66
 on doctrine of equivalents, 207, 208,
    209, 211
 on estoppel, 223
 on experimental use exception to in-
    fringement, 214
 on intellectual property, 50
 on nonobviousness, 93, 95
 on obviousness, 219
 on prior use, 85, 218
 review by, 34
 on *United Carbon Co. v. Binney &
    Smith,* 133
 on *U.S. v. Dubilier Condenser Corp.,*
    54–55
Swain v. Guild, 214
Swearing behind the reference, 86
Switzerland, 194
Synthetic Products Co. (SPC), 7, 8
Systemix, 17
SZESZIPAR, 77–78

Tabuchi v. Nubel, 128
Taiwan, 195
Takamine, 63
Tangible vs. intangible property, 49–50, 53
   derivatives of biological materials,
      51–52
   federal vs. state patent law rights, 50
   materials derived from human donors,
      51
   plants as tangible property, 178
   use of bailments to transfer biological
      material, 52–53
Techniques
   biotechnology, 17–19
   diagnostic, 20
Technology, predictability of, and enable-
     ment, 118–119
Tennessee Valley Authority, 37
Thromboxane synthetase, 71
Tilghman v. Proctor, 79
Tissue plasminogen activator (t-PA),
     209–211
Trade secrets
   defined, 53
   and plants, 177–178
   protection maintained by, 54
   use of, in lieu of patents, 53–54
Transgenic plants, 171, 183
Treaty year, 189
Trial
   findings of fact and, 242–243
   jury, 39, 242, 243, 247
   motions for new, 245
Trialkyl hetero-aromatics, 97
Typhoid, vaccines for, 23

Unexpected results, 103
Uniform Biological Material Transfer
     Agreement, 52
Union Carbide Corporation, 98
United Carbon Co. v. Binney & Smith Co.,
     133
United Kingdom, 188, 191
United States Patent Quarterly, 34
Universities
   licenses vs. trade secrets at, 54

   outside funding of research at, 58
   and ownership of intellectual property,
      57–58
UpJohn, 143
UPOV, *see* International Union for the Pro-
     tection of New Varieties of Plants
Use
   experimental, 86, 214–215
   prior, 84–85
   public, 84–85, 188
Useful arts, defining, 62
U.S. v. Dubilier Condenser Corp., 54–55
Utility, 5, 11, 179
   and anticipatory prior art, 78–79
   practical, 61, 69–71
   requirement, conception and, 157–158
Utility Patent Act, 173, 177
Utility patents, 178–179, 189
   requirements for obtaining, 179

Validity, patent, 201
   of claims, assessment of, 13, 15
   in the courts, 216–219
   presumption of, 217
Vitamin B_{12}, 63–64, 128

Washburn & Moen Mfg. Co. v. Beat 'Em
     All Barbed-Wire Co., 85
Weizmann, Chaim, 3, 6–8, 128
Wellcome Foundation, 209–211
Whittemore v. Cutter, 214
Witnesses, expert, in patent litigation, 243
World War I, 3, 6
Writ of *certiorari,* 34, 36, 41
Written-description requirement, 117,
     130–132, 158
Wyzanski, Charles, 242

Yeast, 16, 66
Yoder Brothers, Inc. v. California–Florida
     Plant Corp., 173–174

Zygotes, genetic transformation of, 21–22